I0138951

A NAZI PAST

A NAZI PAST

Recasting German Identity
in Postwar Europe

Edited by

David A. Messenger
and Katrin Paehler

K UNIVERSITY PRESS OF KENTUCKY

Copyright © 2015 by The University Press of Kentucky

Scholarly publisher for the Commonwealth,
serving Bellarmine University, Berea College, Centre College of Kentucky, Eastern
Kentucky University, The Filson Historical Society, Georgetown College, Kentucky
Historical Society, Kentucky State University, Morehead State University, Murray
State University, Northern Kentucky University, Transylvania University, University of
Kentucky, University of Louisville, and Western Kentucky University.
All rights reserved.

Editorial and Sales Offices: The University Press of Kentucky
663 South Limestone Street, Lexington, Kentucky 40508-4008
www.kentuckypress.com

Library of Congress Cataloging-in-Publication Data

A Nazi past : recasting German identity in postwar Europe / edited by David A.
Messenger and Katrin Paehler.
     pages cm
   Includes index.
   ISBN 978-0-8131-6056-6 (hbk. : alk. paper) — ISBN 978-0-8131-6057-3 (pdf)
   — ISBN 978-0-8131-6058-0 (epub)
   1. Nazis—Germany (West)—Biography. 2. Denazification—Germany (West)
3. Ex-Nazis—Germany (West)—Psychology. 4. Denial (Psychology)—Case studies.
5. War criminals—Germany (West)—Biography. 6. National socialism—Moral and
ethical aspects. 7. Group identity—Germany (West) I. Messenger, David A., editor.
II. Paehler, Katrin, editor. III. Title: Recasting German identity in postwar Europe.
   DD243.A44 2015
   943.086092′2—dc23   2014049366

This book is printed on acid-free paper meeting
the requirements of the American National Standard
for Permanence in Paper for Printed Library Materials.

∞

Manufactured in the United States of America.

∦∦∪⊐ Member of the Association of
       American University Presses

Contents

Part 3. Unique Recastings in Postwar Germany

Abbreviations

ACC	Allied Control Council
BND	Bundesnachrichtendienst (Federal Intelligence Service)
CDU	Christlich Demokratische Union Deutschlands (Christian Democratic Union of Germany)
CIC	Counterintelligence Corps
FDP	Freie Demokratische Partei (Free Democratic Party)
GDR	German Democratic Republic
IMT	International Military Tribunal
NSDAP	Nationalsozialistische Deutsche Arbeiterpartei (National Socialist German Workers' Party)
ODESSA	Organization der ehemaligen SS-Angehörigen (Organization of Former SS Members)
OSS	Office of Strategic Services
RSHA	Reichssicherheitshauptamt (Reich Security Main Office)
SA	Sturmabteilung (NSDAP Stormtrooper section)
SD	Sicherheitsdienst (Security and Intelligence Service of the SS)
SHAEF	Supreme Headquarters of the Allied Expeditionary Forces
SPD	Sozialdemokratische Partei Deutschlands (Social Democratic Party of Germany)
SS	Schutzstaffel (NSDAP Protection Squadron)

Introduction

David A. Messenger and Katrin Paehler

He made it through denazification without many problems. He was categorized as a "follower." He stood trial but was acquitted. He received a mild sentence. His sentence was commuted. He went on to make a career in the Federal Republic of Germany or made good elsewhere. At the very basic level, this book grew out of a deceptively simple question: how did members of Nazi Germany's functional elites manage to recast their past experiences in such a way as to move on to successful careers and lives in postwar Europe? What type of active roles did these men—and a few women—play in the process through which they recast themselves, their former activities, and their convictions? What type of networks existed that made this process easier? This volume addresses these and other questions by focusing on the career paths, ideas, and agency of select individuals known to have had "Brown Pasts." Some of these names are familiar; others are less known. The eleven case studies assembled here investigate the private recasting processes of Nazi functional elites, such as presumed lesser German war criminals, SS members, party functionaries, administrators of spoliation and genocide, and intelligence agents, as well as the networks they created and used to make these processes possible. Rather than running from their pasts, these individuals embraced selective parts of their biographies during the Third Reich and made them congruent with the conservative character of the Federal Republic and the ideological contest of the emergent Cold War.

It is well known that a good number of former Nazi functionaries ascended to positions of influence in the Federal Republic of Germany. Like clockwork, West Germany encountered scandals. Some of them were of domestic origin, as for example the case of Untersuchungsausschuss Nr. 47 (Investigative Committee No. 47), which, in response to newspaper reports in 1951, dealt with former Nazis in the Foreign Office.[1] Others originated outside of the Federal Republic, such as the infamous Waldheim affair, when former United Nations Secretary-General Kurt Waldheim's past as a Wehrmacht officer came to light during his run for Austria's presidency in 1985.[2] More frequently than not, such scandals emerged from the "other" Germany—the German Democratic Republic—which hoped to score points in the Cold War's German-German propaganda battle. Most notable in this context is the *Brown Book,* published in East Berlin in 1965 and designed to draw the world's attention to former Nazis in positions of influence in the Federal Republic. The materials, swiftly rejected by the West German government as Communist propaganda, were an embarrassment for the Federal Republic. The *Brown Book* was also, at least for the time being, the culmination of a constant flow of information and accusations originating in the GDR. As Ulrich Brochhagen has shown, these East German information releases did not remain domestic or even German-German issues; rather, they often led to diplomatic issues for the Federal Republic.[3] West German journalists also did much to draw the West German public's attention to former high-ranking Nazis in position of power and influence. So did the Student Movement, which from the late 1960s onward mobilized a counterpublic that challenged the West German establishment and its "fascist" tendencies. Recent years have seen scholarly treatments of the same issues. By and large, the studies confirm the reality that many former Nazis moved more or less seamlessly into their postwar careers.[4]

Scholars have focused on the various reasons for this development. For example, they have studied the policies that either made it possible for former Nazis to embark on postwar careers or at least did not prevent them from doing so. One focus has been on the limits of denazification. As established at the Potsdam Conference, denazification was meant to destroy the National Socialist German Workers' Party (NSDAP) and its affiliated organizations. The goal was to negate Nazi institutions and laws, arrest and intern war criminals, remove Nazi officials from public and "semipublic" life, and eliminate National Socialist influence from the German education system. The Allied Control Council (ACC) took charge of these efforts and was aided by laws developed within each occupied zone. Combining ideas of reeducation and punishment, the architects of denazification saw internees as potential threats to security, order, and stability, and they sought to remove Nazism from German political and cultural life. Similarly, they hoped to render Germany's economy and politics less militaristic.[5] The best way to do this, in the minds of Allied planners, was to remove people from positions of influence and power.

In its implementation, denazification fell well short of its ambitions.[6] For one, putting every suspect on trial on the basis of his or her membership in Nazi organizations was too impractical, given the nearly 2 million individuals who qualified in the U.S. zone alone. As a result, both the International Military Tribunal in Nuremberg and subsequent trials emphasized major war criminals and representative institutions, like the SS, big business, and the medical establishment. And even at Nuremberg, many people who qualified under earlier definitions of war crimes were not included.[7] In addition, daily occupation operations on the ground demanded experienced individuals who might have had Nazi pasts. In the summer of 1945, food shortages, high unemployment, and the need simply to have functioning municipal governments compelled Allied soldiers and commanders to enlist local businessmen, government employees, and others in reconstruction efforts rather than arrest them. In the U.S. zone, the military—first the fighting and later the occupational force—was responsible for carrying out investigations. Sometimes they were assisted by members of the Office of Strategic Services (OSS) and the Army's Counter Intelligence Corps (CIC), but many times they were not. The public safety teams of the military government, charged with primary responsibility for carrying out what came to be the first round of denazification investigations, were sorely understaffed.[8] The need for German assistance in administration and the need for manpower to help with investigations resulted in the creation of local denazification panels, or *Spruchkammern,* run by Germans.[9] Ultimately, the U.S. military governor of Germany, General Lucius D. Clay, granted amnesties based on age, income level, and the existence of disabilities.[10] What was true for the U.S. zone of occupation held true for the others, too, and even in the Soviet zone, one found similar approaches to the same issues, albeit with a mind to Stalin's goal of future political and ideological dominance.[11] In short, denazification never achieved what it had set out to do. Among the most positive things to be said about the denazification effort is Michael R. Hayse's observation that, while as a "program for dispensing justice" it was a failure, denazification managed to achieve "the professional exclusion of the most prominent National Socialists . . . relatively well." It was a way of weeding out the worst, but it lost its impact on the lower levels. Moreover, the "lower levels" began fairly high up, and many people slipped through the system.[12]

Denazification also proved unpopular among the German public, a fact that contributed to the program's early demise. Many Germans considered denazification to be "victor's justice," administered by people with a scant understanding of Nazi Germany's realities or, later on, by local *Spruchkam-*

mern that frequently let the "big fish" go and punished the "small fry." Popular perceptions of injustice aside, most people were labeled as "fellow travelers" and received negligible punishments. The denazification effort was, in the words of Lutz Niethammer, nothing less than a giant "fellow traveler factory" (*Mitläuferfabrik*).[13] And as the Federal Republic of Germany emerged from occupation in 1949, local officials who had stringently enforced denazification lost in elections. Consequently, in September 1949, the new West German chancellor Konrad Adenauer spoke against the perceived injustices of denazification and sought to move beyond it.[14] Earlier, Adenauer had already stated the need to "punish the guilty, [extend] forgiveness and [make possible] reintegration for the misled or the fellow travelers."[15] The Christian-Democratic politician's plea made sense to a lot of West Germans. As Norbert Frei, Robert Moeller, and others have shown, there was widespread solidarity among members of the former Nazi racial community as the Bonn Republic emerged. The amnesty and the release of prisoners in the late 1940s and early 1950s was in part a reaction to popular protests, which the Protestant and Catholic churches and the press had mobilized.[16] Clearly, the population's overall reluctance to see "victor's justice" as beneficial to Germany, as well as the piecemeal watering down of denazification, allowed many to escape the consequences of their earlier activities.

The failures of Allied and German denazification efforts serve as an important backdrop to the investigations in this volume. But the chapters assembled here have a different vantage point. They focus less on top-down policies than on the agency of individuals impacted by these policies. How did former Nazis, with histories of involvement in espionage, wartime atrocities, and mass murder, make their way in the new postwar world? What stories did they tell about themselves? What narratives did they construct, individually or as groups? How did these self-styled accounts influence policies and affect career paths? This book focuses largely on mid-level Nazi functionaries and explores how they sought to recast their own pasts and to mold their stories to fit the new context in which they found themselves. They created—to employ Robert Moeller's apt phrase—a usable past, and in doing so they were prepared and eager to counter Allied policies from the start.[17] The shortcomings of denazification gave them room to exercise their agency. They used the gap between the denazification policy's rhetoric and its reality to put in place their own accounts of the past. And the emergence of the Cold War allowed them new avenues to pursue in the process of recasting. The chapters that follow thus provide the connection between the immediate experience of political and military defeat and denazification and the later integration of former Nazi functionaries into (West) German society. They show the processes of reshaping identities and envisioning futures—collectively and individually.

The methods used to recast one's identity in the postwar era were varied. But what unites these case studies is a singular realization: many ex-Nazis did not run from their pasts but instead developed ideas and networks of associates that *drew upon* their identity as Nazis. Some offered themselves as assets to the Allies in the process of reconstruction, selling themselves as insiders, not as criminals. Others, as Donald Bloxham has suggested, portrayed themselves as nationalists of a distinct manner.[18] They thereby moved away from Nazism but asserted a revived and revised form of conservative nationalism.

This volume makes regular use of the term *recasting*, and it is therefore worth noting the resonances of this term. The phrase "recast identity" is often applied to the case of West Germany, while in regard to East Germany "forging a Socialist identity" is common. In one respect, the difference between the two is negligible. Both refer to melting something down and giving it a different form. However, "forging" implies force—the beating or hammering of a heated object into an entirely new form. To be sure, Frank Biess makes it clear that in the GDR there was no need "to undergo a radical change but [returning POWs] needed rather to integrate their already existing mental dispositions into new symbolic, social, and political contexts."[19] Yet "to forge" still implies a more brutal and involuntary process and, at least outwardly, a renunciation of the past. The term also carries with it associations of the USSR's forced industrialization in the 1930s, of high Stalinism, and of Nikolai Ostrovsky's famous 1930s novel *How the Steel Was Tempered* (*Kak zakayalas' stal'*). "Recasting," in contrast, connotes a less violent process of reshaping or of presenting existing elements in a different light or configuration. For the purposes of this volume, it refers to a process that allowed people to adopt new personas compatible with the prevalent norms of West German society. One could even think of it as a private *Vergangenheitsbewältigung*—coming to terms with the past, making sense of it, and renarrating it. In the introduction to their edited volume on urban memory, Gavriel Rosenfeld and Paul Jaskot note that at first glance it appears that in the early years there was a desire in the Federal Republic of Germany " to marginalize" Nazism's architectural artifacts. Yet the devil is in the details, as they also observe that this was not "a period of complete amnesia." Rather, it was defined by "highly selective memory," an insight that accords with recent scholarship that sees postwar West Germany as anything but silent about the Nazi years.[20] Just as cityscapes were recast, so were individual and group identities in postwar Europe.

Scholars have already drawn attention to the role of common and even coordinated narratives crafted during denazification proceedings, in the so-called subsequent trials, in the business community, or among Germany's professional elites.[21] Indeed, at the time the public often embraced these portrayals of innocence and victimhood, which colored views of Nazi Germany and its crimes for decades to come. The eleven chapters of this book indicate that the building of such narratives began early, stretched across the globe, and often brought together unexpected actors. The chapters in this volume give a face to processes too frequently described in depersonalized terms and thus broaden our understanding of how the "politics of the past" played out in post–World War II Germany.

Two key questions attend the story of postwar recasting: How was it possible for so many people to integrate almost seamlessly into postwar society? And why were they accepted so readily? This volume's authors offer answers that go beyond issues of postwar exigency and the need for people to administer the reconstruction of a devastated country. The stories these Nazi functional elites told about the past made sense not only to themselves but also to many ordinary Germans who were also trying to come to grips with their experiences during the Nazi years. In the early 1930s, many Germans negotiated their way into Nazism, as Peter Fritzsche has shown.[22] In the late 1940s, they were negotiating themselves out of it. And what had helped people in the 1930s to embrace the Nazi project—the grab-bag nature of much of the Nazi *Weltanschauung*—now helped them disassociate from it. George Browder suggests that the existence of "ideological conjunctions" (antiliberalism, anti-Marxism, nationalism, racism, anti-Semitism) between "radically racist Nazis" and a broader swath of conservative Germans of different stripes allowed the former "to suck in vast numbers of allies."[23] Twelve years later, it allowed these very allies to recast themselves in a national conservative fashion. Shed of its most unsavory elements, such as genocidal anti-Semitism, many elements of the Nazi *Weltanschauung* remained *salonfähig*, now domesticated for consumption in the Federal Republic. There is, of course, anti-Communism and the barely deracialized reference to Asiatic hordes poised to overrun Western Europe; there is a more generalized xenophobia; there is the strong law-and-order approach; and there is a focus on community—no longer phrased in clearly racial terms as a *Volksgemeinschaft* but as a value-conservative, postdefeat, broadly Christian *Schicksalsgemeinschaft* (community of fate). And it was there to stay for many years to come.

The volume is organized in three sections, each one looking at a particular type of recasting. Part 1 deals with war criminals and their postwar trials and interrogations. Daniel E. Rogers begins with an examination of Hans Globke, the most prominent among West German political figures and civil servants to have survived and prospered in the Federal Republic despite involvement in Nazi Germany's anti-Semitic policies. In the Third Reich he had held the moderately high civil service rank of *Ministerialrat* in the Reich Ministry of the Interior; he coauthored a commentary on the Nuremberg race laws of 1935. Nonetheless, Globke served as Konrad Adenauer's chief adviser and chief of staff from 1949 to 1963, although he did not achieve the title of *Staatssekretär* until 1953. During his long service by Adenauer's side, Globke drew the fire of those who believed him an unacceptable holdover from the Nazi era. Rogers argues that a decisive factor in Globke's resurgence was his willingness to testify at trials in Nuremberg in 1946 and 1948. The quality and quantity of his testimony created the image of a man who had nothing to hide about himself, even though he had been so close to the apparatus of mass murder that he knew of it early. In later years, Globke and his defenders therefore could assert truthfully that he had been checked thoroughly by the Allies, had revealed the full extent of his involvement with Nazi Germany's anti-Semitic policies, and represented no danger to the fledgling liberal democracy being established in West Germany.

Similarly, Katrin Paehler investigates Walter Schellenberg's late-wartime and postwar attempts to fashion a usable past, a profitable future, and a worthwhile place in German and Allied history books out of the ashes of his career as the head of Heinrich Himmler's intelligence service and as Himmler's self-appointed foreign minister. Basing her analysis mainly on Schellenberg's postwar interrogations by the Western Allies and on testimonies and writings about his career, role, and associations in Nazi Germany, she argues that Schellenberg took an unusual—and largely successful—tack in his defense. Rather than downplaying his role in Nazi Germany or disavowing his relationship with many members of Nazi Germany's state and party hierarchy, Schellenberg attempted to use them to his advantage, as he cast himself as the ultimate insider, Western-leaning diplomat, and humanitarian thwarted in his attempt to bring peace. Thus, Schellenberg created a usable past for himself and, even if he was not able to make a future out of it, a narrative that still holds influence.

To conclude the first section, Hilary Earl examines the postwar trial and subsequent life of Martin Sandberger, one of the fourteen *Einsatzgruppen* leaders originally sentenced to death in one of the twelve "subsequent" trials held in Nuremberg. Sandberger had been leader of Sonderkommando

1a, one of the four SS-*Einsatzgruppen,* or mobile killing units, that operated in the Baltic States between June 1941 and August 1943. The units under his command killed tens of thousands of people, if not more. Because of good timing and luck, Sandberger was released from prison in May 1958. From then on until his death in March 2010, he lived his life in anonymity, never speaking to anyone about what he had done during the war, that is until Walter Mayr, a *Spiegel* reporter, found him in an exclusive Stuttgart nursing home a month before he died. Mayr was surprised by the remarkable mental acuity of the elderly man who, at age ninety-nine, had the presence of mind to keep silent. How could one recast oneself after being found guilty? Sandberger, as one of the few individuals who served time among all the cases examined in this volume, offers an interesting perspective on how some of the most notorious SS leaders reintegrated back into German society after they were tried and sentenced. Having served his term "like a man" contributed much to Sandberger's ability to reintegrate into society.

The second section examines a variety of efforts through which networks of individuals came together to assist one another, either directly or indirectly, in the process of recasting. David A. Messenger begins by examining an unusual network: former Nazi intelligence agents and diplomats who remained in Spain after serving there in World War II. After the cessation of hostilities in Europe, the United States demanded that Spain, which remained a dictatorship after 1945, repatriate more than sixteen hundred of these individuals to occupied Germany, where they would face the usual denazification procedures. Spain was reluctant and agreed to do so only in certain cases and after a drawn-out process. As a result, these men, part of the well-connected German colony in Spain, took up their own defense. The language and arguments used by these ex-functionaries and agents of the Nazi regime in Spain offer a unique insight into the recasting of identities far from the center of denazification processes in occupied Germany. It shows how Nazi elites in Spain explained their wartime activity, drew on explanatory models germane to their environment, and made a claim for apolitical, economic, and activist futures in Franco's Spain.

Susanna Schraftstetter examines another network that gathered in North Rhine–Westphalia around Siegfried Zoglmann, who had been an official in the Hitler Youth and in the Office of the "Reichprotector" of Bohemia and Moravia as well as a member of the Waffen-SS. Zoglmann's postwar career benefited from a network of Nazis from the Sudetenland in post-1945 West Germany. Active in the Witikobund, an ultra-right-wing organization of expellees, and in the Sudetendeutsche Landsmannschaft, Zogelmann and other former members of the Reichsjugendführung in the Sudetenland found their way into the North Rhine–Westphalian FDP (Freie Demokratische Partei). Schraftstetter examines to what extent this network helped in the denazification process and also provided Zoglmann and his colleagues a "spiritual home."

Thomas W. Maulucci looks at an even more united group of "recasters": career diplomats in the German Foreign Ministry who had begun their service before 1933. Very quickly they developed a strategy that emphasized the differences between themselves as the core group of officials in the Auswärtiges Amt on the one hand and Nazi "outsiders" brought into the ministry on the other. The latter became convenient scapegoats for the Foreign Office's activities during the Third Reich. Maulucci stresses that interned German diplomats interviewed by Allied authorities were developing this story—the idea of "two foreign offices" in existence during the Nazi era, which remained important for the Foreign Office's self-image well into the 1970s—as early as mid-1945.

The book's second section, with its focus on the role of networks in the recasting process, is rounded out by Kerstin von Lingen's examination of former Wehrmacht and SS officers who had served at the Italian front. A sharp distinction between the "clean Wehrmacht" on the one hand and the "dirty Nazi War" of the SS on the other framed the discourse among army veterans between 1945 and 1955. Affiliation with one group or the other, as defined by War Crimes Trials and denazification courts, divided the former comrades-in-arms and became a determining factor in who was to receive a second chance in postwar West German society. In Italy, however, there was no visible divide between the two groups, in contrast to other theaters of war. Lingen explicates how personnel who had served in Italy insisted that the Italian war had been fair and decent and how, once evidence presented in court challenged this narrative, these men engaged in feverish behind-the-scene-debates and discussions about concepts such as military honor and service. The debates became particularly prevalent as war crimes trials got under way in Italy in the late 1940s and as movements for release began to appear in the 1950s. What emerges is a coordinated, scripted recasting meant to serve these men and whatever futures they sought for themselves.

The final section of the volume considers a series of case studies in which the uniqueness of the individual defined the process of recasting. It draws attention to the underappreciated facts that there existed many, very different options for recasting one's past in postwar Germany; that many met with considerable success; and that many audiences were receptive to them. In chapter 8, Florian Altenhöner investigates the unique case of Alfred Nau-jocks. Naujocks was a hit man, counterfeiter, agent, and terrorist who, on the last day of August 1939, led the raid on the Gleiwitz radio station, which Nazi propaganda used as a pretext for the German invasion of Poland. From 1934 to 1941 he was a high-ranking member of the Sicherheitsdienst (SD) of the SS. By 1944 he headed the German counterterrorism (Gegenterror) campaign in Denmark. In the following years, Naujocks was interrogated, served as a witness at the International Military Trial at Nuremberg, and was charged and sentenced for murder in Denmark. Released by the Danes, he returned to Germany in the 1950s. Upon his return, Naujocks did not remain silent about his past; rather, he became almost a mainstay in the German media. In West Germany, Naujocks was portrayed not as a Nazi perpetrator but rather as an adventurer. In East Germany, however, Naujocks was pre-sented as a willing perpetrator. These different versions of Naujocks's story, and his own role in managing the narrative in West Germany, provide much insight into the mind-set of the German public of the time and how they approached recasting and its proponents.

Gerald Steinacher then considers the case of former SS officer Karl Nicolussi-Leck, who, like other former Nazis and SS members, trans-formed from a political actor to a seemingly apolitical businessman. Hav-ing voluntarily joined the Waffen-SS in 1940, Nicolussi-Leck served in the ranks of the Wiking Tank Division and was mainly deployed on the east-ern front; for his service he received the Knight's Cross of the Iron Cross in 1944. In 1947 the former SS-*Hauptsturmführer* was released from an American POW camp and returned to his home region of South Tyrol in northern Italy. There he initially worked as an escape agent for former Nazis and SS officers on their way to South America and the Middle East, developing close relationships with Argentine authorities in Italy. In 1948 he immigrated to Argentina, where he started a new career in private busi-ness. Together with former SS officer Horst Carlos Fuldner, he became involved in large projects of the Perón government and eventually began working for the German company Mannesmann. In the 1950s he returned to Europe and started a series of companies, most of which were affiliates of Mannesmann Germany, a company in which some of the key players were Leck's erstwhile SS comrades, such as Paul Hafner. In Leck's case, his SS connections thus served him twice.

Elisabeth Kohlhaas's study of Gertrud Slottke adds gender to the consid-eration of recasting. During the war, Slottke held a seemingly subaltern posi-tion with the Nazi occupation authority in the Netherlands but was, de facto, in charge of its Judenreferat, the Jewish Desk. After the war, Slottke—who originally hailed from Danzig—recast herself as a dual victim: her enthusiasm for Germany had been abused by "the Nazis" and her home had been destroyed and taken over by "the Russians." She subsequently became active in refugee and expellee organizations. Having escaped responsibility for her wartime activities in the immediate postwar period—very few women were held responsible for their participation in Nazi crimes and, even if they were, punished for it rather than acquitted—her past caught up with her in the 1960s. Jointly with her former supervisors, she was brought to a much-noted trial at the Landgericht München in 1967 and sentenced to several years in prison. Slottke was thus one of the very few female former Gestapo employees who stood trial in the Federal Republic of Germany and whose recasting efforts—different from those of her male counterparts and largely related to her gender—eventually fell apart.

Finally, Norman J. W. Goda considers Heinz Felfe, an SS officer from Dresden who became the head of West German Counterintelligence in 1955. Felfe was a key figure in the Western intelligence establishment, having also worked on joint German-U.S. operations. But he was also a double agent; the KGB had already recruited him in 1951. In this position Felfe managed to wreck West German counterintelligence operations until his arrest in 1961. He also burned hundreds of agents working for West German and U.S. intelligence and caused incalculable damage to NATO intelligence operations. How a self-admitted "ardent Nazi" secured important intelligence positions in the Soviet and West German intelligence establishments is symptomatic of the use of former Nazi officers by both East European and Western intelligence establishments and demonstrates the many constituencies that were willing to involve former Nazis in their own postwar enterprises—if they recast themselves according to the exigencies of the Cold War.

Recent years have seen an increasing interest in the immediate postwar era: denazification, the postwar fates of Nazi Germany's elites, and their impact on postwar German society and its discourses have attracted historians' and the public's attention. This book is located at the nexus of these three historiographical trends; through its individual chapters, it addresses some of their blind spots. It helps us to understand better the West German condition of a long postwar period.

Notes

1. For a recent discussion of Untersuchungsausschuss Nr. 47, see *Das Amt und die Vergangenheit: Deutsche Diplomaten im Dritten Reich und in der Bundesrepublik*, ed. Eckart Conze, Norbert Frei, Peter Hayes, and Moshe Zimmermann (Munich: Karl Blessing, 2010), 466–88.

2. International Commission of Historians, *The Waldheim Report* (Copenhagen: Museum Tusculanum, University of Copenhagen, 1993).

3. Albert Norden, *Kriegs- und Nazi-Verbrecher in der Bundesrepublik: Staat—Wirtschaft—Verwaltung—Armee—Justiz—Wissenschaft* (Berlin: Staatsverlag der Deutschen Demokratischen Republic, 1965); Ulrich Brochhagen, *Nach Nuernberg: Vergangenheitsbewältigung und Westintegration in der Ära Adenauer* (Hamburg: Junius, 1994), chap. 15.

4. See, for example, Norbert Frei, Ralf Ahrens, Jörg Osterloh, and Tim Schanetzky, *Flick: Der Konzern. Die Familie. Die Macht* (Munich: Blessing, 2009); Ulrich Herbert, *Best: Biographische Studien über Radikalismus, Weltanschauung und Vernunft* (Bonn: Dietz, 1996); Ernst Klee, *Was sie taten, was sie wurden: Ärzte, Juristen und andere Beteiligte am Kranken- und Judenmord* (Frankfurt: Fischer TB, 2004); Philipp Gassert, *Kurt Georg Kiesinger 1904–1988: Kanzler zwischen den Zeiten* (Stuttgart: DVA, 2006); Norman Goda, *Tales from Spandau: Nazi Criminals and the Cold War* (Cambridge: Cambridge University Press, 2008); Lutz Hachmeister, *Der Gegnerforscher: Die Karriere des SS-Führers Franz Alfred Six* (Munich: Beck, 1998); Lutz Hachmeister, *Die Herren Journalisten: Die Elite der deutsche Presse nach 1945* (Munich: Beck, 2001); Lutz Hachmeister, *Schleyer: Eine deutsche Geschichte* (Munich: Beck, 2004); Kerstin von Lingen, *Kesselring's Last Battle: War Crimes Trials and Cold War Politics, 1945–1960* (Lawrence: University Press of Kansas, 2009); Kerstin von Lingen, *SS and Secret Service: "Verschwörung des Schweigens"; Die Akte Karl Wolff* (Paderborn: Ferdinand Schöningh, 2010); Daniel E. Rogers, "Restoring a German Career, 1945–1950: The Ambiguity of Being Hans Globke," *German Studies Review* 31, no. 2 (2008): 303–24.

5. Konrad H. Jarausch, *After Hitler: Recivilizing Germans, 1945–1995* (Oxford: Oxford University Press, 2006), 25, 74.

6. See, for example, Perry Biddiscome, *The Denazification of Germany: A History, 1945–1950* (Stroud, UK: Tempus, 2007); Tom Bower, *The Pledge Betrayed: America and Britain and the Denazification of Postwar Germany* (Garden City, NY: Doubleday, 1982); Klaus-Dietmar Henke, "Die Trennung vom Nationalsozialismus, Selbstzerstörung, politische Säuberung, 'Entnazifizierung,' Strafverfolgung," in *Politische Säuberung in Europa: Die Abrechnung mit dem Faschismus und der Kollaboration nach dem Zweiten Weltkrieg*, ed. Klaus-Dietmar Henke and Hans Woller (Munich: DTV, 1991), 21–83; Lutz Niethammer, *Die Mitläuferfabrik: Die Entnazifizierung am Beispiel Bayerns* (Berlin: Dietz, 1982); Hinrich Rüping, "Zwischen Recht und Politik: Die Ahndung der NS-Taten in den beiden deutschen Staaten nach 1945," in *The Nuremberg Trials: International Criminal Law since 1945/Die Nürnberger Pro-*

zesse: Völkerstrafrecht seit 1945, ed. Herbert Reginbogin and Christoph J. M. Saffer-ling (Munich: K. G. Saur, 2006), 199–208; Clemens Vollnhals, ed., *Entnazifizierung: Politische Säuberung und Rehabilitierung in den vier Besatzungszonen 1945–1949* (Munich: DTV, 1991); Patricia Heberer and Jürgen Matthäus, eds., *Atrocities on Trial: Historical Perspectives on the Politics of Prosecuting War Crimes* (Lincoln: University of Nebraska Press, 2008).

7. Hilary Earl, *The Nuremberg SS-Einsatzgruppen Trial, 1945–1958: Atrocity, Law and History* (Cambridge: Cambridge University Press, 2009), 40.

8. Perry Biddiscombe, *The Denazification of Germany, 1945–1950* (London: Tempus, 2006), 62.

9. Ibid., 63, 72–73.

10. Ibid., 65.

11. Norman M. Naimark, *The Russians in Germany: A History of the Soviet Zone of Occupation, 1945–1949* (Cambridge, MA: Harvard University Press, 1995), chap. 1.

12. Michael R. Hayse, *Recasting West German Elites: Higher Civil Servants, Busi-ness Leaders and Physicians in Hesse between Nazism and Democracy, 1945–1955* (New York: Berghahn Books, 2003), 147.

13. Niethammer, *Die Mitläuferfabrik.*

14. Daniel E. Rogers, "The Chancellors of the Federal Republic of Germany and the Political Legacy of the Holocaust," in *The Impact of Nazism: New Perspectives on the Third Reich and Its Legacy,* ed. Alan E. Steinweis and Daniel E. Rogers (Lincoln: University of Nebraska Press, 2003), 232.

15. Jeffery Herf, *Divided Memories: The Nazi Past in the Two Germanies* (Cam-bridge, MA: Harvard University Press, 1997), 221.

16. Norbert Frei, *Adenauer's Germany and the Nazi Past: The Politics of Amnesty and Integration,* trans. Joel Golb (New York: Columbia University Press, 2002); Rob-ert Moeller, *War Stories: The Search for a Usable Past in the Federal Republic of Ger-many* (Berkeley: University of California Press, 2001).

17. Moeller, *War Stories.*

18. Donald Bloxham, "The Genocidal Past in Western Germany and the Experi-ence of Occupation, 1945–6," *European History Quarterly* 34, no. 3 (2004): 327.

19. Frank Biess, *Homecomings: Returning POWs and the Legacies of Defeat in Postwar Germany* (Princeton, NJ: Princeton University Press, 2006), 145.

20. Gavriel D. Rosenfeld and Paul B. Jaskot, eds., *Beyond Berlin: Twelve German Cities Confront the Nazi Past* (Ann Arbor: University of Michigan Press, 2008), 15. Moeller, *War Stories.*

21. Kim C. Priemel and Alexa Stiller, eds., *Reassessing the Nuremberg Military Tri-bunals: Transitional Justice, Trial Narratives, and Historiography* (New York: Berghahn Books, 2012), 2–15, as well as a number of the individual chapters. See also S. Jonathan Wiesen, *West German Industry and the Challenge of the Nazi Past, 1945–1955* (Chapel Hill: University of North Carolina Press, 2001), in particular the fascinating case study on Siemens in chap. 1. Also on this issue, see Hayse, *Recasting West German Elites.*

22. Peter Fritzsche, *Life and Death in the Third Reich* (Cambridge, MA: Belknap Press, 2009).

23. George C. Browder, *Hitler's Enforcers: The Gestapo and the SS Security Service in the Nazi Revolution* (New York: Oxford University Press, 1996), 7.

Part 1

Recast Identities in War Crimes Trials and Interrogations

1

Hans Globke at Nuremberg

Testimony as Rehabilitation, 1948–1949

Daniel E. Rogers

Throughout Konrad Adenauer's tenure as the first chancellor of the Federal Republic of Germany, between 1949 and 1963, Hans Globke remained at Adenauer's side as his closest adviser, while the new chancellor built agencies, formulated policies, and reacted to challenges and crises. But during the first four years of that period, because of controversies surrounding Globke's career during the Nazi era, Adenauer satisfied himself with giving Globke merely the reality, rather than also the title, of his closest adviser. Only after Adenauer won his first reelection in 1953 by a comfortable margin did he promote Globke to the office of *Staatssekretär,* analogous to the position of chief of staff in an American administration. Globke was the gatekeeper, paperwork manager, and chief adviser on process to the chancellor. With this promotion, Globke became the most prominent among West German political figures and civil servants to have survived and prospered in the Federal Republic despite involvement with Nazi Germany's anti-Semitic policies. Even after withering and repeated attacks on Globke by opposition Social Democrats, journalists, and the East German Communist government, Globke held Adenauer's confidence and made himself, deliberately or not, indispensable.[1]

The attacks on Globke were possible in the first instance because of Globke's career path and actions during the Nazi era. Although a member of the Catholic Center Party when Hitler became chancellor, Globke continued as a bureaucrat in the Reich Ministry of the Interior, reaching the high mid-level rank of *Ministerialrat.* He worked in the department handling issues surrounding marital status. From 1935 until the end of the Nazi regime, his immediate supervisor was Wilhelm Stuckart, a Nazi *Alter Kämpfer* (old fighter) who had been a party member since before the Beer Hall Putsch of 1923. In 1936 Stuckart and Globke coauthored a commentary on the Nuremberg race laws of the previous year. While the legal community might have been more widely aware of Stuckart because of the commentary, Stuckart's later, historical infamy stemmed largely from his attendance at the Wannsee Conference of January 1942, where he represented the Interior Ministry at a meeting called to settle procedural, jurisdictional, and legal questions hindering the speedy mass murder of Europe's Jews.[2] Captured by the Allies in 1945, Stuckart was ultimately placed on trial in the Wilhelmstrasse, or Ministries, case from 1947 to 1949. He was charged, among other offenses, with crimes against humanity.

In August 1948, Globke was called to testify at Nuremberg—unusually, he was a witness for both the prosecution and the defense (not merely called by one side and cross-examined by the other).[3] It was not the first evidence Globke offered in a war crimes trial. He provided written testimony at the most famous trial of all, the International Military Tribunal in 1946, by submitting an affidavit concerning the annexation of French territories after the German victory there in 1940.[4] His testimony concerning the two men who had been minister of the interior in the Nazi era was not needed. There was enough evidence from other sources that Wilhelm Frick, who had been the minister until 1943, had participated in mass murder; at Nuremberg he was convicted and hanged. The second minister of the interior after 1943, Heinrich Himmler, had killed himself in May 1945. Thus Globke's main opportunity to testify fully did not come until August 1948, in the trial of his former boss, Stuckart.

The quality and quantity of the testimony Globke provided revealed a witness who had nothing to hide about himself, even though he was so close to the apparatus of mass murder that he had known of it early. In the Wilhelmstrasse trial, Globke was given a rare chance, because he was not accused of any crime himself, to fully air his side of the story under oath and in a forum presumably very hostile to Nazis. Globke's testimony was open, expansive, and usually free of defensiveness. Anyone poring over the trial transcripts looking for evidence to use against Globke during the later attacks on him would not find a man who hid or evaded, but rather one who quickly admitted that he knew of mass murder without having participated in it or having been able to affect its course. Moreover, and most decisively of all for himself and his former superior, Stuckart, Globke portrayed Stuckart as a very rare bird indeed: a Nazi with a humane side and tolerance for dissent among his subordinates. That Stuckart was found guilty in 1949 but sentenced only to time already served may have owed much to how Globke portrayed Stuckart's leadership of his department and his role within the Interior Ministry and the Nazi Party.

Globke's testimony at Nuremberg was thus consistent with previous and later assertions about his level of involvement or noninvolvement with Nazi anti-Semitic policies and practices. If his meteoric rise from Allied internee in 1945 to the chancellor's most valuable aide by 1949 is to be fully understood, along with his survival for fourteen years thereafter despite frequent attacks, his testimony should be credited with fortifying his image as a careful and truthful civil servant who did the best he could under the stress of the time. An analysis of Globke's testimony reveals four distinct areas in which he could demonstrate his candor while also mitigating his personal culpability for crimes against Jews: Stuckart's relatively benign character, Globke's bureaucratic resistance to Nazi racial oppression, Globke's knowledge of the Holocaust as it was under way, and the reasons Globke stayed at his job even though it was so close to mass murder and persecution. In each of these four aspects of his testimony, Globke laid the groundwork for a future career at the highest levels of West German politics. He was able to build upon this benign portrayal of his Nazi years to recast his identity and provide his boss, Adenauer, with ammunition to use in his defense.[5]

First, in his testimony, Globke cast Stuckart in a generally highly positive light. On one level, Globke's self-interest required such testimony, regardless of how Stuckart had behaved in the Nazi era. For Globke, much depended on the outcome of Stuckart's trial. If Globke, via a guilty verdict for Stuckart, had been found to have been working for a mass murderer, Globke's future would have been bleak. Thus, while at the time of Stuckart's trial, Globke had no idea he would ever be more than a local government official in Aachen, one must take into account a certain self-interest in portraying Stuckart mildly.[6] Despite recognizing that Stuckart was a "convinced National Socialist" and even enjoyed wearing his SS uniform, Globke pictured the defendant as a moderate or even kindly Nazi.[7] The likelihood that Globke himself did anything reprehensible while working for the kind of boss he portrayed on the witness stand remained low indeed.[8] If Globke had served such a man, his activities during the Third Reich could have easily remained noncriminal.

As portrayed by his former subordinate on the witness stand, Stuckart believed it essential that the law exist independently of its political context, that Germany, even the Nazi Germany he had helped create, be a *Rechtsstaat,*

a government of laws. Stuckart resisted some measures he regarded as arbitrary and cruel.[9] Globke provided specific, albeit limited, examples of cases
in which Stuckart intervened to assist certain so-called half Jews[10] and even
so-called full Jews: "Through the measures prepared and issued by Department 1 numerous people, among which there were full Jews, ahd [sic] been
spared the treatment as Jews and . . . they owed their lives to Department 1
under the leadership of Stuckart."[11]

According to Globke, Stuckart did not totally support the Nazi Party's
measures toward either full Jews or less-than-full Jews and frequently subverted the wishes of the party chancellery on Jewish questions.[12] Stuckart
believed that "mixed race" individuals should be absorbed into the entirety of
the German people and not excluded, much less eliminated.[13] If necessary, he
favored sterilizing the "mixed race" rather than more extreme measures such
as deportation or murder.[14] Not only did Stuckart object to the most extreme
policies toward those considered less than fully Jewish; he and his department also interceded to save the lives of "numerous" people, Globke alleged
from the witness stand.[15]

His attitudes as a boss made him tolerant of a regime critic in his midst,
namely Globke, who was not silenced when he uttered criticisms of the party
or the regime in Stuckart's presence.[16] And Globke could make himself look
like a daring anti-Nazi while testifying that it was only Stuckart's intervention
with security services (RSHA) leader Ernst Kaltenbrunner that allowed Globke
to escape arrest after the July 20, 1944, assassination plot against Hitler:

> After the 20th of July and as a result of my participation in the
> attempted revolution, Kaltenbrunner wanted to have me arrested.
> Subsequently, Kettner, who was Stuckart's adjutant, told me that
> Stuckart went to Kaltenbrunner and he told him if he was able to
> introduce evidence against me, in that case, of course he had to
> arrest me, but if it was only a question of suspicion against me, he
> was to abstain from undertaking any arrest, and Kaltenbrunner, for
> the time being, adhered to this, at first at least, and the arrest war-
> rant was issued subsequently only but could no longer be put into
> actual effect when it was issued because the Gestapo officials who
> were charged to carry out the arrest, in view of the approach of the
> Americans, were compelled to recede.[17]

Furthermore, Stuckart was openly critical of the party's radical claims in front
of Globke and other subordinates and had clearly expressed, for instance,

his opposition to the violence of November 1938, *Kristallnacht*.[18] Stuckart's frequent opposition to party initiatives led to bureaucratic infighting of the highest order, at least for Nazi Germany: Globke recalled that Stuckart asked him to participate in investigations of a rumored Jewish ancestry of RSHA chief Reinhard Heydrich, not because Stuckart especially hated Jews, but to try to undermine Heydrich's radical leadership of anti-Jewish policies.[19]

Stuckart's opposition to including those considered less than full Jews in the most extreme measures of discrimination and violence earned him the suspicion and enmity of certain party and SS officials.[20] He might have tried to placate them by acting tough in meetings, but when back among his colleagues, he acted moderately and sometimes subversively.[21] Globke believed that Heinrich Himmler, who assumed the role of Stuckart's superior as minister of the interior in 1943, shunned Stuckart and would not often take his phone calls. Globke also estimated that Stuckart probably was in Hitler's presence only about ten times in total and thus had no influence at the highest level of all.[22] In short, he was no SS insider, despite his honorary SS rank and the uniform he liked to wear.[23]

Second, Globke elaborated a theory of successful bureaucratic obstruction in the Third Reich, of which he and Stuckart had been a part. Globke could truthfully state that he had never been a member of the Nazi Party, while keeping quiet about the fact that in 1940 he had applied for membership and had been rejected.[24] Instead of being a party member, he asserted, he had participated for years in the resistance movement.[25] On the stand at Stuckart's trial, there were ample opportunities for Globke to portray his service in the Interior Ministry as helping Jews rather than hurting them. For instance, in 1935, when some courts had been following the Nazi spirit rather than the letter of the law by refusing to marry "Aryans" and Jews, Globke had, he testified, attempted unsuccessfully to intervene with the Justice Ministry. He sought to have the Justice Ministry remind the courts of the law. Before that effort could have borne fruit, though, the Nuremberg Laws were issued, flatly forbidding "interracial" marriages.[26]

As Globke saw it, those such as himself who wished to hinder Nazi racism in general, or like Stuckart, who desired to block merely some isolated policies, could only succeed if they could articulate some danger to Germans at large or to the regime. Appeal to the letter of the law or humanitarian objections always led to a strengthening of party resolve to push through the most radically oppressive measures.[27] As a specific example, Globke offered Stuckart's opposition to Heydrich's efforts to treat so-called full and half Jews the same—in other words, to subject to deportation and death all those with two or more grandparents who were deemed fully Jewish. The only chance to block party zealots was to discuss the disadvantages to Germany as a whole, not to argue for the humane treatment of anyone.[28]

Globke offered another important example of his bureaucratic resistance, this time concerning regulations requiring Jews to add the forenames "Israel" or "Sara." In 1938, Stuckart's department had been confronted with party demands, specifically from Martin Bormann, chief of staff to the deputy Führer, that all Jews be forced to identify themselves with the mandatory *last* name of "Yid" ("Jüdd" or "Itzig" in German).[29] At first, with Stuckart's approval, Globke attempted to circumvent the party demand through the time-tested technique of bureaucratic inaction.[30] When the party and Minister of the Interior Frick insisted anyway, Globke and his colleague Hermann Hering suggested a compromise that would lessen the impact: requiring Jews to identify themselves with an additional *fore*name. Globke asserted that this was a milder solution, although Jews who never knew of the debates behind the scenes regarded the change to forenames as a harsh and humiliating new policy, for which Globke would often be criticized later in his life.[31] Knowing that if the Interior Ministry did nothing, the proposal might reach Hitler, who always agreed to the most radical proposal, Globke believed his had been a milder and therefore better policy for Jews: "It was generally known within the Ministry of the Interior that Hitler, in all basic questions as far as Jews were concerned, always agreed to the more intensified measure. As a consequence of this, one had to try to deal with the matter without a final decision on the part of Hitler and achieve the best possible result and [Bernhard] Loesner [sic] always again and again tried to do this and in that he had the full support of Stuckart."[32]

The trial allowed Globke to enter this perspective into the record, which later gave him and his defenders evidence to support a more benign take on his involvement in the name-change policy.

Perhaps the most difficult thing for Globke to try to explain away, both during the trial and later during his revived career, was his 1936 coauthorship with Stuckart of a commentary on the Nuremberg Laws.[33] Nazified courts would use Stuckart and Globke's commentary (and three others) to help them apply the Nuremberg Laws to individual cases. Globke and his defenders would often argue that his and Stuckart's commentary was the mildest of the four.[34] Regardless, Globke's name was on the title page of an instrument of persecution, and he had earned at least modest royalties from it. Yet here as well, Globke would cast his work as benefiting Jews if one understood the full context of the times, as an act of hidden bureaucratic obstruction. When

the prosecution asked him about Stuckart's racist introduction to the commentary, Globke's immediate response, which earned him an admonishment
from the prosecutor, was a rare display of defensiveness. He tried to explain
his motives for helping to write the commentary rather than addressing the
query about Stuckart's words that had been posed to him:

> Q: Didn't Stuckart in this preface vigorously endorse the racial ide-
> ology of Hitler, quoting "Mein Kampf" again and again?
> A: That is true. I was sorry to read that preface, but since I con-
> sidered the purpose of the commentary to help wherever possible
> those discriminated against, we had to put up with this preface if
> the National Socialist authorities were to get by this commentary
> [*sic*] at all.
> Q: I'm not asking about you, Dr. Globke, but only about Stuckart.[35]

Third, Globke admitted knowledge about the mass murder of Jews without being compelled by his questioners. Stuckart's trial gave him the opportunity to place on the record, under oath and before a hostile cross-examiner,
statements about his knowledge of the mass murders of the Holocaust. But
he set what he felt were important limits to his knowledge that would free
him from any self-incrimination regarding the genocide.

Globke denied ever hearing of the Wannsee Conference directly from
Stuckart, who had been in attendance (and who has, in subsequent cinematic
renditions of the conference, been made to look like the only mildly good
guy in attendance).[36] He further denied ever discussing the murder of the
Jews directly with Stuckart.[37] Yet Globke did immediately admit that he came
to learn about the systematic mass murders of Jews. He asserted that he only
heard the term *Final Solution* after the war[38] but learned during the war of the
mass murders themselves. This knowledge came from informal discussions
in official circles and from returning soldiers, not because policies or official
directives were passing through his department.[39] When Stuckart's defense
counsel, Curt von Stackelberg, offered him a chance to downplay his level of
knowledge about the killings, Globke did not take it:

> I have just told you I did not know the "final solution of the Jew-
> ish question" as a terminus technicus until after the capitulation.
> Consequently, although the expression "final solution of the Jewish
> question" might have been used, I never took it to mean the physical
> extermination of all Jews. I knew that Jews were being killed in large

numbers, and I was always of the opinion that there were Jews who were not killed, who were still living in Germany or in Theresien-stadt or elsewhere, in a sort of Ghetto.

You thought that there were excesses but no systematic extermination?

No, I don't want to say that. I am of the opinion—and I knew that at the time—that the extermination of the Jews was carried on systematically, but I did not know that it was supposed to apply to all Jews.[40]

Globke also denied ever having seen the infamous *Einsatzgruppen* (mobile killing squads) reports that had recounted in exact detail the murders of Jews inside the Soviet Union in 1941.[41] Yet, he acknowledged without any hesitation his knowledge of plans and procedures to kill the disabled among the German "Aryan" populace. He knew, he testified, of plans to kill those "no longer worthy of life."[42] Likewise, he asserted that he was aware that the interior minister who supervised Stuckart and himself, Wilhelm Frick, was responsible for killing the "mentally insane."[43]

Fourth and finally, Globke provided for himself the beginnings of a consistent story as to why he had remained behind at his job in the midst of such horror, why he had not resigned:

In Department 1 it was possible to help many people who had been discriminated against by National Socialist methods and this actually happened in numerous cases. I had, all the same, the intention every now and then to leave the Ministry of the Interior voluntarily, especially when Himmler took over the leadership of this ministry. The reason, I remained in office, was that my friends in the resistance movement, the Bishop of Berlin and others, requested me and urged me to disregard my own personal interests and to remain in office, because if I left, their last source of information about the Ministry of the Interior would vanish and thus the last possibility to gain an insight into their plans. It was comparatively easy for me to make up my mind in their direction because I was convinced that Dr. Stuckart would not request me to do anything which was against my conscience or would never request me to do any punishable act. And finally, after all, what more could I have done in the Third Reich than participate in a conspiracy for years, an activity which had as its ultimate aim the killing of Hitler.[44]

While Adenauer's and Globke's political opponents argued that Globke could have done less, rather than more (namely, by not writing the commentary or participating in the renaming regulations for Jews), Globke was providing himself and his later defenders with a line of argumentation that proved daunting, not the least because it may well also have been correct. As Adenauer's Christian Democratic Union deliberately and successfully courted the support of millions of Germans who had gone along with the Nazis (the so-called *Mitläufer*), having a man at his side who had advanced his career during those years while keeping himself free of personal guilt proved to be no political hindrance.[45] It gave the domestic opposition and many abroad something to complain about or lament, yet Adenauer ultimately served as chancellor longer than Hitler. Globke, of course, was by Adenauer's side the entire time. With an exculpatory version of his past documented under oath before an American military tribunal, Globke had helped himself rise high long before he knew he would ever have the chance.

In that Nuremberg courtroom in August 1948, Globke could hardly have dreamed that only a year later he would be one of the closest aides of the newly elected federal chancellor. Rather than deliberately furnishing the court with a version of his and Stuckart's pasts that would enable total rehabilitation, it is more likely that Globke was framing his experiences in the most helpful way possible so that his future would be less hindered. Having already successfully emerged from his own denazification process the year before as *unbelastet* (cleared), Globke need not have worried that he would be worse off than any other German who had lived through the Nazi regime as an adult.[46] It was, instead, a question of his suitability for a career like the one he had been building during the Weimar Republic, in the highest reaches of the Prussian civil service. An extended network of mutual connections brought him to Adenauer's attention in the late 1940s.[47] Yet it was Globke's careful, self-exculpatory, and unrefuted testimony at the trial of Wilhelm Stuckart that allowed him to put down in that most weighty of all public records, the transcript of a war crimes trial, a version of his life that made his astounding rise and extended tenure possible.

Notes

1. Also indispensable is the only full biography of Globke to date: Erik Lommatzsch, *Hans Globke (1898–1973): Beamter im Dritten Reich und Staatssekretär Adenauers* (Frankfurt: Campus, 2009). Specifically on Globke's postwar resurgence, see

Daniel E. Rogers, "Restoring a German Career, 1945–1950: The Ambiguity of Being Hans Globke," *German Studies Review* 31, no. 2 (2008): 303–24.

2. See Mark Roseman, *The Wannsee Conference and the Final Solution: A Reconsideration* (New York: Picador, 2002).

3. RG 238, U.S. Military Trials at Nürnberg, M897, roll 14, 15422, U.S. National Archives and Record Administration, College Park, MD (hereafter NARA).

4. Lommatzsch, *Hans Globke,* 136.

5. Adenauer cited Globke's dealings with the Allies, presumably including Globke's trial testimony, when he defended Globke from attacks in the Bundestag. Adenauer claimed that Globke had been fully examined by the Allies. See a summary of these statements by Adenauer in *Der Spiegel,* April 4, 1956, 18–19, including the assertions by Adenauer that "die Besatzungsbehörden hätten Hans Globke überprüft, und Juden hätten sich bei ihm für ihre Rettung bedankt."

6. Globke was the city treasurer of Aachen at the time of his testimony in Stuckart's trial.

7. RG 238, M897, roll 14, 15761, 15638, NARA.

8. The movie industry picked up on, and reinforced, this mild view of Stuckart. Twice it has portrayed him as opposing security services chief Reinhard Heydrich at the Wannsee Conference, intervening to try to save the lives of so-called *Mischlinge,* or persons of "mixed blood," part Jewish, part "Aryan." See Heinz Schirk's *Die Wannseekonferenz* (1984) and Frank Pierson's *Conspiracy* (2001), both made for television. In the latter, Stuckart was played by actor Colin Firth, who is not known for portraying darker characters.

9. RG 238, M897, roll 14, 15446, NARA.

10. RG 238, M897, roll 14, 15450, roll 15, 15832, NARA.

11. RG 238, M897, roll 15, 15871, 15872, NARA.

12. RG 238, M897, roll 14, 15247, NARA. Globke asserted that at one point Stuckart worked himself into a nervous collapse from opposing the party on such measures. RG 238, M987, roll 14, 15449, NARA.

13. RG 238, M897, roll 14, 15459, NARA.

14. RG 238, M897, roll 14, 15472, NARA.

15. RG 238, M897, roll 15, 15872, NARA.

16. RG 238, M897, roll 14, 15247, NARA.

17. RG 238, M897, roll 14, 15426, NARA.

18. RG 238, M897, roll 14, 15463, 15630, NARA.

19. RG 238, M897, roll 14, 15433, 15455, NARA.

20. RG 238, M897, roll 14, 15461, NARA.

21. RG 238, M897, roll 14, 15462, NARA.

22. Hans Globke, "Eidesstattliche Versicherung," April 29, 1948, 6, RG 238, M897, roll 116, NARA.

23. RG 238, M897, roll 14, 15434, NARA.

24. Erik Lommatzsch, "Hans Globke und der Nationalsozialismus: Eine Skizze,"

Historisch-politische Mitteilungen 10 (2003): 104; Lommatzsch, *Hans Globke*, 60–61.

25. Globke, "Eidesstattliche Versicherung," 1.

26. RG 238, M897, roll 14, 15477, NARA.

27. RG 238, M897, roll 14, 15451, NARA.

28. RG 238, M897, roll 14, 15474, NARA.

29. RG 238, M897, roll 14, 15465, NARA; Timo Klemm, *"Dem Namen nach zu urteilen . . ."—Antisemitische Namenpolemik und Namenpolitik als Mittel nationalsozialistischer Feindbildmalerei* (Munich: GRIN, 2007), 26n66.

30. RG 238, M897, roll 14, 15465, NARA.

31. RG 238, M897, roll 14, 15466, NARA; Victor Klemperer, *I Will Bear Witness: A Diary of the Nazi Years, 1933–1941,* trans. Martin Chambers (New York: Random House, 1998), 264.

32. RG 238, M897, roll 14, 15452, NARA.

33. Wilhelm Stuckart and Hans Globke, *Reichsbürgergesetz vom 15. September 1935, Gesetz zum Schutze des deutschen Blutes und der deutschen Ehre vom 15. September 1935, Gesetz zum Schutze der Erbgesundheit des deutschen Volkes (Ehegesundheitsgesetz) vom 18. Oktober 1935: Nebst allen Ausführungsvorschriften und den einschlägigen Gesetzen und Verordnungen* (Munich: Beck, 1936).

34. Hans Globke, "Aufzeichnung," in *Der Staatssekretär Adenauers: Persönlichkeit und politisches Wirken Hans Globkes,* ed. Klaus Gotto (Stuttgart: Klett Cotta, 1980), 251–52.

35. RG 238, M897, roll 14, 15640, NARA.

36. RG 238, M897, roll 15, 15831, NARA.

37. RG 238, M897, roll 14, 15472, 15610, NARA.

38. RG 238, M897, roll 14, 15471, NARA.

39. RG 238, M897, roll 14, 15667, NARA.

40. RG 238, M897, roll 14, 15471, NARA.

41. RG 238, M897, roll 14, 15617, NARA.

42. RG 238, M897, roll 14, 15688–89, NARA.

43. RG 238, M897, roll 14, 15615, NARA.

44. RG 238, M897, roll 15, 15873–74, NARA.

45. Norbert Frei, *Vergangenheitspolitik: Die Anfänge der Bundesrepublik und die NS-Vergangenheit* (Stuttgart: Deutscher Taschenbuch, 1999).

46. Rogers, "Restoring a German Career," 312.

47. Lommatzsch, *Hans Globke,* 142–59.

2

Auditioning for Postwar

Walter Schellenberg, the Allies, and Attempts to Fashion a Usable Past

Katrin Paehler

"For the time being, my services were no longer required."[1] Thus ends the memoir of Walter Schellenberg, formerly the head of Office VI—Foreign Intelligence—of Heinrich Himmler's Reich Security Main Office (Reichssicherheitshauptamt [RSHA]). The pithy phrase provides a telling coda to Schellenberg's almost decade-long effort to remake himself from Himmler's spymaster, closely connected to the highest rungs of party and state and many of Nazi Germany's key projects of racial and political surveillance and policing, into a well-meaning and daring German diplomat with strong Western leanings, a cosmopolitan outlook, and a proven humanitarian track record.

When Schellenberg wrote about his "services" no longer being required—clearly implying that he would have been all too happy to render them again—he was already a very sick man. He did not live to see the eventual publication of his memoir.[2] He had begun crafting the narrative and its main tenets much earlier, and while it did not gain for him a role in postwar diplomacy or intelligence, Schellenberg managed to fashion a usable past that helped him evade many of the potential consequences of his earlier activities. And with the posthumous publication of his memoir, hailed in Alan Bullock's introduction to the English version as "a piece of historical evidence, for none of those who have so far published their memoirs of this period were in a good position to know and to have seen at first hand what took place at the center of power," Schellenberg's recast identity and the narrative connected with it took on

Walter Schellenberg. Bundesarchiv Bild 101III-Alber-178-04A.

tremendous staying power. To be sure, Bullock cautions his readers, noting that it "would [not] be wise to accept Schellenberg as a trustworthy witness where his evidence cannot be corroborated. Naturally enough he presents his own part in these events in as favorable a light as possible and often with some exaggeration of his own importance."[3] In reality, though, Schellenberg's memoir has taken on an oft-uncontested life of its own in historical writing, especially when it comes to Nazi Germany's foreign intelligence efforts and to the very last months and weeks of the war. His recast identity looms large.

Schellenberg's recasting of his professional history is a fascinating case study. Recent years have seen a growing interest in those functionaries of the Third Reich who rose to prominence and influential positions in postwar West Germany.[4] This interest is by no means abating but rather has shifted from the specific facts of individual cases to the processes and sometimes networks through which these men (and few women) created more usable pasts for themselves. How did they make sense of their pasts and disassociate themselves from the roles they had played in Nazi Germany? While there surely existed many different strategies, some common approaches are clearly discernible: one focused on alleged fundamental differences with Nazi ideology; another one disavowed or minimized the role(s) a person had played in Nazi Germany; and a third one (over-)emphasized real and imagined dangers into which an individual's "dissidence" had put him. But most who were successful in recasting their identities had not been notorious in the most obvious senses: they had not been directly and visibly connected to the highest rungs of the party elite; they had not been directly involved in the planning of World War II; and they had no direct, "hands-on" involvement with the Holocaust or with the persecution of Nazi Germany's political enemies. They were mostly members of the "expertocracy," and as such, they had remained largely invisible to the public eye.[5] In a postwar society neither inclined nor truly able to confront the Nazi era, their comparative lack of apparent guilt oftentimes paved their way into postwar futures of considerable influence.[6]

Schellenberg—a party man, SS and SD member, spymaster, and closely associated with a good number of the postwar bêtes noires of Nazi Germany, for example, Himmler, Reinhard Heydrich, and Ernst Kaltenbrunner—took a different, seemingly counterintuitive, and most certainly audacious tack in recasting his past. Rather than disavowing his role in Nazi Germany, Schellenberg created a coherent narrative around three images of himself: the ultimate insider, the cosmopolitan diplomat, and the humanitarian and thwarted bringer of peace. He proffered these images in a constant and stable narrative.

It was laid out in writing before his transfer into Allied custody, reinforced during his interrogations, and expanded upon in his memoir. In other words, Schellenberg entered Allied custody with a coherent narrative as his proverbial calling card and stayed on message thereafter. Tripping him off became difficult and increasingly undesirable, because Schellenberg's persona as the ultimate insider established him as a fountain of seemingly valuable information to the Allies; in the process, he helped to shape and to reinforce Allied perceptions about Nazi Germany and its main players.

Schellenberg's gamble almost paid off. His efforts likely helped him to secure a lighter sentence in Nuremberg and, most certainly, a better postwar image than he deserved. It is anyone's guess what would have happened had he lived longer: after interrogating him at length, the Allies were decidedly unimpressed. However, as a relentless self-promoter and good storyteller, Schellenberg might have been able to secure his professional or economic well-being after all; he did not perceive himself as made for obscurity. Lastly, professional historians have quite frequently all too readily accepted Schellenberg's self-serving renditions of events. This holds true in particular when it comes to information about the last months and weeks of the war, when there are comparatively fewer contemporaneous documents. In short: Schellenberg's narratives, meant to recast his own role in Nazi Germany, hold sway over important swaths of history.[7] For that reason alone, tracing the process through which Schellenberg remade himself is an important undertaking.

Born in Saarbrücken in 1910, Walter Schellenberg studied law at the universities of Marburg and Bonn.[8] He passed his first exam in 1933, roughly around the same time that Adolf Hitler was appointed chancellor. He joined the NSDAP and the SS in 1933 and became involved with the SD shortly thereafter. Over the course of the next six years, Schellenberg carved out a position for himself in the new state's administrative and policing universe. Traditionally trained in law, Schellenberg was clearly an asset for Reinhard Heydrich and a fledging SD that was trying to secure and to define its role.

Between 1938 and the summer of 1941, Nazi Germany began to move even more aggressively against perceived domestic racial and political enemies and also began its assault on the neighboring states; in a sense, the state moved from ideological theory to the theory's—sometimes pragmatic—praxis. Schellenberg's professional trajectory mirrored these developments. He remade himself from a talented bureaucrat—he was intimately involved in the negotiations about the deployment of the *Einsatzgruppen* as designated killing units in the upcoming attack against the Soviet Union—into a theoretician of intelligence and policing. After a stint with the Gestapo's

Counterintelligence Department, he was appointed acting head of Nazi Germany's political foreign intelligence service, Office VI of the RSHA, in 1941. Conducting foreign intelligence under the conditions of a global war was an uphill battle at best, especially as political foreign intelligence remained a poorly defined concept. Schellenberg's office found itself in intramural fights with the military intelligence service, the Abwehr under Admiral Wilhelm Canaris, and the Auswärtige Amt under Joachim von Ribbentrop. Schellenberg proved yet again to be an excellent technocrat of power: he managed to take over the better part of the Abwehr in 1943–1944 but was less successful in his attempts to dispose of Ribbentrop as the foreign minister. But he did established himself as Himmler's main adviser in all matters related to foreign policy, readying Office VI to become Himmler's foreign office with himself at the helm. In this context Schellenberg established contacts with a number of Swedish and Swiss nationals. Ultimately, these contacts assisted Schellenberg in his attempts to sound out for Himmler the possibilities for a separate peace with the Western Allies—an option that also included the distinct possibility of breaking up the anti-Hitler alliance and gaining for Germany a new lease on life. To open up these lines to the West, Schellenberg in 1944 and 1945 used Scandinavian and Jewish concentration camp inmates as bargaining chips. Over the course of these negotiations, especially with Count Folke Bernadotte of Sweden but also with the former president of Switzerland, Jean-Marie Musy, and while Nazi Germany was collapsing, a substantial number of people were freed and transported to safety.[9] And in late April 1945, Schellenberg did, indeed, persuade Himmler to offer surrender to the Western Allies via the Swedish intermediaries. The offer was rejected, because it did not extend to all members of the anti-Hitler alliance. Schellenberg subsequently parlayed his involvement with Bernadotte into an assignment given to him by the new German leader Admiral Karl Dönitz that made travel to Sweden possible. Thus, the end of the war found Schellenberg on one of Bernadotte's properties outside of Stockholm and out of the immediate reach of the victorious Allies.

In neutral Sweden Schellenberg crafted his basic narrative: a thirty-seven-page piece that was soon aptly entitled "Brigadeführer Schellenberg, Amtschef VI, Autobiography Compiled during His Stay in Stockholm, June 1945."[10] Schellenberg wrote it under the protection and sometimes on the properties of Bernadotte or of people close to the Swedish count.[11] According to Schellenberg, it was Bernadotte who persuaded him to write down "the events leading up to the capitulation" while his memory was still fresh, noting "that a work of this kind would be difficult to produce later if it were nec-

essary to depend upon memory for the chronological sequence of events."
Bored by "his forced inactivity" and able to make use of the recollections of
his assistant Franz Göring, who had played an important role in the liberation of numerous concentration camp inmates, and his longtime secretary
Marie-Luise Schienke, who were with him in Sweden, Schellenberg began
to dictate what he remembered to Schienke. Though the endeavor was initially planned as the outline for a book, Schellenberg claimed to have soon
settled on "a short autobiographical summary of events," especially when he
"saw the necessity of voluntarily surrendering to the Americans or the British."[12] Indubitably, such a summary of events would come handy under those
circumstances. Schellenberg subtly suggested that neither the idea for the
piece nor its ultimate format originated with him. The former was Bernadotte's suggestion and the latter due to his realization that voluntary surrender would be the best step to take. The implication was that Schellenberg had
little reason either to be concerned about his past or to be exceedingly proac-
tive about his future. In reality, he was clearly both and had found a perfect
format to address these concerns in his autobiographical sketch. Nine-tenths
of the text deals with Schellenberg's good deeds in the last months of the war,
which he depicted as the logical outcome of his beliefs and earlier activities.

Schellenberg did not write this autobiographical sketch, the proverbial
Urfaust of his defense, in a vacuum. Either shortly before Schellenberg began
writing it or concurrently, Bernadotte embarked on a similar project. His
book *The Fall of the Curtain: Last Days of the Third Reich* was published in
London in 1945.[13] Bernadotte's thin book included passages authored by
Schellenberg and clearly identified as such, yet it seems that the inclusion
of these passages, as well as Bernadotte's overall fairly positive evaluation of
Schellenberg and his activities, led to the persistent claim that *The Fall of the
Curtain* was, indeed, ghostwritten by Schellenberg. These claims, lacking in
solid evidentiary support, have largely been debunked. However, it seems
extremely likely and only natural that the two men, who spent much time
together, discussed their respective writing projects or, as Doerries put it,
their reading of "events and appraisals of people."[14] This was clearly a writers' collective of contaminating closeness, for it is reasonable to conclude
that Schellenberg and Bernadotte smoothed out seemingly minor discrepan-
cies that might have existed. Conversely, though, it is likely that Bernadotte's
plan to publish his recollections reined in most inclinations to overreach
that Schellenberg might have entertained. He needed Bernadotte, his contacts, and his influence; there was nothing to be gained from contradicting
or alienating the Swede.

Relationships worked differently in the case of his assistant Franz Göring, whom Schellenberg asked "to write an eye witness account, in order to supplement and *confirm* certain parts of his story." It is reasonable to assume that Göring took very seriously the implications of Schellenberg's request when he wrote his account, which he claimed to be an extract from his diary.[15] Göring had several reasons to hitch his horse to Schellenberg's wagon: for one, Göring was safe and sound in neutral Sweden in the company of his fiancée, Schienke. Second, his role in Schellenberg's humanitarian activities would help Göring with any questions that might arise in the future about his own record. The better his boss did, the better the outcome would be for Göring as well. This is not to suggest that the three accounts were sanitized beyond recognition, but they did not emerge in a vacuum. The "Autobiography" was Schellenberg's first attempt to control the narrative. He crafted a coherent story that could be confirmed in a seemingly independent fashion: by checking it against the accounts by Bernadotte and Göring, two of the other main players in the events in question. Few people, then and now, were or are aware of the context in which these three pieces came to be.

The "Autobiography" proved a success—in Sweden and beyond. Schellenberg gave copies of it to a number of prominent and influential Swedes.[16] In late May, Schellenberg, ably assisted by Bernadotte, began to negotiate his transfer into American custody. The negotiations were fairly protracted and did not work out exactly as Schellenberg had hoped, for he was to be taken to London after a short time in Frankfurt.[17] When Schellenberg boarded his plane for Frankfurt on June 17, 1945—after almost six weeks in Sweden—the American Assistant Military Attaché Charles E. Rayens, who had negotiated the transfer and seemed reasonably taken by the German, was with him. Also on board was Bernadotte, who was willing to vouch for him and who wanted to ensure that all went well. Schellenberg carried his calling card: additional copies of his "Autobiography." He had pulled off the almost impossible, for he had morphed into his own character witness.

In the following months, Schellenberg was interrogated intensely, at least most of the time. Upon his arrival in Frankfurt and registration at SHAEF, he was initially stashed away in one or several local safe houses. Doerries notes with surprise that Schellenberg was not transferred to one of the two main Allied detention centers for Nazi bigwigs, which were the sites of interrogations about the structure and nature of Nazi Germany.[18] Since Schellenberg had been the head of Nazi Germany's foreign intelligence service, it only made sense, though, to have him interrogated separately and exclusively by members of the Allied intelligence services. And the war in the Far East was not over yet. In his initial talk with Rayens in Sweden, Schellenberg had tried to capitalize on American concerns and made intimations that Rayens could not ignore in good faith, for he reported that "Schellenberg believed that his Japanese section, personnel, specialists and records, could be assembled for the benefit of our army."[19] Schellenberg was selling the mirage of an omnipotent spymaster with global assets. The interrogations began ten days after Schellenberg's arrival in Frankfurt and involved a number of British and American intelligence officials.[20] Their findings were summarized in a lengthy report. Doerries describes the report as "not overly impressive in analysis and conclusion but densely packed with information and data gathered in the obviously rewarding sessions with Schellenberg."[21] Schellenberg was a fountain of information and "entirely cooperative and . . . particularly willing to denounce Kaltenbrunner."[22]

On July 7, 1945, Schellenberg was flown to London for further interrogations.[23] He was immediately transferred to Camp 020, an internment center theoretically under the oversight of the British Home Office but practically run by MI5, the domestic branch of the British Intelligence Service. Over the course of the war, the interrogation of suspected spies and others had been made into an art form in this facility. Interrogators made ample use of psychological intimidation and sensory deprivation; recent research also provides strong circumstantial evidence that some prisoners were tortured. In addition, interrogators used the mystique of the omnipotent British Secret Service to their advantage.[24] For Schellenberg, Camp 020 was a rude awakening. Prominent Swedes had handled him with utmost care, Rayens had afforded him quite a bit of consideration, and it appears that the interrogations in Frankfurt conformed to Schellenberg's expectations. Camp 020 did not. Schellenberg, described by the camp commandant as a "priggish little dandy, fetched up rakishly," was "shocked by his stern reception and sulked peevishly until he was brought face to face with the reality of British contempt for him and his evil works."[25] While there is no indication that Schellenberg was tortured, he was treated more poorly than he expected. He clearly did not appreciate the "light, being hollered at, [or] cold water baths," and he noted that he had been "finished." After eight weeks in a dark cell, he had been ready to kill himself but did not find the opportunity to do so. Or so he claimed in a later exchange with R. W. M. Kempner.[26]

As a witness, Schellenberg was as loquacious and eager as ever. Nothing suggests that his interrogators had to "force [information] out of him."[27] From the first (Frankfurt) interrogation on, it was clear that Schellenberg would talk—and talk he did. The interrogation then formed the basis for the "Final Report on the Case of Walter Friedrich Schellenberg," a detailed summary report of more than 120 pages and twenty-three sometimes extensive appendixes on various topics.[28] The "Final Report" was not the Allies' last word on Schellenberg, but it came close. It is of central importance, for it established a core understanding of Schellenberg, his activities, and his role in Nazi Germany.

The interrogations in London were driven by two main motivations: the wish to understand the man and his service—both of which had been shrouded in mystery and had been sources of anxiety among Western intelligence agencies—and the need to arrest developing security threats, such as postdefeat networks. As such, they sated the immediate interest of the intelligence communities. However, the realities these interrogations unveiled turned out to be an exasperating letdown.[29] Neither Schellenberg nor the service he led lived up to Allied expectations.

Schellenberg was transferred to Nuremberg in early November 1945, where the International Military Tribunal was about to get under way. Amt VI had turned out to be largely a mirage and far from a security threat, but Schellenberg had come to be known as a fountain of information. Slated as a witness for the prosecution, he was further interrogated in view of the upcoming trial. It is a fair assumption that the new surroundings agreed with Schellenberg. For one, he had been trained in law and thus was in his element. His role as a witness also allowed him to flaunt his knowledge of the inner workings of Nazi Germany and its leading personalities. In addition, it gave him an opportunity to settle some scores and to hone his persona as a friend of the West.[30]

"The best thing Schellenberg had going for him after the war was that he had developed the right internal enemies," Richard Breitman quips shrewdly and very truly.[31] They included Ernst Kaltenbrunner, the last head of the RSHA and thus Schellenberg's superior; Foreign Minister Joachim Ribbentrop; the head of Office IV (Gestapo) Heinrich Müller; and sabotage expert Otto Skorzeny. These men counterbalanced nicely Schellenberg's "wrong friends," a category in which Heydrich and Himmler took pride of place. Schellenberg was able to exploit his enmity with Kaltenbrunner to the fullest—there was no love lost between the two men, a fact well known at Camp 020 and apparently a source of amusement—and to use their antagonistic relationship to recast his own past.[32] The Allies, for their part, regarded the enigmatic Kaltenbrunner as particularly unsavory, and after Himmler's suicide, he was the highest-ranking member of the RSHA in Allied hands. His name connected to the much feared, yet largely imaginary "alpine redoubt," Kaltenbrunner was considered a security threat and a potential postwar player.[33] He also fit the image of the proverbial ugly German, down to his dueling scars, which was a nice visual bonus for the upcoming trial. Schellenberg expertly delivered on Allied expectations.

Schellenberg's "Autobiography" focused on the last few months of the war, and it presented Kaltenbrunner as the tale's main villain—his relationship with Kaltenbrunner had long before shifted from general cooperation to outright conflict. Schellenberg left little doubt that it was the head of the RSHA who obstructed his efforts to make contact and negotiate with the Western powers and to free concentration camp inmates. Yet Schellenberg's narrative goes even further: he notes that even Himmler feared the head of the RSHA, since Kaltenbrunner was close to Hitler, subtly implying that Kaltenbrunner might have held influence over Hitler. In effect, the "Autobiography" created two competing centers of power, a dichotomy of good and evil, of reasonable and unreasonable: the former consisted of Himmler and Schellenberg, while the latter comprised Hitler and Kaltenbrunner.

In Schellenberg's narrative, Kaltenbrunner is the man who reproached him for supporting too strongly Count Bernadotte's plans to move Scandinavian concentration camp inmates out of the collapsing Germany; who issued orders in Himmler's name that had not originated with the RFSS; who did not comply with orders coming from Himmler; and who "got Hitler to stop any further trains [of freed Jews] to Switzerland."[34] Whatever went wrong with Schellenberg's plans, the blame was Kaltenbrunner's.

Schellenberg portrayed Kaltenbrunner as an outright dangerous man on two different yet interconnected levels. On the one hand, his eagerness to harm Schellenberg presented an immediate and personal danger to the latter; on the other hand, Kaltenbrunner's proximity to Hitler and his alleged influence with or over the Führer made him dangerous in a broader sense. Schellenberg set the stage for this story line in the opening pages of his "Autobiography," noting that in late 1942 and early 1943, "Hitler and later Himmler" wanted "to imprison me and my associates in a concentration camp for defeatism." The alleged reason was an intelligence report on Russia, and the instigator was Kaltenbrunner. There is no independent confirmation of this threat against Schellenberg, but he very skillfully created the impression of a man under siege. Himmler, who had taken a "personal liking" to Schellenberg, became his shield. In the world that Schellenberg created in his "Autobiography," Himmler was the voice of reason; with him, Schellenberg said, "[I] could always be sure that I myself and my work would always be judged by 'non-party-political' standards."[35] In other words, in a political system in which an intelligence report could lead to accusations of defeatism and in which a man like Kaltenbrunner held power, Himmler became a beacon of nonideological common sense and a natural ally to a man like Schellenberg.

In the broader sense, Kaltenbrunner's influence with and proximity to Hitler made him dangerous. Kaltenbrunner "got Hitler to stop any further trains [of camp inmates as part of the negotiations with Musy] to Switzerland," and Hitler then "forbade any German, under threat of death, to help not only one Jew more, but interestingly enough also any American or English P.O.W." In a roundabout way, Schellenberg experienced Kaltenbrunner's influence in his own interactions with Himmler, for Himmler coveted and clamored for Hitler's approval. In early April 1945, for example, Schellenberg and Musy struck upon the idea of a four-day truce "on land and in the air, in order to use this time to conduct all Jews and other foreign prisoners in an orderly manner through the front lines, and thus show Germany's 'good will.'" Ultimately, Schellenberg held the expectation that this plan would—"beyond the rescue of these people"—segue into the "discussion of a compromise, which would be to everybody's benefit." In other words, the truce would lead to negotiations about a separate peace with the Western Allies. However, none of this could be achieved without Hitler's approval, and Himmler, who by Schellenberg's reckoning personally agreed with the plan's merits, did not dare to discuss it with the Führer. Instead, Himmler consulted "with the chief of the 'Camarilla' which surrounded Hitler, Kaltenbrunner, who then indicated his refusal."[36] All that stood between Schellenberg, a solution to humanitarian crisis in the camps, and the end of the war was Kaltenbrunner.

Similar points are made in the "Final Report," but Schellenberg provided additional, damning details. He gleefully conveyed Kaltenbrunner's bumpy career trajectory (owed largely to Kaltenbrunner's disbarment after his involvement in the 1934 Nazi coup attempt in Austria) and compared it to his own much more successful one. He related Kaltenbrunner's jealousy and his efforts to make Schellenberg's professional life difficult, one of the report's main themes. Kaltenbrunner brought about a deterioration of Schellenberg's position, rebuffed Schellenberg's efforts, attempted to remove Schellenberg from his position in Amt VI, and established himself as a relentless micromanager: "All documents and reports of importance had to be submitted to Kaltenbrunner and signed by him and all important decisions and authorizations were taken by Kaltenbrunner personally." As Kaltenbrunner was Schellenberg's superior, this should not have been a shocking surprise.

After Kaltenbrunner's appointment, Schellenberg also found his own direct access to Himmler, which he had until then enjoyed, much restricted; this was a source of major irritation for him. Conversely, Kaltenbrunner was not amused that Schellenberg kept going over his head and directly to Himmler still.[37] Schellenberg also made much of Kaltenbrunner's attempt to circumscribe more precisely Schellenberg's position in his office and in the RSHA in general or to undermine him by establishing Kaltenbrunner's cronies, such as Otto Skorzeny, Wilhelm Hoettl, or Wilhem Waneck, the men of the "Austrian Group," in Schellenberg's domain. Schellenberg countered by putting his own allies in place.

Schellenberg furthermore reframed events that were indicative of a good working relationship between him and Kaltenbrunner. When, in the aftermath of the usurpation of the Abwehr, Kaltenbrunner "put Schellenberg in charge of Amt Mil," Schellenberg let it be known that this had been "provisional."[38] Schellenberg thus recast a career capstone into a temporary arrangement; indirectly, this also implied that the responsibility for Amt Mil was not his alone. Schellenberg also suggested that Kaltenbrunner forced upon him the rank of Major General of the Police and strongly insinuated that he much preferred his civilian titles.

Kaltenbrunner, according to Schellenberg, remained a threat to him until the end of the war and occasionally tried to have him removed from his position. When this removal happened—on May 1, 1945—Schellenberg was with Himmler in Northern Germany and the *Reichsführer* SS did not take Kaltenbrunner's step seriously. Indeed, Schellenberg stressed that Himmler appeared to regret not having taken a stronger stand against Kaltenbrunner earlier.[39] In sum, Kaltenbrunner was at the root of all problems. There was plenty of information in this report that could be used against Kaltenbrunner, and it was abundantly clear that Schellenberg would be all too glad to provide additional information if the prosecution so desired.

Schellenberg's narrative about Kaltenbrunner and his insidiousness remained stable from the "Autobiography" to the "Final Report." The main difference can be found in the level of detail—whereas the "Autobiography" focuses largely on Schellenberg's "humanitarian" and peace-negotiating efforts in the last months of the war, the "Final Report," in which those very same efforts provide the main plot, covers a much broader swath of history. It gave Schellenberg extended opportunities to paint Kaltenbrunner in an unfavorable light and, conversely, to elevate his own standing. These efforts were not restricted to Kaltenbrunner's political demeanor. Schellenberg also made sure to include a fair sprinkling of juicy personal tidbits, with Kaltenbrunner's vanity taking pride of place. However, if one fed his vanity, Schellenberg slyly advised his interrogators, Kaltenbrunner was also a man who could be played.[40]

Kaltenbrunner's personality and appearance take up even more space in Schellenberg's memoir, written for a broad audience interested in recent history but also, just as much, in salacious details about Nazi Germany's elite. On a basic level, Schellenberg's description expertly delivers on German stereotypes about crude Austrians. Kaltenbrunner was a "giant in stature, heavy in movements—a real lumberjack." He was of "rough-hewn coarseness"; his eyes were "small, penetrating . . . unpleasant . . . like the eyes of a viper seeking to petrify its prey." He had "the hands of a gorilla," which made Schellenberg "feel quite sick," and would "bang on the table" before speaking. Schellenberg also noted Kaltenbrunner's "very bad teeth" and that he "spoke very indistinctively"; but then Schellenberg could "understand his strong Austrian accent only with great difficulty" in the first place. In a few broad strokes but with great alacrity, Schellenberg conjured the epitome of an Austrian hick—crude, savage, and dangerous. And the very opposite of himself.

Discussing Kaltenbrunner's initial appointment, Schellenberg made it clear that the choice of Kaltenbrunner was Hitler's and that he, Schellenberg, would have preferred just about anyone else. But Kaltenbrunner was the "right man for Hitler" and background mattered. Hitler was convinced that "this countryman of his . . . had all the necessary qualifications for the job, of which unconditional obedience and personal loyalty to the Fuehrer were not the least important."[41] Schellenberg's implications were clear—as much as Kaltenbrunner was the right man for Hitler, he (Schellenberg) was not. Indeed, their personalities were "too much opposed for us ever to be able to work together harmoniously." Kaltenbrunner was a "doctrinaire," a "fanatical adherent of National Socialism," and "followed the principle of absolute obedience." Kaltenbrunner, on the other hand, regarded Schellenberg "as just a careerist who held a position because of professional ability," who "had rendered no special service to the movement, and from [Schellenberg's] opinions and associations it appeared that [he] was politically unreliable."[42] Schellenberg cast Kaltenbrunner as an "ideological soldier" and a fanatical Nazi and himself as a professional.[43] The differences could not be any starker.

In a virtuoso performance, Schellenberg then gave credit to Heydrich's personnel politics and suggested that Kaltenbrunner's animus toward him found its origins there. Schellenberg let it be known that Heydrich, as long as he was alive, had blocked Kaltenbrunner's ascent in the SD. But when Kaltenbrunner took on Heydrich's former position, his hatred of his predecessor led him to make mistake after mistake. Schellenberg diagnosed Kaltenbrunner with a "Heydrich Complex" that made him surround himself with his Austrian cronies to counteract Heydrich's still palpable influence in the RSHA. Ultimately, though, Schellenberg claimed that he became its prime victim, as "Kaltenbrunner eventually transferred his 'Heydrich complex' to me. I suddenly became the object of all the animosity he had previously entertained against him [Heydrich]." For example, Kaltenbrunner used the weekly lunches of the RSHA's department heads to attack him "in the most sadistic manner." Schellenberg made sure that his readers understood that "those terrible last years of the war seemed a real torture" to him.[44] Schellenberg took on the mantle of the Austrian bully's victim.

Schellenberg's allegedly antagonistic relationship with Kaltenbrunner serves, in turn, as an explanation for his closeness to Himmler. Schellenberg cast Kaltenbrunner as "evil," like the distant Hitler. Himmler, on the other hand, he portrayed as weak and vacillating, void of strong opinions and convictions, and open to influence from those closest to him. Schellenberg crafted a heightened—and somewhat daring—version of the common exculpatory story of an official staying in his position "to prevent worse." Only in Schellenberg's case, he justified having stayed with Himmler "to make better."

Schellenberg's attempts to recast his relationship with Himmler hinged on his ability to portray himself as a diplomat, a humanitarian, and a thwarted bringer of peace, for among any number of "wrong friends," Himmler certainly takes the prize. To some extent, Schellenberg was in luck, for the "Autobiography" focused, almost in its entirety, on the last two years of their relationship, which included Himmler's last-ditch, well-documented, and very recent peace soundings. The "Final Report" and his later memoir, while more detailed on his other exploits, similarly attempted to frame all of his interactions with Himmler as stepping stones toward his alleged ultimate goal: a separate peace with the West. Other activities of Schellenberg's, which brought him into close contact with Himmler, fell to the wayside, for example, the times he reported to the RFSS on the cultural genocide in recently occupied Poland.[45] In his writings Schellenberg emphasized his slowly growing influence with Himmler. He cast Himmler as "an exception to the whole, corrupt government set-up" and emphasized this over the germane fact that he did, indeed, serve at the RFSS's pleasure.[46] With his own activities fading into the background, Schellenberg used his allegedly long-standing plans to bring about peace as the primary reason for his continuing close relationship with the purportedly pliable Himmler. Schellenberg almost managed to square the circle. He turned his proximity to Himmler from a liability into the very reason for, one, Himmler's offer of conditional surrender and, two, his own humanitarian achievements.

Office VI of the RSHA was Nazi Germany's political foreign intelligence, but most of Schellenberg's postwar statements obscure that. Rather, Schellenberg highlighted his foreign policy initiatives and endeavors. In all his accounts, Schellenberg stressed that his interest had always been foreign policy and that, as a young man, he had hoped to make a career in this field; but his ambition was thwarted by circumstances beyond his control. Even his position at the helm of the political foreign intelligence service was simply a step along the road, for as devoted as Schellenberg was to his office, he let it be known that he thought more broadly and used his service to engage in foreign policy.[47]

Schellenberg focused attention on his comparatively frequent interactions with foreigners of considerable influence if not always impeccable pedigrees, such as the Swedish businessmen Jakob Wallenberg, Axel Brandin, and Alvar Möller; the chief of the Intelligence Section of the Swiss General Staff, Roger Mason; or the former Swiss president Jean-Marie Musy. If professional life in Nazi Germany was sometimes tough for Schellenberg, a fact he never failed to impress on his interlocutors, he apparently never met a Western foreigner with whom he did not feel an immediate connection born out of mutual trust and respect, admiration, and a frank exchange of largely compatible ideas. On the initial meeting with the "head of the Swedish I.S. [Intelligence Service]," Martin Lundquist, the "Final Report" noted that "the two men immediately took a personal liking to each other and henceforth Schellenberg always made a point of seeing him on his visits to Sweden." A meeting with Axel Brandin of the Swedish Match Company in June 1943, ostensibly to deal with the fate of the so-called Warsaw Swedes, "led to an intimate exchange of opinion"; a month later, Brandin's "behavior toward [Schellenberg was] even more friendly than before."[48] Alvar Möller, the company's Berlin representative, was not far behind in his appreciation of Schellenberg and his efforts.[49] These and other meetings allowed for Schellenberg to establish bona fides with well-meaning movers and shakers in neutral countries, which, he surely hoped, might come in handy eventually.

Schellenberg's propensity to brandish his diplomatic credentials and his agreeability becomes even more obvious in his references to his interactions with Jean-Marie Musy and Count Folke Bernadotte, two foreign emissaries who traveled to Germany in late 1944 and early 1945 attempting to negotiate for the release of some of Nazi Germany's camp population. Accompanying Musy to his meeting with Himmler, Schellenberg "was able to convince himself that he and Musy were in fundamental agreement."[50] Reporting on his first meeting with Bernadotte, Schellenberg noted that he "felt immediate sympathy with the Count" and reported that he "spoke openly" about "how [he] personally viewed the political situation." Soon, the men were on "such good terms that [he] was able to give Count Bernadotte some tips . . . in regard to the idiosyncrasies and peculiarities of Himmler."[51]

Schellenberg also ensured that his foreign political successes were known and appreciated by his interrogators. He laid out his various meetings with Roger Masson, the head of the Intelligence Service of the Swiss General Staff, and detailed how this connection ultimately brought him into contact with General Henri Guisan, the Swiss chief of staff. Ultimately, this connection allowed him, with some backing from Himmler, to broker an agreement of neutrality between Germany and Switzerland in 1943. In other words, Schellenberg claimed to have been central in averting a German occupation of the country. Along the way and much to the minister's displeasure, Schellenberg managed to best Ribbentrop.[52] In sum, Schellenberg did his best to represent himself as a reasonable alternative to Joachim Ribbentrop, who, conveniently enough, represented another bête noir of the Allies. It was a dubious alternative to being Himmler's spymaster, but an alternative it was, especially since Schellenberg was adept at portraying Himmler as under his increasing influence. And the very basic fact that Schellenberg did, indeed, have a hand in persuading Himmler to offer conditional surrender to the Western Allies in late April 1945 supported his claim that he should not be regarded as the nefarious spymaster of an SS agency.

The images of the ultimate insider and the cosmopolitan, Western-leaning diplomat converge seamlessly in Schellenberg's overarching master narrative of his life and career in Nazi Germany: the story of the humanitarian and thwarted bringer of peace. There is little doubt about the more basic facts. In the fall of 1943, Schellenberg did meet with an American, Abram Stevens Hewitt, who was connected to the OSS (Office of Strategic Services) in Stockholm; the two men, with scant backing from their respective supervisors, talked about the possibilities of a negotiated peace. Ultimately, nothing came of this.[53] In 1943 and 1944 Schellenberg did bat around ideas and plans as to how to make contact with Western, preferably U.S., representatives on the Continent and beyond; however, rarely did these ideas move much beyond their initial stages. And during the last months of the war, Schellenberg, like others but with more determination and better contacts abroad, did attempt to ransom concentration camp inmates to open lines of communication and possibly negotiations with the Western Allies.[54] Schellenberg's main contact was the well-connected and well-respected representative of the Red Cross, Count Folke Bernadotte; it was Bernadotte who brought to General Dwight Eisenhower's attention Himmler's conditional surrender offer of late April 1945. As is well known, the offer met with rejection. Yet, taken together, the humanitarian effort that led to the release of several thousand concentration camp inmates in the last weeks of the war and the conditional surrender offer from Himmler, late as it was, form the shiny centerpiece of Schellenberg's narrative—a narrative that focuses its attention on his efforts to save people and to bring an end the war. While some of the above, such as the meetings with Hewitt, can be confirmed independently, the problem remains that the main source for the events is Schellenberg's stable and ultimately self-serving narrative, which should be treated with the utmost care.

Schellenberg's "Autobiography" set the tone. Early on, one can find the almost programmatic sentence proclaiming that Schellenberg regarded "these last few weeks" as the "manifestations of long-felt presentiments and forebodings," thus making it very clear that he saw his dealings with Bernadotte and his attempt to bring about a separate peace as central to his life and career and not as last-ditch efforts to save his skin.[55] In this report, Schellenberg gave a very short overview of his career that focused on the "legal" work he allegedly did until 1941, effectively rebranding much of his earlier career in benign terms. He then, equally briefly, developed his burgeoning interest in German foreign policy and his realization that Germany and its decision makers had a "completely false impression of the entire outside world" and "no breadth of political experience." From this realization originated his idea to create a "Central Information office for foreign countries," a choice of words indicating a vision that went beyond that of a foreign intelligence service. According to Schellenberg, "important positions were given to stupid and unworthy men," and he bemoaned the "absence of principle of selection" in Germany's appointment policies. "Anything approaching the selection of the individual" could be found in what Schellenberg deemed "the good elements of the SS." He alluded to Himmler's "alleged brutality" but also noted that he—Schellenberg—never made up his mind about the RFSS. Indeed, he regarded Himmler as "the only man I could see in the whole corrupt Government 'set-up,' who could with any success have stood as a factor for order" and as an "antidote to the obstructive Fuehrer-Ribbentrop policy." Schellenberg's Himmler was "sensible and clever enough to be able to still reach a compromise with the outside world."[56] In short, Schellenberg laid out this fundamental opposition to Nazi Germany's foreign policy and its inept practitioners; remade the foreign intelligence outfit he headed into a foreign policy think tank or even an alternative foreign office staffed by good men; and made a case for his proximity to and reliance on Himmler.

Schellenberg then brandished his difficult-to-verify credentials as an advocate for peace. He claimed to have counseled peace with France in 1940; to have warned of war against Russia in 1941; to have gotten into trouble for his reporting on Soviet potentials in late 1942 and early 1943; to have saved Switzerland from a German invasion on 1943; to have attempted to solve the Ukrainian and Tartar-Crimean questions in the same year; and to have had connections via contacts in Sweden, Spain, and Portugal with British and American personalities. This enumeration of his activities, real or imagined, then serves as the perfect springboard to discuss his interactions with Bernadotte and the genesis of Himmler's offer of conditional surrender. That discussion takes up the next thirty-three pages of this thirty-seven-page document. In these, Schellenberg describes, in sometimes mind-numbing and often impossible to double-check detail, his dealings with Bernadotte and the many obstacles he encountered. Aside from pointing out that he was the one who persuaded Himmler to meet with Bernadotte in the first place and who quietly assisted the Swede in his discussions with different German dignitaries, he let it be known that he saw Bernadotte's visit as the opportunity of "putting into effect [his] original idea of getting Germany out of the war." He did not fail to mention the other side of these efforts either, noting, "There was also the humanitarian side which had always moved me deeply, and about which I felt something absolutely had to be done."[57]

The discussion of the negotiations with Musy, which commenced in fall 1944 and which Schellenberg regarded as an opportunity to provide some background on his newfound humanitarian concerns, allowed him to discuss his involvement with the "Jewish question." It provides for some interesting insights. On the one hand, he claimed, via his recollection of a conversation with Musy during which Schellenberg discussed "thoroughly with him the principles of the Jewish question in Germany," that he "had had no part in the events of the last few years and had no direct influence at all." Schellenberg made sure that Musy knew that he could "therefore" not provide "any concrete help, such as their release from imprisonment, etc." Yet Schellenberg also did not fail to point out that Musy "appreciated [his] silent efforts to do good in individual cases" and that he had "been the protector of many Jewish families, of many partial Jews and mixed couples." Most importantly, Musy was "aware of his attitude to the Jewish question" and "fully understood [his] position" and that he had endangered "not only [his] own life, but what was more important . . . , [his] wife and children." These protestations notwithstanding, Schellenberg still wished, "despite all previous vain attempts[,] to bring about some solution of the Jewish question in Germany—that is to save, so to speak, at the last minute those Jews still alive in Germany."[58] While he claimed to have had neither involvement nor influence in an unnamed policy with which he was in some implied disagreement, he still saw himself as the man who could solve the issue.

Schellenberg portrayed himself as someone thwarted at every corner. He claimed that the January 12, 1945, agreement between Musy and Himmler, which was meant to allow for twelve hundred Jews to leave the country for Switzerland every week in exchange for positive press, was reached owing to his "active intervention." This as well as other schemes to free concentration camp inmates fell apart or hit serious roadblocks because of Kaltenbrunner's interventions with Hitler. Similarly, Schellenberg detailed his efforts to persuade a dithering Himmler to offer conditional surrender to the Western Allies via Bernadotte and his own prominent role in the process; how he eventually succeeded, only to see his efforts come to naught; and, later on, his appointment as *Gesandter* with "plenary powers to negotiate with the Swedish Government," signed by Admiral Dönitz on May 4, 1945. A day earlier, Schellenberg had taken his final leave from Himmler. He made sure to include in his report that Himmler had finally understood the wisdom of his counsel, wishing that he "had only listened to [Schellenberg] sooner." Furthermore, Himmler had trust in Schellenberg, allegedly saying, "Perhaps you are the first German to do something positive for his poor 'Vaterland' again."[59]

Schellenberg clearly strove to establish his credentials in these pages. They were buttressed by the accounts of Bernadotte and Schellenberg's assistant Franz Göring, which largely confirmed Schellenberg's version of the events. These seemingly independent statements also extended credibility to those of Schellenberg's statements that they did not confirm directly: his early career, his early interest in and push for a negotiated peace, his low-level humanitarian efforts, and his descriptions of meetings and what was said in them. Schellenberg did not simply decidedly seize the narrative initiative; he had also taken great strides in establishing himself as a reliable source.

Less blatantly self-serving and more defined by the concrete interests of his largely British interrogators, the "Final Report" still managed to convey Schellenberg's message and keep it intact. Once again, about 30 of the 120 pages of the "Final Report" focused on "Peace Negotiations Preceding Capitulation." Indeed, the compilers of the "Final Report" simply took the "Autobiography," "supplemented by further interrogation where necessary," and integrated it into the report, for allegedly "it was more chronologically and factually accurate than subsequent statements."[60] Schellenberg had already cornered the proverbial market.

Schellenberg's alleged interest in a negotiated peace, which he dates as early as 1942, punctuates the early narrative as well. The timing is a matter of crucial importance, for it seemingly sets Schellenberg apart from those whose interest in a negotiated peace rose as the Germany's military fortune began to decline. This timing, and the fact that in other contexts he had established himself as "trustworthy," might have also allowed Schellenberg to take some sharply calculated risks, for it was all but impossible for his interrogators to double-check some of his statements. Indeed, in many instances his erstwhile interlocutors were dead. Most important in this context is an alleged lengthy meeting with Himmler in Zhitomir, Ukraine, in August 1942. Schellenberg claims to have first proffered to the RFSS the idea of a negotiated, separate peace with the West then and to have received tentative permission to explore options.[61] There is, however, no independent confirmation of the meeting or its content.[62] Whether it happened or not, it was Schellenberg who shaped the narrative, and his rendition of 1942 was defined by plans to make contacts with the West, be it via Spain, Switzerland, or Sweden. Ultimately, nothing came of them, but the responsibility was always with others, for example, Ribbentrop or Kaltenbrunner, or because the "internal political situation was not at the moment propitious and . . . the matter should be left in abeyance for the time being."[63] Schellenberg was to be commended for his many efforts. Schellenberg equally efficiently presented himself as a reasonable and able diplomat. In this case, the broader scope of the report allowed him to provide additional details and to establish patterns that cut across the years, for example, when it came to his dealings with Masson. The first meeting in September 1942, according to the "Final Report," on the initiative of Masson, pleased Schellenberg, for he regarded "Switzerland together with Sweden as an important launching platform for the peace feelers he was planning." A meeting in December of the same year allowed Schellenberg to "reiterate . . . his belief that there should be some way of contacting the Western Powers through Masson. Masson agreed to assist Schellenberg in his peace efforts." Schellenberg, for his part, did "everything in his power to maintain Switzerland's neutrality," even though Ribbentrop did his best to undermine Schellenberg's efforts, which were backed by Himmler.[64] Schellenberg also used the opportunity to showcase in detail and in context his good deeds, as in the case of the Warsaw Swedes. He noted that while doing his utmost to help these men, he had information about the men's guilt, which he shared with

Axel Brandin in late 1943.[65] Schellenberg's humanitarianism extended even to the guilty. The broader scope of the "Final Report" also allowed Schellenberg to discuss in detail his 1943 negotiations with Hewitt, a man connected to the OSS, in Stockholm, which are not really mentioned in the "Autobiography." Similarly, it allowed him to reiterate his interactions with Musy and Bernadotte and his many efforts to persuade Himmler to offer conditional surrender. Complimentary of Musy and Bernadotte's efforts throughout, this tale had but one hero: Schellenberg.

And this is also the central focus in Schellenberg's posthumously published memoir, but Schellenberg had recast himself successfully well before its publication. When he was transferred to Nuremberg, he was no longer primarily Himmler's enigmatic spymaster with dubious foreign contacts and a man whom the Allies had been tracking for years.[66] He had remade himself into a bona fide diplomat and humanitarian with a clearly established exculpatory narrative. He never let go of it.

In many ways, Schellenberg is the odd piece out among those who remade themselves after the war. He did not have a successful postwar career, for he died in the early 1950s. There is no way of knowing what would have happened had he lived. One hopes that his "wrong friends" and the Allied disillusionment with his abilities as a spymaster would have prevented postwar employment in intelligence, but this is far from certain. Schellenberg was good at selling illusions and, as is well known, the Western Allies displayed little compunction for hiring Nazi functionaries if they fit the Cold War needs. But then, Schellenberg did have very little of what those men hawked: real or imagined knowledge about the Soviet Union or countries in the Soviet orbit.[67] Schellenberg had always been a Westerner.

Yet Schellenberg's strategies worked to quite some degree. His insider status made him a valuable commodity for the Allies in their preparation of the postwar trials. In addition, his carefully crafted new persona as a diplomat, supported by well-meaning foreigners who in turn needed to justify their interactions with Himmler and his men and therefore had a vested interested in making Schellenberg look good, separated him from his SS peers. That was no mean feat. Schellenberg had not been involved directly with the *Einsatzgruppen* activities, but had his interrogators managed to focus him less on his so-called diplomatic and humanitarian activities and more on his various roles in the RSHA or as head of the Gestapo's counterintelligence department, a different picture would have emerged. Being tried in Nuremberg as part of the so-called Weizsäcker or Diplomats' Case (Case XI), even if to some extent this was a judicial mopping-up operation by U.S.

prosecutors, indicates that Schellenberg's narrative did not fall on deaf ears. All things considered, Schellenberg got off lightly. Charged on four counts, he was acquitted on Count I, "Planning, Preparation, Initiation and Waging Wars of Aggression and Invasion of Other Countries," and, like everyone else standing trial with him, on Count II, "Planning and Committing Crimes against Peace, War Crimes, and Crimes against Humanity." He was found guilty on Count V, "Crimes against Humanity," and Count VIII, "Membership of a Criminal Organization." In April 1949, he was sentenced to six years in prison, including time served. Schellenberg would thus have been eligible for release in June 1951. He received a medical pardon in March 1950.[68]

Schellenberg's testimony has become an important historical source that has not always been subjected to appropriate scrutiny. This is particularly true when it comes to his accounts of Himmler's activities, especially during the last weeks of the war, the Dönitz government, and efforts to free concentration camp inmates during the last months of the war. Schellenberg, through the "Autobiography," the "Final Report," and his published memoir, set the narrative: he is one of the few people who was there—and wrote about it. In addition, he is not a bald-faced liar, for seemingly independent sources broadly support his version of the events. But the devil is in the details: neither the postdefeat writers' collective in Sweden, nor affidavits by Swiss citizens of dubious political backgrounds, nor the delightful moment when seemingly unrelated interrogations match for once, should absolve one from being critical of any narrative, least of all if it originated with a master obfuscator like Walter Schellenberg. His recast narrative throws a long shadow indeed.

Notes

1. Walter Schellenberg, *The Labyrinth: Memoirs of Walter Schellenberg, Hitler's Chief of Intelligence*, with an introduction by Alan Bullock, trans. Louis Hagen (New York: Harper, 1956; reprint, Cambridge, MA: Da Capo Press, 2000), 412. All citations refer to this edition.

2. On the publication schedule of Schellenberg's memoir, see Reinhard Doerries, *Hitler's Intelligence Chief Walter Schellenberg: The Man Who Kept Germany's Secrets*, with an introduction by Gerhard L. Weinberg (New York: Enigma Books, 2009), 286. Schellenberg died in 1952. The English edition was published in 1956, four years after his death, and three years later, his memoir was released in Germany.

3. Bullock, introduction to Schellenberg, *Labyrinth*, xiii, xvii.

4. The most obvious cases are such individuals as Hans Globke, Hans Filbinger, and Hans Georg Kiesinger, but others who come to mind are Hanns-Martin Schleyer,

a good section of West Germany's diplomatic corps, the media and polling elites, and many of West Germany's most influential postwar historians. Their careers show continuities between Nazi Germany and the postwar Adenauer Republic and lay to rest claims of a *Stunde Null* (zero hour) in May 1945. See, for example, Eckart Conze, Norbert Frei, Peter Hayes, and Moshe Zimmermann, *Das Amt und die Vergangenheit: Deutsche Diplomaten im Dritten Reich und in der Bundesrepublik* (Munich: Karl Blessing, 2010); Hans-Jürgen Döscher, *Seilschaften: Die verdrängte Vergangenheit des Auswärtigen Amtes* (Berlin: Propyläen, 2005); Norbert Frei, *Karrieren im Zwielicht: Hitlers Eliten nach 1945* (Frankfurt: Campus, 2001); Norbert Frei, Ralf Ahrens, Jörg Osterloh, and Tim Schanetzky, *Flick: Der Konzern. Die Familie. Die Macht* (Munich: Blessing, 2009); Ulrich Herbert, *Best: Biographische Studien über Radikalismus, Weltanschauung und Vernunft* (Bonn: Dietz, 1996); Ernst Klee, *Was sie taten, was sie wurden: Ärzte, Juristen und andere Beteiligte am Kranken- und Judenmord* (Frankfurt: Fischer TB, 2004); Philipp Gassert, *Kurt Georg Kiesinger 1904–1988: Kanzler zwischen den Zeiten* (Stuttgart: DVA, 2006); Norman Goda, *Tales from Spandau: Nazi Criminals and the Cold War* (Cambridge: Cambridge University Press, 2008); Lutz Hachmeister, *Der Gegnerforscher: Die Karriere des SS-Führers Franz Alfred Six* (Munich: Beck, 1998); Lutz Hachmeister, *Die Herren Journalisten: Die Elite der deutsche Presse nach 1945* (Munich: Beck, 2001); Lutz Hachmeister, *Schleyer: Eine deutsche Geschichte* (Munich: Beck, 2004); Kerstin von Lingen, *Kesselring's Last Battle: War Crimes Trials and Cold War Politics, 1945–1960* (Lawrence: University Press of Kansas, 2009); Kerstin von Lingen, "Conspiracy of Silence: How the 'Old Boys' Network of American Intelligence Shielded SS-General Wolff from Prosecution," *Holocaust and Genocide Studies* 22, no. 1 (2008): 74–109; Kerstin von Lingen, *SS and Secret Service: "Verschwörung des Schweigens": Die Akte Karl Wolff* (Paderborn, Germany: Ferdinand Schöningh, 2010); Daniel E. Rogers, "Restoring a German Career, 1945–1950: The Ambiguity of Being Hans Globke," *German Studies Review* 31, no. 2 (2008): 303–24.

5. These men were, nonetheless, fundamental for the functioning and wide-ranging radicalization of the system. See Gellately's comments on pencil pushers, the expertocracy, and genocidal thinking. Robert Gellately, "The Third Reich, the Holocaust, and Visions of Serial Genocide," in *The Specter of Genocide: Mass Murder in the Historical Perspective,* ed. Robert Gellately and Ben Kiernan (Cambridge: Cambridge University Press, 2002), 256.

6. On the politics of the past, see the pathbreaking study by Norbert Frei, *Vergangenheitspolitik: Die Anfänge der Bundesrepublik und die NS-Vergangenheit* (Munich: Beck, 1996), published in English as *Adenauer's Germany and the Nazi Past: The Politics of Amnesty and Integration* (New York: Columbia University Press, 2002).

7. For example, Peter Padfield, *Himmler: Reichsführer SS* (New York: Holt, 1991); Yehuda Bauer, *Jews for Sale? Nazi-Jewish Negotiations, 1933–1945* (New Haven, CT: Yale University Press, 1994). Indubitably, any work dealing with either of these topics has to rely on Schellenberg's memoirs, his other writings, or his interrogations to

some extent. My own work is certainly no exception. However, his musings should be treated with the utmost care.

8. There exists no book-length biography of Schellenberg, but for information on Schellenberg's biographical background, see George Browder, "Walter Schellenberg: Eine Geheimdienst-Phantasie," in *Die SS: Elite unter dem Totenkopf. 30 Lebensläufe*, ed. Roland Smelser and Enrico Syring (Paderborn, Germany: Schöningh, 2000), 418–30; and Reinhard R. Doerries, *Hitler's Last Chief of Foreign Intelligence: Allied Interrogations of Walter Schellenberg* (London: Frank Cass, 2003), 3–55; as well as Doerries, *Intelligence Chief,* the most detailed biographical account of Schellenberg yet. My own unpublished manuscript, tentatively entitled *Making Intelligence Nazi: The SD, Foreign Intelligence, and Ideology* (to be published by Cambridge University Press) also contains much detail on Schellenberg's life and career, but it is not meant as a biography either. See also Schellenberg, *Labyrinth;* RG 242 Foreign Records Seized, Berlin Document Center (BDC), A 3343, SSO, reel 074B, frames 206–7, Lebenslauf, U.S. National Archives and Records Administration (hereafter NARA).

9. In his introduction to Doerries's most recent book, Gerhard Weinberg comments that the liberated concentration camp inmates could not have cared less whether Schellenberg's humanitarianism was real or a means to an ulterior end; this point is well taken and absolutely true. In any evaluation of Schellenberg's thinking and many schemes, though, Schellenberg's motivations become an important issue. Gerhard L. Weinberg, introduction to Doerries, *Intelligence Chief,* x.

10. This piece can be found in a number of places, for example, RG 226 Office of Strategic Services, entry 125A, box 2, folder 21, NARA. Doerries includes it as Appendix I in his recent book on Schellenberg; his editorial comments are extremely valuable. Doerries, *Intelligence Chief,* 294–349.

11. During his month-long stay, Schellenberg moved around a bit; his exact residences and their sequence are difficult to pin down. See Doerries, *Intelligence Chief,* 224–33 and passim; and Paehler, *Making Intelligence Nazi,* chap. 9.

12. "Final Report on the Case of Walter Friedrich Schellenberg," RG 319 Records of the Army Staff, IRR, XE 001725, Walter Schellenberg, folders 7 and 8, NARA (hereafter "Final Report"). See also Doerries, *Intelligence Chief,* 229; Paehler, *Making Intelligence Nazi,* chap. 9.

13. Count Folke Bernadotte, *The Fall of the Curtain: Last Days of the Third Reich* (London: Cassell, 1945).

14. For a thorough discussion, see Doerries, *Intelligence Chief,* 227–28.

15. The emphasis is mine. Göring's account can be found in a number of places as well, for example RG 226, entry 125A, box 2, folder 21, NARA. This serves as the basis for Göring's later affidavit written on Schellenberg's behalf. Eidesstattliche Erklärung, Franz Göring, February 24, 1948, RG 238 War Crimes Records, M 897, reel 114, frame 1016–31, NARA. Doerries included Göring's account in *Intelligence Chief,* 350–56.

16. He gave his "Autobiography" to the Swedish foreign minister, Christian

Ernst Günther, and the Swedish representative of the World Jewish Congress, Hillel Storch. Storch had Schellenberg initial every page of his copy to authenticate it. "Final Report," 117. See also Doerries, *Intelligence Chief,* 229; Paehler, *Making Intelligence Nazi,* chap. 9.

17. For details, see Doerries, *Intelligence Chief,* 230–33; Paehler, *Making Intelligence Nazi,* chap. 9.

18. Doerries, *Intelligence Chief,* 233–34.

19. Rayens to Bissel, assistant chief of staff, G-2, Washington, May 30, 1945, RG 226, entry 119 A, box 26, folder 29, NARA. Doerries cites a few documents that suggest heightened interests in the British and American intelligence community to keep Schellenberg stashed away, at least for some time. Doerries, *Intelligence Chief,* 234.

20. Doerries, *Intelligence Chief,* 234. Circumstantial evidence suggests that Hugh Trevor-Roper (Lord Darce) was among the men who interrogated Schellenberg in Frankfurt. One stands to reckon that Trevor-Roper developed his conviction that Schellenberg was a consummate liar—a notion that permeates his books—right then and there.

21. Report on Interrogation of Walter Schellenberg, June 27–July 12, 1945, RG 226, entry 125A, box 2, NARA. In other words, the first interrogation took place on June 27, 1945, a detail Doerries confirms in a reference to the actual interrogation (as opposed to the summary report). It is then even more curious that he notes that "Schellenberg was kept inactive as long as fourteen days at the safe house in Frankfurt," for he arrived on June 17, exactly ten days before his initial interrogation. Doerries, *Intelligence Chief,* 234n453, 235. Schellenberg left for London on July 7, 1945; thus July 12, 1945, presumably refers to the date on which the report was completed. However, there is the possibility that the report includes information from interrogations conducted in England before July 12, for it also contains tidbits about Schellenberg's flight to London on July 7.

22. SHAEF Forward to War Room, July 2, 1945, RG 226, entry 119 A, box 26, folder Schellenberg, NARA.

23. Report on Interrogation of Walter Schellenberg, June 27–July 12, 1945, RG 226, entry 125A, box 2, NARA.

24. Ian Cobian, *Cruel Britannia: A Secret History of Torture* (London: Portobello Books, 2012), 2–74. I thank one of the anonymous readers for alerting me to this book; *Camp 020: MI5 and the Nazi Spies, the Official History of MI 5's Interrogation Centre,* ed. Oliver Hoare and with an introduction by him (Richmond, UK: Public Record Office, 2000), 18–22, 81, 119–31, 363–65. As Schellenberg had always regarded the British Secret Service as the epitome of the ideal intelligence service—and the service on which his organization should model itself—it is reasonable to assume that Schellenberg was also convinced that the British knew everything that needed knowing already.

25. *Camp 020,* 365.

26. Interrogation of Walter Schellenberg by R. W. M. Kempner (in German),

November 13, 1947, Institut für Zeitgeschichte (IfZ), ZS 291/V. In the context of Cobian's findings, the "dark cell" and the "cold water baths" take on a more ominous tone, but not enough to call Schellenberg's treatment torture. After all, Cobian's findings also suggest that torture was used in perceived emergencies—that is, during the Blitz, when British officials believed the invasion to be imminent—and on German personnel who had murdered British POWs; Cobian also stresses that "violence was often not needed." Cobian, *Cruel Britannia*, 15, 23–32. Doerries claims that, despite British medical examinations to the opposite effect, Schellenberg was neither "fit" nor "in the right condition for what the British had in store for him," for he was "a very ill prisoner." Doerries, *Intelligence Chief*, 239. While it is clear that Schellenberg had been dealing with various poorly defined ailments for some time, there is little clear evidence to support Doerries's assessment. The opposite is true for Doerries's claim that Schellenberg was "normally not one to dramatize." Doerries, *Intelligence Chief*, 240. Schellenberg tended to be quite dramatic when it came to himself. See, for example, his lengthy justification during his divorce proceedings or the pertinent sections in his memoir. Bundesarchiv Berlin–Lichterfelde (BAL), R 58, Anhang I/49. The National Archives in Washington, DC, also own a copy of these documents. I thank Robert Wolfe for informing me about the NARA holdings.

27. Doerries, *Intelligence Chief*, 240.

28. The "Final Report" can be found in a number of places, for example, RG 319, IRR, XE 001725, Walter Schellenberg, folders 7 and 8, NARA. It was among the lesser-known documents on Schellenberg and not frequently used by historians; the recent declassification effort at NARA has uncovered the same document in thus-far-classified CIA and FBI files. Doerries published the "Final Report" and its appendixes in *Hitler's Last Chief*; however, his suggestion that the report was not known overshoots.

29. See, for example: Counter Intelligence War Room, London, War Room Monthly Summary No. 4, July 23, 1945, RG 319, entry 134A (Impersonal), box 5, XE 003641 German Intelligence Service, NARA; The German Intelligence Service and the War, December 1, 1945, RG 319, entry 134A (Impersonal), box 5, XE 003641, German Intelligence Service, NARA. For a more charitable reading of the British assessments, see Doerries, *Intelligence Chief*, 240.

30. See Paehler, *Making Intelligence Nazi*, chap. 9; and Doerries, *Intelligence Chief*, 243. According to Doerries, there were additional interrogations of Schellenberg by the American CIC as well as "trips" to various cities in the American zone, presumably for fact-finding purposes. No details seem to be known about these trips.

31. Richard Breitman, "Nazi Espionage: The Abwehr and the SD Foreign Intelligence," in *U.S. Intelligence and the Nazis*, ed. Richard Breitman, Norman J. W. Goda, Timothy Naftali, and Robert Wolfe (Washington, DC: National Archive Trust Fund, 2004), 113.

32. *Camp 020*, 81, 363. "Schellenberg was found anxious to indict his former chief. Kaltenbrunner . . . responded with gratifying tu quoques" (363).

33. Peter Black, *Ernst Kaltenbrunner: Ideological Soldier of the Third Reich* (Princeton, NJ: Princeton University Press, 1984), 260.

34. "Brigadefuehrer Schellenberg, Amtschef VI, Autobiography, compiled during his stay in Stockholm, June 1945," RG 226, entry 125A, box 2, folder 21, 7; 8; 11; 21, NARA (hereafter "Autobiography").

35. Ibid., 3–4.

36. Ibid., 11.

37. "Final Report," 42–46.

38. Ibid., 47, 74.

39. Ibid., 100, 108, 110.

40. See, for example: "Autobiography," 6.

41. Schellenberg, *Labyrinth*, 331, 332. Schellenberg claims that he was not alone in his dismay about Kaltenbrunner's teeth, for Himmler eventually sent him to the dentist.

42. Ibid., 333, 334.

43. Black, *Ernst Kaltenbrunner.*

44. Schellenberg, *Labyrinth*, 333, 334. Heydrich is given comparatively short shrift in the "Final Report," an indication of just how successful Schellenberg was in drawing attention away from his work with and for Heydrich and his role in actively shaping the tasks Heydrich had given to him. In his memoir written for the public at large and meant to make money, Schellenberg paints an intriguing and quite lurid picture of Heydrich, which draws on gendered stereotypes and animal comparisons to drive home the point of Heydrich's insidiousness and untrustworthiness (11–14).

45. On the so-called AB-Aktion in Poland and Schellenberg's role in it, see Paehler, *Making Intelligence Nazi*, chap. 3.

46. Breitman, "Nazi Espionage," 113.

47. See Schellenberg, *Labyrinth*, 2–3; "Autobiography," 2; "Final Report," 10.

48. "Warsaw Swedes" was the moniker for seven representatives of the Swedish Match Company, arrested in Warsaw in 1942 for having supported the Polish resistance. The men were tried in 1943; their sentences ranged from the death penalty to life in prison to acquittals (which did not translate into the men's release). Negotiations between high-ranking members of the Swedish Match Company and Schellenberg as well as other German authorities eventually led to the conversion of the death sentence into lifelong prison sentences, and ultimately to the release of the men. Schellenberg claimed credit for the positive outcome of this incident.

49. "Final Report," 18, 36–37, 43, 55, 79, 83, 85.

50. Ibid., 79.

51. "Autobiography," 6–7. Almost the same words can be found in the published autobiography: Schellenberg, *Labyrinth*, 384.

52. "Final Report," 41, 45, 46. It is worth noting how Schellenberg played down his contacts with members of the Japanese delegation in Berlin (85).

53. Richard Breitman, "A Deal with the Nazi Dictatorship? Himmler's Alleged

Peace Emissaries in Autumn 1943," *Journal of Contemporary History* 30 (1995): 413–30; Doerries, *Intelligence Chief,* 106–9; Paehler, *Making Intelligence Nazi,* chap. 8; Raymond Palmer, "Felix Kersten and Count Bernadotte: A Question of Rescue," *Journal of Contemporary History* 29 (1994): 39–51.

54. Doerries, *Intelligence Chief,* chap. 4; Paehler, *Making Intelligence Nazi,* chap. 8.

55. "Autobiography," 2.

56. Ibid., 2–3.

57. Ibid., 4, 6.

58. Ibid., 9.

59. Ibid., 32.

60. "Final Report," foreword.

61. Ibid., 30.

62. See Paehler, *Making Intelligence Nazi,* chap. 8.

63. "Final Report," 30.

64. Ibid., 35, 41–42, 45–46.

65. Ibid., 49, 55.

66. For a good sampling, see the many intelligence snippets in the most recent release of Schellenberg's CIA Name File, RG 263 Records of the Central Intelligence Agency, entry ZZ 18, box 112, NARA.

67. See any number of name files in RG 263, entry ZZ 18, NARA.

68. See also Doerries, *Intelligence Chief,* 253–75; Paehler, *Making Intelligence Nazi,* chap. 9.

3

"Bad Nazis and Other Germans"

The Fate of SS-*Einsatzgruppen* Commander
Martin Sandberger in Postwar Germany

Hilary Earl

In a book about the children of leading Nazis, *My Father's Keeper*, Stephan
Lebert writes that in Germany "there has been a theory of history doing the
rounds, based on silence and a simple formula: there are the bad Nazis and
then there are the other Germans." This is a great myth, writes Lebert. The
truth is that there were only perpetrators, "first and second class, and maybe
third too."[1] SS officer Martin Sandberger, a brilliant and driven university student who earned a PhD in law and was leader of Sonderkommando 1a, the
SS unit in charge of killing racial and political enemies of the Reich in Estonia, was a first-class perpetrator. However, after serving only ten years in an
Allied prison for crimes he committed on the eastern front, he became one
of those mythical "other Germans" Lebert writes about, who seamlessly reintegrated into German society, his criminal past all but forgotten and ignored.
This process was not unique to Sandberger; rather, it was part of the larger
reconstruction (and rehabilitation) of German society in the context of the
Cold War. This was a process by which the perpetrators themselves were not
the only ones interested in remaking the past. The forces for forgetting came
from all directions, from German society and government and even from the
Americans, who at the height of the Cold War started to recast Germany as a
democratic nation and therefore an ally, not an enemy.

 Sandberger was captured and arrested in May 1945 and was tried by the
Americans at Nuremberg in 1947–1948 in a group trial against two dozen

Martin Sandberger. Courtesy United States Holocaust Memorial Museum.

SS-*Einsatzgruppen* leaders. The *Einsatzgruppen* were the mobile killing units attached to the German Army during the Nazi campaign in the east. They were hybrid killers, giving orders in the field, and they were also the vanguard of the "Final Solution," killing Jews before the death camps officially became operational. Between July 1941 and 1943, four units of *Einsatzgruppen,* along with reinforcements and local helpers, killed—in open-air shootings—between 1 and 1.5 million Soviet civilians, including the mentally ill, Soviet commissars, and Jews, in what has been dubbed "the Holocaust by bullets."[2] The evidence against Sandberger was overwhelming, and thus the court at Nuremberg found him guilty and sentenced him and thirteen of his colleagues to death by hanging.[3] As with so many of those tried after the war, Sandberger's death sentence was commuted, and he was released from prison in 1958. One would think that his criminal past would have impeded his career as a professional; instead it seemed to have had the opposite effect. With the exception of two judicial processes initiated against him and subsequently dropped, from the day he was released from prison until his death on March 30, 2010, he lived his life as if his Nazi past had not existed, never speaking to anyone about what he had done during the war—that is, until Walter Mayr, an investigative journalist for *Spiegel,* found him "hiding in plain sight" in an elite Stuttgart nursing home a month before he died.[4]

This chapter seeks to understand the process by which a man such a Sandberger made and unmade himself under shifting contexts of the war and postwar periods; how a seemingly average German became a major perpetrator of the Nazi regime and then how, after the war and a public trial of some importance that clearly exposed his complicity in the most heinous crimes of the regime, he was still able to reintegrate into German society and live a life free from public shame and humiliation. What factors enabled a man such as Sandberger to become an ordinary German? Was he simply a beneficiary of the politics of ambiguity of the postwar period and the amnesties of the day, or did he play an active role in his own postwar reintegration and rehabilitation and the construction of a new identity? When you ask whether someone has changed his identity, it begs the question who he was to begin with. This seems like a good place to start this story: Who was Martin Sandberger before he became a Nazi?

Karl Martin Sandberger was born on August 17, 1911, in the district of Charlottenburg, Berlin.[5] Even though he was born in Prussia, Sandberger's identity was that of a southwestern German, a region of the country where his family had deep roots. His father, Karl Viktor, a merchant by trade who became a plant manager for I. G. Farben, was born in Königsbronn, and his mother, Hedwig, in Müsingen.[6] The couple married in 1910 in Stuttgart. According to his SS racial profile, Sandberger was able to trace his family tree back hundreds of years. In fact, his records show a long line of Evangelical (Lutheran) Christians, including a number of church ministers and other ancestors who were deeply rooted in the state of Baden-Württemberg, mostly in and around Stuttgart.[7] Sandberger was a religious man, but like all serious party members, he officially renounced formal religion and became *gottgläubig* when he joined the SS on May 11, 1935.[8] Geography, religion, and the history of his family are important to understanding Sandberger's postwar transformation. As we will see later, when he set out to remake his life, it was in this region of Germany, and it was with the help of prominent religious and political figures from Württemberg who enabled him to do so and with such success.[9]

Because he was so young, Sandberger did not have much of an established life before he joined the Nazi Party; in fact his only pre-Nazi identity, aside from his connections with Stuttgart and the Evangelical Lutheran Church, was as a student. Between 1917 and 1933 Sandberger had what could be described as a typical educational experience for someone who was preparing for a life in the German civil service.[10] By all accounts Sandberger was an excellent student, regularly receiving high grades.[11] He attended a *Volksschule* and then a *Reform Gymnasium,* from which he received his *Abitur* in 1929. He then went to several universities before transferring to Tübingen in 1931, where he received his PhD in law in 1933. Importantly, this is also where he was introduced to Nazism for the first time.[12]

Martin Sandberger was part of a cohort of German youth whose involvement with the Nazi Party was the direct result of their university experience. It was this same experience, ironically, that enabled Sandberger and others like him to later extricate themselves from their involvement in the regime. Education has always been a social leveler, and in a society as stratified as Germany was in the first half of the twentieth century, it is not surprising that someone like Martin Sandberger, the son of a merchant, would seize the opportunity for social mobility.[13] Michael Wildt has shown quite convincingly that German universities were prime recruiting grounds for the Reichssicherheitshauptamt (RSHA), one of the most important party organizations to participate in the implementation of Nazi racial policy, especially the "Final Solution."[14] Nearly every leader of the *Einsatzgruppen* came from this organization, and most of these men were unusually well educated.[15] The cultural political milieu that operated at German universities tended toward the political Right, and like their professors, German students tended to be nationalists, anti-Communists, and anti-Semitic, a perfect match for the burgeoning Nazi Party. In the period following Hitler's release from prison, when the party was trying to remake itself, the National Socialist German Students League (NSDStB) was founded; it was where many young university students—including the young Martin Sandberger—discovered their political calling.[16]

Sandberger cut his teeth on politics while he was an active member and then the leader of the NSDStB at the University of Tübingen. Acting as a rallying point were a number of particularly prominent professors who were also virulent anti-Semites, including a philosophy professor by the name of Max Wundt.[17] It was also while at Tübingen that Sandberger met Carlo Schmid for the first time. This turned out to be an important relationship for Sandberger after the war, because Schmid, an active figure in Konrad Adenauer's government, lobbied for his amnesty. As a student Sandberger was well suited to the radical political milieu he had entered. According to his own record, he joined the Student League as soon as he arrived at the university in the autumn of 1931, quickly rose through its ranks, and in November joined the party with membership number 774,980, and then in 1933, after the Nazi seizure of power, he became a leader of the NSDStB.[18] Sandberger appears to have been predisposed to politics and a leadership role, making a reputation for himself as a leader when he demanded that the university raise the Nazi flag on campus while also encouraging attacks on "undesirable" university professors.[19]

Sandberger's political career took off just as he was establishing himself in the law, when in May 1935 he was recruited to the Sicherheitsdienst (SD).[20] By all accounts, he worked exceptionally hard and was promoted regularly. Shortly after joining the SD, he married Eva Kirschstein, a fellow National Socialist with a doctor of philosophy degree, and by 1941 they had had three children together, twins Bärbel and Jörg in 1938, and Frank in 1941.[21]

Sandberger began his work with the mobile SS units with the invasion of the Soviet Union on June 22, 1941.[22] He was part of a cohort of young SD-RSHA men hand selected by Bruno Streckenbach, head of personnel of the RSHA, to lead a mobile killing unit in the east. Personnel were often not decided on until the very last minute, because the job was so important, and thus Heydrich and Himmler did not want to take any risks in selecting the wrong person. Sandberger, as it turns out, was the youngest of eleven section chiefs chosen to lead a *Kommando*, and the preponderance of these men had law degrees, had come out of the SD, and were born after 1900.[23] In other words, they formed a cohort of smart and youthful men, with demonstrated commitment to the movement and experience—the perfect candidates to lead the ideological war in the east.

The formation of the *Einsatzgruppen* took place one month before they were deployed, in Pretzsch, a small German town on the Elbe River, bordering Soviet territory, where a training school for security police was located.[24] Here the men were briefed about their assignments (what they were told is a matter of debate among historians of the Third Reich and the Holocaust) and given some rudimentary training.[25] Sandberger was assigned to head Sonderkommando 1a of Einsatzgruppe A, led by Franz Walter Stahlecker, which operated in and around Lithuania, Latvia, and Estonia. Einsatzgruppe A was the largest of the four units, comprising more than nine hundred personnel, yet Sandberger's *Sonderkommando* was "the smallest of the four Security Police commandos operational in the Baltics," consisting of just 195 men.[26] Its objective was to occupy Estonia and the region between the Gulf of Riga and Lake Peipus, where they arrived in early July.[27]

Sandberger commanded a unit that oversaw the killing of all Estonian Jews, and thus, according to Anton Weiss-Wendt, Sandberger held the power of life and death.[28] Before the "Final Solution" as a European-wide project of assembly-line killing was put into motion in the summer of 1942, between 1 and 1.5 million Jews were murdered in the Soviet Union, primarily in open-air shootings in small towns and villages such as those found in Estonia, the smallest of the Baltic states. According to Yitzhak Arad, Estonia had a "negligible Jewish minority," perhaps as few as 4,500 at its peak, but only 1,200–1,500 Jews at the time of the German occupation in the summer of 1941 (German records suggest it was slightly higher, about 2,000).[29] Even though there were few Jews in Estonia, Sandberger and his unit "aggressively and actively sought to implement a [final] solution" there; this fact tells us something about his ideological commitment to the regime.[30]

Sandberger and his unit made fast work of their task. For twenty-four months, until the fall of 1943, he oversaw the murder of all Estonian Jews, the persecution and murder of Gypsies, and the arrest and murder of anyone else deemed undesirable, including political enemies and Communists. Under Sandberger's watch, some 60,000 persons were investigated, 5,634 were murdered, 5,623 were sent to concentration camps (it is unclear how many survived), and 18,893 were incarcerated in prisons (also unclear how many survived).[31] All of Sonderkommando 1a's work was reported to Berlin, and the reports formed a substantial portion of the evidence used against Sandberger at Nuremberg to prove his guilt.[32] In December 1943, after a brief stint in Italy, he returned to Germany, where he worked for the RSHA until the end of the war.

Sandberger spent the last weeks of the war worrying about his future. When the writing was on the wall and surrender was imminent, he decided to go into hiding and made his way to Austria, where he lived in a small mountain farmhouse incognito as a civilian. Realizing he only had a small window of opportunity before he would be arrested, wearing civilian clothes and referring to himself as "a lawyer," SS *Obersturmbannführer* Martin Sandberger surrendered himself to the 42nd Counter Intelligence Corps (CIC) Detachment of the 42nd Infantry Division of the U.S. Army in Kitzbühel, Austria, on May 25, 1945.[33] He immediately "requested to be taken to [a] SHAEF [Supreme Headquarters of the Allied Expeditionary Forces] Intelligence [office] in order to give what [he claimed] was valuable information in regard to the German Secret Service and German Intelligence."[34] He was transferred to Camp 020. Described by American counterintelligence agents as well-educated, intelligent, and capable, Sandberger gave the Americans detailed accounts of plans for the creation of a small and efficient secret intelligence service and how this might be put at their disposal (as opposed to that of the Russians).[35] While Sandberger's name was listed on the Central Registry of War Criminals and Security Suspects wanted list, he was not officially arrested until October 18, 1946, by the 318th HID ("H" Intelligence Detachment), who held him responsible for war crimes. Specifically, he was charged with sending four hundred to six hundred Estonian Jews to Pleskau, a work camp in Sandberger's area of responsibility, where they were subsequently executed; this action made him a bona fide war criminal.[36]

Sandberger began the work of reconstructing his identity immediately. He tried to convince his captors that he was one of those "good Nazis." Almost as soon as he was arrested, he set out to write his own history and bury or at least mitigate his guilt. One intelligence report notes that he was the epitome of "politeness, correctness and co-operation," for he was known to volunteer information. When asked to make conclusions about his role in criminal activity, the reports all say the same thing: the 1941–1943 period of Sandberger's career is a problem; however, he is a nice guy who just wants to "return to the legal profession for which he originally trained."[37] This view of Sandberger's professional life as a "career interrupted" is significant, and it was an argument he returned to over time when he was more easily able to convince others of his clean record during the war.

Until his trial in September 1947, Sandberger was held in detention and interrogated on numerous occasions, always appearing to be helpful to his captors. His luck ran out, though, when in the summer of 1947, the American Office of Chief of Counsel for War Crimes (OCCWC), the legal organization that administered the twelve Subsequent Nuremberg Trials, decided it had enough evidence to indict and try Sandberger and twenty-three of his colleagues for the crimes they had committed in the occupied eastern territories.[38] Sandberger was charged with war crimes, crimes against humanity, and membership in criminal organizations.[39] Against Sandberger the prosecution had sixteen individual pieces of documentary evidence, almost all of which were written by his own hand, including sworn affidavits and his field reports from his time in Estonia. There were excerpts from several Operational Situation Reports he had authored, as well as his personnel records from the SS, all of which was particularly damning.[40] On the stand Sandberger did not deny knowledge of the order to murder the Jews, as did some of his codefendants; however, he was extremely evasive, and his responses were often so convoluted that the tribunal had difficulty making sense of them. Described as "round-faced and juvenile-looking" (not surprising since he was the youngest defendant in the dock), Sandberger maintained his innocence throughout the trial, claiming that on at least seven separate occasions he asked to be released from his job in Estonia.[41] His claim rings false, however, since no *Einsatzgruppen* personnel were forced to stay in the east for longer than eight weeks (Sandberger stayed for twenty-six months), and those who did stay for extended periods did so by choice. Denying his past and positioning himself as a victim of Nazism and an object of history was crucial to Sandberger's later reintegration.

In terms of the specific charges, Sandberger denied he was responsible for any illegal executions—the implication, of course, is that there is such a thing as a legal execution. He told the tribunal he never openly protested the *Führerbefehl*—the Hitler order to murder all Soviet Jews—even though he sincerely objected to it, because he feared disobedience or dissent would lead to his own "martyrdom." This myth is still alive today. Like many of the *Kommando* leaders, Sandberger did not kill anyone himself; rather, he gave orders to others who carried out the executions. There is absolutely no evidence that he questioned the validity (morally or legally) of his orders. Instead he seems to have believed the order was legal since it came directly from Hitler, via Heydrich, and morally what was good for Germany was good for him.[42] Even in the face of numerous documents pointing to his culpability, he denied any wrongdoing whatsoever and maintained this position until his death in 2010. He blamed the Estonian police and Home Guard for all "illegal executions," because they hated the Jews for the role they allegedly played in the Communist takeover of their country.[43] The few executions his group carried out, he said, followed fair trials, the same procedure offered all suspected criminals, including Jews. Jews were executed not because they were Jews, Sandberger insisted, but because after exhaustive investigations it was determined they were Communist functionaries and therefore a legitimate security risk.[44]

It is worth keeping in mind that Sandberger's SS personnel record cites the "better than average intensity in his work" in the east as well as his "irreproachable politics" as reasons for promotions he received when he returned from Estonia, strongly suggesting that his later account of the activities of his group was fictitious.[45] The presiding judge, Michael Musmanno, recalled that Sandberger "conveyed the impression of someone telling tall stories," many of which were preposterous, especially Sandberger's claim that each individual slated for execution was entitled to have his case reviewed and that indeed this was done.[46] That Sandberger thought the court would believe him seems outrageous, but to admit guilt would have been tantamount to questioning the convictions he had nurtured since his youth; and perhaps more importantly, it would have meant an automatic verdict of guilt and potentially his own death. Thus it was easier to blame others, and this is exactly what he did.

Quite telling of Sandberger's disposition was a palpable sense of the righteousness of the cause as well as his own infallibility. Ideology is a powerful motivator. It ensures a level of certainty that can only come when one relinquishes one's own moral choice in favor of the prevailing one the ideology embraces. Sandberger was a servant of the state, an obedient agent who felt as if he had no personal responsibility for what he participated in. There can be no doubt that National Socialist ideology shaped his worldview and morality, and ultimately it contributed significantly to his aberrant behavior. It also gave him a moral out; by blaming the state for his actions, he could claim no personal responsibility. Genocide is a corporate act and is not committed by individuals, even though the individual forms part of the collective. The absence of individual intent is what enables the state to get individuals who otherwise would not kill, to kill. Perpetrators such as Sandberger feel innocent because they acted in the interest of something bigger than themselves, the state. The absence of remorse is something we see in virtually all Nazi perpetrators, and understanding this absence is central to understanding their behavior and their ability to fit seamlessly back into ordinary postwar society.

Regardless of how Sandberger cast himself, evidence did not lie. He had taken a consenting part in the murder of innocent civilians. The tribunal found him guilty of war crimes and crimes against humanity. He, along with thirteen of his colleagues, was sentenced to death by hanging. In the first Nuremberg trial, sentences were carried out immediately; by the time sentences were pronounced in the *Einsatzgruppen* trial, however, the political context in which the American trials were operating had changed substantially. American officials were now far less eager to hang immediately those they had sentenced to death, and this hesitance afforded Sandberger the opportunity to convince American officials and Germans who might support him that he was really a good man who had been misguided in his youth.

Immediately following the conclusion of the trial, Sandberger's lawyer, Kurt Mintzel, sent an appeal to Lucius Clay, the U.S. military governor. The petition included nine supporting documents. Among other things, the documents claimed that Sandberger did not agree with the Führer's order to kill all Jews. This was an issue that the tribunal had already ruled on and therefore not a basis for an appeal.[47] The petition also claimed that Sandberger was a man of "good character," as evidenced by the supporting documents from important officials in the church, the government, and the legal profession. Among these documents was a letter from Theophil Wurm, bishop of the Evangelical Church of Württemberg from 1933 and one of the most active opponents of the American war crimes trial program in Germany. Wurm claimed Sandberger was a loyal Christian and had been unjustly convicted by American courts. Mintzel also included a letter from Carlo Schmid, a well-known legal scholar (one of the authors of the German Basic Law, or das Grundgesetz) and vice president of the German Bundestag. Schmid had known Sandberger from his student days in the faculty of law at Tübingen, and during the Nazi period Sandberger had had some contact with Schmid, even helping him avoid arrest at one juncture.[48] Schmid claimed that Sandberger "should be given an opportunity to prove himself anew in life," that prison had "cleansed him," and that he would be more help eliminating Nazism outside of prison "than if he remained forever in his cell."[49] In spite of the very real crimes committed by the Nazi regime, the German people did not support the death penalty and neither should the United States, argued Schmid.[50] Schmid and Wurm's arguments are important to understanding the transformation from bad to good of men such as Sandberger. When public officials who hold moral sway do not see you as a murderer, it is easy to reintegrate into your community. Importantly, both Schmid and Wurm actively and persistently campaigned for Sandberger, although Wurm died on January 28, 1953, before his charge was released in 1958.[51]

The Sandberger family followed up the original appeal with a petition for clemency. Written by Sandberger's father, the petition was heartfelt and indicative of a general postwar attitude that positioned Germans as objects of history and the young Sandberger in particular as a victim of Hitler and the party. In it we learn that the young Martin possessed a good Christian character and that he was a naive idealist, duped into supporting the National Socialists while he was a student. We also learn that the young Sandberger was not one of those "fanatical *bad* Nazis," nor was he pathological in any way, but rather a "kind" boy who was always ready to help others and that ironically it was *this* nature that got him involved with the Nazis in the first place. Disassociating Sandberger from the crimes of the regime undoubtedly was intended to rehabilitate Sandberger's moral character. One of the accompanying letters the Sandberger family included in their petition attested to this. He was not and never had been "hostile to Jews," his father asserted; after all, his family had lots of Jewish friends. Letters from a Jewish couple living in England were included in the petition. His son's only crime seemed to be that he "had fallen victim to a political error." Sandberger was a loving husband and father, and they affirmed that, as a Christian, he "rejects hatred and retaliation."[52] For these reasons, and many more, the Sandberger family pleaded with General Clay for mercy for their son.

Sandberger had an army of supporters beyond those who knew him well. These included the populist Republican senator from North Dakota, William Langer, who seems to have come to Sandberger's defense from his own position as an active and vocal anti-Communist, but also from his connection with ministers of various Lutheran congregations in the Midwest who had taken up Sandberger's cause.[53] Frederick Libby, the executive secretary for the National Council for the Prevention of War, wrote several letters to President Truman pleading for Sandberger's release, based on the specious argument that Truman and Sandberger had common experiences: both had served in war and both had had to do unpleasant things. In Sandberger's case, he carried out executions, which, Libby noted, "must have cost him as much soul-torture as [the president's] decision to drop the atomic bomb."[54] Sandberger had dozens of supporters in Germany as well, the most surprising of whom may have been Inge Scholl, the surviving sister of the brother and sister team executed by the Nazis in Munich in 1943. Scholl, for some unfathomable reason, wrote a letter claiming that she was convinced that Sandberger "did not take part in any criminal actions" for which he was prosecuted. She believed if released from prison he would be "a useful, perhaps even valuable member of human society" and therefore should be granted amnesty.[55]

The fact that Sandberger had friends in high places, including the church, which was one of the few organizations after the war that had any moral credibility, meant that he stood a better than average chance of securing sentence revision. However, it is also important to remember that his case was not isolated; hundreds of convicted war criminals stood to gain their freedom from the clergy's work, not just Sandberger. In this way his fate was wrapped up in the larger campaign to reverse all death sentences and free convicted war criminals.[56]

At the forefront of the campaign was a group of nationally minded German clergy, a group one scholar considers to have been the "most effective helpers of National Socialist [war] criminals."[57] Theophil Wurm, bishop of the Evangelical Church of Württemberg, whose son Hans was an early joiner of the Nazi Party, was the most vocal opponent of the Americans and one of the most important helpers of Sandberger.[58]

On the legal front, Wurm and other highly positioned clergy employed the assistance of former Nuremberg attorneys to help in their campaign to discredit the war crimes trials. Rudolf Aschenauer was foremost among those active in the opposition movement. Aschenauer, a young and ambitious lawyer from Munich and a former Nazi Party member, was a devout Catholic. He had a close relationship with Bishop Neuhäusler, another vocal opponent of the American war crimes program, who was his legal adviser.[59] The German clergy worked with Aschenauer to establish the Committee for Church Aid for Prisoners, or Komitee für kirchliche Gefangenenhilfe, an organization whose main aim was to legally assist so-called destitute war criminals housed in Landsberg prison—the committee also acted as the coordinating body for their lobbying efforts.[60] The Protestant and Catholic churches financed the organization, and they retained Aschenauer and fellow attorney Georg Fröschmann (a personal friend of bishop Hans Meiser, *Landesbischof* of Bavaria, a former Nazi Party member, and a member of the SA) as their principal attorneys, whose job it was to offer legal advice to the Landsberg prisoners.[61] Thanks to backing by the German churches, Aschenauer amassed a substantial client list immediately.[62] The work of the kirchliche Gefangenenhilfe helps explain why so many ex-Christian Nazis, including Martin Sandberger, returned to the church during this period.[63] Even if they weren't true believers, it was in their interest to pretend to be, since they would get free legal help in exchange.

Between 1948 and 1951, Wurm, in particular, lobbied on behalf of Sandberger and his colleague Eugen Steimle, a fellow *Einsatzgruppen* leader who had also been a prominent and active member of the Evangelical church before the Nazi "seizure of power."[64] With the help of Wurm, after his release from prison in 1954, Steimle got a job at a *Gymnasium* in Wilhelmsdorf teaching German history. As Sandberger did after he was released from prison, Steimle lived his life unimpeded until he died in 1987.[65] The German clergy took up the work of freeing some of the least known but most committed mass murderers of the Third Reich because, as they convinced themselves, the men were not war criminals but "decent human [beings]" deserving of Christian charity, and besides, even if they were not, the trials were unfair.[66] Not only were they vengeful and an expression of victor's justice, they argued, but the laws under which the defendants were tried were ex post facto; and, worst of all, the Americans lacked the "moral authority" to try these men.[67] To free the war criminals, they initiated letter-writing campaigns, lobbied American officials, and used the press to call into question the jurisdiction and integrity of American war crimes policy, especially convictions, all during a period when the American political leadership was seriously concerned about reintegrating Germany back into the community of nations as a bulwark against their new enemy, the Soviets.[68]

It is difficult to assess whether Martin Sandberger genuinely believed he was a victim of Allied justice—certainly others in his position did—because he was oddly silent on the issue himself. It is also not easy to determine from his behavior in prison. He was one of the longest-serving German prisoners in Landsberg; he received dozens of visitors over the years, including many involved in lobbying efforts against the Americans; yet all the prison records suggest he accepted his fate, that he could almost be described as contrite. Whether this was a strategy is impossible to determine. What we can say with certainty is that those who supported him understood the need to recast him, lest he be branded a bad Nazi. Of course, rebranding takes time. In the 1950s the war was still too present and those Americans involved in war crimes trials still too angry to allow men such as Sandberger out of prison.

John McCloy, Clay's replacement and the head of the High Commission for Germany (HICOG), the new political body that came into being after the election of Konrad Adenauer as the first chancellor of the new Federal Republic of Germany in September 1949, was the man responsible for saving Martin Sandberger's life. When McCloy replaced Clay in 1949, sixteen Nuremberg prisoners remained on death row at Landsberg prison. Among these were all fourteen of those sentenced to death in the *Einsatzgruppen* case, including Martin Sandberger.[69] These sixteen men were referred to as the "red jackets," owing to the distinctive red jacket the condemned men wore while awaiting execution.

McCloy was responsible for reviewing their cases. His attitude toward the war criminals issue differed significantly from that of his predecessor, who had adopted an unwaveringly hard line. Like many in Washington, the new high commissioner believed that a strong Germany and improved German-American relations could act as a bulwark against the expanding Soviet Union.[70] McCloy was under a tremendous amount of political pressure at home as well as in Germany. Along with the endless stream of requests for clemency, German officials also pressured him to grant amnesty to war criminals, including all those with death sentences. Amnesty, the Germans concluded, would not only go a long way toward improving relations between the two nations; it would also have an important and lasting "moral effect . . . among the [German] population," who uniformly rejected the American judicial process as it applied to its citizens.[71]

From the very beginning of his tenure, McCloy was not inclined to carry out the death sentences of the sixteen condemned men in Landsberg, but neither was he inclined to grant amnesty to any or all war criminals.[72] He realized that some solution to the war criminals problem was necessary, especially since such a broad spectrum of Germans, including the clergy, professionals, and officials of the Federal Republic, demanded amnesty.[73] Many Germans were of the opinion that even if justice had been served at Nuremberg, it was inhumane to make the condemned men wait any longer to have their sentences carried out.[74] As Bishop Wurm stressed to McCloy, "none of the prisoners knows whether or not today is the last day of his life," and thus "the severity of the death sentence is increased to an unheard of degree and is at variance with all feelings of decency."[75] McCloy vehemently disagreed with Wurm's interpretation of suffering, but nonetheless he was persuaded that some course of action was necessary if relations between the former enemies were to improve.

His solution was to establish an impartial body to review all remaining sentences: the Advisory Board on Clemency, or "Peck Panel," as it was called because its chair was David W. Peck, a presiding judge of the New York Supreme Court's Appellate Division.[76] The panel's principal task was to make recommendations for sentence reductions, clemency, and commutations of death sentences for the Nuremberg convicted and thereby, McCloy hoped, "solve" the war criminals problem that now stood in the way of healthy German-American relations.[77]

The Advisory Board on Clemency began its work in the spring of 1950, and for six weeks the board speedily, some might say carelessly, reviewed all petitions submitted by the war criminals, and there were a lot of them—Martin Sandberger's legal team alone submitted fifty-eight petitions—reviewed all of the judgments of the twelve Nuremberg tribunals (nearly thirty-three hundred pages), interviewed 105 of the petitioners personally, and heard oral arguments from as many as ninety attorneys.[78] The panel was mandated to temper justice with "charity and generosity" and thus consider all mitigating issues.[79] Too much charity toward the perpetrators, they were warned, though, "would be a mistake as it would undo what Nuremberg has accomplished."[80] The panel nonetheless found many reasons to recommend sentence reductions—but not for Martin Sandberger, whose case for mitigation they found wanting.

The Advisory Board submitted its report to McCloy on August 28, 1950. The Korean War had broken out in June, and McCloy was duly convinced that now, more than ever, the United States needed Germany as an ally against the bourgeoning Communist threat. German opposition groups also took advantage of the changing political situation, using the war criminals issue as a quid pro quo for the rearmament of Germany as protection against Communism in Europe. In fact, by late 1950, most Germans, even those who had been victims of Nazism, viewed the American war crimes trials as an attack on German sovereignty, and many Germans wrote the high commissioner demanding clemency for those convicted by U.S. tribunals and still incarcerated, such as Martin Sandberger was. Even Adenauer personally requested that McCloy commute all pending death sentences.[81] It was under tremendous pressure, including threats of death and political upheaval, that McCloy considered the Advisory Board's recommendations. Not wanting to execute anyone over the Christmas holiday, McCloy waited until January 31, 1951, to announce his decisions regarding sentence modifications.

Only five men did not have their death sentences commuted, and they were hanged on June 7, 1951.[82] In the other cases, McCloy was much more lenient. For instance, whereas the panel had upheld Martin Sandberger's death sentence, it was McCloy's decision to commute it to life in prison, seemingly on the basis that Sandberger was young and stood a good chance of reintegrating into German society. It was also noted that he was a model prisoner who denied killing anyone illegally and that he had been absent from his command when those who were killed illegally were murdered.[83] Under McCloy's decision, Sandberger would be eligible for parole on May 25, 1960.

McCloy's successor, James Bryant Conant, a former president of Harvard University, became the U.S. high commissoner in 1953 and then ambassador to Germany in 1955. Conant presided over the final release of all remaining war criminals tried by the Americans, including Martin Sandberger. On August 31, 1953, Conant created the Interim Mixed Parole and Clemency

Board, which included one representative each from Britain, France, and the United States and two representatives from Germany.[84] The job of the Interim Board, as for the Peck Panel before it, was to find ways to release imprisoned war criminals without challenging the legal basis for which they were tried.[85] Sandberger acquired more supporters at this juncture, including Carl Friedrich von Weizsäcker, a friend of his sister's, who got his father's lawyer, Helmut Becker, on board. Becker was part of a group of leading German jurists (referred to as the Heidelberg Circle because one of its founders, Eduard Wahl, was a professor of international law at Heidelberg University) who worked together to coordinate a strategy to free all war criminals from Allied prisons.[86] They were a highly influential group, and Becker took his task seriously. Beginning in August 1953, he submitted petitions on Sandberger's behalf every six months. Becker's petitions always contained appeals from notable Germans, including Carlo Schmid, whom he talked into supporting Sandberger again. It will be recalled that Sandberger and Schmid knew each other from the early 1930s, when Sandberger was studying law at Tübingen. Schmid had been a mentor of Sandberger's at that time, but this was not the reason he felt compelled to stand up for his former charge; rather, it was because Sandberger had saved Schmid from arrest by the Gestapo, who were investigating claims that he was harboring Jewish students in his house.[87] As it turned out, Schmid owed Sandberger his life. As payback, he wrote a glowing letter spelling out in detail Sandberger's many strengths, not the least of which was that prison had purged him of his misguided ideas of youth, and claimed that if given the opportunity, Sandberger would resume his career as a "gifted" jurist.[88] Between 1953 and 1955, the Interim Board granted parole or clemency to twenty-four Landsberg prisoners, including four who had been prosecuted alongside Sandberger in the *Einsatzgruppen* case; in spite of Schmid's support, Martin Sandberger was not one of them.[89]

Sandberger's prison records suggest he was a popular man. Not only did his extended family visit him regularly, but he had repeat visitors from a wide range of elites from postwar German society. Helene Elisabeth, Princess von Isenburg (1900–1974), the force behind *Stille Hilfe,* visited Sandberger in prison on several occasions, as did Prince Friedrich von Schaumburg-Lippe, who seems to have acted as a sponsor for Sandberger. He had visits from high-ranking ministers and lawyers, and even Werner Best visited him on multiple occasions. His future boss, Bernhard Mueller, came several times during his final years of incarceration as well.[90] Whether these were individuals he had known before he was incarcerated is impossible to determine; however, it seems quite clear that his wife lobbied everyone she could for his release.

When Germany gained full sovereignty in 1955, the Interim Board became a permanent fixture and was renamed the Mixed Clemency and Parole Board, or Mixed Board for short.[91] The new body reviewed the clemency and parole applications of the remaining Landsberg prisoners, of which there were only seven from the Nuremberg trials left in prison, including Sandberger.[92] Between 1955 and 1958, when he was released from prison, Sandberger applied for parole on ten separate occasions, and his supporters became more high-ranking with each application. He even managed to get a heartfelt letter from the German president, Theodor Heuss, but to no avail.[93] Each time he filed an appeal it was denied.[94] His prison records from this time tell us something about his preparations for release and his reintegration into German society.

Sandberger's time in prison was not squandered. He spent the last ten years of his incarceration transforming himself and preparing to seamlessly reintegrate into German society. He focused all of his attention on his future career as a lawyer, taking courses when they were offered and blocking out and simply ignoring what he had done to land in prison in the first place. Katharina von Kellenbach has argued that what made men like Sandberger capable of killing so easily was the "professional ethos" of a disciplined SS officer, which allowed them to "overcome empathy" for their victims. Ironically, it was this same characteristic that enabled Sandberger to feel unburdened by what he had done and to move on after the war.[95] Von Kellenbach believes this was the norm, but by all accounts Sandberger was unusual, a "model prisoner," by which prison officials seemed to mean he was no longer a "bad Nazi" but rather a "good German."[96] The new and improved Martin Sandberger was patient and "extremely cooperative" with American officials, and, importantly for someone who desired to fit back into society, he harbored no ill will toward anyone. In fact, according to the prison warden, he had "resolved himself to make the best of the situation"; it was "god's will." Perhaps most importantly of all, the warden noted that Sandberger was "truly repentant" and regretted "ever having become associated with Hitlerism," and as such he would make a "good citizen" in the new Germany.[97] Sandberger had reason to be optimistic. While he accepted his legal fate, he was also ready to "return to normal society," where, according to his parole plan(s), he had secured an apartment, two sponsors (he actually had many more over the years), and two potential jobs, one teaching for the Evangelical Academy in Bad Boll (Kreis Göppingen), which he ultimately declined because it wasn't financially lucrative enough, and the other with the Lechler business firm in Stuttgart.[98] It was just a matter of time before the handful of war criminals would be released, and Sandberger was well equipped for that transition.

By 1957 it was only a matter of time before Sandberger would gain his freedom. There were only four war criminals remaining in Landsberg prison, Sandberger and two of his *Einsatzgruppen* colleagues (Ernst Biberstein and Adolf Ott) and Otto Brinkmann, who had also been sentenced to life in prison for crimes against humanity. The Americans hoped to transfer them to German custody as part of the Transition Treaty, but the Germans would settle for nothing less than full freedom.[99] In early 1958, the Americans finally relented and agreed to release all four prisoners. With little trouble and no fanfare, Martin Sandberger and his three fellow prisoners—Nazi Germany's last remaining war criminals—were released from prison on May 5, 1958. Ten years and one month after he was originally sentenced to death, Sandberger's life sentence was commuted to time served.[100] Still a young man at the age of forty-six, Martin Sandberger was completely free and transformed, ready to return to his family and community in Stuttgart and start the third chapter of his life as a good citizen of the new West German state.

As one writer has aptly noted, Sandberger had a "soft landing in postwar Germany," never challenged for what he had done. Sandberger believed that his lengthy prison term (in comparison to others) had cleansed him of his guilt, and no one ever said differently. After his release from prison, he had help from a number of people, including his brother Bernhard, who was a CDU member of the Baden-Württemberg parliament. Ultimately it was Bernhard Müller who provided Sandberger the opportunity to become an "ordinary German." Müller was the general manager of the Lechler firm (it is not clear what type of company Paul Lechler was, only that it had close ties to the Evangelical Church in Württemberg), and he hired Sandberger as his legal adviser when he was released from prison in 1958. In prison, Sandberger had taken specific classes in tax law that served him well in this position. Prison had not stymied his ambition; just as he had as a young man in Nazi Germany, Martin Sandberger worked his way up the corporate ladder and became a fairly successful corporate lawyer.[101]

Sandberger tried to forget about his Nazi past, but as fate would have it, not long after he was released from prison, he was called as a witness in the Ulm *Einsatzgruppen* trial; two years later the Central Office for the Investigation of National Socialist Crimes in Ludwigsburg interviewed him, and in 1970 the Stuttgart public prosecutor's office initiated investigations against him for the crimes he had committed in Estonia. He was three times lucky. On July 13, 1972, all charges were dropped. After the fall of Communism in 1990 and the opening of the archives in the east, new evidence surfaced, but somehow Sandberger again fell under the radar—that is, until Walter Mayr found him in an affluent Stuttgart nursing home only months before his death on March 30, 2010. What did Sandberger say to the *Spiegel* journalist? Nothing. Sandberger knew enough to keep his mouth shut. By age ninety-eight he had learned his lesson that it was better to say nothing at all; the past was the past, and as he told Mayr, "What I remember is completely irrelevant." Reverting to an old position and forgetting his past was familiar behavior for a man whose past remained an open secret.[102]

How is it that a man who willingly spent two years of his life actively killing people could say that his memory was "completely irrelevant"? A keen observer of postwar German society, Norbert Frei, has argued that the silence that allowed for the amnesties of National Socialist perpetrators and their release from prison also "served to satisfy larger collective emotional needs of a society which had undergone a singular political and moral catastrophe."[103] Put more simply, through the desire for rehabilitation German society facilitated the reintegration of war criminals such as Sandberger. Germans wanted to believe that men such as Sandberger were victims, not perpetrators. But context was not the only reason for forgetting. The fact that a perpetrator's immediate community was unable and unwilling to critically engage with his crimes undoubtedly went some way toward building a place where he could live unfettered by his criminal past. While Sandberger laid the groundwork for his new identity, it could never have been accomplished without the help of a forgiving and forgetful nation. To be sure, Sandberger needed the help of the important and highly placed individuals who coordinated and organized his release, but this took place within the larger context of postwar German society's desire to forget its immediate past. It was that same quiescent society that enabled a man such as the one Martin Sandberger had become under the Nazis to forget his criminal past. This highlights an important fact: identity is never fixed; rather, it is fluid and malleable depending on the place of the individual in society. In a country where there were more fellow travelers than people who were not, Sandberger was easily able to reconcile his past Nazi identity with his present position as a prominent lawyer. In some ways Martin Sandberger did not have to recast his identity entirely; all he had to do was to forget the past, rejoin his fellow Germans in life, and pick up where he might have left off had the Nazi period never taken place; Germans and Cold War Americans did the rest. As it turns out, his was a life barely interrupted. His point of entry to reconciliation and reintegration was the Cold War. This allowed him unchallenged access to his postwar German community, and everyone around him complied, even those who had originally branded him a perpetrator.

The Sandberger case forces us to ask whether trials are little more than a pointless exercise. As Donald Bloxham has so aptly noted, trials afforded Germans the opportunity to "either identify themselves against indicted criminals or with them." I would add another category: to simply forget.[104] The truth is that Sandberger's reintegration was never challenged. Those in moral positions, as well as those in the political arena, embraced the ambiguity of his past and in this way were able to deny his guilt, which ultimately enabled him to rejoin his family and professional life. Thus it was with conviction in 2010 that he could say to Walter Mayr that what he remembered about his Nazi past was "irrelevant." It was what Germany and his fellow citizens forgot that mattered.

Notes

I would like to thank Maria Wesoly and Rainer Vogeley for their help translating documents written in Sütterlin script and also for their encouragement and friendship while I was in Berlin doing research.

1. Stephan Lebert and Norbert Lebert, *My Father's Keeper: The Children of Nazi Leaders—an Intimate History of Damage and Denial,* trans. Julian Evans (Boston: Back Bay Books; Little, Brown, 2000), 17–18.

2. Patrick Desbois, *The Holocaust by Bullets: A Priest's Journey to Uncover the Truth behind the Murder of 1.5 Million Jews* (New York: Palgrave Macmillan, 2008).

3. For a history of the trial, see Hilary Earl, *The Nuremberg SS-Einsatzgruppen Trial: Atrocity, Law, and History* (New York: Cambridge University Press, 2009).

4. Walter Mayr, "The Quiet Death of a Nazi: Martin Sandberger's Last and Only Interview," *Der Spiegel* ONLINE *International,* April 15, 2010, www.spiegel.de/international/germany/the-quiet-death-of-a-nazi-martin-sandberger-s-last-and-only-interview-a-687922.html, accessed June 3, 2012.

5. Fragebogen #39957 and Lebenslauf of Martin Sandberger, Rasse und Siedlungshauptamt-SS (ehem. BDC), Signatur F 140, document #3792, Federal Republic of Germany, Bundesarchiv Berlin–Lichterfelde (hereafter BA-L).

6. Mayr, "Quiet Death of a Nazi," 2.

7. Fragebogen #39957 and Lebenslauf, Martin Sandberger, Rasse und Siedlungshauptamt-SS (ehem. BDC), Signatur F 140, document #3792, BA-L.

8. Personal-Akte Martin Sandberger, file #6,249, undated, SS-Führerpersonalakten, Signatur 60-B, BA-L.

9. Sandberger family to Lucius Clay, June 1948, in RG 153 (AG), War Crimes Branch, Nuremberg Administrative Records 1944–1949, box 11, 86-3-5 folder, U.S. National Archives and Records Administration, College Park, MD (hereafter NARA).

10. Benno Müller-Hill, "The Idea of the Final Solution and the Role of the Experts," in *The Final Solution: Origins and Implementation,* ed. David Cesarani (London: Routledge, 1996), 62.

11. Lebenslauf-Sandberger, Stuttgart, September 9, 1936, SS-Führerpersonalakten, Signatur 60-B and Personal Bericht of Martin Sandberger, BA-L. Sandberger's dissertation from the faculty of law at Tübingen was completed on February 3, 1934, three years after he joined the party. It is titled "Die Sozialversicherung im nationalsozialistischen Staat." Müller-Hill, in "Role of the Experts," 65, describes it as a "91-page apology for the social security system in Nazi Germany."

12. Lebenslauf-Sandberger, Stuttgart, September 9, 1936, SS-Führerpersonalakten, Signatur 60-B, BA-L.

13. Michael Wildt, *Generation des Unbedingten: Das Führungskorps des Reichssicherheitshauptamtes* (Hamburg: HIS, 2003), 75–76.

14. Ibid., 67–80.

15. Ibid., 74–75.

16. Ibid., 82–83.

17. Ibid., 89–92.

18. Personal-Akte Martin Sandberger, undated, SS-Führerpersonalakten, Signatur 60-B, BA-L; Eidesstattliche Erklärung, Parteikorrespondenz ehem, BDC, Signatur K150, #9233 frames 0254–0256, BA-L.

19. Wildt, *Generation des Unbedingten,* 100–101.

20. Personal-Akte Martin Sandberger, SS-Führerpersonalakten and Lebenslauf Martin Sandberger, September 9, 1936, Bundesarchiv-Licterfelde, Führerpersonalakten, Signatur 60-B, BA-L.

21. Personal Akte, Personal Bericht, and RSHA report, October 10, 1944, Martin Sandberger, SS-Führerpersonalakten, Signatur 60-B, BA-L.

22. Ronald Hedland, *Messages of Murder: A Study of the Reports of the Einsatzgruppen of the Security Police and the Security Service, 1941–1943* (London: Associated University Press, 1992), 25.

23. Wildt, *Generation des Unbedingten,* 548–50.

24. Interrogation Summary No. 2403, Martin Sandberger, May 23, 1947, in National Archives Microfilm Publication M1019, Records of the United States Nuremberg War Crimes Trials Interrogations, 1946–1949, roll 61.

25. The issue under debate is whether the *Einsatzgruppen* were briefed on their extra-military task and whom they would target and when.

26. Anton Weiss-Wendt, *Murder without Hatred: Estonians and the Holocaust* (Syracuse, NY: Syracuse University Press, 2009), 87.

27. Wildt, *Generation des Unbedingten,* 578–79. Weiss-Wendt says there were only 105 members of SKO 1a in *Murder without Hatred,* 87; Arad, *The Holocaust in the Soviet Union* (Lincoln: University of Nebraska Press, 2009), 126.

28. Weiss-Wendt, *Murder without Hatred,* 84.

29. Operational Situation Report USSR No. 111, "Reports: Jews in Estonia," Octo-

ber 12, 1941, in *The Einsatzgruppen Reports: Selections from the Dispatches of the Nazi Death Squads' Campaign against the Jews in Occupied Territories of the Soviet Union, July 1941–January 1943,* ed. Yitzhak Arad, Shmuel Krakowski, and Shmuel Spector (New York: Holocaust Library, 1989), 183.

30. Wildt, *Generation des Unbedingten,* 583.

31. Ibid., 588–89.

32. Individual Responsibility of Sandberger, A 1a and KdS Estonia, undated, Richard Dillard Dixon Records of Nuremberg War Crime Trials #3567, Southern Historical Collection, Manuscripts Department, Wilson Library, University of North Carolina at Chapel Hill (hereafter SHC).

33. Memorandum of the 42nd CIC Detachment, 42nd Infantry Division, U.S. Army, May 25, 1945, RG 319, Records of the Army Staff, Records of the Office of the Assistant Chief of Intelligence, Records of the IRR, box 191, Sandberger folder, and FBI Files, Sandberger 56543, NARA.

34. Memorandum of the 42nd CIC Detachment, 42nd Infantry Division, U.S. Army, May 25, 1945, RG 319, box 191, Sandberger folder, NARA.

35. Preliminary Interrogation Report (PIR) of Martin Sandberger, June 23, 1945, in RG 319, box 191, Sandberger folder, and FBI File on Sandberger, 56543, NARA.

36. Confidential CIC Report, Case No. 31C 6592 994 of Martin Sandberger, undated, RG 319, box 191, Sandberger folder, NARA.

37. T. P. Bagge, Conclusions about Martin Sandberger, CIC Report, Camp 020, October 1945, RG 319, box 191, Sandberger folder, NARA.

38. For a complete history of the trial, see Earl, *Nuremberg SS-Einsatzgruppen Trial.*

39. Press release, September 1947, 5-1-4-62, Nuremberg Military Tribunal, Office of the Chief of Council for War Crimes Press releases, 1947, Telford Taylor Papers, Columbia University, Diamond Law Library, New York, NY.

40. Individual Responsibility of Sandberger, A 1a and KdS Estonia, in RDD Records, SHC.

41. Michael A. Musmanno, *The Eichmann Kommandos* (London: Peter Davies, 1962), 174.

42. Testimony, Sandberger, November 7, 1947, in National Archives Microfilm Publication M895, Records of the United States Nuremberg War Crimes Trials, United States of America v. Otto Ohlendorf et al. (Case 9) (hereafter Trials), 2154 and 2157, and November 13, 1947, 2310. See also Sandberger's claim that he supported the total "extermination" of the intelligentsia of the occupied eastern territories. Quoted in Weiss-Wendt, *Murder without Hatred,* 93.

43. Trials, November 7, 1947, 2184, and November 13, 1947, 2249–53.

44. Trials, November 7, 1947, 2184, and November 12–13, 1947, 2245–65.

45. Memorandum, SS Standartenführer Ehrlinger, July 20, 1944 (NO 5045), in Trials, roll 12, frames 0402–03.

46. Musmanno, *Eichmann Kommandos,* 174.

47. Petitions to the Military Governor filed by defendants in Case 9, April 26, 1948, in RG 466, U.S. High Commissioner for Germany, Prisons Division, War Criminal Case File, box 4, Case 9 folder, NARA.

48. Pfarrer Seidel to Landesbischof Theophil Wurm, May 11, 1948, D1/311.2, Landeskirchliches Archiv Stuttgart (hereafter LKA); and Norbert Frei, *Adenauer's Germany and the Nazi Past: The Politics of Amnesty and Integration* (New York: Columbia University Press, 2002), 226.

49. Schmid quoted in Michael Wildt, *An Uncompromising Generation: The Nazi Leadership of the Reich Security Main Office* (Madison: University of Wisconsin Press, 2009), 386.

50. Petra Weber, *Carlo Schmid, 1896–1979: Eine Biographie* (Munich: C. H. Beck, 1996), 476–77.

51. Petitions to the Military Governor filed by defendants in Case 9, April 26, 1948, in RG 466, box 4, Case 9 folder, NARA.

52. Petition for Clemency, Submitted to General Clay by Family Sandberger, June 9, 1948, RG 153 JAG Army, War Crimes Branch, Nuremberg Administrative Records 1944–1949, box 11, 86-3-5 folder, NARA.

53. William Langer to Clarence R. Huebner, May 25, 1949, in RG 338 JAD, War Crimes Branch, Records of Post-Trial Activities 1945–1957, box 11, petition of Martin Sandberger folder, NARA.

54. Frederick Libby to Harry Truman, May 10, 1949, in RG 238 Advisory Board on Clemency for War Criminals, Office of the HICOG, Correspondence 1947–1950, box 12 E212, Martin Sandberger folder, NARA.

55. Inge Scholl to John McCloy, March 30, 1950, in RG 466, box 30, Sandberger folder, NARA.

56. Michael Phayer, *The Catholic Church and the Holocaust* (Bloomington: Indiana University Press, 2000), 143.

57. Ernst Klee, *Persilscheine und falsche Pässe: Wie die Kirchen den Nazis halfen* (Frankfurt: Fischer Taschenbuch, 1991), 7. See also Daily Intelligence Digest no. 133, "Clergy Continues to Favor Cause of Interned Nazis," March 15, 1946, in RG 260, OMGUS, Information Control Division, Opinion Survey Branch, box 145, Daily Intelligence Digest folder, NARA; and Wurm to Justice Lawrence, September 19, 1946, D1/272, NL Wurm, LKA.

58. Klee, *Persilscheine und falsche Pässe,* 14–15, 61–71; and Phayer, *Catholic Church,* 138–44. Wurm's son was found to be a follower by the denazification court in Wiesbaden and was sentenced to one year in prison. Wurm to Ambassador Murphy, January 19, 1949, D1/272, NL Wurm, LKA.

59. Klee, *Persilscheine und falsche Pässe,* 78–79.

60. "Komitee für kirchliche Gefangenenhilfe," *Süddeutsche Zeitung,* March 27, 1950, 305/94 Kriegsgefangenen Allgemeines 1950, Federal Republic of Germany, Bundesarchiv-Koblenz (hereafter BA-K); Klee, *Persilscheine und falsche Pässe,* 79.

61. Memorandum, Special Agent Joe R. Cox to the JAG, re: Rudolf Aschenauer

and the Church Aid Society, September 5, 1950, 1–5, in RG 338, box 5, Aschenauer folder, NARA; and Evangelical Landeskirchenrat to Rudolf Weeber, May 24, 1949, D1/293, NL Wurm, LKA. For synopses of Aschenauer and Fröschmann's postwar activities, see the reports by the CIC, Internal Route Slip, October 10, 1950, in RG 338, box 5, Aschenauer folder, NARA.

62. Klee, *Persilscheine und falsche Pässe,* 80; Weeber to Frederick Libby, February 11, 1949, D1/293, NL Wurm, LKA. Tom Bower, *Blind Eye to Murder: Britain, America and the Purging of Nazi Germany: A Pledge Betrayed* (London: Andre Deutsch, 1981), 320, states that Fröschmann had more than three thousand Landsberg inmates on retainer at one point.

63. Bower, *Blind Eye,* 6–7.

64. Wurm took up the case of Eugen Steimle. Erich Meyer to Frau Steimle, April 12, 1948, and Dekan (signature illegible) to Weeber, June 7, 1949, D1/311.6, NL Wurm, LKA.

65. Klee, *Persilscheine und falsche Pässe,* 8.

66. Vermerk, Wurm, September 1, 1950, "Mein Besuch in Landsberg zum 9. August 1950," B305/148 Deutsche Kriegsverurteilte in Landsberg Einzelfälle, BA-K; and Wurm to Robert Kempner, March 30, 1948, D1/289, NL Wurm, LKA.

67. Wurm to Kempner, January 28, May 5, 1948, D1/289, NL Wurm, LKA.

68. Taylor to Clay, memorandum, re: Inspection of War Criminal Prison No. 1 (Landsberg), June 3, 1949, RG 466, box 1, Nuremberg Subsequent Proceedings Medical Reports folder, NARA. Wurm lobbied Clay for the creation of an appellate court. Because Clay refused to establish one, Wurm and the Nuremberg defense attorneys embarked on a media campaign to gain public support. Various newspaper articles, D1/332, NL Wurm, LKA, and Major Joseph L. Haefele to Theater JA, memorandum, September 16, 1948, in RG 338, box 9, Bishop Wurm folder, NARA.

69. HICOG Frankfurt to U.S. Secretary of State, cable, October 5, 1949, in RG 466, box 28, 321.6 War Criminals folder, NARA.

70. Thomas Alan Schwartz, "John J. McCloy and the Landsberg Cases," in *American Policy and the Reconstruction of West Germany, 1945–1955,* ed. Jeffry Diefendorf, Axel Frohn, and Hermann-Josef Rupieper (Washington, DC: German Historical Institute and Cambridge University Press, 1995), 436.

71. German Federal Government to the High Commissioner, undated, circa July–September 1949, B305/141/36–40 Deutsche Kriegsverurteilte im Landsberg 1949–1952, BA-K.

72. McCloy told Neuhäusler, "I have not committed the United States to a program of wholesale commutation of sentences of war criminals." McCloy to Neuhäusler, January 16, 1951, D1/295, NL Wurm, LKA.

73. Gebhard Müller to Adenauer, October 21, 1949, B120/395 Nürnbergerprozesse, BA-K.

74. In early 1950, Konrad Adenauer wrote McCloy that "the death penalty in the Federal Republic of Germany was abolished. . . . Under these circumstances it would

be felt by the German people as particularly harsh, if nearly five years after the end of the war executions were still carried out on German soil by the American occupation powers." Adenauer to McCloy, February 28, 1950, B305/142/14–15 Deutsche Kriegs-verurteilte im Landsberg 1949–1952, BA-K.

75. Wurm to McCloy, January 27, 1950, D1/295, NL Wurm, LKA.

76. John Bross to Gerald Fowlie, memorandum, May 18, 1950, RG 238, box 2, Clemency Committee General folder; "Clemency Board Member Completes Prelim-inary Survey," Press Release No. 312, May 2, 1950, RG 466, John J. McCloy, Classi-fied GR 1949–1952, box 13, D(50) 1273–1318 folder, both NARA; and Besprechung, Bowie mit Aschenauer, April 1, 1950, B305/142/25, Deutsche Kriegsverurteilte im Landsberg 1949–1952, BA-K.

77. Moran to Gerald Fowlie, memorandum, Re: Neuro-psychiatric examinations, July 12, 1950, in RG 238, box 2, Clemency Committee–General folder, NARA.

78. Fowlie to Peck, Snow, and Moran, July 24, 1950, RG 238, box 1, Research for the Board folder; Supplemental letters and petitions requesting clemency for Martin Sandberger, July 1950, in NARA RG 238, box 10, Ohlendorf Case 9 folder, NARA.

79. McCloy instructed them to be as charitable as possible. Rules of Procedure in Clemency Board Hearings, July 22, 1950; Fowlie to Peck, Snow, and Moran, July 20, 1950, RG 466, box 36, War Crimes Clemency Board Operational History folder, NARA.

80. Peck Panel quoted in Bower, *Blind Eye,* 421.

81. Schwartz, "McCloy and the Landsberg Cases," 444–45.

82. Ibid.

83. Summary of McCloy's decision regarding Sandberger, September 1, 1950, in RG 466, box 6, Report of HICOG Advisory Board on Clemency for War Criminals, part II folder, NARA.

84. Edwin Plitt was the U.S. member, and later Spencer Phenix was; Gustave Laroque was the French member; and Edward Jackson was the British member. Hell-muth von Weber, Emil Lersch, and Gottfried Kuhnt were the German members. The Mixed Board began its work on August 11, 1955. See Vermerk, B305/758, Adolf Ott; and Vermerk, "Kriegsverurteilte in der Bundesrepublik," B305/53, Bereinigung des Kriegsgefangenenproblems—Gemischte deutsche—alliierte Ausschusse zu Überprü-fung der Urteile, both BA-K.

85. John Mendelsohn, "War Crimes Trials and Clemency in Germany and Japan," in *Americans as Proconsuls: United States Military Government in Germany and Japan,* ed. Robert Wolfe (Carbondale: Southern Illinois University Press, 1984), 253.

86. Frei, *Adenauer's Germany and the Nazi Past,* 121–23.

87. Ibid., 227.

88. Schmid quoted in ibid., 227–28.

89. Mendelsohn, "War Crimes and Clemency," 253–54.

90. Inmates Records of Visits and Visitors, 1952–1958, in RG 466, Prison Records for Martin Sandberger, NARA.

91. Foreign Service Despatch, U.S. Embassy Bonn, re: Composition of Mixed Board on War Criminals in Western Allied Custody, September 16, 1955, in RG 466, box 164, 321.6 folder, NARA.

92. Mendelsohn, "War Crimes and Clemency," 252–54.

93. Frei, *Adenauer's Germany and the Nazi Past,* 228.

94. Supplement to the Records Officer's Report concerning Sandberger, petition for parole 1955, in B305/785 Martin Sandberger; Dr. Emil Lersch, Chair of the Board, to James B. Conant, November 28, 1956, in B305/836; and Minutes of the meeting of the Board, November 7, 1956, in B305/836, all BA-K.

95. Katharina von Kellenbach, *The Mark of Cain: Prison Chaplains Counsel Perpetrators of the Shoah* (forthcoming from Oxford University Press).

96. Institutional Record of Martin Sandberger, WCP#1430, September 24, 1957, RG 466, box 14, Sandberger folder, NARA.

97. Institutional Record of Martin Sandberger, WCP#1430, February 13, 1958, RG 466, box 14, Sandberger folder, NARA.

98. Parole plan for Martin Sandberger by Deforest A. Barton, Parole Officer, September 17, 1957, RG 466, box 14, Sandberger folder, NARA.

99. Frei, *Adenauer's Germany and the Nazi Past,* 229.

100. Order of American Ambassador David Bruce with Respect to the Sentence of Martin Sandberger, May 9, 1958, RG 466, box 14, Sandberger folder, NARA.

101. Mayr, "Quiet Death of a Nazi," 6.

102. Ibid., 2.

103. Norbert Frei, *Vergangenheitpolitik: Die Anfänge der Bundesrepublik die NS-Vergangenheit* (Munich: C. H. Beck, 1996), 401.

104. Donald Bloxham, "Prosecuting the Past in the Postwar Decade: Political Strategy and National Myth-Making," in *Holocaust and Justice: Representation and Historiography of the Holocaust in Post-War Trials,* ed. David Bankier and Dan Michman (Jerusalem: Yad Vashem; New York: Berghahn Books, 2010), 37–38.

Part 2

Networks of Recasting

4

Petitions to Franco

Arguments and Identities of Ex-Nazis in the Effort to Avoid Repatriation from Spain, 1945–1950

David A. Messenger

On September 10, 1945, in Berlin, the Allied Control Council for Germany (ACC), made up of France, Great Britain, the Soviet Union, and the United States, passed a resolution ordering all Germans who had been officials or intelligence agents of the Nazi regime and now found themselves in territories that had been neutral during the war to return to Germany and face denazification proceedings. Furthermore, the ACC requested that governments in states where such Germans resided were to deport these individuals to the territory under control of the ACC, occupied Germany. These Germans were Nazi diplomatic personnel, National Socialist leaders, economic officials of state and para-state organizations, and intelligence agents, who, had they been in occupied Germany, would have been subject to denazification measures such as automatic arrest, interrogation, and hearings or trials. Spain was the European country with the largest number of Allied-identified "obnoxious Germans," and the authoritarian regime of General Francisco Franco had extensive dealings with the Nazi regime, going back to Adolf Hitler's decision to intervene on Franco's side in the Spanish Civil War.

The Spanish government agreed that the ACC had the right to request repatriation, but, as a sovereign nation, it reserved its right to carry out its own investigations of those named and to determine whether they deserved to be deported under Spanish law. The process of Allied identification and subsequent Spanish investigation was well known among ex-Nazis in the

German colony. As a result, they took to their own defense. The archives of the Spanish Foreign Ministry contain hundreds of petitions by former Nazi intelligence agents seeking exemptions from the repatriation lists. The language and arguments used by these ex-agents of the Nazi regime in Spain offer a unique insight into the recasting of identities far from the center of denazification processes in occupied Germany. It is no surprise that many arguments used inside Germany were repeated in Spain. German Catholics in Spain, as in occupied Germany, put forward very specific arguments about religion and Nazism. Yet the possibility of being in Spain also allowed these individuals to argue that they had been motivated by ideology and had made a political commitment through their service to the Nazi regime—a commitment made to Franco, not Hitler. This was obviously an argument unique to Spain. This chapter will assess the range of arguments used by ex-Nazi agents in Spain to explain their wartime activity and examine their efforts to claim a future in Franco's Spain.

As Ronald Newton has written about the German colony in Argentina, between 1933 and 1939 a major transformation occurred within the German colony in Spain, masterminded by operatives of the National Socialist Party, which resulted in a new situation whereby "with few exceptions the communal organizations—religious, educational, welfare, musical, sport, social—had declared their formal adhesion to Hitler's New Order. . . . Teaching cadres in the larger schools came to be dominated by recently arrived apostles of the New Germany, most of them party members, the children of leftist and Jewish parents were driven off . . . [and the] German Labor Front organized the employees of many German firms."[1] In Spain, the process of Nazi influence over the Germany colony was well under way when civil war broke out in July 1936. Yet it was the war that brought numerous German intelligence operatives to Spain, first with the dispatch of the Condor Legion, Germany's air force contingent in Spain, and later, by 1937, with military intelligence, Abwehr agents, sent to monitor British Gibraltar.[2] As the war in Europe expanded to encompass the entire continent by 1941, primarily through German occupation of conquered states and territory, some seventy-five hundred Germans were resident in Spain; by 1944–1945, that number had grown to around twenty thousand.[3] These Germans consisted of a small group involved in business and other activities since the 1920s or earlier; a significant number who came during the Spanish Civil War, for either military or business purposes; and a large number sent during World War II for military intelligence, diplomatic and cultural relations, and economic reasons as well.

By 1938–1939, the Abwehr detachment in Spain, KO-Spanien, became one of the largest foreign operations of German military intelligence before World War II, with two hundred personnel and more than one thousand sub-agents as well as a close relationship with Franco's intelligence services. From 1939 to 1944, the organization was led by Gustav Leissner, alias Gustavo Lenz, and then by Arno Kleyensteuber. It included sections on intelligence gathering versus the Allies; sabotage in the vicinity of Gibraltar, Morocco, and Algiers; counterespionage versus Allied intelligence in Spain; and specific intelligence-gathering operations related to French Morocco, Allied aviation, the Atlantic coast, and the Canary Islands, as well as to Gibraltar and the Straits (Operation Bodden).[4]

Military intelligence was not the only game in town, for the Gestapo was also heavily engaged in Spain. Formal German intelligence operations in Spain began with the Police Treaty signed between Germany and Franco's Burgos-based government on July 31, 1938. The first official police attaché sent to Spain from Berlin was a representative of the Sicherheitsdienst (SD), or the Security and Intelligence Service of the SS.[5] It sent Paul Winzer to Madrid, where he remained until August 1944; he was killed in a plane crash shortly thereafter.[6] Close collaboration between the SD and the Spanish Dirección General de Seguridad (DGS) was carried out on issues such as the internment of Spanish Republican activists in occupied France. There also was the dispatch of SD agents to all German consulates across Spain to monitor the German colony and, after 1941, the use of SD agents sent by its head of foreign intelligence, Walter Schellenberg, to gather intelligence that was more than just of military value against Spain and the Allies.[7] SD agents were placed not only in German consulates, but also in a number of German firms, many with ties to the SS.[8] Over time, the SD desired to expand its operations in Spain and came into increasing conflict with the Abwehr. This was not unexpected; the SD, working alongside the Gestapo, had long sought to increase its activities and responsibilities compared to the Abwehr in all regions of Europe.[9] Finally, in March and April 1944, Hitler allowed Himmler to direct the SD to take control of the Abwehr and consolidate foreign intelligence operations under Schellenberg.[10]

Allied pressure on Spain in the last year of the war to intern and to deport German agents largely failed; very few individuals from Allied lists were arrested. Once the war ended, in May 1945, the Spanish government made an effort to demonstrate its desire to conform to Allied wishes and dramatically increased the internment of suspect Germans, but the policy was short-lived, and from a maximum of some two hundred internees in June 1945, all but four were released by June 1946.[11] Within the American Embassy in Madrid, the fear that the German colony in Spain could develop into a source for the maintenance of Nazi ideology, intelligence operations, and potential sabotage was prominent.[12] The Spanish failure to expel German agents during the last year of the war underlined the necessity of a new, postwar policy. Developments within occupied Germany concerning the internment of Nazi officials and agents, and specifically the decision to create categories of individuals subject to automatic arrest, also influenced thinking about Nazis outside of occupied Germany.[13] Together, the work of Allied policymakers in Germany on denazification and the concerns of American personnel in Madrid and other neutral states resulted in the beginning of a program of forced repatriation. This was made official with the adoption of the term "obnoxious Germans" to define the targets and was officially enacted by the ACC in September 1945. The American and British embassies in Madrid compiled a list of some sixteen hundred Germans desired for repatriation, including all military and diplomatic personnel, espionage agents, and Germans linked to businesses that had strong ties to the Nazi regime.

Of the total number of Germans desired for repatriation, approximately 265 were deported from Spain in 1946 and 1947. Others returned voluntarily to Germany, and the British and American embassies established the British-American Centre for Repatriation of Germans in Madrid to process these cases. However, voluntary repatriation rarely involved those ex-Nazi intelligence agents most desired by the victorious wartime powers. For example, of the 207 Germans who left for Bremen voluntarily on board an American ship in August 1946, only two were from the agents' list compiled by the British and Americans as top priority.[14] In a last-gasp effort to force the Spanish government to act, the Allies came up with a list of 104 "hard-core" cases in 1947, but no members of this final group were ever deported from Spain.[15]

Part of the reason for the failure of repatriation was the attitude of the Franco regime. Many within it took actions to protect Germans inside Spain and to implement their own espionage and repatriation investigations, without any concern for timeliness or efficiency. Notices appeared in Spanish newspapers in May 1946 inviting Germans to voluntarily repatriate to Germany via maritime transport that had been arranged by the United States and Great Britain, but rarely were Germans forced to leave.[16] When debate in the United Nations over Spain's international position led to charges that Spain hid Nazis, a full publicity campaign outlining Spanish policies of internment and police oversight of Germans in Spain was launched.[17] In most cases, Germans on the Allied lists had to report weekly to local police or spend some time in internment, usually at the spa resort town of Caldas de Malavella near Girona.

The atmosphere created by the regime's tepid response to Allied demands meant that many Germans felt no need to disavow their ties to Nazism and its history within the German colony. Indeed, the continuation of Nazism remained a prominent part of life in the German colony in Spain. Yet at the same time, Germans who either were targeted for repatriation or feared they would be took their own initiative in requesting permission to stay in Spain and made new arguments about their commitment to Franco's regime. Those with ties to Nazi espionage were chief among these. In the midst of Francoist Spain, they had a unique opportunity to justify their wartime past and reframe their experiences without immediately facing the specter of denazification.

German Advocacy

The earliest investigations were of the most prominent and publicly visible individuals associated with Nazi activity in Spain, and many of these individuals, knowing they would be investigated, directly contacted British and U.S. officials to plead their cases. The most infamous case in this respect was that of Johannes Bernhardt, the director of SOFINDUS, the Nazi firm that managed all trade between Spain and Germany during World War II. Bernhardt was, simply put, the most engaged German in Spain from the beginning of the Spanish Civil War through to the postwar period. A member of the Nazi Party's Auslandorganization (Party organization abroad) in Spain, he had been instrumental in securing Nazi Germany's assistance of Franco in the military rebellion of July 1936.[18] He later went on to lead Hispano-Marroquí de Transportes, S.L., which, partnered with the company Rohstoff-Waren-Handelsgesellschaft, A.G. (ROWAK), managed all trade between Germany and the Francoist zone during the Civil War.[19] SOFINDUS was one of the offshoots of ROWAK, created in 1939 to manage all German investments in Spain. Bernhardt was its director from the beginning. He worked closely with Hitler's director of the Four-Year Plan, Hermann Goering, in developing German economic plans for Iberia, which also often coincided with military intelligence operations. The linkages between German economic activity in Spain and German espionage were tight, and the distinction between private, state, and para-state assets to be examined after the war was rarely clear-cut. Bernhardt and SOFINDUS were involved in a number of operations that, ostensibly commercial, were linked to supplying and assisting the German military. One of the largest, and latest, was the supply of German troops in France from the Cantabrian coast between January and March 1945.[20] Beyond these specific operations, employment with SOFIN-DUS and its many subsidiaries often provided cover for SD agents like Walter Mosig.[21] For this, Bernhardt ended the war with the SS rank of *Oberführer.*[22]

Bernhardt and SOFINDUS were of immediate priority to Allied investigators at the end of the war. Bernhardt himself offered to work with Allied investigators in June 1945.[23] Yet this was not all Bernhardt was up to, for he continued to maintain a prominent position among the German colony in Spain as well as with his contacts in the Spanish government. Such offers to assist Allied investigations were not uncommon, either in Spain or in occupied Germany, where SS men in particular often volunteered their services.[24] Bernhardt himself eventually met with American and British Embassy officials in Madrid in July 1945. His initial statement to these investigators demonstrates a good deal about the inability of the Nazi community in Spain to separate their work for the German cause, their ties to Spain and the Franco regime, and their fear for whatever fate they might face at the hands of the Allies:

> We know that Germany has lost the war; we are without a country and we do not know what the future will bring us. We live in a neutral country to which we have been united for many years in certain common interests and from time to time with certain friendships. Everything we have done here has been done with all due correctness and if occasionally there were certain "actions," it was always done with consent. We dispose of good, proved friendships. We are disposed to place ourselves at your disposition, believing we can be useful. I only request that you not ask things that go against our and my honor. Our idea must be to think, if possible, in a constructive manner so that we not become slaves but can work and be useful in constructive labor in Europe.[25]

Certainly one must be cautious of Bernhard's words—he was, after all, being interviewed by U.S. and British officials as the leading Nazi in Spain. However, his words are significant as representations of important sentiments within the Nazi community in Spain. The end of the war left them, in Bernhardt's description, stateless. In the interwar period, numerous states denaturalized various groups, usually for ethnic reasons, as the Nazis did to German Jews. Now Bernhardt was turning the idea of statelessness on its head by claiming statelessness in the minimal sense of someone losing the state's protection.[26] Of course there was a government in postwar Germany, provided by the occupiers, the Allied Control Commission. Yet because Bernhardt did not recognize Allied occupiers of Germany as the legitimate government there, he considered himself stateless.

However, Bernhardt and other Germans in Spain had another option besides seeking international protection as stateless, an option that was not going to be offered in any event. There was another state that could protect them—Spain. While acknowledging the lack of any legal tie between Germans resident in Spain and the regime of Franco, he used the word *united* to describe the relationship of Germans resident there with the Spanish state. The ties that Bernhardt had made in Spain, personal and otherwise, were used to reject any consideration of repatriation to occupied Germany, to claim a status that, even if not a legal one, would serve some of the same purposes, especially to protect them from repatriation.

Across Germany, Allied occupation and reeducation policies coexisted with a continuity of a bureaucratic, professional, political, military, and clerical elite that consistently "sought to undermine its [Allied policy] foundations to the end of creating a 'usable past' on which German national identity could be reconstructed."[27] If one perceives the search for "obnoxious" Germans in neutral states like Spain as part of a broad Allied denazification program, then Bernhardt's interpretation of his position in Spain was simply a different take on the consistent unpopularity of denazification measures inside Germany.[28] As Jeffrey Herf has written about Konrad Adenauer and the emerging Christian Democratic position on denazification in 1946 and 1947, "The best way to overcome Nazism was to avoid a direct confrontation with it."[29] Arguably, that sentiment was shared by the so-called obnoxious Germans in Spain, although they could do more than ignore it—as Bernhardt demonstrated, they could draw upon other ties, those with Spain, to divert attention away from the immediate past or to cast that experience in a different light.

Service to Franco: Germans as Nationalist Crusaders

The Germans most likely to take up the pen in their own defense were those who knew they were on the top priority lists for repatriation; they had been among the most active Nazis during World War II: agents and party and diplomatic officials. Before we examine the words of these Germans themselves, it is important to outline the memory of the Civil War in the Francoist discourse of the time, for this discourse proved one of the most used by

Germans seeking to stay in Spain. As Paloma Aguilar has written, official discourse allows us "to study the kind of version of the Civil War that the regime wished to convey to the generation that had not lived through the war, as well as to those that had taken part in it."[30] In this instance, German veterans of the Civil War could use that discourse to shape their own defense against Allied desires for deportation to occupied Germany.

Aguilar argues that the key to the early use of the war's memory came in Franco's argument that his coup and the subsequent civil war were a necessary evil required to provide legitimacy to government, a legitimacy that he believed the Second Republic had failed to produce. In the view of Franco and his movement, because the Second Republic did not contain political violence, defend the Church, and protect the unity of national territory, it was illegitimate. The fact that the right wing saw the influence of outsiders, especially the Soviets, as part of the Second Republic's makeup only added to the charges against it.[31] Even if civil war was necessary, however, and not a choice, it was nonetheless purifying, and the total defeat of the enemy renewed Spain. The language associated with depicting the war in this way was "crusade," "war of national liberation," or the "glorious uprising." As Aguilar concludes, "It was a matter of good against evil, of Spanishness against anti-Spanishness, of believers against atheists, of law-abiding people against anarchists, of reason against barbarians."[32]

It is useful to consider the initial post–Civil War period of 1939–1947 or so as a revolutionary transitional era, one in which Franco's state was engaged in significant nation-building. There were aspects of social engineering present, such as in an attempt to purge the state of the enemies who were the losers of the Civil War and to build up new ideas of citizenship and patriotism. These were present in the concentration camps established by Franco after 1939, called the "laboratories of the New Spain" by the historian Javier Rodrigo. The concentration camps were set up to punish and, in many instances, kill opponents of the regime. But they also had a "social function of indoctrination [and] re-education."[33] This moment of great focus on establishing a "New Spain" could easily be tapped into by others, such as the Germans facing repatriation. In textbooks used in the education system and in the public celebrations of the war's key dates, July 18, 1936 (the beginning of the coup against the Second Republic), and April 1, 1939 (the end of the war), such language and imagery was prevalent in Spain of the 1940s. Commitment to this memory of the conflict was especially strong among Nationalist military officers, with whom the German military attachés and intelligence agents had considerable contact.[34]

Antonio Cazorla-Sanchez has built on these ideas in describing what Spaniards understood as citizenship in the late 1940s, writing that "nationalism and dictatorship were used interchangeably" in official language. Citizens accepted the regime's argument that democracy meant a return to chaos and civil war, and they supported the regime in mass demonstrations when the United Nations condemned it in December 1946. As Cazorla-Sanchez writes, "Spaniards may or may not have completely believed these assertions, but the mere possibility of again falling into civil strife drove ordinary people to support the notion that peace could only be preserved by Franco."[35] From this foundation, Spaniards reinterpreted what it meant to be a Spanish citizen, and many did indeed participate in the regime's projection of community and identity. Just as Spaniards participated in this time of upheaval and redefinition of loyalty and citizenship, so too did their German neighbors, in seeking to defend themselves from the threat of repatriation.

The first part of their argument was to underline service in the Condor Legion during the Spanish Civil War as a service to Spain, not to Germany. Many people could justify this claim with evidence of direct service to Franco as well as service in the Condor Legion. One such example was Max Nutz, a former employee of the German Embassy who served as an interpreter for the Air Attaché in Madrid from 1939 to 1943. Nutz had come to Spain in 1926 after serving in Morocco with the Spanish Foreign Legion. He settled in Alicante, where he was an active member of the German colony there and joined the NSDAP in 1934. During the Civil War, he served in the Condor Legion. He argued, however, that any service to the Nazi cause was only based on "patriotism and obligation"; the work that had inspired him the most was service in Morocco and in the "War of Liberation," fighting for Spain.[36] Similarly, Alfred Giese wrote that he considered Spain "my second country," given his twenty years of residency and that his work in the Condor Legion during the "war of liberation" had led to his being awarded two Spanish military medals, the Cruz de Caballero de Isabel la Catolica and the Cruz de Caballero de la Orden de Mehdauia. He thus found his arrest in 1945 shocking, especially considering his "service to Spain."[37]

Meino von Eitzen was a top target for American and British intelligence, arrested by Spanish authorities in December 1944 based on American evidence that he was a German intelligence agent, and he turned out to be one of the last internees held by the Spanish in Caldas de Mallavella camp in mid-1946.[38] Because of his prominence as a spy, Spanish foreign minister José Lequerica considered von Eitzen too "political" to be granted special consideration or protection on the part of the Spanish government.[39] In his bids for early release from internment, von Eitzen provided copies of his Condor Legion membership, his military awards from Spain, and his membership in the Falange, Spain's fascist movement, which went back to 1936. Von Eitzen also had letters of support from the head of the civil government in Vigo confirming no German political activity, as well as from the office of Francisco Franco himself verifying military and political service for Spain.[40] Eventually an official in the Ministry of the Navy, Salvador Moreno, advocated on von Eitzen's behalf, underlining his service not only to the Condor Legion, but also to the Spanish Navy in Vigo.[41]

Alfred Genserowsky also played on his ties to serving Spain. Genserowsky was identified by the Office of Strategic Services (OSS) as the leading Abwehr agent in San Sebastian, and he played a prominent role in coordinating Abwehr naval intelligence activity in northern Spain with agents of the Spanish military, especially the Spanish High Command.[42] His name first appeared on Allied lists for expulsion in March 1944.[43] Orders were issued for his internment in Caldas de Malavella in May 1945, and one of his collaborators within Spanish Military Intelligence, Jose Jimenez y Mora, was arrested by Spanish officials for being too close to Nazism.[44] In appealing his own order for internment, Genserowsky noted that he was "an ex-combatant in the Spanish Crusade of the Nationalist columns."[45] His petition was supported by General Martinez de Campos of the Spanish High Command, who emphasized that Genserowsky had been injured during the Spanish Civil War when he acted as a translator for the Condor Legion and that he was "un mutilado [wounded veteran]."[46] Although Genserowsky eventually decided to conform and was voluntarily deported to Germany in August 1946, he was never arrested while in Spain and was permitted to settle in Segovia until he left. He returned to Spain in April 1948.[47]

As early as 1944, before the war ended, investigations into potential German agents carried out by the Dirección General de Seguridad were curtailed if service in the Civil War was the background of the person under investigation. One of the earliest investigations of Germans based on American and British accusations of spying focused on three individuals, Hans Kellner, Ricard Herberg, and Alfred Klaevisch. None of them were deemed to be spies; and the points mentioned most prominently were, first, their time of residence in Spain, which in all cases began in the 1920s or earlier, and, second, their service to the Nationalist cause in the civil war. In Klaevisch's case, he worked for the Spanish Red Cross during the Civil War and then for the Naval Ministry; Herberg worked in Germany during the Civil War to help Spanish refugees; Kellner not only served the Condor Legion but acted as a liaison for the legion with the Spanish Air Force and continued to train pilots for the Spanish Air Force after the Civil War.[48]

In the case of Otto Hinrichsen, the most notable German activist in Bilbao during the war, his long-term residency in Spain and his service in the Condor Legion led to a position within the Spanish Army itself. This, and his subsequent work in Bilbao, made him, in the eyes of one member of the Spanish Foreign Ministry, an "ideological enthusiast" for the Franco regime, and his inclusion on Allied repatriation lists was an "injustice."[49]

The arguments that one might expect in 1944 still held prominence for the Spanish much later. In 1947, the American and British embassies, facing the real failure of the repatriation program in terms of the number of people actually deported from Spain, came up with a final list of 104 Germans wanted for deportation.[50] The Political Economy division of the Spanish Ministry of Foreign Affairs categorized the names into three tiers: first, intelligence agents, most of whom probably would have to go; a second tier of friendly Germans who could be forced out if the Anglo-Americans became insistent; and a third category of Germans to be protected without question. In this third group there were certainly many Germans who had been, and continued to be, leaders in industry, such as Karl Albrecht of AEG, Karl Andress Moser of Merck, and Johannes Bernhardt, the former head of SOFINDUS. However, those with ties to the Condor Legion also appeared prominently on the list, for example, Erich Gabelt and Alfred Menzell.[51] Naturally these figures were of economic and political importance within the German colony, and all had Spanish defenders. But the fact that their service in the Condor Legion would be mentioned here, as late as 1948, demonstrates the success of seeing prominent Nazi activists and diplomats primarily as veterans of the Spanish Civil War.

Germans as Nationalists and Anti-Communists

While service to Spain as a way of explaining Nazi and German activity during the war was the most common tactic taken by Germans wanted for repatriation, the more overtly political manner in which Franco cast the Civil War after the conflict was not absent. In particular, this meant depicting one's service to Spain not only as part of the Nationalist "crusade" against the Spanish Left, but also as a crusade against international Communism, which could be used to bring in their service to Germany as cut from the same cloth. As the international political environment changed following the World War II, and the Cold War conflict between the United States and the

Soviet Union, between democratic capitalism and totalitarian Communism, emerged, Franco was quick to position his regime to articulate its anti-Communism.[52] Indeed, Franco had begun making such arguments with officials from the United States even before the war ended. In March 1945, he spoke with the new U.S. ambassador to Madrid, Norman Armour, and argued that Spain accepted the defeat of Nazism but refused "to be indifferent to the dangers presented by communism in postwar Europe."[53] Even earlier, in October 1944, Franco had written a personal letter to British prime minister Winston Churchill expressing his fear that the end of the war would bring a massive expansion of Bolshevism and Soviet hegemony in France and Italy.[54] And even before the Civil War ended in 1939, "de-Marxification" was an important element of Franco's prison system.[55]

Franco's portrayal of service to Spain as service against Communism went back to his interpretation of the Civil War as a crusade not only against "anti-Spain," but in particular against Communism in Spain. Similar arguments came from many Germans with histories of service in Spain during the Civil War. One example emerged in the petitions of Friedhelm Burbach, a former German consul-general in Bilbao. Burbach, as consul in one of the communities with a significant German population, had a difficult argument to make to convince others that he had not acted as the official representative of the Nazi regime. However, like many, he had a history in Spain, having been awarded the military Imperial Order of the Yoke and Arrow by Franco. He wrote his petition directly to Franco as "Head of State and Grand Master of the Order." A resident of Spain before the outbreak of the Civil War, he connected with Johannes Bernhardt in 1936 as part of the group of Germans who advocated with the Nazi regime to assist Franco's rebellion. He argued, in 1946, that they should not be seen as Germans getting involved in the internal affairs of another country; their role in the Spanish Civil War was justified because it was not a purely civil war, but a "dispute between nationalism and the ideas of order and civilization against Communism." In a second statement, Burbach outlined his role at the outbreak of the Civil War in 1936 in the Basque region, where he coordinated the evacuation of the German colony from Republican territory; here, he claimed to have been personally responsible for moving some seven thousand Germans by ship back to Germany to escape "red" zones and that more than one thousand Spaniards also were saved in this way. He requested that Franco and the Spanish government interpret his actions to assist Spaniards as a "humanitarian labor of saving Spaniards persecuted and condemned to death" by the Communist-Republican side.[56]

What is significant in Burbach's petition to Franco is that he never sought to distance himself from the Nazi regime. Nor does he claim that service to Nationalist Spain overrode his service to Germany—as consul-general since 1936, this would have been even more difficult for him to do than for those who fought in the Condor Legion. What he did do was to argue that the shared battle against Communism united Nationalists and Nazis and that his service must be interpreted in that light and that light alone. A Nazi, acting as a Nazi, therefore requested Franco's assistance in resisting the U.S. order for his repatriation as an "unjust situation."[57] It is worth noting that Burbach made similar arguments in petitions to the U.S. Embassy, with the important difference that he highlighted his opposition to Nazi anti-Semitism, which was not mentioned in his letters to Spanish officials. Yet the anti-Communist element remained strong, for Burbach emphasized in a letter to Harry Hawley of the U.S. Embassy that his work in evacuating Germans and Spaniards from Bilbao in 1936 could only be interpreted as "the humanitarians' work of all the nations we call civilized," given the fate that awaited those "politically condemned by Spanish reds."[58]

This line of argument can also be seen in one of the most notorious cases, that of Kurt Meyer-Doehner, the former naval attaché of the German Embassy in Madrid. In petitioning the Spanish Ministry of Foreign Affairs to prevent his deportation from the village of Pozuelo de Laracon outside of Madrid, Meyer-Doehner outlined his appointment as naval attaché to the Condor Legion at the end of 1936, the position that brought him to Spain for the first time. Like others, he characterized his service not as service to Germany, but to Spain, outlining all of the Spanish (but not the German) military awards he won during the Civil War. He then emphasized that he brought his family to Spain in 1938, before the end of the conflict, and not only raised his four German-born children in Spain but had three more once in Iberia. Since he had no contact with his German family, except that he knew his mother had died and his family home had been bombed by the Allies, he had no desire to return to Germany. Most significantly for this analysis, however, was his argument that returning to Germany with young children would mean a return to the Soviet zone, where his family residence had been, and that this would expose himself and his children to a leftist government and education system. His desire "to maintain my family and educate and baptize my children" could only be realized in Spain.[59] Implicit in this writing are suggestions not just of exposure to leftist ideas, but also that Communist regimes would remove children from their families and prevent religious education and practice. This mirrored the conceptualization of the Republican movement present in Spain at the time, which was portrayed not only as leftist, but also as foreign.[60]

The connection of the Spanish Civil War and World War II as fights against the same Communist enemy is very clear in the petition for exemption from deportation made by Richard Enge in April 1946. Enge had been employed by the German Embassy in Madrid during the war on a contract basis, as an assistant to the commercial councilor. His experience in Spain, where he had lived since 1919, was primarily with the Banco Aleman Transatlantico, a leading German investment firm. His petition for assistance to avoid deportation mentioned the loss of his home and personal assets during the Spanish Civil War, on account of an attack by "reds" in Madrid; he then noted that if he returned to what family he had left in Germany, he would be in the "red" zone of occupation.[61] Without explicitly stating it, the implication was that Enge would suffer the same fate twice if repatriated. And there was no need to be blunt about what a terrible fate it would be to be under Communist rule.

The public projection of the Franco regime as having emerged from civil war to conquer a foreign, atheist socialism consistently shaped the rhetoric of the period after the Civil War, into World War II, and afterward.[62] It is thus unsurprising that the Spanish government responded favorably to Germans wanted for repatriation when they picked up elements of the general Francoist argument and applied them to themselves. Their commitment to fight "reds" made them compatible with the mission of the Spanish government; it made them, in essence, good Nationalists in the present, as well as in the past. Alfred Menzell combined past and present when he explained his decision to fight in the Spanish Civil War in the Condor Legion as a result of his having lived in "red Barcelona" for a year after the outbreak of the conflict.[63]

Another target of the Allies, also arrested and interned from late 1944 through mid-1946, Walter Leutner, highlighted not only his many years of residency in Spain but also his service in the Condor Legion in the "war of liberation" and the fact that this experience led him to be hired by the Spanish Army as an instructor. He served Spain in its "Glorious Moment" and was most comfortable in the uniform of Spain.[64] He urged the Spanish government to consider these facts, rather than his work for the German Embassy in 1940–1941 and the German Consulate in Barcelona from 1941 until his arrest in November 1944.[65]

Catholic, Not Nazi

Leutner also opened another line of argument commonly used by Germans threatened with repatriation to add to their credentials as loyalists in the service of Franco. He underlined the fact that he had never been involved with either the SS or the Gestapo and that he was a "good Catholic."[66] Indeed, he went so far as to state that membership in the NSDAP would have been "absolutely incompatible with my religion."[67] Implicit here was that Catholicism and a devotion to Catholicism proved a commitment to Franco's Spain rather than Hitler's Germany. The Archbishop of Toledo, Cardinal Enrique Pla y Deniel, built on such arguments and forwarded to the Spanish government a list of German Catholics to be protected from repatriation.[68] Similarly, Gottfried von Waldheim, former German consul general in Barcelona, used the existence of Catholic supporters to imply opposition to Nazism. In his efforts to document that he was not a member of the Nazi Party, and therefore did not deserve deportation despite his prominent diplomatic position, Waldheim petitioned not only the Spanish Foreign Ministry, but also the U.S. Embassy in Madrid, sending them testimonies from German Jews and Catholics from within and outside of Spain.[69]

The use of Catholicism to distance oneself from the NSDAP, and to justify one's actions as service to Spain, matched up well with the role of Catholicism in Francoist memory of the Civil War. Catholicism's concept of sacrifice and martyrdom fit well with Francoist rhetoric about coming through a "crusade."[70] The religious mission of the Francoist regime was equal in its propaganda to its focus on Franco as *Caudillo* and broader themes of nationalism.[71] Indeed, in many prison camps the celebration of the anniversary of Franco's coup, July 18, was followed on July 19 by ceremonies and discussions of "La Religión y la Patria."[72] Thus Catholicism was used by Germans in Spain in two contexts, first as a way to downplay their commitment to Nazism and second, and most importantly, to further reinforce their loyalty to Franco's Spain.

There are numerous cases in which Germans sought for repatriation simply stated they were Catholic on the assumption that this made it impossible to be a true Nazi. Jose Lipperheide Henke, a prominent Bilbao mining company executive, expressed surprise at the Anglo-American request for his repatriation to Germany, given that he was "a Catholic by birth and conviction," which explained why he never was involved with the NSDAP.[73] His brother and business partner, Federico Lipperheide, was president of the Association of German Catholics in Spain and also a "fervent Catholic," according to the Archbishop of Toledo.[74] While the association was created for community-building purposes, its use in the defense of Germans threatened with repatriation suggests that German Catholicism could be politicized as a means to distance Germans from Nazi activities. Both brothers were on the Allied lists for repatriation, Federico especially for his ties to Nazi propaganda agents and the importation of German propaganda films into Spain during the war.[75] In the case of Federico, the many letters of support received on his behalf in the Ministry of Foreign Affairs and the U.S. Embassy in Madrid almost always mentioned his Catholicism as evidence of his anti-Nazi stance, despite Allied evidence to the contrary. Most significantly, Fr. José Maria Huber, head of the Association of German Catholics in northern Spain, wrote that Allied accusations against F. Lipperheide were false in large part because Nazism "would not be compatible with his catholic convictions, demonstrated by his incorporation into the movement Acción Catolica."[76]

Similarly, Georg Wolfgang Scuebel, former head of the Reichsbahn in Spain and the German tourist office in Barcelona, explained in his interrogation that as a result of his being Catholic he was only a "nominal" member of the NSDAP, having joined in 1938 for employment purposes.[77] Initially arrested by Spanish authorities and held in Yserias Prison for repatriation before being released, Antonio Oboril mentioned his Catholicism as well as that of his wife and two children.[78] In all of these cases, there was an implicit assumption that being Catholic was incompatible with being a Nazi. As a result, a commitment to Catholicism should be enough to exempt someone from denazification and, in these cases, deportation from Spain.

This line of argument was not uncommon in occupied Germany. Indeed, there is definitive evidence of a postwar construction of the argument that Nazism was anti-Christian and thus committed Christians were inherently anti-Nazi; much of this also fed into the emergence of Christian Democracy as a legitimate political movement in Germany after the war.[79] Certainly many of these arguments had truth at the center of them, but the fact that they were also constructed and coordinated by various religious leaders, both Protestant and Catholic, is significant.[80]

In Spain, the coordination of a Catholic movement to counter repatriation was overt. The dispatch of German Catholic priests to Spain in the summer of 1945, primarily through religious orders, and their involvement in linking the Catholic Church and Germans was another concerning trend remarked upon by the Allied informant Roger Tur.[81] Similar reports came from Bilbao, where prominent priests in the German community such as Father Lang had taken residence in convents; a source reported that there could be plans in the works to hide fugitive Germans within religious orders.[82]

A number of prominent priests played significant roles in the advancement of Catholicism as a defense in the face of repatriation. The two most

notable were Fr. José Maria Huber, head of the Association of German Catholics in northern Spain, and Fr. Josef Boos, head of the Association of German Catholics based in Barcelona. Boos took it upon himself to argue against
repatriation as an overarching policy, writing to the Foreign Ministry in
Spain that his role was solely a "moral one" to advocate against the separation of families if fathers and husbands were on the repatriation list and to
prevent German Catholics in Spain from being exposed to "the material and
moral misery" of occupied Germany.[83] Father Huber also defended German
Catholics against repatriation. Both Huber and Boos drew support from the
Church hierarchy, most notably Cardinal Enrique Pla y Deniel, Archbishop
of Toledo.[84] The cardinal wrote in praise of the work of Boos and Huber
in defending Catholics from repatriation, asking Foreign Minister Martín
Artajo to call on his own "sentiments of justice and Christian charity" in
defense of "our German co-religionists."[85]

The activism of Boos and Huber typically involved sending lists of names
to be exempted from deportation to the Ministry of Foreign Affairs.[86] Boos
used a number of arguments linked to religion to justify his requests that
repatriations not be carried out in the cases of the men he defended. He
wrote that in all cases he was involved with, the separation of a father from
the family should be reason enough to exempt an individual from repatriation, for material reasons but also to avoid the "disgrace" that would fall upon
single mothers in Spain's Catholic communities. He also stated that it was his
"moral obligation" as a Catholic leader to advocate the exercise of international law that allows for the "defense of each individual person."[87]

Beyond making an argument against repatriation, Church leaders like
Boos and Huber also took a significant role in supporting those Germans
interned at Caldas de Malavella and other camps through fund-raising.
Ostensibly, the purpose of such activity was to provide food and clothing
for the interned. Begun as a program to help those in need within the German colony during World War II, the program continued afterward. One
of the chief fund-raisers was Karl Albrecht, the head of AEG in Madrid,
described as "one of the most dangerous Germans in Madrid from the
political and party point of view."[88] In the autumn of 1945, he began to visit
many pro-Nazi members of the German colony in Madrid accompanied by
two priests, seeking donations for Germans held in Spanish custody; those
priests were Boos and Huber.[89] Indeed, the largest fund, the Correa Fund,
was set up and administered by Boos and was based in Barcelona. In addition to using funds for the support of internees in the Spanish camps, early
intelligence reports in 1946 suggested that the funds raised within the Ger-

man colony were distributed primarily to the wives and families of interned Abwehr members.[90]

Allied officials were eager to learn of the role that such Church-sponsored activities had within the German colony. One contact U.S. officials had was Father Conrad Simonsen, of the Order of Cappucines in Madrid. Simonsen reported to Earle Titus of the U.S. Embassy on the role of Church leaders in the process of developing arguments that used Catholicism as a defense against repatriation; he believed that many Nazis were finding refuge within the Catholic community, regardless of their personal views on religion. Such organized activities, approved by the Church and civil authorities in Spain, suggested the acquiescence of the Spanish government in assisting or at least facilitating the networks of support that emerged in the aftermath of World War II. To Simonsen, this amounted to "considerable mischief" that went beyond simply supplying internees with food and other goods, and he implied that the continuation of Nazi identity, now within the framework of the Catholic Church, was really what was happening.[91] Another source of information within the German colony that U.S. officials used was Pastor Bruno Mohr, the head of the German Protestant Church in Madrid. Mohr was a close friend of the former German Embassy employee Hans Rothe, who served as an informant for the U.S. Embassy and American intelligence and thus passed on Mohr's findings. By 1947, when Rothe left for the United States, Mohr was put in direct contact with the U.S. Embassy and continued to supply intelligence on Nazism within the German colony. As the leader of the Protestant Church in Spain, Mohr visited Germans held in Spanish internment camps while their repatriation status was being investigated. On one of these trips, in January 1946 to the camp at Carranza, which had four hundred internees, Mohr observed how monies raised for the maintenance of internees, often by Catholic priests, were directed to certain prisoners, the more vocal pro-Nazi elements, to administer. Thus, such funds were linked not only to charity but to the intent, in Rothe's words, "to animate political life within the camps."[92]

To a variety of U.S. officials, it became clear that there was a consistent defense of Nazism and individual Nazis from German Catholic leaders, who worked openly within the broader Catholic institutions in Spain, with the aim of maintaining a Nazi presence in Spain, even if it was one without overt political or espionage goals.[93] Fearful that German Catholics and Nazis would become compatible in people's minds, Father Simonsen and other prominent German Catholics actively worked with the U.S. Embassy and created a group of anti-Nazi German Catholics to advocate for themselves with both the U.S. and the Spanish governments.[94] This group did not achieve the significance of those already established, however, and did not win the support of leading Church officials in Spain, either. Earle Titus of the U.S. Embassy wrote that the Church's assistance was sought by many former Nazis so as to "enable them to have the protection of the church by posing as the defenders of Catholicism against Bolshevism."[95] Such a strategy, of course, was well under way across Europe, not only in Spain. In Italy, many former Nazis were rebaptized as Catholics in the belief that this could assist their hiding, even though it was against Canon Law; Gerald Steinacher has called this a form of "church denazification."[96] Moreover, many leading priests in Rome and other parts of Italy were deeply involved in the hiding of wanted German war criminals in monasteries and other Church properties.[97]

Simonsen, although concerned about the politicization of Catholicism as a defense against Nazism, was not immune to making the same arguments himself. He did so in the case of Baron Joaquim von Knoblach, the honorary German consul in Alicante during World War II and earlier. Writing on his behalf, Simonsen underlined that his primary work as honorary consul before the war had been to organize the evacuation from Alicante of Germans and Francoist supporters in 1936 when the Republicans attacked; he then joined the Francoist side and was subsequently transferred to the Condor Legion at the end of 1936. However, he was never a member of the Nazi Party and had attempted to resign as consul, but his resignation was not accepted by the German government.[98] Luis Carrero Blanco, subsecretary of the government, characterized von Knoblach's actions as "great service to Spain" and not as activism in favor of Nazi Germany.[99]

While much of the religious defense against claims of Nazism bore similarities to arguments made in Germany, there was a specific Spanish variant. The interpretation given by Carrero Blanco in von Knoblach's case suggested that not only did Catholicism simply make it impossible to be a Nazi, but that religious belief also demonstrated loyalty and service to the Franco regime. In many cases, like von Knoblach's, individuals' religion was combined with their service during the Civil War in order to make a complete argument that they supported Franco's Spain. Such rhetoric mirrored the regime's own linkage of national renovation and religious inspiration. Hubert Hahn, an SD agent arrested by the Spanish in May 1945, as the war ended, and still in prison at Yserias in March 1946, wrote an appeal against his own deportation and signed his request to be released as "an admirer of Spain and a fervent Catholic."[100] The bringing together of "pro-Spanish" and "Catholic" was more deliberate than simply stating that one's Catholicism made it impossible to be a committed Nazi. Moreover, this led naturally to claiming that one was better categorized as "Spaniard" than as "German."

Germans as Spaniards

The final strategy for Germans defending themselves against the threat of repatriation, of those who spoke up and tried to shape their own fate in the face of U.S. policy and the Spanish government's response, was to be even more blunt than the petitioners already examined and simply argue that they were, in effect, Spaniards. For the most part they were Germans who had lived in Spain since before the Nazi rise to power in 1933. They usually had come to Spain for business and only became involved in politics and service to the Nazi state much later. Most of them had married Spanish women and had children born in Spain. These people, however, made up the core of the Abwehr in Spain, which by 1944 employed 220 people directly and had more than one thousand agents, most of whom came from the German colony already in existence in Spain or were employees of German businesses that developed in Spain after 1936.[101] Friedrich Burkhardt combined his conversion to Catholicism, his first marriage to a Spaniard, his service in Franco's army, and his residence in Spain since 1913 to declare Spain as "my second country"; he did, he claimed, only a little work for the German Embassy during the war and viewed what happened to Germany under Nazism as "a Spaniard."[102] According to OSS records, Burkhardt had served the Abwehr in Seville, where he was based, from 1943 onward.[103]

Marriage was the primary argument through which the claim to effectively be Spanish was made, with length of time in Spain usually also a featured component. In most cases these two circumstances went hand in hand. This was true whether the petitioner was on one of the priority lists and his arrest was potentially imminent or whether he was on a lower priority list and was simply contacted by the U.S. and UK embassies and asked to consider voluntary repatriation. In the first instance, higher-priority candidates for repatriation, such as Wilhelm Meyer, protested the Spanish order to intern him at Caldas de Malavella in May 1945. He cited his residency in Bilbao for thirty-two years and his marriage to a Spaniard for twenty-four years and noted that his only political activity was not as a German, but as a Spaniard, joining the Falange during the Civil War.[104] In the second instance, for expulsion candidates of lower priority, Max Ludwig Muller-Bohm, for example, received requests for voluntary repatriation from his local police in Barcelona and from the British-American Repatriation Centre in February

1946. He argued against these requests based on his residency in Spain since 1930 and his marriage to a Spaniard. He went on to note that his two children were born in Barcelona and baptized in the Sagrada Familia Cathedral. To him, these facts mattered more than his absence from Spain to work in Germany during the Republican period in Barcelona, his work in Tetuan, Spanish Morocco, from 1938 to 1943, or his membership in the German Labor Front (DAF) of the Nazi Party.[105]

These arguments also proved to be the most convincing to Spanish officials, many of whom used the same arguments in petitioning their Ministry of Foreign Affairs to protect their German friends under the line of argument that whether these Germans were actual Spanish citizens did not matter. When citizenship was not possible, the Spanish government used the idea of Germans "incorporated into Spanish life." This phrase was first used by the political director of the Foreign Ministry, Roberto Satorres, in a December 1945 discussion with American and British officials, indicating that it referred to Germans with many years' residency in Spain, a Spanish spouse, or children of Spanish nationality.[106] In the case of Alfred Menzell, formerly of the German naval attaché's office, one of the leading figures in Spanish government, Luis Carrero Blanco, wrote to Artajo with Francisco Franco's approval. He advocated that Menzell be exempted from repatriation in part on the basis of his residency in Spain since 1918, his marriage to a Spaniard in 1925, and the birth of three children on Spanish soil. These facts, argued Carrero Blanco, meant Menzell's inclusion on a repatriation list could only be a "bureaucratic error."[107] This, despite the fact that the U.S. Embassy made the protection of Menzell by Spanish officials, including the security services, a major point of complaint in a subsequent meeting with Artajo, suggesting he was in fact one of the prominent targets for repatriation.[108]

Conclusion

Most of the Germans with ties to Nazi espionage, diplomacy, and party activity facing Allied repatriation policy in Spain sought to avoid deportation to occupied Central Europe. In many cases, they were able to draw upon arguments used within occupied Germany and Austria. This was especially so of Catholic Germans, whose reinterpretation of their recent past echoed interpretations used by Catholics at home. However, the advantage of being in Spain also allowed them to tap into interpretations of the war used by the Franco regime itself. In these instances, service in wartime could be connected to Civil War service, even if for Germany in the Condor Legion, to represent a long-term commitment to Francoism, not Nazism. Anti-Communism played an important role in this, as well as more broadly defined Spanish nationalism.

Given the international politics of the time period and the reluctance of the Franco regime to cooperate with the Allied Control Commission in rounding up Germans and Austrians after the war, it was unlikely that the postwar repatriation of "obnoxious" Germans would have any chance of success. Francoist stalling was clear and consistent throughout this time period, for the Spanish regime did not accept the legitimate right of the ACC to order deportation, and any agreements made with the United States and Britain were concluded purely for "political" reasons, to preserve the regime's position with the Western powers.[109] The result was the minimal level of cooperation.[110] By 1947, the onset of the Cold War and the beginning of the end of denazification in occupied Germany combined to weaken support within the U.S. government to pursue the remaining cases for deportation from Spain.[111]

Nonetheless, interpretations of the recent past used by Germans in Spain are worth examining. In their petitions to the Franco regime, these Germans, of various backgrounds and various levels of commitment to Nazism, used their unique situation to make arguments that were often more political than one might suspect. In placing themselves within the Spanish context, as advocates of Francoism, they defended their personal histories as advocates of nondemocratic regimes. Here, then, we have an instance of denazification that was not developed with an eye to the inevitability of democracy and change as perceived by the victorious Allied powers in western Germany or occupied Austria. Even if we interpret those who used Catholicism as employing a tool to distance themselves from Nazism, the implication in Spain was that their future lay there, within the context of a very pro-Catholic government, a regime that would elevate the status of Catholics more than whatever might come into existence in Germany. The appeal to Catholicism in Spain, therefore, needs to be interpreted as a political commitment to Francoism in a way that Catholicism as a means of distancing oneself from Nazism was not in occupied Germany. Naturally, in each case of a German in Spain, it is impossible to measure the level of an individual's commitment to Nazism, or democracy, or anything else, with the evidence gathered from Spanish and American official archives. Yet it is striking that these individuals not only were attempting to limit the extent of denazification proceedings they may have faced; they also were seeking to make a commitment to Francoism, which provides a strange twist on the development of denazification outside of occupied Germany that the members of the Allied Control Council could never have foreseen when they developed a policy to hunt Nazis in neutral states like Spain.

Notes

Portions of this chapter were published in David Messenger, *Hunting Nazis in Franco's Spain* (Baton Rouge: Louisiana State University Press, 2014).

1. Ronald Newton, "The United States, the German-Argentines, and the Myth of the Fourth Reich, 1943–47," *Hispanic American Historical Review* 64, no. 1 (1985): 85–86.

2. Manuel Ros Agudo, *La guerra secreta de Franco (1939–1945)* (Barcelona: Crítica, 2002), 209–10.

3. Carlos Collado Seidel, "España y los agents alemanes 1944–1947: Intransigencia y pragmatism politico," *Espacio, Tiempo y Forma, Serie V., Historia Contemporánea* (1992): 436.

4. Ros Agudo, *La guerra secreta*, 210–17.

5. RG 226 Office of Strategic Services, entry 127, box 28, "Haig Files," January 31, 1946, U.S. National Archives and Records Administration, College Park, MD (hereafter NARA).

6. RG 457 National Security Agency/Central Security Service, "The German Intelligence Series: Spain," October 1, 1944, NARA. This document from 1944 clearly defines Paul Winzer as different from Walter Eugen Mosig, another SD agent in Spain, although other sources, including the German Wikipedia (http://de.wikipedia.org/wiki/Paul_Winzer, accessed February 28, 2012), argue they were one and the same. My research indicates a high likelihood that they were in fact two different people.

7. Ros Agudo, *La guerra secreta*, 191–201.

8. RG 226, entry 190A, box 24, NARA, contains information on one such case of an agent under cover in a trading firm, that of SD agent Walter Schwedke and the Hamburg-based business Harder & De Vose; see the series of memos by the OSS, beginning July 11, 1946, in this file.

9. Katrin Paehler, "Foreign Intelligence in a New Paradigm: Amt VI of the Reich Main Security Office (RSHA)," in *Secret Intelligence and the Holocaust*, ed. David Bankier (Jerusalem: Yad Vashem, 2006), 279.

10. Richard Breitman, "Nazi Espionage: The Abwehr and SD Foreign Intelligence," in *U.S. Intelligence and the Nazis*, by Richard Breitman, Norman Goda, Timothy Naftali, and Robert Wolfe (Cambridge: Cambridge University Press, 2005), 107.

11. RG 226, entry 210, box 35, British Passport Control Officer to British Chancery (copied to U.S. Embassy), June 27, 1946, NARA.

12. Carlos Collado Seidel, *España: Refugio Nazi* (Madrid: Temas de hoy, 2005), 54.

13. Most important here were a series of policies developed as the war ended and the occupation of Germany began: the Supreme Headquarters of the Allied Expedi-

tionary Forces (SHAEF) November 1944 "Directive for Military Government in Germany," which emphasized the necessity of automatic arrest and internment of various Nazi Party members; the U.S. Joint Chiefs of Staff Resolution 1067 for U.S. Occupation Policy; and the Allied Control Council (ACC) Directive 24, issued in January 1946, which used JCS 1067 as a model to outline ninety-nine categories of Nazis subject to automatic arrest and detention. See Perry Biddiscombe, *Denazification: A History, 1945–1950* (Stroud, UK: Tempus, 2007), 33–39; and Frank M. Buscher, *The U.S. War Crimes Trial Program in Germany, 1946–1955* (New York: Praeger, 1989), 19.

14. RG 226, entry 127, box 3, U.S. Embassy Madrid to State Department, September 10, 1946, NARA.

15. Jose María Irujo, *La lista negra: Los espías Nazis protegidos por Franco y la Iglesia* (Madrid: Aguilar, 2003), 140–43.

16. *ABC* (Madrid) and *ABC* (Sevilla), May 18, 1946.

17. *ABC* (Madrid), May 7, 1946.

18. Wayne H. Bowen, *Spaniards and Nazi Germany: Collaboration in the New Order* (Columbia: University of Missouri Press, 2000), 29.

19. Stanley Payne, *Franco and Hitler: Spain, Germany and World War II* (New Haven, CT: Yale University Press, 2008), 29.

20. Ros Agudo, *La guerra secreta*, 133.

21. Ibid., 200.

22. Ibid., 321.

23. RG 226, entry 183, box 8, Report XX-7785, June 28, 1945, NARA.

24. Hilary Earl, *The Nuremberg SS-Einsatzgruppen Trial, 1945–1958: Atrocity, Law and History* (New York: Cambridge University Press, 2009), 49.

25. RG 226, entry 183, box 8, Memo. of Conversation with Logie, Copeland and Milton, Bennett and Horwin and Bernhardt, July 26, 1945, NARA.

26. Seyla Benhabib, *The Rights of Others: Aliens, Residents and Citizens* (Cambridge: Cambridge University Press, 2004), 55.

27. Donald Bloxham, "The Genocidal Past in Western Germany and the Experience of Occupation, 1945–6," *European History Quarterly* 34, no. 3 (2004): 307.

28. Jeffrey Herf, *Divided Memory: The Nazi Past in the Two Germanies* (Cambridge, MA: Harvard University Press, 1997), 202.

29. Ibid., 225.

30. Paloma Aguilar, *Memory and Amnesia: The Role of the Spanish Civil War in the Transition to Democracy,* trans. Mark Oakley (New York: Berghahn Books, 2002), 30.

31. Ibid., 46.

32. Ibid., 61.

33. Javier Rodrigo, *Cautivos: Campos de concentración en la España franquista, 1936–1947* (Barcelona: Crítica, 2005), 127, 128.

34. Michael Richards, "From War Culture to Civil Society: Francoism, Social Change and Memories of the Spanish Civil War," *History and Memory* 14, nos. 1–2 (2002): 99.

35. Antonio Cazorla-Sanchez, *Fear and Progress: Ordinary Lives in Franco's Spain, 1939–1975* (Oxford: Wiley-Blackwell, 2010), 25.

36. Archivo Renovado (R) 2159/6, Nutz to Ministry of Foreign Affairs, January 22, 1946, Spain, Archivo General del Ministerio de Asuntos Exteriores, Madrid (hereafter AMAE).

37. R 2159/3, Giese to Ministry of Foreign Affairs, July 31, 1945, AMAE.

38. RG 226, entry 210, box 35, British Passport Control Office to British Embassy Madrid, copied to U.S. Embassy, Madrid, June 27, 1946, NARA.

39. R 21690/4, Lequerica to Carrero Blanco, November 22, 1944, AMAE.

40. R 2159/4, von Eitzen to Ministry of Foreign Affairs, August 11, 1945, AMEA; R 2159/6, von Eitzen to Ministry of Foregn Affairs, January 18, 1946, AMAE; R 2159/6, Casa Civil de El Jefe del Estado y Generalissimo de los Ejercitos to Artajo, February 20, 1946, AMAE.

41. R 2160/4, Moreno to Lequerica, November 15, 1944, AMAE.

42. RG 226, entry 127, box 1, Agent SAINT BC 012 to SAINT BC 001, May 19, 1945, NARA.

43. R 2159/1, British Embassy Madrid to Ministry of Foreign Affairs, March 16, 1944, AMAE.

44. RG 226, entry 127, box 1, Agent SAINT BC 012 to SAINT BC 001, May 31, 1945, and August 31, 1945, NARA.

45. R 2159/3, Genserowsky to Foreign Minister, May 28, 1945, AMAE.

46. R 2160/4, Martinez de Campos to Lequerica, June 16, 1945, AMAE.

47. R 5161/7, DG Seguridad General Memo., May 7, 1948, AMAE.

48. R 2159/1, DG Seguridad General to DG Politica Exterior, Ministry of Foreign Affairs, August 8, 1944, AMAE.

49. R 2160/4, Memo., Ministry of Foreign Affairs, no date, AMAE.

50. Irujo, *La lista negra,* 140–43.

51. R 5161/5, Yturralde y Orbegosos, to Carceller, March 4, 1948, AMAE.

52. Florentino Portero, *Franco aislado: La cuéstion espanola, 1945–1950* (Madrid: Aguilar, 1989), 72–76.

53. Armour to Secretary of State, March 24, 1945, in *Foreign Relations of the United States,* 1945 (Washington, DC: Government Printing Office, 1967), 5:668.

54. Joan Maria Thomàs, *Roosevelt, Franco and the End of the Second World War* (New York: Palgrave Macmillan, 2011), 177.

55. Rodrigo, *Cautivos,* 138.

56. R 2159/6, Burbach to Franco, April 12, 1946, AMAE.

57. Ibid.

58. R 2159/6, Burbach to Hawley, copied to Ministry of Foreign Affairs, April 27, 1946, AMAE.

59. R 2159/6, Meyer-Doehner to Artajo, April 24, 1946, AMAE.

60. Richards, "From War Culture to Civil Society," 98.

61. R 2160/4, Enge to Ministry of Foreign Affairs, April 17, 1946, AMAE.

62. Sasha D. Pack, *Tourism and Dictatorship: Europe's Peaceful Invasion of Franco's Spain* (New York: Palgrave Macmillan, 2006), 40.

63. R 2159/6, Menzell to Atajo, April 24, 1946, AMAE.

64. R 2159/2, Leutner to Ministry of Foreign Affairs, December 9, 1944, and January 2, 1946, AMAE.

65. R 2159/6, Leutner to Artajo, January 11, 1946, AMAE.

66. Ibid.

67. R 2159/2, Leutner to Ministry of Foreign Affairs, January 2, 1946, AMAE.

68. R 5161/19, Cardinal Enrique Pla y Deniel to Artajo, June 8, 1946, AMAE.

69. R 2160/4, von Waldheim to Baldwin, U.S. Embassy (copied to Ministry of Foreign Affairs), June 27, 1946, AMAE.

70. Richards, "From War Culture to Civil Society," 102.

71. Rodrigo, *Cautivos,* 133.

72. Ibid., 137.

73. R 2159/6, Lipperheide Henke to Ministry of Foreign Affairs, April 20, 1946, AMAE.

74. R 5161/19, Cardinal Enrique Pla y Deniel to Martin Artajo, June 18, 1946, AMAE.

75. RG 226, entry 127, box 28, Agent 23715/C to 23700, "Incoming British," no date, NARA.

76. R 2160/1, Huber to Ministry of Foreign Affairs, May 30, 1946, AMAE.

77. RG 260, Records of U.S. Occupation Headquarters, entry 421 (A), box 585, Interrogation of Georg Wolfgang Scuebel, Hohenasperg, Germany, June 28–29 and July 1, 1946, NARA.

78. R 2159/6, Oboril to Ministry of Foreign Affairs, Februry 23, 1946, AMAE.

79. Richard Steigmann-Gall, *The Holy Reich: Nazi Conceptions of Christianity, 1919–1945* (New York: Cambridge University Press, 2003), 266.

80. See Mark Edward Ruff, "The Postmodern Challenge to the Secularization Thesis: A Critical Assessment," *Schweizerische Zeitschrift für Religions- und Kulturgeschichte* 99 (2005): 385–401.

81. RG 84, Records of Foreign Service Posts of the State Department, entry 3162, box 97, U.S. Embassy to State Department, January 19, 1946, NARA.

82. RG 226, entry 127, box 2, "Note from Recent Haig Reports (Incoming British)," no date, NARA.

83. R 2161/1, Boos to Ministry of Foreign Affairs, June 1, 1946, AMAE.

84. R 5161/19, Cardinal Enrique Pla y Deniel to Artajo, June 8, 1946, AMAE.

85. R 5161/19, Cardinal Enrique Pla y Deniel to Artajo, May 13, 1946, AMAE.

86. R 2160/2, Memo., DG Politica Exterior to DG Seguridad General, June 5, 1946, AMAE.

87. R 2160/1, Boos to Artajo, June 1, 1946, AMAE.

88. RG 226, entry 190A, box 23, Gillie Howell Memo., February 26, 1946, NARA.

89. RG 84, entry 3161, box 98, Titus to Park, November 18, 1946, NARA.

90. RG 84, entry 3162, box 97, Rhodes to Ford, January 21, 1946, NARA.

91. RG 226, entry 190A, box 27, Memo by Titus, December 2, 1945, NARA.

92. RG 226, entry 210, box 35, Rothe Report, January 16, 1946, NARA.

93. RG 65 Federal Bureau of Investigation, box 152, FBI–U.S. Embassy Report, February 10, 1947, NARA.

94. R 5161/19, Simonsen to Ministry of Foreign Affairs, January 26, 1946, AMAE.

95. RG 226, entry 190A, box 27, Memo by Titus, December 2, 1945, NARA.

96. Gerald Steinacher, *Nazis on the Run: How Hitler's Henchmen Fled Justice* (Oxford: Oxford University Press, 2011), 154.

97. Ibid., 101–58.

98. R 2160/4, Simonsen to Doussinague, July 22, 1945; copied to Artajo on November 16, 1945, AMAE.

99. R 2160/4, Carrero Blanco to Doussinague, February 19, 1946, AMAE.

100. R 2159/6, Hahn to Ministry of Foreign Affairs, March 1, 1946, AMAE.

101. Ros Agudo, *La guerra secreta,* 217.

102. R 2160/1, Burkhardt to Ministry of Foreign Affairs, no date, AMAE.

103. RG 226, entry 127, box 3, "Consolidated List of Persons Who Worked for the German Intelligence Services in Spain, Compiled from Sources within Germany," September 26, 1946, NARA.

104. R 2159/3, Meyer to Minister of Foreign Affairs, May 26, 1945, AMAE.

105. R 2159/6, Muller-Bohm to Ministry of Foreign Affairs, March 29, 1946, AMAE.

106. R 5161/19, Satorres, Note of Meeting with Baldwin and Bramwell, December 28, 1945, AMAE.

107. R 2160/4, Carrero Blanco to Artajo, September 4, 1946, AMAE.

108. RG 226, entry 210, Titus to Bonsal, November 29, 1946, NARA.

109. R 5161/19, Memo., Ministry of Foreign Affairs, July 10, 1946, AMAE.

110. David A. Messenger, "Beyond War Crimes: Denazification, 'Obnoxious' Germans and US Policy in Franco's Spain after the Second World War," *Contemporary European History* 20, no. 4 (2011): 473.

111. Ibid., 477.

5

Siegfried Zoglmann, His Circle of Writers, and the Naumann Affair

A Nazi Propaganda Operation in Postwar Germany

Susanna Schrafstetter

In 1991 the famous spy novelist John Le Carré wrote in a new introduction to *A Small Town in Germany,* his 1967 thriller, "The West Germany of Konrad Adenauer was not all lovely by any means: old players from the Hitler time were two-a-penny, whether they were such men as Adenauer's own éminence grise Herr Globke," or "such luminaries of the Free Democratic Party as Herr Achenbach," or "the ebullient Herr Zoglmann, who only eighteen years before had been a high-ranking figure in the Hitler Youth."[1] By 1991 Globke and Achenbach had become emblematic of those former National Socialists who had managed to rebuild careers in West Germany after the collapse of Nazism. By contrast, Siegfried Zoglmann has remained an underexamined "old player from the Hitler time." The head of the Reich Youth Leadership (Reichsjugendführung) in Bohemia and Moravia, an editor of Hitler Youth newspapers, and a member of the Waffen-SS, Zoglmann enjoyed an illustrious career in the Free Democratic Party (FDP). As a member of the Bundestag from 1957 to 1976, he served as deputy chairman of the FDP parliamentary group until 1968. In 1969 he entered the political limelight for his spectacular breakaway from his party in protest against Chancellor Willy Brandt's Ostpolitik. Yet in 1952–1953, Zoglmann had played a part in the notorious Naumann Affair. In January 1953 British authorities, using their prerogatives under the Occupation Statute, had arrested a number of former National Socialists for attempted subversion of the FDP. The conspiracy, named after its main protagonist, Werner Naumann, the former deputy of Joseph Goebbels in the Propaganda Ministry, involved a diffuse circle of former Nazis active at high levels of the FDP in the state of North Rhine–Westphalia. Zoglmann was one of the conspirators who also ran a circle of journalists that provided the propagandistic platform of the conspiracy. While West German democracy had not been under immediate threat from the activities of the Naumann circle, the subsequent investigation highlighted the political activities and influence of former Nazis and certain failures of the earlier denazification process.

Much has been written on the Naumann Affair and its repercussions on German politics and *Vergangenheitsbewältigung* (coping with the Nazi past), as well as on its impact on Anglo-German relations.[2] Most recently, Kristian Buchna's detailed study of the subject has led to considerable attention from the media and to renewed questions about whether the FDP has failed to confront its problematic postwar past.[3] Buchna detailed the connections among former Hitler Youth officials in the Naumann circle, including Zoglmann. However, both the investigation into the affair in 1953 and the historiography since then have centered largely on the key protagonists, especially Werner Naumann himself; Friedrich Middelhauve, the head of the FDP in North Rhine–Westphalia; Wolfgang Diewerge, Middelhauve's personal assistant, who had been a high-ranking official of Goebbels's Ministry of Propaganda; and Ernst Achenbach, a former attaché in the German Embassy in Paris during the Nazi period and a member of the FDP State Board (Landesvorstand) in North Rhine–Westphalia. By contrast, Zoglmann's role in the conspiracy, and his activities in National Socialist networks more generally, have attracted little attention. Zoglmann was not only a politician but also a journalist. As editor of the FDP weeklies *Die Plattform* and *Die Deutsche Zukunft,* he oversaw the dissemination of revisionist ideas and cultivated a close circle of former Nazis in Germany and Austria, providing them with an ideological home and an outlet for their political views. Zoglmann was at the center of this journalistic network of former National Socialists that understood itself as the propagandistic spearhead of the national rallying (Nationale Sammlung) envisaged by the Naumann circle. Among them were the key protagonists of the Naumann conspiracy (often publishing under pseudonyms) as well as a range of lesser-known, second-tier National Socialist journalists and writers such as Werner Beumelburg, Günter Kaufmann, once a top assistant to Baldur von Schirach, or Wolfgang von Wolmar, former head of the press department in the Reich Protectorate of Bohemia and

Opening of the 5th Training Camp of the Curatorium for the Education of Youth in Bohemia and Moravia in Mnicha Palace, Prague, November 22, 1942. *Right to left:* Willy Dressler, Siegfried Zoglmann, Ernst Schaschenk, unidentified, Emanuel Moravec, unidentified. Bpk, Berlin/Art Resource, NY.

Moravia. The network, its papers, and their contributors have never been examined in detail; they are at the center of the following analysis.

Born in 1913 in Neumark/Sudetenland (today Všeruby, Czech Republic), Siegfried Zoglmann was the fifth son of the farmer Josef Zoglmann and his wife Maria. He attended the German Trade Academy in Plzeň, graduating in 1931. He was already a Nazi activist by this time, having joined the German National Socialist Workers Party in the Sudetenland and its youth organization in 1928 (at age fifteen). After leaving school he was employed as a party activist, engaged in editing work. Following his arrest by Czech officials in 1933 on account of his political activity, for which he served a short prison sentence, Zoglmann fled to Germany in 1934, where he joined the NSDAP and the Hitler Youth.[4]

In 1935 Zoglmann was appointed head of the Foreign Press Office (Auslandspressestelle) of the Reich Youth Leadership, a position he held until 1939. In this position, he served as editor of the Hitler Youth newspapers *Der Morgen* and *Der Pimpf* from February to July of 1937 and coauthored further publications.[5] Especially striking in the volumes of *Der Morgen* and *Der*

Pimpf edited by Zoglmann was the strong focus on Hitler. While his successor published several issues in a row without articles on Hitler, the volumes that appeared between March and July 1937 were full of articles about, and pictures of, the Führer.[6] Similarly, Zoglmann's 1938 publication *Sudetenland Marschiet* was fully focused on Hitler as liberator and savior of the Sudetenland.

In 1939 Zoglmann was sent to the Reich Protectorate of Bohemia and Moravia as a representative of the Reich Youth Leadership. Subsequently, he volunteered for service in the Waffen-SS, and in March 1943 he was assigned to the Leibstandarte Adolf Hitler. He was posted to the eastern front in March 1943. From July 1943 he participated in the occupation of northern Italy, where he engaged, in his own words, in "anti-guerilla warfare [*Banden-bekämpfung*] in Istria."[7] *Bandenbekämpfung* was a cynical Nazi euphemism for killing anyone suspected of real or perceived activity against the German occupation. In November Zoglmann returned to the eastern front. He spent the first half of 1944 at the SS-Junker-Schule Braunschweig in Posen (Poznań), from which he graduated with high marks. His superiors remarked that, as an "old fighter" and Hitler Youth leader, he showed a special interest in National Socialist ideology. They also noted, somewhat cryptically, "He has a special talent for organizing celebrations."[8] In October 1944 Zoglmann, now promoted to *Untersturmführer*, returned to the front, where he served as *Ordonanzoffizier*, personal adjutant to *Sturmbannführer* Karl Rettlinger, the commander of the SS-Panzerjäger Abteilung 1.[9]

In 1955 Zoglmann claimed that at the end of the war he had moved to Bavaria to work at his cousin's farm, in the hope that this would facilitate the issuing of a release certificate (*Entlassungsschein*) from the American author-ities, as agricultural laborers were desperately needed at the time. He claimed to have been released by the Americans shortly after reporting to the U.S. POW camp in the town of Landshut.[10] However, he did not provide an exact date of his release, and Zoglmann's CIA file maintains that he was captured in Austria and interned there until August 1945. Also unclear are his where-abouts until 1950, when he resurfaced in Düsseldorf and became press officer of the FDP for North Rhine–Westphalia. All of Zoglmann's CVs contain gap-ing holes for the years 1945–1950.

According to a report in his CIA file, Zoglmann remained in Austria until 1949 to avoid denazification proceedings in Germany.[11] Given that no evi-dence of Zoglmann's denazification, or of his professional activities between 1945 and 1950, could be found, the view of the CIA report seems credible. How it was that he came to surface in North Rhine–Westphalia thus remains an open question. What is clear is that by 1950, several old acquaintances of

Zoglmann were in charge of administering the FDP Landesverband (state or regional association) North Rhine–Westphalia, headed by Friedrich Middelhauve. "Eminence grise" behind Middelhauve was former Nazi diplomat Dr. Ernst Achenbach, who used his good connections to industrial circles to raise funds for the regional FDP to employ a general manager.[12] Achenbach's choice for the job was Heinz Wilke, a former Hitler Youth (HJ) leader. Wilke and Zoglmann knew each other from their time together at the Reich Youth Leadership. Two other FDP officials, Günter Prager and Heinz Lange, had also been among Zoglmann's fellow HJ regional leaders (HJ-*Gebietsführer*) in the Sudetenland. Prager and Zoglmann had engaged in intrigue together against Konrad Henlein in 1939–1940.[13] By 1950, Prager was general manager of the FDP in the Ruhr district, where Lange ran a subsection before becoming head of the Young Liberals in North Rhine–Westphalia in 1952.[14] Who moved whom into leadership positions and who was who before 1945 are nicely described on a spreadsheet found in the personal papers of vice-chancellor (and FDP member) Franz Blücher. While it was Wilke who brought Zoglmann on board, Wolfgang Döring, who had served as captain of a tank unit in the Wehrmacht during the Second World War, helped Walter Brand, former editor-in-chief of *Die Zeit* and founding member of the Sudetendeutsche Heimatfront, to start a new career in the FDP. Willi Weyer, another leading member of the FDP in North Rhine–Westphalia, hired former HJ-*Gebietsführer* Günter Prager.[15] Table 5.1, at the end of this chapter, provides a list of key personalities and their positions before and after 1945.

In December 1950, Zoglmann started as managing editor of the weekly FDP paper *Die Plattform* under Friedrich Middelhauve, who was editor-in-chief of the paper as well as head of the Landesverband North Rhine–Westphalia.[16] The paper was renamed *Die Deutsche Zukunft* in December 1951, and Zoglmann remained as managing editor of this weekly with a circulation of forty thousand copies. Under both its old and its new banners, the paper was notorious for its right-wing positions, but neither its staff nor its articles have been examined by historians. *Die Plattform* and *Die Deutsche Zukunft* were official organs of the FDP during its formative phase, and as such they were instrumental in presenting the party's ideas and values both to party members and to the wider public.

During the investigation into the Naumann Affair, FDP officials took a close look at the role of *Die Deutsche Zukunft* as a possible organ of the Naumann conspirators. The scrutiny of the paper focused on two main areas: the political background of the paper's staff and the extent of Werner Naumann's personal influence on personnel and content. Zoglmann was questioned on both counts. The investigation showed clearly that Zoglmann had been in charge of hiring the staff. It also revealed that scrutiny of the paper had been lax and that the investigators had asked the wrong questions. The extent of Naumann's direct personal influence was, in a sense, not relevant, as the paper fully reflected Naumann's ideological agenda. Zoglmann was questioned only about the background of a small group of section editors (*Resortleiter*).[17] In two cases, Zoglmann was able to hide compromising pasts. In any event, the section editors had played only minor roles in shaping the ideological direction of the paper. Much more important had been the regular political commentators, about whom no questions were posed. It was an illustrious group that contributed regularly to *Die Plattform* and *Die Deutsche Zukunft*. Most of them had come from three closely interrelated National Socialist networks: the Reich Youth Leadership, Sudetengerman National Socialists, and the Ministry of Propaganda. Some of the commentators did try to hide their true identities behind pseudonyms. One byline that appeared frequently was "Amadeus," but in other cases the fictional names employed by the commentators were less easily recognizable as pseudonyms. A substantial number of articles in *Die Plattform* and *Die Deutsche Zukunft* were published under such false names. One must ask whether the routine use of pseudonyms provided the members of the Naumann circle (and others with similar political tendencies) with an outlet for their opinions. The tone of the articles would certainly support that view.

One member of the Naumann circle who published commentary without disclosing his identity was Wolfgang Diewerge. His name never appeared in the paper, but he was a regular contributor—which became clear during the Naumann investigation. He also made suggestions about which topics should be covered. A former Nazi propagandist specializing in anti-Semitic pamphlets, Diewerge had been hired as personal secretary to Middelhauve. Diewerge was widely seen as "Naumann's man" in the FDP, and hence Zoglmann was questioned about Diewerge's role at the newspaper. Zoglmann's response was highly contradictory. While claiming that Diewerge's influence on the paper had been minimal, Zoglmann also admitted that Diewerge had attended staff meetings and that it had been necessary for Zoglmann regularly to purge the "Klumpfuss" (club foot) from Diewerge's articles. This reference to Goebbels was Zoglmann's way of referring to Diewerge's compulsive anti-Semitic mind-set.[18] Obviously, Zoglmann had readily accepted Diewerge's contributions. But he had the investigators believe that he had been annoyed with Diewerge's inability to hide his virulent anti-Semitism in his articles.

Whether Diewerge and Zoglmann had known each other before 1945 remains unclear. Both had served in the Leibstandarte Adolf Hitler.[19] As head of the foreign press section of the Reich Youth Leadership, Zoglmann must have had regular contact with the Propaganda Ministry. Had they in fact known each other previously, their relationship may well have been tense, as suggested by Zoglmann's ridicule of Diewerge to the investigators. On the other hand, this may have been a tactic used by Zoglmann for self-protection. The fact remains that Diewerge regularly contributed to the FDP papers and exercised influence over content. It has been suggested that Zoglmann might have been under pressure from Friedrich Middelhauve to accept Diewerge's influence, but there is little evidence that this was the case.[20] First, Zoglmann stated clearly that he could have rejected Diewerge's suggestions had he wanted to. Second, the investigations into the Naumann Affair clearly established that Zoglmann was fully in charge of personnel at *Die Deutsche Zukunft*.[21] Finally, the other regular commentators who contributed to the paper under Zoglmann shared Diewerge's views and background.

It was likely Diewerge who introduced to *Die Plattform* and *Die Deutsche Zukunft* his old collaborator, Professor Friedrich Grimm, who became a regular contributor. Once a prominent lawyer for the Nazi movement and regime, Grimm had been involved (with Diewerge) in the planned Nazi show trial of Herschel Grynszpan. He had also served as legal adviser to the former ambassador to France, Otto Abetz, and more generally as a propagandist for German foreign policy. Grimm sought a prominent role in postwar Germany as an advocate for German war criminals, a vocal supporter of a general amnesty, and a Nazi apologist.[22]

Carl Albert Drewitz, a Nazi propagandist and short-time *Pressereferent* of Goebbels in 1938, had worked for the Deutsches Nachrichtenbüro, the Nazi news agency, before he came to *Die Plattform* through a Düsseldorf connection.[23] When Drewitz was questioned as part of the Naumann investigation, he mentioned that when he had started working as freelance journalist in Düsseldorf in 1950, he shared an apartment with Heinz Schmidt, another FDP official who was in charge of advertising in *Die Plattform* and *Die Deutsche Zukunft*. There had been another person living with Heinz Schmidt—Siegfried Zoglmann.[24] While Zoglmann and Drewitz only met in 1950, Zoglmann and Schmidt had worked together at the Reich Youth Leadership during the Nazi era.[25] From there, Schmidt had gone to work for the German Embassy in France under Ernst Achenbach. The glowing *Persilschein* Schmidt had written for Achenbach's denazification might have helped Schmidt secure a job with the FDP.[26] Zoglmann justified Drewitz's employment with the argument that he was in charge of cultural affairs and never wrote anything political. This was a lie. Drewitz was a regular contributor on current affairs and history.

One of the most prolific writers for *Die Deutsche Zukunft* and *Die Platt-form* was Wolfgang Wolfram von Wolmar. Before 1945, SS-*Hauptsturmfüh-rer* von Wolmar had supervised the Czech press in the Reich Protectorate of Bohemia and Moravia. Under von Wolmar, the Czech press had been sys-tematically pressured to make anti-Semitic propaganda a dominant feature of its work.[27] Closely scrutinized, the press had received regular orders in "press club" meetings organized by Wolmar. After Jews in the protectorate were ordered to wear the yellow Star of David in September 1941, Wolmar raged when he learned that some "Aryan" factory workers had donned the star out of solidarity with their Jewish co-workers. He called this "a scandal-ous shame for the entire Czech people."[28] In a meeting with Czech newspa-per editors, he ordered them to publicize the policy that "Aryans" wearing a star would be treated like Jews and to admonish Czech businessmen to avoid further association with Jews.[29] On October 10, 1941, Wolmar participated in a meeting with Reinhard Heydrich, at which the "evacuation" of Jews from the protectorate was discussed.[30] Particular emphasis was placed on the ques-tion of how and when the press had to report on the coming events. Follow-ing the beginning of the deportations, Wolmar uttered his frustration with Czech journalists and the Czechs more generally, who showed "inappropri-ate sympathy with the Jews." To combat this, Wolmar ordered the press to set up special newspaper columns (*Denunziationsrubriken*), where Czechs could denounce fellow citizens who showed sympathy with the Jews.[31]

In November 1939 Wolmar had provoked the execution of three Czech men following a complaint by one of his staff that two of the Czechs had ver-bally abused him. A Czech policeman arrested the two men only reluctantly. Receiving the news late in the evening, Wolmar went straight to the police station, suspended the policeman from his position, and notified the SS-*Gruppenführer, Staatssekretär* Karl Hermann Frank, who ordered the execu-tion of all three Czechs. Wolmar drafted the "sentence" to be read out to the Czechs, who would be executed for attempted murder.[32] The exact circum-stances of this crime remained unclear. After the German surrender, Wolmar was wanted by Czechoslovakia as a war criminal.[33] Zoglmann nonetheless took Wolmar on as a permanent staff member at *Die Deutsche Zukunft*, dis-guising his past as that of a "reserve officer." Zoglmann "knew Wolmar well, from way back."[34] Indeed, the parallels in the two men's CVs are remark-able. Wolmar had joined the German National Socialist Workers Party in the Sudetenland in 1929, one year after becoming a member of the party's youth organization. After a brief arrest in Czechoslovakia in 1933 because of his political activity, he fled to Germany in 1934. In 1939 he was sent back to Prague as head of the press department in the Reich protectorate. He volunteered for the Waffen-SS, and starting in 1943 he served in the SS-division Prinz Eugen. After 1945 he hid in Austria under a false name.[35] He published in *Die Plattform* and *Die Deutsche Zukunft* under his alias, Felix Haen, but he also used other false names, among them Berndt Jannsen.

Dr. Manfred Zapp served as the newspaper's "expert" for international relations. The author of many books, Zapp had been the chief Nazi propagandist in North and South America.[36] In 1938 he became head of the Trans-Ocean News Service bureau in the United States. Transocean had once been a reputable news agency but was then transformed into a propaganda mill controlled by the Propaganda Ministry. Following his transfer from South America to the United States in 1938, Zapp was indicted for espionage activities in 1941. Zapp and his associate Günter Tonn were sent back to Germany in exchange for two American journalists who had been arrested by Nazi authorities.[37] Zapp was then transferred to the German Embassy in Ankara. After the war, Zapp, the son of a Düsseldorf industrialist, searched for a new job. He received a recommendation from an old acquaintance in Washington, Herbert Blankenhorn, who had written "that he [Zapp] plans to start an administrative job in the Rhineland after his 'debrowning' ["Entbäunung"— (*sic*)]."[38] Whether this recommendation landed him a job at *Die Plattform* remains unclear, but the ties between the Goebbels ministry and the Trans-Ocean News Service seem a plausible explanation.

Heinz Wilke, previously of the Reich Youth Leadership, and Walter Brand, the founder of the Sudetendeutsche Heimatfront, wrote regularly for *Die Plattform* and *Die Deutsche Zukunft*, as did Günter Kaufmann, former head of the press department of the Reich Youth Leadership. In 1940 Kaufmann had headed the Reich Propaganda Office in Vienna, and he had also served as a top assistant to Baldur von Schirach.[39] Another columnist was Nazi writer Werner Beumelburg, one of Hitler's most outspoken supporters from German literary circles.[40] The author of countless Nazi novels and an official reporter of the Condor Legion's bombing campaign in Spain, Beumelburg had compiled the "war diary" of Hermann Goering, which was supposed to become a comprehensive propaganda volume on the war.[41]

The political direction of *Die Plattform* and *Die Deutsche Zukunft* was clear. Aside from commentary on contemporary political issues, most space was devoted to World War II and the legacies of the Nazi past. The supposed heroism of the Wehrmacht and the SS in battles in which the Germans came "this close to winning" was a recurring theme, as was the belittling of German war crimes and an emphasis on Allied crimes against German expellees. Memoirs and revisionist histories by former Nazi officials were reviewed extensively. German victimization at the hands of the Western Allies received extensive attention, as did appeals to end denazification and release German war criminals. The following examples—drawn from among many—provide an overview of the papers' key themes.

The specialist for anti-Western, and specifically anti-American, sentiment was a certain "W. Breidenbacher," who regularly raged against Allied victimization of Germany. Under the headline "Everything Is the Germans' Fault," Breidenbacher ranted about Allied commissioners who had asked Adenauer "to deprive North Koreans of materials by inhibiting West German exports to the Eastern bloc." He wrote, "This time Generals of German blood cannot be hanged, this time—unfortunately—they were not involved. Hence it had to be the German merchant, German industry, German trade that were—as the biggest smugglers of all time—accused of planning to stab the UN in the back."[42] Breidenbacher also wrote a defamatory personal attack against Ludwig Rosenberg, a member of the board of the German Trade Union Association (and its chairman starting in 1962). A Jewish-German trade union activist, Rosenberg had been forced to flee the Nazis in 1933, returning to Germany from exile in London after the war. Under the headline "Another Amt Rosenberg," Breidenbacher claimed that Rosenberg had become an enemy of Germany during his exile and that, since his return from Britain, he had been fueling the propaganda machinery in preparation for a seizure of power by the trade unions.[43] The victim had been turned into the perpetrator. As there is no record for the existence of a real journalist by the name of W. Breidenbacher, the name was in all probability the pseudonym of one of Zoglmann's FDP friends.[44]

The piece on Rosenberg appeared in the July 20, 1951, edition of *Die Plattform*, together with an unsigned article on the Battle of El Alamein. Titled "The Victory [in Alamein] Dangled by a Thread," it claimed that German troops may well have won the battle had they not accidentally drunk some salt water. Placed directly beneath the El Alamein story was a piece, also unsigned, on the annual Lippoldsberger Dichtertreffen, a meeting of poets organized by Hans Grimm, the author of *Volk ohne Raum*, a book published in 1926 that is widely seen as a blueprint for Nazi expansionist ideas. *Die Plattform* did not neglect to mention that the Nazi poet Grimm "declared that today it is more important than ever to show the German *Volksgenossen* that there is a free, healthy German poetry growing out of the German soil like trees."[45] The issue appearing on the anniversary of the failed coup of July 20, 1944, against Hitler contained a highly polemical piece by Egmont Roth on the German military resistance. Defaming the men of July 20 was a major theme—*Die Plattform* ran a whole series in 1951–1952 titled "Bendlerstrasse: Betrayal and Espionage in Hitler's Secret Service."[46]

Felix Haen, aka Wolfgang von Wolmar, typically contributed articles devoted to France, contemporary political affairs, and sentimental war stories. In a lengthy review of the memoirs of Otto Abetz, Wolmar endorsed the author's claims that Hitler had wanted peace after Poland was defeated and that France and Britain had been at fault for refusing it.[47] A similar piece, titled "Who's Fault Was Rotterdam," contended that the Dutch general Henri Winkelmann had foolishly provoked the bombing of the city, an action that was "still branded a German war crime in international propaganda."[48] Nobody took responsibility for this unsigned article.

It was also common for the contributors to use their articles to whitewash one another. Celebrating the professional career of Professor Friedrich Grimm, Günter Kaufmann, former head of the press department of the Reich Youth leadership, defended Grimm's record with a summary of dubious accomplishments: "The Cairo trial of Jews against Germany, the Gustloff trial, the Berne Zionists' trial, the trial against Grünspan, the murderer of vom Rath—all those are the big political trials before the start of the Second World War in which Grimm can still effectively defend the idea of the rule of law."[49] Kaufmann had a long postwar record of distributing Nazi propaganda that continued well into the 1990s.[50] In 1999 he published *Auf Teufel komm raus: Unwahrheiten und Lügen über die nationalsozialistische Jugendbewegung*, which not only exposed him as an unreconstructed National Socialist who had learned absolutely nothing, but also contained a section entitled "People Who Shouldered Responsibility in the Hitler Youth and in the Democratic Rechtsstaat." It provides a list of sixty-six "exemplary" Germans, among them Siegfried Zoglmann, Heinz Schmidt (FDP), Heinz Lange (FDP), Horst Huisgen (another former HJ-*Gebietsführer* who was part of the Naumann circle), Wolfgang Döring, and Otto Abetz.

In 1951 one of the contributions by Carl Albert Drewitz was a eulogy to the Dönitz government. It concluded with the lines, "Looking back, one has to say that the Dönitz government accomplished something practically impossible. Much pain and suffering could have been avoided, if the Allies had followed the competent advice of the caretaker government of the Reich. . . . The circumstances under which the arrests of Admiral Dönitz, his cabinet, and the members of the OKW took place were humiliating. Those responsible for these orders should be ashamed of themselves."[51] In addition to articles published under his own name, Drewitz also likely penned other articles signed "C. Albert."[52]

In November 1951 *Die Plattform* published an article by Felix Rothberg about the "Sudeten German Tragedy." The author juxtaposed the murder of Sudeten Germans, for which he gave the highly exaggerated number of 700,000, with the German massacre of Czechs in Lidice, which had claimed 184 lives. The author then asked how it had been possible for a people like the Czechs to fall into such a murderous frenzy (*Blutrausch*). According to Rothberg, the Czechs had never had it as good as they did under the Germans. When in the final days of the war, Dr. Benesch called on his people to change sides, the Czech people had to silence their bad conscience as collaborators. Now they had to demonstrate to the Allies that only under the pressure of violent German rule had they collaborated. The Czechs had to rise against the German oppressors, "a bloody and cruel fake revolution had to be unleashed," and Dr. Benesch called on the Czechs to take everything from the Germans.[53]

An even more defamatory version of the article appeared six months later in *Die Deutsche Zukunft*. The argument was similar—with one exception. The author claimed that Dr. Benesch had also been responsible for both the assassination of Reinhard Heydrich and the Lidice massacre. Supposedly, Benesch had wanted both the assassination and the massacre in order to turn the Czechs against the Germans. The piece included a full page of pictures, among them a stamp featuring Heydrich's image that had been issued after his assassination and a picture of Wenceslas Square in Prague over the caption, "After 1945 the worst mass torture of Germans took place here."[54] The number of German victims had risen from 700,000 in the earlier article to 800,000 in this one. This time Egmont Roth, not Felix Rothberg, signed as author. Most likely, Felix Rothberg (occasionally Dr. Felix Rothberg) and Egmont Roth were pseudonyms used by an author who frequently contributed to *Die Plattform* and *Die Deutsche Zukunft*. Real journalists with those names did not seem to have existed.[55] Egmont Roth often signed for the most vicious articles in both papers.

From 1954 onward, *Die Deutsche Zukunft* and *Der Fortschritt,* the extreme-right-wing paper of the Hilden industrialist Gert Spindler, closely cooperated. Zoglmann became editor-in-chief of both papers.[56] Spindler was a confidant of Naumann and a close associate of Walter Brand and Zoglmann, and Zoglmann had been invited to Spindler's notorious Altenburger Treffen, meetings who attendees included former National Socialists at Spind-

ler's estate in 1950–1951.[57] Interestingly, at *Der Fortschritt* the editorial comment alternated between "SZ" and "ER"—the writing style is very similar.[58]
Following the demise of *Der Fortschritt* in 1960, Egmont Roth also wrote for
the FDP paper *Das freie Wort*.

In the 1980s Egmont Roth contributed to *Das Ostpreussenblatt*, the
weekly paper of the Landsmannschaft Ostpreussen, in his usual vein. The
editor-in-chief of *Das Ostpreussenblatt* was an old acquaintance of Zoglmann, Hugo Wellems, a former HJ-*Bannführer* and former official of both
the Reich Youth Leadership and the Goebbels Ministry. During the war he
had led the NS-Propagandaamt in Kowno. After Siegfried Zoglmann left the
FDP in protest against Brandt's Ostpolitik in 1971 to form a new party, the
German Union, Hugo Wellems served as its press liaison. He also served as
editor-in-chief for the *Deutschland-Journal*, a newspaper published by the
Nordwestdeutscher Zeitungsverlag, which Zoglmann had bought in 1958.
Zoglmann had also been a member in Wellems's Staats- und Wirtschaftspolitische Gesellschaft, which used obscure big business financial donations
to mobilize against Ostpolitik.[59] Who ultimately wrote under the pseudonym
Egmont Roth cannot be clarified with certainty.[60] What is certain is that
either the person was close to Zoglmann or it was Zoglmann himself.

Following the Naumann Affair, Siegfried Zoglmann was asked about
the 1952 version of the Lidice article, as it had caused some protest. A couple of concerned voices had used it as evidence to complain that the FDP
paper possessed a Nazi agenda.[61] Zoglmann was confronted with complaints
about "Führerverherrlichung"—glorification of the Führer—in his paper. He
claimed to have reread the piece on Lidice, maintaining that it may have been
"misunderstood." He also said that, at the time, the article must have slipped
his attention.[62] *Die Plattform* and *Die Deutsche Zukunft* had a clear ideological
agenda. There was a heavy emphasis on relativizing German crimes, on the
glorification of the German military effort, on the promotion of "revisionist"
history, on the victimization of Germans by the Western Allies, and, above
all, on the suffering of the Sudeten Germans (and all ethnic German expellees more generally). It was not, as one critic claimed, "Führerverherrlichung."
While "Führerverherrlichung" is evident in Zoglmann's publications from the
late 1930s, he was smart enough to understand that crude Hitler apologias
and anti-Semitism would be politically and legally unacceptable in postwar
Germany. The themes, centering on the exculpation of National Socialism
and the millions who had supported it, formed the framework for the paper's
main aim—promoting the national rallying ("Nationale Sammlung") envisaged by the Naumann circle.[63] *Die Deutsche Zukunft* provided the fanfare and

popular mobilization for the "German Program" of the FDP in North Rhine–Westphalia, which Zoglmann had coauthored with Middelhauve, Diewerge, and others. Framed in black, white, and red and announced at the state party conference (*Landesparteitag*) in Bielefeld to the sound of Franz Liszt's *Les Preludes*—as Kristian Buchna observed, this was the music that had introduced news from the Russian front during the Third Reich—the "German Program" centered on the notion of a *Deutsche Sammlung,* claiming, "[The] German Reich was the traditional way of life of our people."[64]

In his calls for a national rallying in *Die Deutsche Zukunft,* Zoglmann presented the FDP as a genuinely new party of the German youth, one without ties to the Nazi or Weimar pasts. According to Zoglmann, it was also the only party that did not owe its formation to the Allied powers, as it had been built by a new generation emerging from POW and internment camps. "These young forces," Zoglmann wrote, "who had consciously overcome the collapse of a totalitarian state which they had served out of youthful drive and utterly selfless enthusiasm—always a prerogative of the young—are the basis on which a combative and committed democracy can build the solid walls of its new house."[65] New, different from the other parties, young, genuinely German, formed in the "land of our people's destiny" ("Schicksalsraum unseres Volkes"), the FDP in North Rhine–Westphalia was, in actuality, a club of middle-aged former Nazi functionaries eager to seek positions of influence and power in the guise of a purportedly new movement, advertising some all-too-familiar characteristics of fascist parties—youthful, new, different, combative, genuinely national. The language was intended to appeal to old and young alike. Zoglmann's call for a rallying of Germany's youth appeared repeatedly in *Die Deutsche Zukunft.*[66] On one occasion it was garnished with the claim that if the SPD were to come to power, the result would be much worse than Hitler's having come to power in 1933.[67]

In 1951 Zoglmann attended meetings of the NS-Bruderschaft, where he declared that he had only joined a democratic party because he thought this would be the best way for former Nazis to return to power.[68] Zoglmann accepted the necessity of playing by the rules of parliamentary democracy. His circle's major goal was to facilitate a merger of the FDP with the parties on the Far Right, most importantly the Deutsche Partei, into a "united front of the righteous."[69] Zoglmann's party colleague Reinhold Maier, the prime minister of Baden-Württemberg, who represented the opposite end of the political spectrum in the FDP, described the threat realistically at the FDP party conference in Bad Ems in November 1952: "It [the danger] lies in the possibility that a national movement of the far-right is formed which does not necessarily present itself as radically anti-democratic, . . . but sees democracy as an issue of lesser importance, and, as a consequence, willingly or unwillingly, develops authoritarian structures. . . . You can win the first round with a move to the right and, at the same time, more or less remain within the framework of parliamentary democracy. The second round will be won by members of a younger generation in that movement. They have strong elbows."[70] The "united front of the righteous" would be led by people like Werner Naumann, and Zoglmann's paper was its most vocal organ. Naumann had also tried to make suggestions about hiring of newspaper staff to Zoglmann—something that Zoglmann later denied.[71] Some of Wolfgang Diewerge's testimony indicated that Naumann may have worked on the final draft of the program with Diewerge, Middelhauve, and Döring.[72] Whether or not Naumann had any direct contact with Zoglmann is irrelevant, as the political tenor of the FDP papers and the background of their staff speaks for itself.

The "united front of the righteous" extended into Austria, where old contacts were maintained. The investigation into the Naumann Affair identified Zoglmann as a "liaison to Austrian National Socialists."[73] Given the likelihood that Zoglmann had hidden himself in Austria between 1945 and 1950, this is not all that surprising. The connections were manifold. Zoglmann was in direct contact with Alfred Frauenfeld, former *Gauleiter* of Vienna and *Generalkommissar* for Tauria (Crimea). Fearing arrest in Austria, Frauenfeld lived in Germany after the war. Frauenfeld was also a friend of Günter Kaufmann, one of the former Reich youth leaders and a former head of the Reich Propaganda Office in Vienna, who wrote for *Die Deutsche Zukunft*. When they were prisoners of war, Frauenfeld wrote numerous articles under various pseudonyms for the camp newspaper, which was edited by Kaufmann.[74] Quite possibly, he continued writing under pseudonyms for *Die Plattform* and *Die Deutsche Zukunft*. Werner Naumann was in contact with a Salzburg lawyer, Dr. Hans Freyborn, a founding member of the Verband der Unabhängigen (VdU), who intended to send greetings to Zoglmann "from very old friends."[75] Freyborn had been a writer for the *Völkischer Beobachter*. The VdU (League of the Independent) was a reservoir of former Austrian National Socialists formed in 1949 under the leadership of Viktor Reimann, deputy to the editor-in-chief of the *Salzburger Nachrichten,* which was notorious as a hotbed of former National Socialists.[76] Middelhauve, Döring, and Wilke went to Salzburg in the summer of 1952 to meet with Freyborn and VdU members to discuss the German Program.[77] Wolfgang Wolfram von Wolmar worked not only for *Die Deutsche Zukunft,* but also for the *Salzburger Nachrichten*.[78] Middelhauve reported about the meeting with the VdU members: "We totally agreed in our discussions. Because the VdU also is an organization, a political party, that thinks that we are one great Volk that has to come together, no matter what the political path to do so might be."[79]

These activities came to an abrupt halt with the British raid against the Naumann circle in January 1953. While *Die Deutsche Zukunft* raged against the British intervention, presenting it as an attack against all Germans that was intended to torpedo the friendly relations between Bonn and Washington, the national leadership of the FDP (Bundesvorstand) started its own investigation.[80] The Bundesvorstand saw Zoglmann's role critically—during the Bundesvorstand's discussion of the affair in April of 1953, his resignation seemed almost a foregone conclusion.[81] One member of the Bundesvorstand, Alfred Günzel, acknowledged—self-critically—that "we had looked at *Die Deutsche Zukunft* with a little concern but what we should have really admitted to ourselves is that *Die Deutsche Zukunft* tried desperately hard to look like *Der Angriff* [the National Socialist newspaper for Berlin]."[82] (A certain similarity in the logo is indeed discernible.) However, in a June 1953 memorandum from the FDP Landesverband (state association) of North Rhine–Westphalia, Zoglmann's role in the affair was whitewashed, and the Landesverband did not see any reasons to take any action against him.[83] Zoglmann was given ample opportunity to present himself in the best possible light during questioning by leading members of the FDP in North Rhine–Westphalia. As Kristian Buchna and others have shown, none of the FDP dignitaries who had been compromised by the affair had to face any serious consequences.[84] Friedrich Middelhauve remained head of the Landesverband and deputy head of the party until 1956. Ernst Achenbach and Siegfried Zoglmann proceeded to become members of the Bundestag and leading personalities of the FDP on a national level. And while Naumann had to bury his dreams about political revival, his trial ended with an acquittal.[85]

The report of the FDP Bundesvorstand about the affair questioned whether *Die Deutsche Zukunft* should be allowed to continue, concluding that, at the very least, the direction of the paper had to change.[86] In the wake of the scandal, however, nothing changed at *Die Deutsche Zukunft*. The same people kept writing for it, and some of them, including Zoglmann and Roth, also wrote for its right-wing ally, *Der Fortschritt*. Later, both Wolmar and Egmont Roth published in *Das freie Wort*, the new major FDP weekly paper founded in 1956. By the 1960s, complaints about the right-wing tendencies in *Das freie Wort* multiplied.[87] Among them was one by Hans Reif, who noted bitterly that if one talked to members of the FDP Bundesvorstand about the problem, one noted nothing but "tired resignation."[88] Efforts to terminate Wolmar's contract were subverted.[89] Clearly, Egmont Roth and Wolmar had powerful friends in the FDP. In 1966 the Central Office for the Investigation of National Socialist Crimes in Ludwigsburg started to investigate Wolmar's activities in Prague. One of the witnesses who testified in favor of Wolmar was Siegfried Zoglmann.[90]

The cases of *Die Plattform, Die Deutsche Zukunft,* and the other right-wing newspapers mentioned in this chapter raise broader questions about the extent to which former National Socialists were able publish their views in newspapers—often under the guise of pseudonyms—in postwar Germany and Austria. Appearing in the organs of ostensibly democratic parties was intended to legitimize their viewpoints. One might discount the influence of a paper with a circulation of forty thousand copies, but *Die Deutsche Zukunft* clearly was not the only newspaper of its kind. Also, some of these former National Socialists were eager to publish their views, writing for several papers, including major newspapers. According to Zoglmann, Wolmar also wrote for the *Süddeutsche Zeitung,* one of Germany's most prominent newspapers.[91]

Siegfried Zoglmann's role in the Naumann Affair had been central. His network of old National Socialists writing in the FDP newspapers provided the groundwork for the "national rallying" championed by the German Program. Men such as Wolfgang von Wolmar, Manfred Zapp, Günter Kaufmann, Friedrich Grimm, Werner Beumelburg, and many voices that preferred to remain anonymous, set the tune. Zoglmann himself had coauthored the German Program and orchestrated the propaganda from his newspapers. Neither Zoglmann nor the content of his papers and the background of his writers were thoroughly investigated following the Naumann Affair.

Siegfried Zoglmann survived the affair unscathed and went on to become a member of the West German parliament in 1957, deputy leader of the FDP parliamentary group, and an influential member of the Foreign Affairs Committee. In 1970 he left the FDP to form a new party, the Deutsche Union, before joining the Christlich-Soziale Union (Christian Social Union) in 1974. Much more could and should be said about his activities after 1953, some of which seem no less dubious than his role in the Naumann Affair. This concerns not only his (brief) efforts at forming a new party but also his activities in the Witikobund, a far-right-wing association of Sudeten Germans, and his activities as lobbyist for weapons sales.[92] For his role in the Naumann Affair alone, Zoglmann qualifies as one of the shadiest figures in postwar German politics.

Table 5.1. Zoglmann's Network: Who Was Who before and after 1945?

Name	Position Held before 1945	Position Held after 1945
Siegfried Zoglmann	Head of the Foreign Press Office of the Reich Youth Leadership (1936–1939), HJ-*Gebietsführer*, head of the Reich Youth Leadership, Reich Protectorate of Bohemia and Moravia Waffen-SS, Leibstandarte Adolf Hitler	Managing editor of *Die Plattform, Die Deutsche Zukunft*, and *Der Fortschritt*; member of the Landtag (state parliament) of North Rhine–Westphalia, 1954–1958; member of the Bundestag, 1957–1976; since 1958, owner of the Nordwestdeutscher Zeitungsverlag
Wolfgang W. von Wolmar	SS-*Hauptsturmführer*, Waffen-SS, head of the press department in the Reich Protectorate of Bohemia and Moravia	Staff writer for *Die Plattform* and *Die Deutsche Zukunft*
Günter Kaufmann	Head of the press department of the Reich Youth Leadership, top assistant to Baldur von Schirach, head of the Reich Propaganda office in Vienna	Regular contributor to *Die Plattform* and *Die Deutsche Zukunft*
Egmont Roth		Contributor to *Die Plattform* and *Die Deutsche Zukunft*; most likely the name was used as pseudonym
Felix Rothberg		Contributor to *Die Plattform* and *Die Deutsche Zukunft*; most likely the name was used as pseudonym
Felix Haen		Pseudonym used in *Die Plattform* and *Die Deutsche Zukunft*
W. Breidenbacher		Pseudonym used in *Die Plattform* and *Die Deutsche Zukunft*

Manfred Zapp	1938–1941, head of the Trans-Ocean News Service office in the United States	Regular contributor to *Die Plattform* and *Die Deutsche Zukunft*
Carl Albert Drewitz	Pressereferent of Joseph Goebbels (1938), Ministry of Propaganda, Deutsches-Nachrichtenbüro (Nazi News Agency)	Section editor and regular political commentator at *Die Plattform* and *Die Deutsche Zukunft*
Friedrich Grimm	Lawyer for the Nazi regime, Nazi propagandist	Lawyer, legal representative for German war criminals, regular contributor to *Die Plattform* and *Die Deutsche Zukunft*
Wolfgang Diewerge	Nazi propagandist, specialist for anti-Semitic pamphlets, Ministry of Propaganda Waffen-SS, Leibstandarte Adolf Hitler	Personal assistant to F. Middelhauve, contributor to *Die Plattform* and *Die Deutsche Zukunft*
Walter Brand	Editor-in-chief of *Die Zeit*, the newspaper of the Sudetendeutsche Partei; arrested and imprisoned in 1939; imprisoned in various concentration camps until 1945	Regular contributor to *Die Plattform* and *Die Deutsche Zukunft*
Werner Beumelburg	National Socialist writer	Contributor to *Die Plattform* and *Die Deutsche Zukunft*
Heinz Wilke	HJ-*Führer*, Reich Youth Leadership	General manager (*Geschäftsführer*) of the FDP in North Rhine–Westphalia, contributor to *Die Plattform* and *Die Deutsche Zukunft*
Günter Prager	HJ-*Gebietsführer*	General manager (*Geschäftsführer*) of the FDP in the Ruhr district
Heinz Lange	HJ-*Gebietsführer*	Head of the Young Liberals in North Rhine–Westphalia
Heinz Schmidt	Reich Youth Leadership, German Embassy, France	In charge of advertising at *Die Deutsche Zukunft*
Friedrich Middelhauve	Businessman, not a member of the Nazi Party	Head of the FDP in North Rhine–Westphalia
Wolfgang Döring		1950–1956 Managing director (*Hauptgeschäftsführer*) of the FDP in North Rhine–Westphalia

Willi Weyer		Member of the Landtag of North Rhine–Westphalia, 1950–1954 and 1958–1975; 1956–1972, head of the FDP in North Rhine–Westphalia
Ernst Achenbach	Attaché in the German Embassy, Paris	FDP politician, member of the Landtag (state parliament) of North Rhine–Westphalia, member of the Bundestag
Otto Abetz	German ambassador, Paris, 1940–1944	Tried in France, imprisoned until 1954, died in a car accident in 1956
Gert Spindler	Hilden industrialist, Paul Spindler Werke KG	Organizer of the Altenburger Treffen, whose attendees included former National Socialists; owner of the newspaper *Der Fortschritt*
Hugo Wellems	Hitler Youth Leader, head of the Nazi Propaganda Office Kowno	Journalist and publisher, editor-in-chief of the *Deutschland Journal* (published by the Nordwestdeutscher Zeitungsverlag, owned by Zoglmann) and *Das Ostpreussenblatt*
Werner Naumann	State secretary in the Ministry of Propaganda, personal assistant to Joseph Goebbels	Arrested in 1953 for attempted subversion of the FDP by former National Socialists
Alfred Frauenfeld	*Gauleiter* of Vienna, *Generalkommissar* for Tauria (Crimea)	Position in private industry, maintained numerous contacts to former National Socialists
Hans Freyborn	Lawyer, writer for the *Völkischer Beobachter*	Lawyer, founding member of the Verband der Unabhängigen (VdU)

Notes

1. John Le Carré, *A Small Town in Germany* (1991; New York: Scribner, 2008), vii.

2. On the Naumann Affair, see Kristian Buchna, *Nationale Sammlung an Rhein und Ruhr: Friedrich Middelhauve und die nordrheinwestfälische FDP, 1945–1953* (Munich: Oldenbourg, 2010); Norbert Frei, *Vergangenheitspolitik: Die Anfänge der Bundesrepublik Deutschland und die NS-Vergangenheit* (Munich: Beck, 1996); Jürgen Dittberner, *Die FDP: Geschichte, Personen, Organisation, Perspektive. Eine Einführung*

(Wiesbaden: Sozialwissenschaften, 2005); Christof Brauers, *Die FDP in Hamburg, 1945 bis 1953* (Munich: M-Verlag, 2007).

3. *Der Spiegel,* November 29, 2010; Zweites Deutsches Fernsehen (ZDF), *Frontal 21,* November 16, 2010.

4. NS-Archiv, ZA VI 0312A.07, Leiter der Personalabteilung an Staatsekretär: Lebenslauf Siegfried Zoglmann, October 20, 1943, Federal Republic of Germany Bundesarchiv Koblenz (hereafter BA-K). It is not clear exactly when Zoglmann joined the party and the Hitler Youth. In his SS file Zoglmann stated that he joined the Sudetengerman National Socialist Workers Party in 1928, equating the Sudeten-deutsche "Bruderpartei" with the NSDAP. On Zoglmann's 1943 CV cited above, the date 1934 is given (with the date 1940 crossed out). A CIA dossier of Zoglmann mentions that he may not have been a party member until 1939—that is also what Zoglmann claimed after 1945 to downplay his affiliations with National Socialism.

5. *Der Pimpf* was called *Der Morgen* before May 1937. Heinrich Hoffmann and Siegfried Zoglmann, *Jugend erlebt Deutschland* (Berlin: Kunstpflege, 1936); Siegfried Zoglmann, *Sudetenland Marschiert* (Berlin: Osmer, 1938).

6. Compare volumes of *Der Pimpf* from March to July 1937 to later volumes.

7. SSO SS Führerpersonalakten, Personalakte Zoglmann Siegfried, Lebenslauf, Federal Republic of Germany, Bundesarchiv-Berlin Document Center (hereafter BDC).

8. SSO, SS-Führerpersonalakte, Zoglmann Siegfried, Abgangzeugnis der SS Waffen Junkerschule Braunschweig, allgemeine Beurteilung der Persönlichkeit, BDC.

9. Rudolf Lehmann, *Die Leibstandarte* (Osnabrück: Munin-Verlag, 1982), 3:482.

10. Siegfried Zoglmann, "Dem Unheil entgegentreten von Anfang an," in *Es wird nicht mehr zurückgeschossen . . . Erinnerungen an das Kriegsende 1945,* ed. Reinhard Appel (Bergisch Gladbach: Lingen, 1995), 349–50. See also the huge gap in his CV (1945–1954) on page 392 of this publication.

11. RG 263, Records of the Central Intelligence Agency, entry ZZ-18, box 144, U.S. National Archives and Records Administration, College Park, MD (hereafter NARA).

12. Brauers, *Hamburg,* 462, 464.

13. Ralf Gebel, *"Heim ins Reich!" Konrad Henlein und der Reichsgau Sudetenland, 1938–1945* (Munich: Oldenbourg, 2000), 166–68.

14. Buchna, *Sammlung,* 86–87.

15. N 1080/256, Bl. 001, Der Geschäftsführerstab des Verbandes Nordrhein-Westfalen, undated, BA-K.

16. According to the head of the Berlin Document Center in 1954, Walter Mueller, there was no record that Zoglmann had submitted an editorial licensing application for the British zone, which was required until 1949. Zoglmann must have waited until the licensing requirement was dropped. Mueller was certain that Zoglmann's application would have been denied. RG 263, entry ZZ-18, box 144, Mueller to State Department, October 12, 1954, NARA.

17. LV NRW 26989, Naumann Affäre, 89–92, Archiv des Liberalismus (hereafter AdL).

18. LV NRW 26989, Naumann Affäre, 94–95, AdL.

19. See also Lehmann, *Leibstandarte,* 3:480.

20. Gerhard Papke, *Liberale Ordnungskraft, nationale Sammlungsbewegung oder Mittelstandspartei? Die FDP-Landtagsfraktion in Nordrhein-Westfalen, 1946–1966* (Düsseldorf: Droste, 1998), 172.

21. LV NRW 26989, Sitzung des erweiterten Landesverbandsvorstandes der FDP, Befragung von Herrn Zoglmann, April 29, 1953; see also LV NRW 26987, Eidesstattliche Erklärung, April 24, 1953, AdL.

22. On Grimm, see Frei, *Vergangenheitspolitik;* Roland Ray, *Annäherung an Frankreich im Dienste Hitlers?* (Munich: Oldenbourg, 2000).

23. See *Die Tagebücher von Joseph Goebbels,* im Auftrag des Instituts für Zeitgeschichte, herausgegeben von Elke Fröhlich, Teil I Aufzeichnungen 1923–1941, Band 5 (Munich: Saur, 2000), 162, 350.

24. Ibid., 84.

25. Michael Buddrus, *Totale Erziehung für den totalen Krieg, Hitlerjugend und nationalsozialistische Jugendpolitik* (Munich: Saur, 2003), 93; see also Buchna, *Samm-lung,* 86.

26. NW 1005-G40-463, Entnazifizierungsakte Ernst Achenbach, Landesarchiv Nordrhein-Westfalen (hereafter LA NRW).

27. Jaroslava Milotova, "Die Protektoratspresse und die Judenfrage," *Theresienstädter Studien und Dokumente* 3 (1996): 156.

28. Miroslav Karny, Jaroslava Miltova, and Margita Karna, eds., *Deutsche Politik im "Protektorat Böhmen und Mähren" unter Reinhard Heydrich 1941–1942* (Berlin: Metropol, 1997), 86; Milotova, "Protektoratspresse," 171.

29. Karny, Miltova, and Karna, *Politik,* 86.

30. Livia Rothkirchen, *The Jews of Bohemia and Moravia* (Lincoln: University of Nebraska Press, 2005), 123. See also Karny, Miltova, and Karna, *Politik,* 137.

31. Jaroslava, "Protektoratspresse," 173.

32. Tim Fauth, *Deutsche Kulturpolitik im Protektorat Böhmen und Mähren, 1939 bis 1941* (Göttingen: V&R Unipress, 2004), 35–36.

33. Information provided by the Dokumentationsarchiv des österreichischen Widerstands.

34. NI-2335, NL Dehler, Betr. Deutsche Zukunft, Personalien, undated, AdL.

35. Biographical data from Helge Dvorak, ed., *Biographisches Lexikon der Deutschen Burschenschaft,* vol. 1, *Politiker* (Heidelberg: Universitätsverlag Winter, 2005), 376–77.

36. Manfred Zapp, *Zwischen Wallstreet und Kapitol: Politiker und Politik in den USA* (Berlin: W. Limpert, 1943).

37. Klaus Kipphan, *Deutsche Propaganda in den Vereinigten Staaten, 1933–1941* (Heidelberg: C. Winter, 1971), 205.

38. Herbert Blankenhorn quoted in Birgit Ramscheid, *Herbert Blankenhorn, Adenauers aussenpolitischer Berater* (Düsseldorf: Droste, 2006), 195.

39. Buddrus, *Totale Erziehung,* 1162–63.

40. For details, see Ernst Klee, *Das Kulturlexikon zum Dritten Reich: Wer war was vor und nach 1945?* (Frankfurt: Fischer, 2007), 50. In January 1953, on the tenth anniversary of the battle of Stalingrad, Beumelburg celebrated "the heroes of Stalingrad" on an entire page, *Die Deutsche Zukunft,* January 10, 1953.

41. Hans Sarkowicz and Alf Mentzer, *Literatur in Nazi-Deutschland* (Hamburg: Europa, 2002), 97.

42. *Die Plattform,* June 15, 1951.

43. Ibid., July 20, 1951.

44. On the article by W. Breidenbacher, see also Julia Angster, *Konsenskapitalismus und Sozialdemokratie. Die Westernisierung von SPD und DGB* (Munich: Oldenbourg, 2003), 347–48.

45. *Die Plattform,* July 20, 1951.

46. See, for example, ibid., June 28, 1951.

47. Ibid., May 1, 1951.

48. Ibid., March 8, 1952.

49. *Die Deutsche Zukunft,* December 19, 1953.

50. Günter Kaufmann, *Jugendbewegung im 20. Jahrhundert: Ein Kapitel ihrer Geschichte im Rückblick: Hitlerjugend* (Rosenheim: Kultur und Zeitgeschichte, 1997); Günter Kaufmann, *Auf Teufel komm raus: Unwahrheiten und Lügen über die nationalsozialistische Jugendbewegung* (Berg: Vowinckel, 1999).

51. *Die Plattform,* June 1, 1951.

52. See, for example, ibid.

53. Ibid., November 1, 1951.

54. *Die Deutsche Zukunft,* June 14, 1952.

55. Neither Roth nor Rothberg is listed in the *Journalisten Handbuch* for the years 1956 and 1960 or in the relevant literature. Inquiries at a number of archives yielded no results.

56. Heinz-Dietrich Fischer, *Parteien und Presse in Deutschland seit 1945* (Bremen: Schünemann Universitätsverlag, 1971), 394. *Die Deutsche Zukunft* ceased to exist in 1957, *Der Fortschritt* in 1960.

57. For the net of contacts, see also Kurt Tauber, *Beyond the Eagle and the Swastika: German Nationalism since 1945* (Middletown, CT: Wesleyan University Press, 1967), 142, 275–77.

58. Cf. editorial comments in *Der Fortschritt* for the year 1957.

59. *Der Spiegel,* November 24, 1945. In the 1950s he had been a member of the Deutsche Partei (DP), a small nationalist party, and editor of the DP's newspaper, *Deutsches Wort.* The Staats- und Wirtschaftspolitische Gesellschaft is a privately funded society, politically to the right of the CDN/CSN, that offers public lectures in the areas of history, politics, government, and economics.

60. The editors of the *Preussische Allgemeine Zeitung,* the successor of *Das Ostpreussenblatt,* claim to have no more information about staff working for the newspaper in the 1980s.

61. LV NRW 26989, Sitzung des erweiterten Landesverbandsvorstandes der FDP, Befragung von Herrn Zoglmann, April 29, 1953, AdL.

62. Ibid.

63. *Die Deutsche Zukunft,* September 6, 1952.

64. Buchna, *Sammlung,* 105–6; the "German Program" cited in Edgar Wolfrum, *Geschichtspolitik in der Bundesrepublik Deutschland* (Darmstadt: Wissenschaftliche Buchgesellschaft, 1999), 94.

65. *Die Deutsche Zukunft,* December 6, 1952.

66. See ibid., June 7, September 6, December 6, 1952.

67. Ibid., June 7, 1952.

68. LV NRW 26986, NWDR: Der Fall Naumann, 11, AdL.

69. Theo Rütten, *Der deutsche Liberalismus 1945–1955* (Baden-Baden: Nomos, 1984), 242. These efforts were well under way in 1952 and even included efforts to bribe DP members into cooperation. Brauers, *Hamburg,* 632; *Die Deutsche Zukunft,* June 7, 1952.

70. Reinhold Maier cited in Rütten, *Liberalismus,* 244.

71. LV NRW 26989, Befragung von Drewitz und Zoglmann, AdL. Apparently Naumann suggested Dr. Mahlberg, another ex-member of the Goebbels Ministry, and Albert Urmes, Gaupropagandaleiter in Luxemburg.

72. Buchna, *Sammlung,* 118.

73. LV NRW 27034, Protokoll der Sitzung des Geschäftsführenden Vorstandes am 13. Dezember 1952, AdL.

74. Alfred Frauenfeld, *Und Trage Keine Reu': Vom Wiener Gauleiter zum Generalkommissar der Krim: Erinnerungen und Aufzeichnungen* (Leoni: Druffel-Verlag, 1978), 292.

75. LV NRW 26988, Bericht zur Lage im Landesverband Nordrhein-Westfalen (Neumayer, Dehler, Onnen), June 5, 1953, 12, AdL.

76. Fritz Hausjell, *Journalisten gegen Demokratie oder Faschismus: Eine kollektiv-biographische Analyse der beruflichen und politischen Herkunft der österreichischen Tageszeitungsjournalisten am Beginn der Zweiten Republik,* part 1 (Frankfurt: Peter Lang, 1989), 209.

77. LV NRW 26988, Bericht zur Lage im Landesverband Nordrhein-Westfalen (Neumayer, Dehler, Onnen), June 5, 1953, 12, AdL.

78. In 1950 Wolmar was involved in a bizarre scandal. During the war, he had taken the "Mussolini-Diary," which had been in the possession of Ernst Kaltenbrunner's adjutant, Wilhelm Höttl, and, unbeknownst to the latter, who had considered it lost, sold it to the *Salzburger Nachrichten*—which planned to publish the diary. Another paper, *Der Abend,* got wind of the story and reported about forthcoming fascist propaganda in the *Salzburger Nachrichten* and the paper's close connections to SS circles. *Der Abend,* April 14, 1950, printed in *Unerhörte Lektionen: Journalistische Spurensuche in Österreich 1945–1955,* ed. Fritz Hausjell and Wolfgang Langenbucher (Vienna: Picus, 2005), 184–87. *Salzburger Nachrichten* sued *Der Abend* for slander.

The scandal also revealed that Wilhelm Höttl, Kaltenbrunner's right-hand man, was working as a journalist, writing under the alias Walter Hagen.

79. LV NRW 26988, Bericht über die Lage im Landesverband Nordrhein-Westfalen, June 5, 1953, AdL.

80. *Die Deutsche Zukunft,* January 24, 1953.

81. FDP Bundesvorstand, Die Liberalen unter dem Vorsitz von Theodor Heuss und Franz Blücher, *Sitzungsprotokolle 1949–1954,* bearbeitet von Udo Wengst, herausgegeben von Karl Dietrich Bracher, Rudolf Morsey, und Hans-Peter Schwarz, Bd. 7/1, zweiter Halbband (Düsseldorf: Droste, 1990), 1070–71.

82. Ibid., 934.

83. RWN 172/9, Stellungnahme des Landesverbandsvorstandes von Nordrhein-Westfalen, June 6, 1953, LA NRW.

84. Only Drewitz, Diewerge, and Brand were formally excluded from the party. RWN 172/9, Stellungnahme des Landesverbandsvorstandes von Nordrhein-Westfalen, June 6, 1953, LA NRW.

85. Buchna, *Sammlung,* 197.

86. LV NRW 26988, Bericht über die Lage im Landesverband Nordrhein-Westfalen, June 5, 1953, AdL.

87. Ulrich Keitel, *"Sehr geehrter Parteifreund . . ." Parteiinterne Rundbriefe gegen alte Nazis* (Frankfurt: Societas, 2001).

88. Reif to Keitel, March 3, 1960, in ibid., 23.

89. Keitel to Rubin, January 19, 1961, in ibid., 133–34.

90. B 162/6086, von Wolmar Wolfram, Federal Republic of Germany, Bundesarchiv, Ludwigsburg.

91. LV NRW 26989, Befragung von Drewitz und Zoglmann, 92, AdL.

92. *Der Spiegel,* June 17, 1990.

6

German Diplomats and the Myth of the Two Foreign Offices

Thomas W. Maulucci

In 1970 the West German Foreign Office (Auswärtiges Amt), which considered itself the institutional descendant of the ministry first led by Otto von Bismarck, issued an official history commemorating its own one-hundredth anniversary. What this publication contained about the National Socialist years was revealing. In the preface Foreign Minister Walter Scheel emphasized that the Auswärtiges Amt itself did not establish the overall lines of foreign policy but instead implemented that policy. However, Scheel asserted that while the ministry was an "excellent instrument for statesmen like Bismarck and [Gustav] Stresemann," it had been "one of the worst imaginable" for the National Socialists: "The [foreign] service opposed the will of the usurpers [i.e., the Nazis] with a tenacious, temporizing, if admittedly seldom successful resistance. Where it was implicated in the political crimes of that time, almost always National Socialist henchmen [*Vollzugsgehilfen*] had to be forced upon the service from outside in order to break its internal resistance. A number of outstanding members of the old ministry [*Behörde*] paid for it with their lives."[1] In the same volume Heinz Günther Sasse, head of the Foreign Office's Political Archive (Politisches Archiv), also put the blame for Nazi crimes on the noncareer diplomats bought into the ministry by Joachim von Ribbentrop. "Only rarely had an old member of the office incurred personal guilt out of human weakness or in order to hold their position."[2]

Scheel and Sasse had stated in dramatic form what historian Sebastian Weitkamp later called the "minimal guilt thesis." It posited that the Auswärtiges Amt and the core of career diplomats were passive instruments while outside interlopers made the ministry into a tool for Nazi policies.[3] This thesis was based on the notion that there had been two foreign offices, the "real" one with roots in the pre-1933 period and a criminal version super-imposed upon it by the National Socialists. During the Third Reich, career diplomats indeed had complained about Ribbentrop and his policies, about the massive influx of Nazi outsiders into influential positions in the ministry, and about their own increasing lack of influence. After the war, when faced with internment, denazification, and various criminal proceedings, they expanded these criticisms into a much broader narrative about "two foreign offices" that exonerated the career officials and emphasized their resistance activities. Although greatly exaggerated, this story proved useful to the diplomats in avoiding sanctions and reestablishing their careers, and starting in 1951 it became part of the official history of the new West German Auswärtiges Amt, continuing as such for three decades. However, from the start it also had its critics, including diplomats, and new developments in historical scholarship made it largely untenable by the 1980s.

The Auswärtiges Amt during the Third Reich

The minimal guilt thesis would not have been believable had it not been based in an element of truth.[4] For example, the career diplomats viewed with great suspicion National Socialist foreign affairs organizations like Alfred Rosenberg's Foreign Policy Office (Außenpolitisches Amt), the Auslandsorganisation under Ernst Wilhelm Bohle, and the Ribbentrop Bureau (Dienststelle Ribbentrop). Direct pressure from party outsiders on the ministry itself increased starting in 1936, and after Ribbentrop succeeded Konstantin von Neurath as foreign minister in February 1938, he presided over a massive expansion in the ministry's personnel, from 2,665 to 6,458 by 1943. He also created new structures like the Culture and Radio Division, the Information and Press Division, and the offices that managed relations with the NSDAP and Jewish policy, the Abteilung Deutschland and its successors Referat Inland I and II. In these new divisions members of Nazi organizations, including SS-*Führer,* exercised great influence, as the leading officials were selected largely according to ideological criteria. The career diplomats resented the intrusion of these outsiders, especially when they did not bring the customary qualifications for the service. A postwar analysis of the Auswärtiges Amt's personnel files by the American High Commission in Germany called attention to a real if undercover tension between the two groups when it came to competing for jobs and promotions. By the late 1930s, diplomats who were Jewish or had Jewish wives, or who were thought to harbor democratic or leftist views, had been forced out of the ministry due to Nazi policies. Some career diplomats also found Hitler's turn to an expansionist foreign policy after 1937 alarming because it entailed a risk of a new world war, and the Auswärtiges Amt became an important center of the anti-Nazi resistance.[5]

Despite these differences between the career diplomats and the National Socialists, however, on the whole "the office represented, thought, and acted in the name of the regime."[6] This is indeed the task of any government bureaucracy, even if individual civil servants may object to policies and on occasion seek to undermine them. Few diplomats resigned of their own will after the National Socialists came to power in 1933, and while some, such as State Secretary Bernhard von Bülow (1930–1936), saw it as their patriotic duty to remain in office, many others hoped the Nazis would restore domestic order and national power and take firm measures against German Communists and other supposed enemies of the state. From the start, the Auswärtiges Amt showed no hesitation in justifying anti-Semitic policies to the outside world. Career diplomats also joined the NSDAP and its organizations in large numbers. By 1941 an estimated 75 percent of the ministry's entire personnel were party members or candidates, and by 1944 there were approximately seventy-three SS-*Führer.* There is evidence that support for National Socialist policies in the ministry increased greatly because of German military victories through 1942. Only a very small number of diplomats, well less than 10 percent of the pre-1933 corps, became involved in resistance activities or suffered persecution during the Nazi years. Most importantly, even though they did not initiate the National Socialist policies of war and genocide, the remaining core of career officials regularly cooperated with the party outsiders to implement them. More than sixty years later, work remains to be done to determine the exact responsibility of the career diplomats for wartime crimes and for the Foreign Office's wartime polices overall. But even in areas where the NSDAP outsiders clearly determined the Auswärtiges Amt's policies, such as the Holocaust, many career diplomats proved to be willing accomplices.[7]

The Pre-1945 Origins of the Myth

Diplomats Ulrich von Hassell, Ernst Freiherr von Weizsäcker, and Curt Prüfer all left diaries or collections of personal papers written during the Third Reich that contained some common elements of the myth of the two

Ulrich von Hassell. PA AA,
Bildsammlung.

foreign offices. These documents are especially interesting because they represent a wide range of opinion about National Socialism and date from the time before the career diplomats had an obvious need to justify their activities. Hassell (NSDAP 1933) was placed on temporary retirement (*Wartestand*) in 1938 owing to policy differences he expressed while serving as ambassador to Italy, and then he was permanently retired in 1943, although his various activities and contacts kept him continually informed about developments within the ministry. He initially supported the regime but after the start of World War II joined the resistance and was executed after the failed coup attempt against Hitler on July 20, 1944.[8] On the other extreme, Prüfer (NSDAP 1937) unabashedly admired Hitler. He led the Personnel and Budget Division from 1936 to 1939 and then served as ambassador to Brazil for three years before returning to Berlin in 1942 as ambassador for special assignments (*Botschafter z.b.V.*) in the Middle Eastern Section. In light of Germany's deteriorating wartime situation, in 1942 he began planning to leave the diplomatic service and move with his family to Switzerland, which occurred in September 1943. Despite this, Prüfer wrote in his original wartime diary on July 19, 1943, "The *Führer* is a great, a very great man."[9] Some-

Ernst von Weizsäcker.
PA AA, Bildsammlung.

where in the middle, Weizsäcker (NSDAP, SS-*Oberführer* 1938), who served as Ribbentrop's state secretary from 1938 to 1943, hoped to exercise a positive influence on German foreign policy in order to keep the "Nazi revolution," which he credited with "great social successes" in 1937, from becoming too radical and destructive. Although he wanted to prevent a general European war in 1938–1939, he himself claimed not to be a resistance member. His main concerns were preserving the influence of both the German Reich in the world and the traditional Foreign Office and its career diplomats.[10] Despite their different perspectives on Nazism, the writings of all three men reflected themes that became important parts of the postwar myth of the two foreign offices: Joachim von Ribbentrop was a horrible foreign minister; unqualified Nazi outsiders played an ever-increasing role in the ministry after 1938; and during the same time the traditional diplomatic corps became increasingly impotent and powerless.

All three diplomats agreed that Ribbentrop was disastrous. Hassell wrote in his diary that Ribbentrop was "irresponsible, superficial, unrealistic" (October 10, 1938); "behaving like a lunatic, unbearable in office, and has lost whatever friends he ever had" (August 7, 1939); "the chief danger"

Curt Prüfer.
PA AA, Bildsammlung.

because of his "disastrous counsels" (August 29, 1939); "lusting for war" (August 30, 1939); along with Hitler, "seized by the spirit of criminal recklessness" (August 31, 1939); and with Hitler, General Wilhelm Keitel, and others, guilty of "criminal irresponsibility" for starting the war (September 22, 1940).[11] Through 1941 Hassell's diaries repeatedly mention Weizsäcker's troubles with Ribbentrop.[12] On April 20, 1943, Hassell wrote, "Ribbentrop has now become totally rabid. He hates the entire old Foreign Ministry (in which I also found much to criticize, but for other reasons)."[13] For his part, Weizsäcker described Ribbentrop as Hitler's instrument, who often engaged in fruitless conflicts with other party and government offices.[14] In May 1941 Ribbentrop accused Weizsäcker of always being negative about "great decisions," such as the effort to annex the Sudetenland and the plans to attack France and then the USSR.[15] On April 30, 1943, in one of his last official acts as state secretary, Weizsäcker congratulated Ribbentrop on the occasion of his fiftieth birthday. He wrote with a great deal of sarcasm, "I quite correctly credited him with straightforward policies. At the same occasion H[err] von R[ibbentrop] confirmed that we sought peace with neither the West nor the

East, but that we thought of victory; that means force and no diplomacy [*Politik*]."[16] Despite his greater sympathy for Nazism, Prüfer joined Hassell and Weizsäcker in their dislike of Ribbentrop, whom he considered an unqualified outsider who had replaced the veteran diplomat Neurath. This comes out occasionally in his original diaries from 1942 to 1943, as when he refers to Ribbentrop—in Arabic—as "the crazy administrator" (February 2, 1943) and the foreign minister and his close co-workers as "our noble lords" (February 18, 1943). On November 23, 1942, he also made an unflattering comparison of Ribbentrop to Wilhelm II.[17]

The idea that the German diplomats were at constant loggerheads with Ribbentrop is greatly exaggerated, however. For example, most historians agree that Weizsäcker sought to prevent a general European war in 1938 and 1939, but also that he had nothing against German expansion to the east in principle, especially if it entailed limited risk. Not only did he greet the annexation of Austria with approval; he also played a role in the diplomatic preparations for the annexation of Bohemia and Moravia in March 1939 and the invasion of Poland the following September.[18] There is also the larger question that is the focus of Rolf Lindner's 1997 dissertation: Why and how did he remain state secretary for five years if he did not enjoy the trust of both Ribbentrop and Hitler? Lindner even speculates that Weizsäcker used Hitler's personal support to stay in Berlin in 1937 against Neurath's wishes and then to become Ribbentrop's deputy.[19] For his part, Prüfer displayed no hesitation in participating in an investigation of Martin Luther, the outsider who served as deputy state secretary and head of the Abteilung Deutschland, that led to Luther's removal in early 1943 and thereby helped keep Ribbentrop in office.[20] After the war the criticism of Ribbentrop was sharpened by the diplomats into a narrative of fundamental opposition to his policies and methods.

Complaints about the influx of Nazi outsiders and the marginalization of the traditional Foreign Office and its diplomats also abound in these wartime documents. On December 20, 1938, Hassell wrote, "The pace in the Foreign Ministry, it seems, borders on the unbearable: it is a frantic merry-go-round with everybody's nerves frayed. Even the highest officials, with the possible exception of Weizsäcker, and he to a limited extent, know nothing of the political objectives and general lines of policy."[21] On June 26, 1940, one day after the armistice with France went into effect, Weizsäcker protested against plans to restructure the Auswärtiges Amt by pensioning off twenty-four career diplomats (ironically, Hitler's intervention with Ribbentrop proved decisive in halting the plan).[22] The foreign minister and his state secretary

Joachim von Ribbentrop announces to journalists assembled in the Bundesratssaal in Berlin on June 22, 1941, that Germany has declared war on the Soviet Union. *At the table, starting third from Ribbentrop's right:* Ambassador at Large Karl Ritter; Weizsäcker; Reich Press Chief of the NSDAP Otto Dietrich; Ribbentrop; and Foreign Office Press Chief Paul Karl Schmidt (not to be confused with translator Paul Otto Schmidt). *Wearing glasses and looking down over Schmidt:* Ribbentrop's adjunct Bernd Gottfriedsen. PA AA, Bildsammlung.

continued to clash over internal Foreign Office matters, and the latter clearly had set his sights on a transfer to a foreign post since, as Hassell put it, it was clear that he was "fighting a lost war; the best at the Foreign Ministry [were] becoming fewer and fewer."[23] On July 13, 1941, Hassell wrote, "The dissection of the Foreign Ministry continues, but not in the direction of objective reform. Favors are distributed to the Party mercenaries, the SS and SA," including diplomatic posts in Eastern Europe.[24] In the wake of Luther's failed attempt to depose Ribbentrop in early 1943, Hassel reported that the foreign minister supposedly "had told Hitler that the only thing that mattered in the Foreign Ministry [was] a National Socialist mentality, and he wanted forty SS men, forty SA men and forty Hitler Youth leaders to replace the older members at the Ministry." The recent reassignment of several senior career officials was "a blow struck against the old bureaucracy."[25] Meanwhile, Prüfer's original diaries from 1942 and 1943 note the proliferation of useless bureaucracy in the Foreign Office as well as growing "dilettantism" by officials from Ribbentrop's "outfit." On January 14, 1943, he commented, "The confusion in the office is boundless. Everyone acts on his own authority."[26] As an ambassador for special assignments, he also noted that he personally had no influence in the ministry.[27]

However, only Hassell's diary dwells on the criminal activities of outsiders brought by Ribbentrop into the Foreign Office. Hassell clearly viewed Luther and the Abteilung Deutschland ("the whole unbelievable Luther outfit")[28] as foreign bodies in the ministry and as solely responsible for its extreme anti-Jewish policies. For example, his diary states on November 1, 1941, "[Career diplomat Felix] Benzler, Foreign Ministry representative in Belgrade, had enquired desperately what to do with the 8,000 Jews herded together in the city, and made suggestions as to how he thought the problem should be handled. In the Foreign Ministry (that is, Luther), there was indignation over such softness. Luther contacted [SS-*Obergruppenführer* Reinhard] Heydrich, who sent a 'specialist' to Belgrade at once to clean out the problem."[29] The Jews were then executed in reprisals for attacks against German occupation forces. Benzler, it should be noted, was hardly an innocent party. In his reports advocating deportations, he falsely blamed the Jews for partisan activity in Serbia, an argument that Luther and others seized upon to make them "hostages on call."[30] On the other hand, the Weizsäcker papers are strangely silent about these officials. Only on February 11, 1943, do they mention Luther, Ribbentrop's "special confidant." Weizsäcker wrote that the "Luther putsch" was a "strange intrigue," which no longer had to be taken seriously.[31] A month later he complained that "some of the outsiders [*uns aufgedrängte Elemente*] have behaved very badly [*haben sich übel aufgeführt*]," but to compensate for their removal, there were to be changes to the old corps of officials, too.[32] Nonetheless, various researchers have detailed Weizsäcker's knowledge of the Holocaust and lack of principled opposition to it.[33] A diary entry for November 22, 1942, also confirms that Prüfer knew of the mass murder of the European Jews.[34]

We can only speculate why Weizsäcker and Prüfer chose not to write about these outsiders and their activities in any detail. However, it is also true that of the three men, only Hassell no longer worked in the ministry during the war years, and only he moved toward active resistance, motivated by his outrage over Nazi policies. By 1943 his sharply critical attitude toward his old colleagues who would not stand up to Ribbentrop, including Ambassador to Spain Hans-Heinrich Dieckhoff, Under State Secretary Ernst Woermann of the Political Division, head of the Legal Division Friedrich Gaus, Ambassador to Fascist Italy Rudolf Rahn, and Weizsäcker himself, was also amply evident.[35] Most damningly, Hassell commented on his own efforts to assist a prominent German Jew in August 1942, saying, "Success at either the Foreign Ministry or with the military is doubtful because everybody in the Jewish question has a fear of being a 'Jew lover' (or worse a relation)."[36]

As Weizsäcker wrote to his defense counsel Helmut Becker on July 20, 1948, he considered himself neither a criminal nor a member of the "'resistance' circle in the narrow sense."[37] But even before the war ended, one of Weizsäcker's younger colleagues and close co-workers, Albrecht von Kessel, harbored no such inhibitions about shaping his patron's image. While at the Vatican with Weizsäcker, Kessel wrote a memoir titled *Verborgene Saat* (*Hidden Seed*). In it, he argued that Hitler relied only on Ribbentrop, not the career diplomats, for foreign policy advice. The one exception was the "crown jurist" Friedrich Gaus, "the most despicable and guilty figure ever produced by the Auswärtiges Amt," who willingly assisted the foreign minister.[38] Kessel credited Weizsäcker with using a "side channel" with Hitler to frustrate Ribbentrop's 1940 plan to reorganize the ministry and to make the old style of diplomacy superfluous.[39] Weizsäcker was encouraged to stay in his post by the resistance, both to maintain Germany's international reputation and to preserve the old diplomatic corps, and Kessel called Weizsäcker's reassignment to the Vatican in 1943 "the end of the Foreign Office." By this time he claimed that Weizsäcker already had managed to have "all of the protagonists [*Exponenten*] of our circle"—i.e., younger officials of the "diplomatic resistance"—transferred abroad in order to be ready when the right time came.[40] Kessel's account demonstrated that the veteran diplomats' collective experience during the war could be and easily was synthesized into a broader myth that portrayed them as steadfast opponents of National Socialism.

The Full-Blown Myth: Denazification and War Crimes Trials

In his memoir Kessel wanted to honor friends who had been executed by the Nazis. However, it is also obvious that as a virtual prisoner in Vatican City during the last year of the war, he had ample time to think about what might happen to himself and his colleagues after the conflict ended. When the Third Reich collapsed, German diplomats faced "automatic arrest" and internment, which might last as long as several years. In interrogations with Allied authorities, they repeated the themes found in the wartime papers discussed above in an attempt to paint a good picture of themselves, but they also differentiated themselves from the Nazi outsiders even more sharply.

After internment, denazification and indictment for war crimes raised the stakes even higher for finding plausible and believable justifications for their wartime activities and therefore contributed to the development of the full-blown myth.[41]

In the internment camps, attacks on Ribbentrop became the norm, even for officials closely associated with the NSDAP. For example, Bohle remarked that although there initially had been tensions between his Auslandsorganisation and the Foreign Office, these disappeared after his appointment as state secretary in the Auswärtiges Amt in January 1937, and "full coordination of work was achieved." Once Ribbentrop became minister, however, "bitter conflicts developed," culminating in Bohle's dismissal. He told the U.S. War Department's Owen J. Hale "that Ribbentrop was regarded as unfit for his duties by most of his colleagues. At one time or another all attacked him—Goering, Goebbels, and at the end even Himmler—but up to 1944 his position with the *Führer* was unassailable."[42] Hermann Neubacher, a NSDAP outsider who, starting in 1940, served as Reich plenipotentiary for economic issues in Romania and Greece as well as the Foreign Ministry's special envoy for southeastern Europe in 1943–1944, told Hale that not only did Ribbentrop have "no positive ideas," but he also "sought to avoid responsibility and blame for what was done."[43] When the War Department's George Shuster commented that Ribbentrop honestly seemed to know nothing about German plans to declare war on the USSR—here Shuster had been greatly deceived—and wondered how such a person could have been appointed foreign minister, his interview subject Franz von Papen, of all people, agreed that "the man was a catastrophe, the man."[44]

Those interviewed also tried to obscure the ties between the career diplomats and the NSDAP and its representatives. Although Bohle mentioned Gaus and Ambassador for Special Assignments Karl Ritter as two of Ribbentrop's closest advisers, he downplayed the ties between the Nazi Party and the Foreign Office. Hale wrote that "[Bohle] knew from his records that there were 600 Party members employed in the Foreign Ministry. One could walk all day through the corridors and offices and not see more than three Party buttons."[45] Werner Gregor, in British internment in 1945, commented on a list of his former colleagues through the letter K plus Ribbentrop, Neurath, and Luther (illness prevented him from getting further). He wrote that German diplomats had been reserved toward National Socialism, and only those who were young and ambitious or who had poor prospects for advancement had been attracted to it. In October 1945 Paul Otto Schmidt, the senior Foreign Office translator and the last head of Ribbentrop's personal office, asserted that there was a sharp distinction between the moderate career diplomats such as Weizsäcker, his friend Erich Kordt, and himself, on one hand, and the "Hitler-Ribbentrop extremists" brought into the ministry by the NSDAP, on the other.[46] Werner von Bargen, the Foreign Office plenipotentiary in northern France and Belgium until 1943, expressed "contempt and scorn for the Führer, Ribbentrop and the Nazis in general" and blamed the SS for stirring up Flemish and Walloon nationalists. He claimed that "the Foreign Office exerted no influence in the occupied territories and during his service in Belgium he never received a directive from the Foreign Office." He and other diplomats did not know what to make of vague Nazi plans for a "new order" in Europe, but "as far as the Party was concerned there would be no place in this system for a German diplomatic service and a Foreign Office." Bargen also mentioned that he clashed with the German ambassador to France, the outsider Otto Abetz, and "could not work" with him. Unbeknownst to his interrogators in 1945, Bargen had raised no fundamental objections when asked by the Foreign Office about plans to deport Belgian Jews.[47]

Remarkable testimony along these lines came from Gunther Seyd, who worked in the section Inland from 1942 to 1944 before being drafted into the military and then captured in February 1945. The American interrogator who interviewed him on March 22 described him as an "opportunist" who was a reluctant informant and who, in spite of his disavowals, was still sympathetic to the NSDAP, which he had joined in 1934. Although he had worked only briefly in the ministry in a unit closely associated with the outsiders, Seyd nonetheless praised the old core of career diplomats and criticized the growing influence of the SS, SA, and other extremists associated with the party. "The Foreign Office . . . was generally very wary about accepting anyone other than a professional diplomat into their circle, and took pains to cultivate a kind of politics which would enhance international relations."[48]

Finally, the diplomats emphasized the growing irrelevance of the Auswärtiges Amt under Ribbentrop. This was a constant theme in interviews conducted by the State Department's Special Interrogation Mission in 1945.[49] Other American agencies, such as the War Department, heard much the same story. Gustav Adolf Steengracht von Moyland, who had entered the ministry in 1938 from the Ribbentrop Bureau and who succeeded Weizsäcker as state secretary in 1943, called Hitler a "pathological liar" whose ambitions knew no bounds and who "listened fundamentally only to those who said what he wanted to hear." In the "organized disorganization" that characterized Germany's government administration, "the Foreign Office was virtually eliminated for the duration." Steengracht asserted that "there were no diplomatic discussions with other powers," and even the German diplomats were not consulted about invasions. In particular, Hitler ignored good advice—which Ribbentrop himself was enlisted to deliver—about the dangers of attacking the USSR. The Foreign Office also counseled "sound occupation policies" in the USSR and "self-government" in other parts of occupied Europe. However, in the east "all was hopelessly lost," since the occupation was quickly turned over to party offices and the SS.[50] Gaus told his American interrogators on November 30, 1945, that "as a technical official he was unable to influence the foreign policy of the Third Reich." He had merely served as Ribbentrop's adviser on handling competency conflicts between the Auswärtiges Amt and other ministries and on the drafting of diplomatic notes and other documents.[51] After the attack on the Soviet Union, "Eastern Expert" Gustav Hilger said he was assigned to Ribbentrop as an adviser and "had no real work to do," especially since he "declined" to write propaganda and the minister ignored his warnings about the USSR's strength.[52] Kurt von Kamphoevener described his activities leading negotiations with the USSR on population transfers in Poland in 1939 and with Italy about ethnic Germans in Croatia in 1941. He claimed that Hitler ignored advice from the German ambassador in Belgrade that might have prevented the invasion of Yugoslavia in 1941.[53]

In interviews with Allied interrogators in the internment camps, Heinz Trützschler von Falkenstein and Paul Otto Schmidt pushed the argument about the professional German diplomats' irrelevance during the Third Reich to its logical extent. Trützschler served in the Political Division from 1939 to 1945 and helped compose various "White Books" and the official speaking points (*Sprachregelungen*) provided to diplomatic missions to justify Germany's policies. In September 1945 he contended that "the career officials played no important part in the formulation of high policy during Ribbentrop's ministry" and merely served as technical experts, a situation that only intensified after Weizsäcker's reassignment in April 1943. He added that "a strict security code" had been promulgated around 1942 that "required every official to limit his information to those matters strictly necessary for the performance of his specific duties from day to day." The whole system was designed to prevent the spread of "news of military affairs and certain internal matters" through the government; however, Trützschler admitted that the diplomats evaded many of these restrictions.[54] On May 1, 1946, at Nuremberg, Schmidt went a step further when asked about how German intelligence networks in the Western Hemisphere operated. He provided the following justification for his lack of knowledge:

You see, the system which was perfected to a very high degree was the system of water-tight compartments: that everybody should know just as much as was necessary for his own work and [be] kept away from everybody else's work. There was even an order issued by Hitler to the effect—printed in all the offices later on during the war—that every officer or civil servant should only just know the things that were necessary for him to do his work and not more. That system of what I called a moment ago water-tight compartments was one of the fundamental characteristics of Nazi bureaucracy or the way they handled things, and that is why you find it so difficult now to get to people who really saw anything. There would hardly be a man in Germany.

His interrogator responded bitingly: "Yes, I have found that. Of course one wonders immediately, are these people withholding [information] or is the witness cooperative? It is difficult to make up one's mind."[55]

Later other diplomats attempted to use this argument about their limited knowledge and competence to exonerate themselves, at least until confronted with clear documentary evidence to the contrary. For example, Curt Heinburg, who led the Foreign Office's desk for southeast Europe in the Political Division from 1936 to 1943, flatly denied any knowledge of the deportation of Jews from that region during his interrogation on July 7, 1947, by American prosecutor Robert Kempner, in preparation for the Ministries Trial at Nuremburg. When shown documents that he had signed, Heinburg admitted that he was implicated, although he continued to claim he neither bore responsibility for initiating the policy nor had any idea the Jews were going to be murdered. In subsequent interviews on July 16, July 27, and August 21, he proved much more candid, and on September 5, 1947, he even provided a sworn statement that detailed how the Abteilung Deutschland regularly asked the Political Division for its position on anti-Jewish measures.[56] A similar scenario played out on May 27, 1947, during Kempner's interrogation of Ernst Woermann, deputy state secretary and director of the Political Division from 1938 to 1943. Woermann finally conceded to Kempner that the Foreign Office had initially attempted to protect all foreign Jews in German-occupied territory but then moved to a "policy of the least resistance." "We did not fight in our foreign policy for Jews whose countries did not protect them," including those who were citizens of Germany's own allies.[57] A memo in the files of the West German Federal Chancellery, without author or date but probably from 1951, pointed out that many of the diplomats subjected to preliminary interrogations at Nuremburg did not know that the Allies were in possession of the Foreign Office's files. Therefore they provided false testimony under oath until confronted with papers they had signed or initialed.[58]

An obvious question regards the extent to which the diplomats coordinated their stories with one another. It is unlikely that those captured by the Allies in the winter or early spring of 1945, such as Seyd, had much opportunity to do so before interrogation. However, there are clear signs that coordination increased as time went on. Higher-ranking officials were held together from late April until the start of August 1945 in the "Annex" of the American collection center for prominent enemy personnel called the "Ashcan," located in Belgium and then Luxemburg. They were subsequently relocated both to Nuremberg as witnesses for the International Military Tribunal and to the civilian internment camp at Oberursel. Those who were not in the "Ashcan" were held in Allied camps throughout occupied Germany. Since the diplomats were so widely dispersed, many escaped careful scrutiny of their wartime activities. Because they seemed willing to talk freely and candidly, they also made a good impression on their captors and even recommended themselves as witnesses for upcoming war crimes trials.[59]

The case of Horst Wagner at the Allied Ministerial Collection Center at Hessisch-Lichtenau near Kassel illustrates this phenomenon. Wagner entered the Auswärtiges Amt from the Ribbentrop Bureau in 1939 and later led Referat Inland II from 1943 to 1945. In 1945 he was one of a team of nearly sixty former diplomats supervised by Andor Hencke, the career diplomat who was the last head of the Political Division in the Auswärtiges Amt. The team's mission was to describe the Foreign Office's structures as background evidence for the prosecution at the upcoming International Military Tribunal trials in Nuremberg. These officials had the opportunity to present a sanitized version of their ministry's activities during the Third Reich. Wagner reduced the role of Referat Inland II, which coordinated relations with Heinrich Himmler's SS and Reich Main Security Office (RSHA), as well as the Auswärtiges Amt's participation in anti-Jewish policies, to that of a simple liaison office. His account was not only accepted without question by Allied authorities but even found its way into the *Akten zur Deutschen Auswärtigen Politik,* an official collection of diplomatic documents, in 1979.[60] In his postwar interviews with occupation authorities, Wagner consistently repeated the story that his office was merely a messenger service for communications with party and government offices and had no real responsibilities of its own, and he was even used in March 1948 as a prosecution witness at the Nuremberg Ministries Trial. Already by that time, however, American authorities had accumulated so much evidence about his role in the Holocaust and other crimes that he felt it wise to flee the lightly guarded camp he was being held in, eventually getting to Argentina.[61]

Because of the need to restart their careers, get through denazification, and help former colleagues who faced war crimes trials, other diplomats corresponded with one another throughout Germany already before the end of 1945 and developed a common line of defense. For example, Vollrath von Maltzan, who worked at the Ministry for Economics and Transportation in Hesse and later in the Frankfurt Economics Administration, received requests for help with denazification proceedings from Bargen (his former housemate in Berlin), Hasso von Etzdorf, Rainer Kreuzwald, Wilhelm Melchers, and Erica Pappritz. In sworn statements for denazification boards—*Eidesstattliche Erklärungen,* mockingly called "Persil certificates" in Germany after a famous brand of laundry detergent—he emphasized that all of them had rejected the NSDAP's political and racial ideologies. In fact, only Kreuzwald had not been a party member, and Etzdorf, although linked to the resistance, had belonged to the SA. Maltzan also stated that his friends had all been in conflict with party authorities or experienced career setbacks. His statements had particular weight because he had been forced to leave the Auswärtiges Amt in 1938 because he had a Jewish mother, although he worked for Ambassador Ritter between 1939 and 1942. He credited Etzdorf with intervening on behalf of his sister when both she and his mother were arrested by the Gestapo in 1942.[62] Both his statements and those provided by other colleagues served to underline the differences between the career and the "Nazi" diplomats. Especially notorious was Hans Schroeder, former head of the Foreign Office's personnel division, who wrote many sworn statements for diplomats seeking to distance themselves from the NSDAP and admitted, "I refused no one."[63]

Other lines of defense against denazification were also developed by applicants, including playing up their ties to the resistance and asserting that they had joined the NSDAP or other party organizations in order to stay at their posts and to prevent the worst from happening.[64] This last idea had its roots before 1945 as well. Weizsäcker emphasized in March 1933 that he saw the continued presence of Neurath and Bülow as a "guarantee of reason" in Germany's foreign policy.[65] After the war, junior diplomats and others, including former chancellor Heinrich Brüning, went further and asserted that the Foreign Office leadership had asked younger officials to stay at their posts in order to prevent Nazis from entering the ministry, even if this required them to join the NSDAP.[66] In one variation on this theme, Wilhelm

A diplomat who propagated the story of the two foreign offices: Wilhelm Melchers. PA AA, Bildsammlung.

A diplomat who propagated the story of the two foreign offices: Heinz Günther Sasse. PA AA, Bildsammlung.

Melchers stressed in the materials he prepared for his denazification that he had applied to the NSDAP while stationed in Palestine in 1939, upon the recommendation of acquaintances, including Jews whom he knew, for purposes of "camouflage [*Tarnung*]" so that he could continue to counteract harmful Nazi policies.[67]

In stark contrast to Weizsäcker and other career officials in similar circumstances, Melchers later argued against the deportation of Palestinian and Turkish Jews living in occupied Europe and thereby helped save many of them. But his objection arose from professional concerns about Germany's relations with the Middle East. There is little evidence that he actively attempted to undermine Nazi policies, despite his friendship with diplomats who did resist. His focus on foreign policy perhaps explains why he had no difficulty arguing that Weizsäcker and other career diplomats were also anti-Nazi.[68] In a lengthy account of his own role in the resistance that he submitted to denazification authorities in Bremen in 1946, Melchers recalled that on July 18, 1944, he and Adam von Trott zu Solz, who was executed by the Nazis after the failed assassination attempt against Adolf Hitler on July 20, had expressed their astonishment and admiration that those employed in the ministry already in 1933 had behaved irreproachably ("*tadellos*") over the subsequent eleven years. Melchers quoted Trott as saying "the Nazification attempts of Ribbentrop, Bohle and the notorious Deputy State Secretary Luther were absolute failures. Certainly a lot of undesirable elements found their way into the press, information, radio and *Inland* divisions." But, Trott continued, "the core of the office with the really important divisions was healthy."[69] Here was the story of the two foreign offices fully developed.

However, diplomats only went public with this story in response to Allied war crimes trials. The 1945–1946 proceedings of the International Military Tribunal against the major Nazi war criminals did not produce particular controversy among them. The case against Ribbentrop was clear, and his defense inept. At least twelve diplomats, including Erich Kordt, a former head of his personal office, actually offered to testify against him. The career diplomats did have more sympathy for Neurath, who was one of their own. Kessel, his personal assistant during the two years after he left the ministry, wrote a sworn statement stressing that Nazi foreign policy had become truly expansionist only after Neurath's removal in 1938. Neurath may have been naive in thinking that he could limit National Socialist influence in the ministry by staying in office, Kessel argued, but that was not a crime, nor were his attempts to shelter colleagues whom the Nazis had targeted.[70] Neurath himself argued before the tribunal that he had stayed in office to prevent the worst. But the brutal activities of the SS and the Gestapo during his time as Reich protector in Czechoslovakia gave the lie to this assertion. His contradictory answers while on the witness stand, his unwillingness to take any responsibility whatsoever for what had happened during the Third Reich, and the impression that he had profited financially also damaged his credibility.[71]

The American-led Subsequent Nuremberg Trials from 1946 to 1949 were a different matter. In particular, Case XI, "The United States against Ernst von Weizsäcker et al." (also known as the Ministries Trial), which ran from 1947 to 1949, threatened to bring the entire Auswärtiges Amt into disrepute, not just the supposed "Nazi diplomats," and with it the new careers and future prospects that had begun to open up after the war. Now the diplomats actively collaborated not only to defend Weizsäcker—and later to work for his full pardon—but also to pull together all of the elements of the story of the two foreign ministries. These developments were triggered by a March 17, 1947, statement in the American paper *Neue Zeitung* by Gaus, who was working with the American prosecutors at Nuremberg, that posited the collective guilt of German civil servants. Former diplomats and Weizsäcker's defense team rushed to the counteroffensive, and by 1949 any number of accounts existed that spelled out the story of the two ministries.[72]

A good example is a memo prepared by Melchers in October 1948, entitled "The Balance of Forces in the Foreign Office during the War." It argued that in 1938 the Auswärtiges Amt was still quite homogeneous compared to other ministries because of the specialized nature of its work. Although some had joined the NSDAP as early as 1933 in the false hope of being able to influence Nazi foreign policy, in imitation of Italian diplomats who had stayed on under the Fascists, as time went on the majority of diplomats decided to join the party in order to preserve the career civil service. Only a few Higher Service officials became party members out of true conviction. Ribbentrop deeply mistrusted the career officials but needed their expertise, while these same officials saw the opportunity to exercise "a diversionary, delaying, and braking effect" on his initiatives. The office quickly split into Ribbentrop's own staff on the one hand and the old experts under Weizsäcker on the other. However, the actual situation was very complicated and difficult for outsiders—especially foreigners, the memo stressed—to understand. Owing to the "Führer principle" and Ribbentrop's own peculiarities, the career diplomats played no role in political decision making, and many outsiders flooded into the ministry, with the SS and SD especially well represented among the support staff. However, the foreign minister still needed to work with experts, and Weizsäcker and the Personnel Division assigned trusted diplomats throughout the ministry to keep an eye on things. Weizsäcker did not give these diplomats special instructions, nor had he himself been chosen to lead a resistance movement, but he was nonetheless viewed as the spiritual head of the opposition. The memo asserted that only those who kept this peculiar situation within the Foreign Office in mind could truly understand the diplomatic documents in the archives and determine whether they could be taken at face value. "Camouflaged resistance activity demands fictional cooperation [*Getarnte Gegenarbeit erheischt fiktive Mitarbeit*]."[73] The new twist here was that documents, even those obviously signed or initialed by career officials, did not necessarily mean what they seemed to mean. Erich Kordt argued much the same in his 1950 book on Weizsäcker and the Foreign Office resistance, *Nicht aus den Akten* (*Not From the Documents*).[74] By the 1950s any number of diplomatic memoirs, including Weizsäcker's own and a heavily revised, unpublished version of Prüfer's wartime diaries, pinned full responsibility for the Foreign Office's activities during the Third Reich on Ribbentrop and other outsiders in the ministry.[75]

The story of the two foreign offices had its roots in the experiences of the career German diplomats during the Third Reich. However, only after the war were these elements collected into a coherent account of their opposition to National Socialism. It should be noted that this story was questioned right from the very beginning. In particular, the evidence presented at the Nuremberg Ministries Trial did not support the idea that the career diplomats had resisted Hitler and Ribbentrop. Documents from the trial were used among others by Michael Mansfeld in his 1951 article series in the *Frankfurter Rundschau* to criticize the return of Wilhelmstraße veterans to the Federal Republic's new Foreign Office and by West German prosecutors who, in the mid-1960s, initiated no less than ten proceedings against former diplomats for mass murder.[76] By the early 1960s, a number of scholarly works, including Raul Hilberg's *The Destruction of the European Jews* (1961), as well as the Eichmann Trial, also had called attention to the Foreign Office's role in Nazi crimes.[77]

From the start some career diplomats also questioned aspects of the story, both explicitly and implicitly, even though such criticism remained private. For example, while still in internment, Hencke wrote in a memo for his American captors that some NSDAP outsiders had taken on the career service's mentality and worldview once in office and had become useful diplomats.[78] Discussions within the Circle of Friends (Der Freundeskreis ehemaliger

A diplomat who questioned the story of the two foreign offices: Fritz von Twardowski. PA AA, Bildsammlung.

A diplomat who questioned the story of the two foreign offices: Rudolf Holzhausen. PA AA, Bildsammlung.

Höher Beamter des Auswärtigen Amtes), which for several years, starting in 1948, collected donations from former diplomats and distributed them to needy colleagues and their immediate relatives, revolved around how to treat career diplomats who obviously had collaborated with the NSDAP. One of the circle's coordinators, Fritz von Twardowski, wrote Werner von Fries in December 1948 that, while all members of the Foreign Office were eligible to join, the Circle of Friends would admit only those who had demonstrated "a disposition [*Verhalten*] in accord with the traditions of the professional civil service. We won't accept people like Gaus or Ritter, for example."[79] Three months later, at the meeting of the board of directors, Twardowski raised the question of membership for career diplomats who previously had been prominent members of the NSDAP, such as Alexander Freiherr von Dörnberg zu Hausen, Gustav Adolf von Halem, and Rudolf Rahn. The board agreed that the key question was how these men had treated their former colleagues, not that they had used their party ties to advance their careers. Board member Wolfgang Freiherr von Welck, who had been arrested by the Nazis in 1943 and dismissed from the foreign service the following year, took it upon himself to mollify Gottfried von Nostitz, a member of Hassell's circle who had threatened to leave the Circle of Friends if it admitted "undesirable elements."[80] In September 1948 Twardowski also described the defense's attempt to portray Weizsäcker as a "resistance fighter" at Nuremberg as unfortunate, since witnesses like Kessel could not describe any concrete assignments they had received from the state secretary.[81] To take one final example, Rudolf Holzhausen, who had been forced out of the Foreign Office due to his Jewish wife questioned the very solidarity of the career diplomatic corps. In August 1949 he refused to become a representative (*Vertrauensmann*) of the Circle of Friends because he and his wife felt "they were written off" by the vast majority of their former colleagues after his dismissal.[82] The same year he wrote a memo detailing divisions within the ministry during the war, which asserted that a group of "those who could see again"—including career diplomats—developed only after the war began to turn against Germany.[83] Perhaps the only aspect of the story of the two foreign ministries that was unassailable was Ribbentrop's poor performance as foreign minister.

Nonetheless, the new West German Foreign Office founded in 1951 officially endorsed the story of the two foreign ministries and the minimal guilt thesis. For example, in 1967 the Auswärtiges Amt informed the Federal Justice Ministry that Luther and his "Jewish expert" Franz Rademacher, both brought into the ministry by Ribbentrop, had been the first to make Jewish affairs an instrument of Nazi racial and anti-Semitic policies.[84] In a last major public statement in 1978, the Foreign Office published a brochure entitled *Foreign Policy Today* (*Außenpolitik heute*) that said "the [Auswärtiges Amt] offered a tenacious and temporizing resistance to the plans of the [National Socialist] rulers, without however being able to prevent the worst. The office long remained an 'unpolitical' administration [*Behörde*] and was considered a site of opposition by the National Socialists."[85]

However, the Auswärtiges Amt could not ignore new developments in historical research beginning in the late 1970s. In 1978, Christopher Browning published his landmark book on Referat III D of the Abteilung Deutschland and its role in the Holocaust, to be followed in 1987 by Hans-Jürgen Döscher's investigation of the role of the NSDAP and the SS in the Foreign Office.[86] By this time considerable doubt had also been cast on Weizsäcker's role as a resistance figure.[87] It is also worth bearing in mind that in 1977 lawyers associated with the Central Investigation Center for Nazi Crimes in Ludwigsburg announced that all active investigations against Foreign Office personnel concerning their role in the Holocaust had ended.[88] This fact plus the simple passage of time probably permitted a more open historical discussion for the ministry's current and former employees, even if the 2004 "Obituary Affair [*Nachruf-Affäre*]" and its aftermath clearly indicated that no consensus existed within these circles about how to interpret their ministry's role during the Third Reich.[89]

In any event, by the time of its 125th anniversary in 1995, the ministry had moved toward a more balanced and realistic official history. Ludwig Biewer of the Political Archive wrote:

The low number of active resistance fighters from the foreign service demonstrates that the Auswärtiges Amt between 1933 and 1945 was no hotbed [*Hort*] of resistance against the brown tyranny, but it was just as little a National Socialist institution [*Behörde*] ruled by the SS. The truth lies somewhere in the middle: among the German diplomats there were a few convinced opponents of National Socialism and a few fanatical adherents of this ideology. Alongside them however [were] a considerable number of fellow travelers and those who were indifferent, and also people who wanted and had to come to terms [with it] somehow. In this respect the foreign service was not better but also not worse than other Germans.[90]

Notably, this new interpretation maintained the strict distinction between the career diplomats (the "foreign service") and the Nazi outsiders, a distinction that the controversial 2010 report of the Independent Historians Commission to Examine the History of the German Foreign Office during National Socialism attempted to demolish.[91] But the ministry had finally conceded the ideological overlap and cooperation between the two groups. The story of the two foreign offices was no longer tenable.

Notes

1. Walter Scheel, "Geleitwort," in *100. Jahre Auswärtiges Amt 1870–1970*, ed. Auswärtiges Amt (Bonn: Thenée Druck KG, 1970), 7–8, here 7. All translations are by the author unless otherwise indicated.

2. Heinz Günther Sasse, "Zur Geschichte des Auswärtigen Amts," in ibid., 23–46, here 44.

3. Sebastian Weitkamp, *Braune Diplomaten: Horst Wagner und Eberhard von Thadden als Funktionäre der "Endlösung"* (Bonn: Dietz, 2008), 462–63.

4. Ibid., 463.

5. For an overview of the Auswärtiges Amt during the Third Reich, see Thomas W. Maulucci Jr., *Adenauer's Foreign Office: West German Foreign Policy in the Shadow of the Third Reich* (DeKalb: Northern Illinois University Press, 2012), 22–40.

6. Eckart Conze, Norbert Frei, Peter Hayes, and Moshe Zimmermann, *Das Amt und die Vergangenheit: Deutsche Diplomaten im Dritten Reich und in der Bundesrepublik* (Munich: Karl Blessing, 2010), 13. The present author contributed the sections in this study on denazification and new careers for diplomats after 1945, 342–62.

7. For an overview, see Maulucci, *Adenauer's Foreign Office*, 22–40. On the policymaking role of the career diplomats and the NSDAP outsiders, see Johannes Hürter, "Das Auswärtige Amt, die NS-Diktatur, und der Holocaust: Kritische Bermerkungen zu einem Kommissionsbericht," *Vierteljahreshelfte für Zeitgeschichte* 59, no. 2 (April 2011): 167–92; and Michael Mayer, "Akteure, Verbrechen und Kontinuitäten: Das Auswärtige Amt im Dritten Reich—Eine Binnendifferenzierung," *Vierteljahreshefte für Zeitgeschichte* 59, no. 4 (October 2011): 509–32. On the Foreign Office resistance, see Jan Erik Schulte and Michael Wala, eds., *Widerstand und Auswärtiges Amt: Diplomaten gegen Hitler* (Munich: Siedler, 2013).

8. Gregor Schöllgen, *Ulrich von Hassell 1881–1944: Ein Konservativer in der Opposition*, updated ed., Beck'sche Reihe (Munich: C. H. Beck, 2004); Ulrich von Hassell, *The Ulrich von Hassell Diaries: The Story of the Forces against Hitler in Germany*, trans. Geoffrey Brooks (1946; London: Frontline Books, 2011).

9. Donald M. McKale, *Curt Prüfer: German Diplomat from the Kaiser to Hitler* (Kent, OH: Kent State University Press, 1987), quote 132. The quote about Hitler is from *Rewriting History: The Original and Revised World War II Diaries of Curt Prüfer, Nazi Diplomat*, ed. McKale., trans. Judith M. Melton (Kent, OH: Kent State University Press, 1988), 114.

10. Leonidas E. Hill, *Die Weizsäcker Papiere 1933-1950* (Berlin: Propyläen, 1974), quote 109; Hill, *Die Weizsäcker Papiere 1900-1932* (Berlin: Propyläen, 1982); Ernst von Weizsäcker, *Erinnerungen* (Munich: Paul List, 1950). The most recent scholarly account of Weizsäcker's career is by Lars Lüdecke, "Offizier und Diplomat: Ernst von Weizsäcker in Kaiserreich, Weimarer Republik und 'Drittem Reich,'" in Schulte and Wala, *Widerstand und Auswärtiges Amt,* 225-49.

11. Hassell, *Ulrich von Hassell Diaries,* quotations 6, 35, 43, 44, 45, and 99.

12. Ibid., diary entries of October 10, 1938; August 7, 17-18, 31, 1939; and March 2, 1941, 6, 35, 39, 46, 112.

13. Ibid., diary entry of April 20, 1943, 196.

14. Hill, *Die Weizsäcker Papiere 1933-1950,* 246.

15. Ibid., 252. See also Weizsäcker's note from April 21, 1941, in ibid., 248.

16. Ibid., 337.

17. McKale, *Rewriting History,* 13, 47, 52.

18. See Rolf Lindner, *Freiherr Ernst Heinrich von Weizsäcker, Staatssekretär Ribbentrops von 1938 bis 1943* (Lippstadt: ROBE, 1997), 203-49.

19. Ibid., 154-202. However, Lindner concludes that "[Weizsäcker] pledged [*einsetzen*] his career and diplomatic arts less to Hitler personally than to the nation and Greater Germany" (467).

20. McKale, *Curt Prüfer,* 172-73.

21. Hassell, *Ulrich von Hassell Diaries,* 13; see also the diary entry of August 17-18, 1939, 39.

22. Hill, *Die Weizsäcker Papiere 1933-1950,* 208-11.

23. For example, on June 16, 1942, Weizsäcker offered his resignation after an argument about German military representatives being incorporated into the foreign missions. Ibid., 293; Hassell diary entry of March 2, 1941, in *Ulrich von Hassell Diaries,* 112.

24. Hassell, *Ulrich von Hassell Diaries,* 131. See also the diary entry for August 30, 1941, 138-39.

25. Ibid., diary entry of April 20, 1943, 196.

26. See the diary entries in McKale, *Rewriting History,* 36-39, 109-10.

27. Ibid., diary entry of January 23, 1943, 41.

28. Hassell, *Ulrich von Hassell Diaries,* diary entry of March 6, 1943, 189.

29. Ibid., 146.

30. Walter Manoschek, "The Extermination of the Jews in Serbia," in *National Socialist Extermination Policies: Contemporary German Perspectives and Controversies,* ed. Ulrich Herbert (New York: Berghahn Books, 2000), 163-85, here 172.

31. Hill, *Die Weizsäcker Papiere 1933-1950,* 323.

32. Ibid., 327.

33. See Lindner, *Freiherr Ernst Heinrich von Weizsäcker,* 286-350.

34. Diary entry of November 22, 1942, in McKale, *Rewriting History,* 11.

35. Hassell, *Ulrich von Hassell Diaries,* 176, 196, 210.

36. Ibid., diary entry for August 1, 1942, 169.

37. Hill, *Die Weizsäcker Papiere 1933–1950*, 437.

38. Albrecht von Kessel, *Verborgene Saat: Aufzeichnungen aus dem Widerstand 1933 bis 1945*, ed. Peter Steinbach (Berlin: Ullstein, 1992), 173–74, quote 173.

39. Ibid., 200–201. He neglected to mention that Weizsäcker had presented Ribbentrop with thirty to forty names of officials who could be released and also had argued that this large-scale reorganization at the moment of victory was a slap in the face of the minister's own diplomats who had loyally served the Führer. Hill, *Die Weizsäcker Papiere 1933–1950*, 208–9.

40. Kessel, *Verborgene Saat*, 201–2, 240–41.

41. These issues are well described in Conze et al., *Das Amt und die Vergangenheit*, 319–439.

42. Owen J. Hale, Historical Interrogation Commission, War Department General Staff, G2, Historical Branch, MID, interview with "Ernst W. Bohle, Gauleiter of the NS Foreign Organization (Auslandsorganisation)" at "Ashcan" (PWE No. 32), July 26–27, 1945, RG 165, Records of the War Department General and Special Staffs, Captured Personnel and Materials Branch, Reports Relating to POW Interrogations 1943–1945 (hereafter RG 165), Shuster Files, box 1, U.S. National Archives and Records Administration, College Park, MD (hereafter NARA).

43. Hale, "Historical Interrogation Report: German Wartime Policy in the Balkans" (interview with Hermann Neubacher at MISC-USFET), October 3–4, 1945, RG 165, Shuster Files, box 5, NARA.

44. George M. Shuster, "Conversation with Franz von Papen," Bad Mondorf, July 23, 1945, RG 165, Shuster Files, box 5, NARA. On Ribbentrop's knowledge of plans to invade the Soviet Union, see Michael Bloch, *Ribbentrop* (New York: Crown, 1992), 346, 360–63.

45. Hale interview with Bohle, July 26–27, 1945, RG 165, Shuster Files, box 1, NARA.

46. Maulucci, *Adenauer's Foreign Office*, 72, 79–80.

47. Hale, interview with "Werner von Bargen, Plenipotentiary of the Foreign Office in Northern France and Belgium (until 1943)" at SAIC, August 13, 1945, RG 165, Shuster Files, box 1, NARA.

48. Report 6824 DIC/MIS/NOI-563, "Detailed Interrogation Report on Personalities, German Foreign Office," signed M. S. Hilton, April 14, 1945, RG 165, entry 179C, box 669, NARA.

49. Maulucci, *Adenauer's Foreign Office*, 79.

50. Shuster, "Conversation with Baron Adolf von Steengracht Moyland [*sic*]," Bad Mondorf, July 24, 1945, RG 165, Shuster Files, box 5, NARA.

51. PIR 67, "Preliminary Interrogation Report on Botschafter Friedrich Gaus," December 6, 1945, RG 165, entry 197C, box 657, NARA.

52. "Hilger, Gustav—Counsellor in the German Embassy in Moscow," July 17, 1945, RG 165, Shuster Files, box 3, NARA.

53. Hale, interview with Kurt von Kamphoevener, August 14, 1945, at SAIC, RG 165, Shuster Files, box 4, NARA.

54. Harold C. Vedeler (State Department Special Interrogation Mission), interrogation of Heinz Truetzschler von Falkenstein on September 9, 10, 15, 1945, Wiesbaden, October 25, 1945, RG 59, Records of the State Department, Special Interrogation Mission to Germany 1945–1946 (Poole), NARA.

55. "Testimony of Paul Otto Schmidt, taken at Nuernberg, Germany, 1400–1600, 1 May 1946 by Mr. John Rogge," RG 59, Lot File no. 60 D, box 9, NARA.

56. Curt Heinburg's testimony to Kempner in Nuremberg on July 7, 1947, copy in B 136 [Bundeskanzleramt], vol. 1846/141.02, vol. 2, 2, 4–16, Federal Republic of Germany, Bundesarchiv-Koblenz (hereafter BA-K). The subsequent interviews can be found in *Records of the United States Nuernberg Trials Interrogations, 1946–1949*, National Archives Microfilm Publications 1019 (Washington, DC: National Archives Trust Fund Board, 1977), roll 25, 913–51. See also Hans-Jürgen Döscher, *Das Auswärtige Amt im Dritten Reiche: Diplomatie im Schatten der "Endlösung"* (Berlin: Siedler, 1987), 250–52.

57. Robert M. W. Kempner, *Das Dritte Reich im Kreuzverhör: Aus den Vernehmungsprotokollen des Anklägers* (1969; Düsseldorf: Droste, 1984), 249–54, quote 252.

58. Memo, no author or date (probably late 1951), B 136, vol. 1846/141.02, vol. 2, 3, BA-K.

59. Conze et al., *Das Amt und die Vergangenheit*, 332–37. For example, DeWitt C. Poole of the U.S. State Department's 1945 Special Interrogation Mission thought the diplomats and other officials he interviewed were inclined to "talk freely" and concluded: "There was a surprising measure, one felt in the end, of truthful disclosure." See Poole, "Light on Nazi Foreign Policy," *Foreign Affairs* 25, no. 1 (October 1946): 130.

60. Döscher, *Das Auswärtige Amt*, 303–4.

61. See the dossier of his postwar interviews collected by the Institute for Contemporary History in Munich (IfZ, ZS 1574 Wagner, Horst), available online at www .ifz-muenchen.de/archiv/zs/zs-1574.pdf, accessed September 7, 2012. On his life, see Weitkamp, *Braune Diplomaten*.

62. Maltzan statement for Werner von Bargen, April 10, 1946, B 102 (Bundesministerium für Wirtschaft), vol. 43; Maltzan statement for Hasso von Etzdorf, September 16, 1946, B 102, vol. 43; Maltzan statement for Rainer Kreutzwald, August 16, 1946, B 102, vol. 44; Maltzan statement for Wilhelm Melchers, January 19, 1946, B 102, vol. 44; Maltzan statement for Erica Pappritz, Oct. 14, 1946, B 102, vol. 45, all BA-K.

63. Conze et al., *Das Amt und die Vergangenheit*, 345–46.

64. For examples, see ibid., 346–49.

65. Hill, *Die Weizsäcker Papiere 1933–1950*, 61, quote 69.

66. Maulucci, *Adenauer's Foreign Office*, 29.

67. See, for example, the February 28, 1946, statement he prepared to initiate his case before denazification authorities in Bremen in Federal Republic of Germany, NL

Melchers, vol. 4, Political Archive, Auswärtiges Amt, Berlin (hereafter PA AA).

68. Francis R. Nicosia and Christopher Browning, "Ambivalenz und Paradox bei der Durchsetzung der NS-Judenpolitik: Heinrich Wolff und Wilhelm Melchers," in Schulte und Wala, *Widerstand und Auswärtiges Amt,* 211–24.

69. Wilhelm Melchers, "Darstellung der Teilnahme von Dr. Melchers an der Widerstandsbewegung," February 28, 1946, reprinted in Wilhelm Haas, *Beitrag zur Geschichte der Entstehung des Auswärtigen Dienstes der Bundesrepublik Deutschland* (Bonn: H. Kollen, 1969), 388–408, quote 396. An English version of this document is in NL Melchers, vol. 6, PA AA.

70. Kessel, *Verborgene Saat,* 283–92.

71. Conze et al., *Das Amt und die Vergangenheit,* 376–80.

72. Ibid., 401–21; Maulucci, *Adenauer's Foreign Office,* 82.

73. Melchers, "Das Wiederspiel der Kräfte im Auswärtigen Amt während des Krieges," October 17, 1948, B Z35 (Deutsches Büro für Friedensfragen), vol. 11, 47–57, BA-K.

74. Erich Kordt, *Nicht aus den Akten . . . Die Wilhelmstrasse in Frieden und Krieg; Erlebnisse, Begegnungen und Eindrücke, 1928–1945* (Stuttgart: Union Deutsche, 1950).

75. Paul Seabury, "Ribbentrop and the German Foreign Office," *Political Science Quarterly* 66, no. 4 (December 1951): 532–55, here 533; McKale, *Rewriting History.*

76. Maulucci, *Adenauer's Foreign Office,* 161–62; Weitkamp, *Braune Diplomaten,* 440–41.

77. Maulucci, *Adenauer's Foreign Office,* 249–50.

78. Ibid., 31.

79. Fritz von Twardowski to Werner von Fries, December 10, 1948, R 143449 (Bestand Freundeskreis), PA AA.

80. "Vorstandssituzung des 'Freundeskreises' am 31. Januar 1949," dated February 4, 1949, Hamburg, R 143449 (Bestand Freundeskreis), PA AA.

81. Twardowski to Melchers, September 8, 1948, R 143449 (Bestand Freundeskreis), PA AA.

82. Rudolf Holzhausen to Twardowski, August 1, 1949, R 143449 (Bestand Freundeskreis), PA AA.

83. Maulucci, *Adenauer's Foreign Office,* 32.

84. Auswärtiges Amt "*Schnellbrief*" to the Federal Justice Ministry, January 27, 1967, cited in Weitkamp, *Braune Diplomaten,* 463.

85. Cited in Conze et al., *Das Amt und die Vergangenheit,* 14.

86. Christopher R. Browning, *The Final Solution and the German Foreign Office: A Study of Referat D III of Abteilung Deutschland, 1940–43* (New York: Holmes & Meier, 1978); Döscher, *Das Auswärtige Amt.*

87. Besides Döscher, 188–90, see Rainer Blasius, *Für Großdeutschland—gegen den großen Krieg: Staatssekretär Ernst Freiherr von Weizsäcker in den Krisen um die Tschechoslowakei und Polen 1938/39* (Cologne: Böhlau, 1981); Daniel Koer-

fer, "Ernst von Weizsäcker im Dritten Reich: Ein deutscher Offizier und Diplomat zwischen Verstrickung und Selbsttäuschung," in *Die Schatten der Vergangenheit: Impulse zur Historisierung des Nationalsozialismus,* ed. Uwe Backes, Eberhard Jesse, and Rainer Zitelmann, 2nd ed. (Frankfurt am Main: Ullstein, 1992), 375–402; and Marion Thielenhaus, *Zwischen Anpassung und Wiederstand: Deutsche Diplomaten 1938–1941: Die politischen Aktivitäten der Beamtengruppe um Ernst Freiherr von Weizsäcker* (Paderborn: Schöningh, 1984).

88. Weitkamp, *Braune Diplomaten,* 444.

89. The "Obituary Affair" was triggered by then foreign minister Joschka Fisher's decision not to publish in the ministry's internal newsletter official obituaries containing the phrase "the Foreign Office will hold [him or her] in honored memory" for deceased members of the foreign service who had been members of the NSDAP. Many current and former Foreign Office diplomats resented this new practice and in 2005 published their own obituaries in prominent German newspapers for Franz Krapf (NSDAP 1936, SS 1933, SS-*Obersturmführer* 1938, later the Federal Republic's ambassador to Japan and at NATO) and Wilhelm Günter von Heyden (NSDAP 1935, later consul general in Hong Kong and Macau). The affair resulted in the Foreign Office establishing an "Independent Historians' Commission" to study its role in the Third Reich and continuities with the Federal Republic, which in 2010 published its study as Conze et al., *Das Amt und die Vergangenheit.* Conze et al., *Das Amt und die Vergangenheit,* 705–711.

90. Ludwig Biewer, "125. Jahre Auswärtiges Amt. Ein Überblick," in *125. Jahre Auswärtiges Amt. Ein Festschrift,* ed. Auswärtiges Amt (Bonn: Auswärtiges Amt, Referat Öffentlichkeitsarbeit, 1995), 96.

91. Conze et al., *Das Amt und die Vergangenheit.* On the debate over *Das Amt und die Vergangenheit,* see "Forum: The German Foreign Office and the Nazi Past," *Bulletin of the German Historical Institute, Washington, DC* 49 (Fall 2011): 51–109. For references to virtually all of the important articles and reviews that have appeared in Germany, see Wikipedia.de contributors, "Unabhängige Historikerkommission—Auswärtiges Amt," *Wikipedia, die freie Enzyklopädie,* http://de.wikipedia.org/wiki /Das_Amt_und_die_Vergangenheit, accessed October 22, 2013.

7

Hitler's Military Elite in Italy and the Question of "Decent War"

Kerstin von Lingen

For Hitler's military elites, the surrender in May 1945 meant not only a national catastrophe, for which the officers had to take professional responsibility, but also social degradation and de-legitimation. From the moment of defeat, but even more during internment and their later testimony at Nuremberg's International Military Tribunal, Hitler's officers fought for a reconstruction of their "military honor": to win the memory battle, while also hoping to continue their professional military careers with immaculate personal records.

A sharp distinction between the "clean Wehrmacht" and the "dirty Nazi War" of the SS framed the discourse among Hitler's army veterans between 1945 and 1955. The affiliation with one group or the other, as defined by war crimes trials and denazification courts, divided the former comrades-in-arms and became a determining factor in who was to receive a "second chance" in postwar German society. What was at stake after 1945 was the very individual definition of what "honorable" behavior during war meant and how this concept had an impact on the feeling of total defeat and professional disaster. Discussions with different groups reveal varied narratives if one takes a closer look at individual theaters of war, as this chapter does with its focus on the German military elite in Italy. The chapter focuses in particular on a group of German officers who brought about the first surrender in Europe on May 2, 1945.

This chapter deals with group identities of former Nazi military elites,

Gero von Schulze-Gaevernitz visited German headquarters in Bolzano on May 12, 1945, to express his thanks for the officers' cooperation during the surrender of the southern front. Enjoying a relaxed moment in the courtyard of SS headquarters are (*left to right*) Hans Röttinger, Gaevernitz, Heinrich von Vietinghoff-Scheel, and Karl Wolff; *in the background:* SS officers Eugen Wenner and Eugen Dollmann. NARA RG 226, entry 110, box 01, OSS photos. Photograph by T. S. Ryan.

comparing Wehrmacht and SS officials who served in the Mediterranean theater of war in Italy. It looks at their postwar defense strategies in automatic arrest or prisoner-of-war camps, in denazification courts, and during war crimes trials and is based on sources such as official army records, trial proceedings, private correspondence, and the records of individuals' lawyers. The group under consideration consists of a relatively homogeneous set of high-ranking officers of Army Group C in the Mediterranean theater, who—after months of secret negotiations in Switzerland—surrendered about eight hundred thousand men in northern Italy on May 2, 1945; this action, coordinated by Allied intelligence, was code-named Operation Sunrise.[1] A group of conspirators, formally under the command of Field Marshal Albert Kesselring, who had already left to achieve the overall command for southern Germany, was grouped around his successor as commander in chief in Italy, Lt. Col. General Heinrich von Vietinghoff-Scheel, on one side; the SS-staff was grouped around Supreme SS and Police Leader SS-*Obergruppenführer* Karl Wolff. This group of officers from the Wehrmacht and the SS had established close ties during the final year of war and especially during the occupation of Italy; these ties were reaffirmed when negotiating secret surrender. Thus, there was no visible divide between the two groups, as was the case in other theaters. Commander-in-chief Vietinghoff emphasized in an affidavit that there had never been such a fair and decent war as the one fought in Italy; and most of the officers agreed with him.[2] However, in court, hard evidence challenged this narrative.

Italy was a special case for German officers; following the Allied landing on Sicily in July 1943 and the subsequent armistice with Italy in September 1943, Germany lost its noblest and oldest ally. Italy came under German occupation and its status shifted from Axis partner to occupied enemy territory. Two special areas of northern Italy were annexed to the Reich: the so-called operational zones *Alpenvorland* (basically southern Tyrol) and *Adriatisches Küstenland* (the area around Trieste), which came under the respective rule of *Gauleiter* (party district leaders) Franz Hofer and Friedrich Rainer. For the rest of Italy, the Wehrmacht, under Field Marshal Albert Kesselring, and the rear troops, under SS-*Obergruppenführer* Karl Wolff, were forced to conduct a war of retreat from Sicily to the Alps, especially after the Allies took Rome in spring 1944. Their retreat was hindered by acts of sabotage carried out by the Italian resistance movement Resistenza.[3] From the start, ambushes by the Resistenza posed a significant problem for the Wehrmacht.[4] The unbelievably brutal German "retaliation measures" indicate the perceived severity of the threat that confronted the Wehrmacht in the "second war behind the front," which cost nearly ten thousand civilian lives between 1943 and 1945.[5] Rampant fear among the ranks of German soldiers, coupled with bitterness over the death of comrades, and the inability to move about freely and securely in the territory of a former Axis ally led to overreactions by individual units, which quickly took the form of a coordinated antipartisan campaign—euphemistically called the "war on bands" (*Bandenbekämpfung*).[6] Even if its scale still differed quantitatively from the war in the east,[7] the brutality of the measures differed very little from practices common on the eastern front.[8]

The Allied war crimes trials after 1945 were the first platform on which to reconstruct military identity and to separate the army from the record of the SS; consequently, these trials benefited the formation of an agreed-upon version of veterans' identity. Concurrently with the distinctions established in court, a debate developed among veterans about military codes such as honor and duty—terms that had to acquire new meaning in order to make sense of wartime sacrifices. This was part of a hidden agenda of former officers that allowed them to reconstruct a useful group identity, to justify actions of the past, and to create plausible roles for themselves in the future. Ex-Wehrmacht soldiers came together for the first time during the occupation period in POW and internment camps, and from this experience and the process of recasting their identities emerged the first demands that formed the basis of a concrete veterans' policy. Of particular interest were issues such as German rearmament and the reestablishment of the army; for most officers, the opportunity for individuals to return to military service was crucial, as there were few other options.[9] Wehrmacht officers' relationships to former SS officers soured, and they soon distanced themselves from their former comrades-in-arms, as they became aware that some SS officers had been given more favorable conditions by the disclosure of "insider knowledge" about the eastern enemy and about spy networks, so that they benefited from their dirty wartime experiences.[10]

Research on Hitler's military elite is located in a field of tense dialogue that encompasses a record of war crimes and a discourse of victimization. It concentrates on questions about the experience of total defeat and the nature of war crimes trials, pension debates, and discussions about financial recognition for former wartime service, as well as the broader public discourse about military guilt.[11] Norbert Frei coined the term *Vergangenheitspolitik* to describe the political process that took place between West Germany and its Allies and by which (West) German society tried to deal with the legacies of the Third Reich.[12] The term refers not only to issues of amnesty, integration, and setting the boundaries of how to talk about Nazism, but also to policies adopted in trials or for the benefit of veterans and to the lobbying and public-relations campaigns that this group conducted on its own behalf. All of their lobbying helped to influence the atmosphere of the early 1950s in Germany and molded a so-called *Schlußstrich* mentality: the desire to wipe clean the slate and conclude the Allied war crimes program and the debate about pardoning prominent generals.[13]

Former Wehrmacht officers played an active role in the construction of their memory of the war, focusing on differences between themselves and the SS, emphasizing their decency as compared to their SS counterparts. Theoretical works, such as studies by Anderson and Assmann on national communities and their coming to terms with a traumatic past, have underlined the impact of memory formation on group identity.[14] According to French scholar Maurice Halbwachs, societal groups create for themselves a "frame of reference" to give meaning to crucial national events.[15] Koselleck introduced into the debate the distinction between narratives with the intent of *giving* meaning (*Sinnstiftung*) and those *requesting* meaning (*Sinnforderung*), between active and passive interpretations, between the results of one's own experience and a socially accepted national narrative.[16] So, how was the idea of a "clean" military perceived and created? How did such a common group identity actually benefit individual officers in the early postwar period? How was the segregation between Wehrmacht and SS accomplished, given the degree of close collaboration during war years?

In the group under investigation here, the lines between Wehrmacht and SS blur. After the war, the Sunrise conspirators developed a narrative about honor and duty that differed from that of other veterans, because they had to defend their surrender from the allegation of military treason and, in addition, their version against competing narratives. It is remarkable that this internal dispute went unnoticed by the public for many years.

Coining a Narrative: The Generals at Nuremberg

Criminal proceedings, in particular the International Military Tribunal (IMT) at Nuremberg and the subsequent trials at Nuremberg and in other European locations, and public debate revealed the extent of the army's involvement in war crimes and led to a social rejection of career officers. For Hitler's military elite, the IMT meant a humiliation that had to be endured on top of military defeat and internment. Unaccustomed to being called to account for their actions, some leading officers tried to erase the shame by using the military tactics of "forward-defense" (*Vorwärtsverteidigung*) and prepared a lengthy memorandum that dealt exclusively with the heroic resistance of the regular army officers against Hitler and his "clique of criminals" from the SS.[17] When the IMT trial started on November 20, 1945, it became apparent that Wehrmacht officers considered it their honorable duty—and a trial tactic—never to give any details to the prosecutors and to avoid standing witness against former comrades. In the beginning, this courtesy extended even to SS officers. The ranks of comradeship still held firm.

Hans Laternser, who subsequently acted as attorney in the trial against Kesselring in Italy, played a key role in creating the new group identity, as he was the defense lawyer who represented the Wehrmacht General Staff in Nuremberg. Owing to his defense strategy, one particular charge was dropped for lack of evidence: namely the allegation that the senior Wehrmacht leadership constituted a criminal organization. This strategy could only work at the cost of demonizing the SS and thus destroying the wartime comradeship. A memorandum prepared by high-ranking officers of the former General Staff, Franz Halder, Erich von Manstein, Walter Warlimont, and Siegfried Westphal and the former commander-in-chief of the Wehrmacht, Walther von Brauchitsch, played a crucial role in this defense strategy.[18]

Laternser's text emphasized the strict separation between the army and the SS, the strategic powerlessness of army commanders, their ignorance of internal Nazi affairs, and their alleged objections to war crimes.[19] The whole manuscript argued for the separation of ordinary military affairs from SS crimes. The Wehrmacht, the memorandum stated, had distanced itself tacitly from dirty warfare on the eastern front. Parallel to this dirty war, the army officers emphasized, an honorable war took place, in which the army commanders were disconnected from SS troops and *Einsatzgruppen* (mobile killing squads). This Generals' Memorandum (*Generals Denkschrift*) paved the way for a recasting of military identity and served as a guideline for the memory of the war. It also prefigured subsequent narratives of the Wehrmacht's clean war, which were not challenged until the mid-1990s by the Wehrmacht Exhibit and the subsequent historiographical debates.

In testimonies, however, some generals remembered that the war in the east was not always honorable, as the memorandum suggested. When Hans Röttiger, one of the officers and Kesselring's later chief of staff in Italy, was interrogated at the IMT, he testified to SD crimes he had witnessed while serving as staff officer with Army Group 4 in Russia under the command of General Gotthard Heinrici. He underlined that everybody in the higher Wehrmacht ranks knew that Jews and partisans were executed without trial in Russia.[20] Röttiger was silenced quickly during cross-examination by the defense counsel, Laternser.[21] There were also personal threats against him within the witness wing of the Nuremberg prison; it was claimed that Röttiger had "sold out" to the Allies.[22] He later hastened to declare to the court that his statement had been "misunderstood."[23] This is one of the rare examples of an officer's honest testimony in court. In general, officers on trial tended to separate themselves from their real wartime experiences, to keep silent about crimes, and to close ranks.[24]

Although the defense did win in rejecting the charge that the General Staff was a "criminal organization," the Nuremberg judgment represented a devastating critique of Hitler's Wehrmacht.[25] The Allied judges did not follow Laternser's distinction between clean Wehrmacht and dirty SS but, in their final sentence, described the German Army as a general "disgrace to the honorable profession of arms." Furthermore, the judges bitterly criticized the generals for their unwillingness to assume command responsibility.[26] Chief U.S. Judge Robert Jackson made it clear that he would have preferred to see the individual generals convicted in the IMT trial; failing this, however, he announced that there would be further trials. Given that nearly 20 million men served in the Nazi armies during the war, another trial of Hitler's officers could become quite decisive in proving widespread complicity in Nazi crimes. The subsequent trials at Nuremberg did indeed include four more trials dealing with crimes committed during the war.[27]

Accounting for Crimes: The Trials in Italy

However, another narrative and defense strategy emerged at Nuremberg as well: the notion of a decent war in Italy as opposed to the dirty war on the eastern front. This narrative gained momentum during the preparations for the trial against the German military leadership in Italy, namely, Field Marshal Kesselring. It should be noted that when reference is made to German war crimes in Italy, Kesselring's name is generally linked with that of Karl Wolff, the highest SS and police commander in Italy, because the Wehrmacht and the SS were complicit when it came to antipartisan warfare in Italy.[28] Initially two big trials, one for each leader, were scheduled for war crimes against civilians in Italy.[29] However, Wolff enjoyed a degree of protection—especially from the American intelligence establishment—that was not available to Kesselring. There are strong indications that powerful American forces, most notably in the ranks of the Office of Strategic Services, were protecting Wolff, even though no concrete evidence to this effect has been found in the records.[30] As a result, Kesselring's was the only trial to go forward.

It is noteworthy that even though Wehrmacht commanders under interrogation repeatedly referred to SS responsibility for the massacres, the SS leadership was largely spared prosecution, because of the lack of evidence.[31] A more pragmatic approach, which dictated that the Wehrmacht trials, considered "simpler" by the prosecution, should be prepared first, prevented SS members from being tried for war crimes early on, before the Allies' taste for trials dissipated. SS officers in particular also appear to have been given more favorable conditions for the disclosure of insider knowledge or as a reward for services rendered to the Allies, although Allied military authorities repeatedly denied this. One striking example is the Sunrise surrender in Italy: in 1946, SS *Sturmbannführer* Heinrich Andergassen, from the SD headquarters in Bozen, sentenced to death by a British military court, stated for the record that Wolff had reached an agreement with Allen Dulles according to which, in return for Wolff's efforts to achieve a partial surrender on the southern front, the Allied courts would not try any war crimes committed by the SS.[32] In addition, it was also the custom among SS men to assume responsibility in place of higher-ranking comrades, allowing the latter to go unpunished.[33]

The most significant trial with respect to memory politics about the Italian theater of war was the British Military Court conducted against the former commander-in-chief in Italy, Field Marshal Albert Kesselring. It lasted from February to May 1947 and was held in Venice. Kesselring was found guilty both of having ordered the executions of 335 Italian hostages in the Ardeatine Caves near Rome and of inciting his troops to commit atrocities against Italian civilians during the summer of 1944. The German lawyers defending Kesselring used the trials as a platform to rehabilitate the reputation of the Wehrmacht as the "clean" force in battle, while justifying its actions in the name of exigency. The fact that international law was ambiguous on the permissibility of hostage and reprisal killings benefited Kesselring.

The Kesselring trial was perceived as an exemplary trial by both sides. The defense hoped to present the court with a picture of fair and decent warfare in Italy—a picture that the media disseminated throughout the world. The prosecution worked around two fixed points. On the one hand, they had to address the proportionality of the reprisal killings in the Ardeatine Caves near Rome, where 335 hostages had been shot in March 1944. On the other hand, they had to address the issue of whether Kesselring's *Bandenbefehle* (antipartisan orders) of June 1944 had been deliberately couched in such a manner that they could be interpreted as giving license to murder. After all, they had resulted in nearly ten thousand dead civilians during the summer campaign of 1944.

The trial offered both the accused and his witnesses a platform from which to tell a story of soldierly solidarity in the wake of defeat. Kesselring stood trial as a placeholder, and many of his witnesses used the metaphor of the "final Italian battle" to describe the trial in private correspondence; they saw it as a battle that had to be won to ensure that the Wehrmacht could at least look back on a moral victory in the lost war.[34] The officers considered themselves duty-bound to "line up" for this "final battle in Italy" to save the "honor" of Kesselring and of the "decent Germans soldiers in the Italian theatre" and to vindicate what they had agreed upon as the "truth."[35] Kesselring's attorneys also viewed the pending trial as an investment in the future of the German military, thus emphasizing memory politics.[36] What was at stake in Venice in 1947 was nothing less than a public rehabilitation of the reputation of German military leadership in Italy and the justification of Kesselring's military actions in particular. The appointment of a distinguished defense team, Laternser being among the most prominent lawyers of the time, showed that the German side understood the symbolic nature of the Kesselring trial and used it to draw a positive picture of the war in Italy—a picture that, in turn, could be used to construct an official war memory. The old military rank structures still held sway, and the General Staff coordinated the witness statements.[37] The legal team assembled for the trial was greatly helped by the fact that many members of the officer corps were still interned in the autumn of 1946; this facilitated the collection of affidavits on Kesselring's behalf during the first phase.[38] The erstwhile brothers-in-arms interned in Allendorf worked together to prepare affidavits for their revered field marshal. The veterans' statements corroborated one another to such an extent that they were almost interchangeable.

Kesselring's own view of his actions was that of a nonpolitical soldier who had done only his duty, thereby building on myths used earlier at Nuremberg that argued that the generals were victims of their profession. Kühne has named this phenomenon "the self-victimization trap."[39] The code word *duty* was used to absolve any officer from any individual sense of guilt he might feel and from the obligation to define his own position and responsibility within the larger political frame, which had been revealed to be a criminal regime.[40] For example, Kesselring made the following observation during the prosecution's opening statement: "The prosecutor's demands are too great: should I verify all my orders? This goes beyond the power of an individual and a military staff charged with conducting a war, who wanted nothing to do with such pettiness and degradation."[41] This note revealed Kesselring's attitude—an attitude that utilized military categories of "good" and "bad" soldiers. It also left it to the SD and SS troops to wage war on the civilian population, thus meeting Kesselring's demands for a "pacified hinterland." In contrast, his view of the Wehrmacht soldier was a positive one: "Soldiers will understand that one cannot do everything, that criminal activity takes place behind the lines of honest warfare, and that one cannot intervene in the command areas of others."[42]

For strategic reasons, Laternser—who had initially avoided calling witnesses from the ranks of the SS—also requested statements from Waffen-SS general Max Simon and SS *Obergruppenführer* Willy Tensfeld and Alois Brunner.[43] The request reveals that Kesselring was well aware of the atrocities that had taken place in Italy.[44] The SS officers approached by Laternser clearly used the opportunity to exonerate themselves of any suspected involvement in antipartisan warfare. This is exemplified by the statement of SS *Obersturmbannführer* Ekkehardt Albert, chief of operations of the Sixteenth Panzer Grenadier Division, who was interned with other veterans of the war in Italy at camp Allendorf.[45] Albert stated that his troops had been unaware of Kesselring's orders. Since it was the Sixteenth SS Panzer Grenadier Division that had carried out numerous massacres, Albert's statement was particularly valuable to the defense, buttressing the idea that the troops had committed atrocities on their own initiative rather than as a result of Kesselring's order. However, Laternser was reluctant to use Albert's affidavit, since in court he might have testified to the close ties between the Wehrmacht and the SS in Italy. In a telegram following the operation in Marzabotto, which resulted in the killing of nearly eight hundred civilians, Kesselring had indeed congratulated the commander of the Sixteenth Panzer Grenadier Division on his "success in combating partisans," and he put the commander forward for promotion. There can therefore be no doubt that Kesselring was aware of the Sixteenth Panzer Grenadier Division's activities behind the lines, thus shedding light on the complicity between the Wehrmacht and the SS in operations against so-called partisans.[46]

The complicity was evident also during cross-examination, when some witnesses gave substance to the charge that the Wehrmacht failed to ensure what British prosecutor Richard Halse termed the "humane" execution of the shootings, meaning with more traditional military-style firing squads. For example, Kesselring's former intelligence officer, Ernst Zolling, stated that they "paid no further attention to the reprisal" once the execution order had been transferred to the SD.[47] The affidavit by General Joachim Lemelsen, whose last posting had been as commander-in-chief of the Fourteenth Army in Italy, was also unambiguous. As a long-serving officer, Lemelsen had told the British interrogation officers that he felt that Kesselring's antipartisan orders "posed a grave risk to discipline and order, given the critical situation at the time and the fact that emotions were running high among the troops."[48] Lemelsen grasped the basis of the charges against Kesselring earlier than his colleagues: he understood that Kesselring was charged with issuing orders that could be viewed as a license to kill—and given the military and political tensions prevailing at the time, they were seen as such, at least by the SS troops. He thus demonstrated that the Wehrmacht had by no means completely forfeited its sense of justice.

In court, Laternser confronted Lemelsen with his affidavit. Under the scrutiny of former comrades, the general tried to take back his words, term-ing the affidavit "a major error."[49] However, his courtroom avowals of soli-darity with Kesselring came too late. General Lemelsen's reputation among his fellow soldiers seems to have suffered heavily as a result of his Venice testimony. Lemelsen's affidavit was criticized as going against the rules laid down in Nuremberg never to testify against a German comrade.[50] In court, however, Kesselring tried to downplay any disunity among German officers; instead, he stressed the loyalty that existed within the military. He acknowl-edged that Lemelsen's affidavit had left him with a "bitter aftertaste" and that he was "extremely sorry that he now had to once again raise this matter between two officers in public."[51] The *Times* carried these references to the military honor code and the "imperative of silence" in full, thus stressing military solidarity more than Lemelsen's noble attempt to find the truth.[52]

The judges sentenced Kesselring to be shot, but the outcome of Kessel-ring's "final battle" was certainly not decided by the verdict of the court. After it was announced on May 6, 1947, it became apparent that the fight would continue on another level during the years to come. Kesselring's reaction to the death sentence reveals the pattern of recast identity used in Italy, most notably in a letter dated May 6, 1947, which Kesselring later also included in his memoirs. The letter expressed his views on the death penalty: although he had sought an acquittal, he said he would "welcome" the execution. An acquittal would have "demonstrated to world opinion that there were and are millions of decent Germans," but the death sentence imposed would also be of public benefit "because it would create a martyr for the German peo-ple, whose memory and continued presence could provide an impetus to the youth." Because of the exemplary function he saw himself performing, he decided to "continue fighting until the end for justice for myself and my soldiers."[53]

The growth of a "veterans of Italy" legend, which had started during the trial, now continued with a fictitious closing statement by the former field marshal that was, indeed, authored by Laternser.[54] Until the trial, Kesselring's image had been that of the upstanding general who assumed responsibility for his subordinates' errors and would, if necessary, pay for them with his life. Laternser's closing statement reinvented that image. Kesselring was now presented as a general suffering the insult of a wrongful conviction. Tried in combat, he now demanded "justice." This image of the soldier on duty was also presented to the outside world. Expressions of personal regret or reflec-tions on the trial would merely get in the way of this newly sculpted image.

However, Kesselring's sentence was later commuted to life imprisonment, partly owing to the eruption of political controversy in London, led by former prime minister Winston Churchill and supported by Field Marshal Harold Alexander.[55] Numerous English politicians deplored "British victors' justice," church leaders preached reconciliation, and senior British officers raised their voices to praise Kesselring's military skill. They were all given plenty of media coverage, thus creating the British version of the "upright and fair Italian theater of war." In addition, these men triggered a debate on the very purpose of war crimes trials—a bitter debate that continued to rage in England until Kesselring's release in 1952. It showed the British victory in court to be a Pyrrhic one, at least with respect to memory politics.

Kesselring's Venice trial was of particular importance to the subsequent rehabilitation campaigns, because it established the elements of the positive narrative that cast the war in Italy as a legal and "clean" one. Even from the British side, there was an interest as early as 1947 in establishing the Italian theater of war as clean, for there was no interest in a discussion on whether British arms shipments and supplies sent to the resistance had, in fact, escalated the partisan war in Italy.[56] Once it became clear that lower-ranking officers awaiting Italian trials were likely to get a lighter sentence than the ones that were to be handed down to their senior officers, it became politically impossible to execute Kesselring.[57] In February 1948, the British Foreign Office announced the end of the British war crimes program for Italy: "The decision is that no Germans will in future be tried by British Military Courts for war crimes committed against Italian victims."[58] All these factors combined to form a fog of exculpation and obfuscation from which, just a short time later, the myth of the unjustly convicted field marshal was to emerge.

The other high-ranking commander in Italy was lucky as well: Supreme Police Commander and SS-*Obergruppenführer* Karl Wolff escaped Allied prosecution altogether, for he was actively shielded by U.S. intelligence authorities with whom he had conducted the surrender negotiations in Switzerland.[59] Three factors—strategic cooperation on the part of the accused, Dulles's personal commitment, and the political interests of the Western Allies—facilitated Wolff's evasion of prosecution. There can be no doubt, however, that, as Himmler's adjutant, Wolff was aware of the extent of the Holocaust. Yet his role in organizing rail transports of Jews from the Warsaw Ghetto to Treblinka Extermination Camp became the basis for criminal proceedings against him in the Munich Regional Court in 1962 only. As it was, Wolff's involvement in the Holocaust already had been briefly discussed in Nuremberg during preparations for the trial against Oswald Pohl and other officers from the SS Economics and Administration Department, and it would have been possible to put him on trial at that time, but the issue was then dropped "for political reasons."[60]

The Allied failure to prosecute Wolff had its origins in the agreement on a partial surrender in northern Italy. The German capitulation on the southern front was in the American interest, and it was vital that the anti-Soviet nature of the negotiations be concealed from the public after the war. Wolff had been able to offer the Allies the advantage of a relatively self-contained theater of war, which made a hand-over of arms easier. Moreover, the Western Allies had a vital political interest in curtailing the Soviet sphere of control and not allowing it to extend to southern Europe.[61] In 1946, the American head of the military mission in Moscow, General John Deane, judged that Sunrise had represented the turning point in American policy toward the Soviet Union: after that, the United States displayed a new self-confidence in its dealings with Stalin.[62] The military benefits offered by a partial surrender were obvious. In this regard, the hand-over of southern Tyrol and the Trieste harbor played a key strategic and military role.[63] And thanks to the peace agreement, two Allied armies in Italy were spared and could be redeployed to southern Germany to counter any further advance of the Red Army in the final days of the war.

Cold War considerations helped to delay decisions and thus helped Wolff evade justice. The Western Allied authorities' willingness to address Nazi crimes—whether those crimes were committed in concentration camps or in the context of antipartisan warfare—changed over time. By the time Wolff was brought before a denazification court in 1948, it had become clear that shielding him represented a politically calculated trade-off. Thanks to Allied interventions, the denazification court stated that Himmler's adjutant was deemed to have been only a nominal member of the SS and thus placed in Category III as a "minor offender." The German judge underlined, "The defendant leaves the Court without a taint."[64] Wolff's four-year sentence was offset against the time he had already served, and he was released immediately after the sentence was handed down. Thanks to Dulles, Karl Wolff was able to find his way back into civilian life and was not subjected to an employment ban.[65]

It was quite decisive for Wolff's case that Dulles had attributed to him in numerous statements the image of a gentleman waging a clean war in Italy.[66] Sympathy stemmed from their personal contact during the surrender negotiations, but also from Wolff's desire to protect the economic, political, and ideological interests of the United States and its political allies. U.S. intelligence in this way also helped mold the image of a decent war in Italy.

Once the general line of the honorable SS men in Italy was accepted, other SS staff benefited from Wolff's deal as well: some of them received assistance to escape to South America, while others, among them Eugen Dollmann, Eugen Wenner, and Guido Zimmer, were used by the CIA.[67] The benefits of this doubly bolstered narrative of a clean war in Italy were striking: Wolff escaped punishment in Nuremberg, his denazification trial was a farce, and only when in 1962 international pressure demanded that Wolff be brought to justice for his involvement with the Holocaust did the United States' protective shield for this SS commander crumble. However, Wolff himself felt supported for the rest of his life in his view that he was an honorable SS man, alien to the dirty war of some of his comrades in the east.

Wolff also benefited greatly from the campaign for Kesselring's release, because it linked his name with the Italian theater of war, which had become idealized. This campaign of great symbolic value to all sides started as early as 1947 and went on until the release of Kesselring in 1952; it demonstrated the close links between diverse interest groups inside and outside Germany. The efforts to secure the field marshal's release went beyond personal interventions by his friends: a range of individuals representing churches, lawyers' groups, veterans' associations, and opponents of industrial dismantlement were also active on Kesselring's behalf. After 1948, as the Cold War emerged, the reconciliatory attitudes of Lord Maurice Hankey, Sir Basil Liddell Hart, Bishop Bell, and Winston Churchill led to a reconsideration of the imprisonment of German officers.[68] Joined by a group of U.S. senators, these individuals were not interested in the release of Kesselring as a person. In advancing their arguments that the Wehrmacht had fought an honorable war, their motive was to use former generals to spur rapid German rearmament in order to help in the fight against the common (Communist) enemy in the east. In terms of public opinion, "war criminals" were rehabilitated and transformed into "comrades." Preexisting German arguments regarding the officers' personal integrity, the imperative of obeying orders, and errors made by the British during the trials were now knitted together with the argument for a joint defense against the east. German advocates for Kesselring did not ignore these new ideas. "Justice, not mercy" was the phrase used by the war criminals' lobbyists in their attempt to interpret Kesselring's release in 1952.

By analyzing the campaign for Kesselring, it becomes clear that one of the aims espoused by the campaign for clemency for the officers imprisoned in Germany was to achieve a shift in German public opinion and a more positive attitude toward the Wehrmacht's military legacy. It was hoped that the rehabilitative efforts would enable the German public—in particular ordinary soldiers who had served in Italy—to attach retrospective purpose to their war service, thus helping foster public acceptance of German rearmament.

In this way, the rearmament debate influenced and distorted the debate on German war crimes to such an extent that several issues became confused: the crimes committed during the war against civilians and POWs, the crimes committed by the National Socialists against concentration camp inmates, and the frequently arbitrary sentences imposed on German POWs still in Soviet custody were linked to the continued imprisonment of Wehrmacht generals. Even Chancellor Adenauer, who had initially regarded the issue of war criminals as tangential to his policy of Western integration, quickly recognized the integrative power of the demand for the release of those officers still in custody and its potential to contribute to the republic's domestic stabilization. The public rehabilitation of the soldiers' honor—and the exceptions made for some "good SS men"—paved the way for public repression of large parts of the memory of the Nazi war. Yet it is undeniable that in the early 1950s the representatives of officers' interests, in interviews and memoirs, did not establish the idea of a "clean Wehrmacht" but rather cemented what had already been built during the IMT and trials like the one against Field Marshal Kesselring.[69]

Controversies behind the Scenes: Honorable War in Italy?

The success of the veterans' organizations, at least in their lobbying for the so-called war criminals in 1951 and 1952, must not blind us to the fact that there was a time of reflection among officers' circles during the immediate postwar period. The knowledge that they had served a criminal cause resulted, for many, in adopting a new position—but only in private. The external impact was quite different: veterans' associations and politicians were in favor of well-known military leaders' taking the lead in the debate on rearmament and pushing ahead the "politics of honor" for the benefit of the Wehrmacht. Only rarely, as in the case of the debate over Kesselring's memoirs, did controversies occur—but only behind closed doors.

This lends itself to an analysis of war images that became important over the course of demands for rehabilitation.[70] The narrative concentrated on the dictum of a "clean" or "decent war" and was actually a paradox: it conceded that war crimes had occurred, but only on the eastern front—in short, no such crimes had ever taken place in Italy. This laid the cornerstone for a strategy to exculpate a considerable number of veterans. With the blessing of their officers, nearly eight hundred thousand men could feel exonerated from all guilt for war crimes. There was hardly an officer from the Italian theater of war who contradicted this positive image of the war in his memoirs.[71]

A closer investigation of the discourse, however, leads to a blurred picture. Ties of comradeship had bound most of the Italian veterans to a policy of silence about Kesselring's dishonorable role in the last hours of the Italian war, when he had refused to surrender and had threatened the Sunrise negotiators with court-martial. When Kesselring filed a request for release in 1951, all his officers rallied again in court—as they had done before in Venice—to testify that Kesselring had never meant to kill Italian civilians; even Röttiger spoke for his chief, although they had been on opposite sides of the surrender debate.[72] The officers testified bluntly that the Italians were notorious liars and thus Italian witnesses who gave testimony about civilian massacres could not be trusted.[73]

The internal discussion at the officers' level shows how the narration of the Sunrise events and their participants became a constitutive factor for the postwar evaluation of German officers who had served in Italy.[74] The officers were divided into two opposing camps: those who had wanted to fight to the bitter end and the "capitulators." Kesselring, General Friedrich Schulz, and his chief of staff, Fritz Wentzell, argued that the surrender had been a betrayal of Army Group E in Yugoslavia, because the agreement had cut off their possible retreat to the Western territories. A group of leading Sunrise negotiators and generals led by Hans Röttiger, including the then army commanders Traugott Herr and Joachim Lemelsen, and backed by Ambassador Rudolf Rahn and SS general Karl Wolff, defended their negotiations as an example of responsible actions taken to end the war. The matter in question was the following: in the final days of the war, Kesselring had opposed capitulation by arresting members of the Sunrise group, but he claimed in his memoirs not to remember this episode. In his memoirs Kesselring reinterpreted the arrest of the negotiators as a patriotic act to save the Yugoslavian front, which needed to be held a few days longer to enable additional combat units to retreat to Western territories.

The strong resistance against Kesselring's self-serving view of the Sunrise negotiations reveals the existence of a line of demarcation in the collective memory of the war that no one was permitted to cross, not even the commander-in-chief himself.[75] It is remarkable that Wolff, as an SS officer, was accepted on the basis of his rank in the Waffen-SS into the positively connoted circle of comrades and thereby overcame the distinction made in the Nuremberg IMT trials between the Wehrmacht and the ordinary

SS, the latter having been demonized in politics since 1951 as the "true criminals."

The main objective during this first phase of the war's aftermath—roughly until 1949—when narratives were still in flux, was to defend the negotiators against this accusation. As the denazification trials ran their course and societal awareness about the war changed, the early surrender started to be seen in a positive light, and the correspondence reveals that, starting in 1950, many an officer began to polish up his biography in retrospect and to "admit" his participation in the negotiations. However, the main Sunrise protagonists actively began to challenge such attempts in 1953.

In prison, Kesselring had the opportunity to write studies for the Historical Division of the U.S. Army, whose German Section was run by the former chief of the general staff of the Wehrmacht, Franz Halder. Halder, who had fallen into disgrace with Hitler in 1944, conducted this war history section just as strategically as he had once conducted operations in the war, but this time it was his clear aim to win at least the memory battles. In a draft study about the cessation of hostilities in Italy, Kesselring continued to propagate the explanation that the surrender had been the option necessary to protect his soldiers in light of the threat posed by Communist forces advancing from the Balkans.[76]

His former chief of staff, General Röttiger, objected to Kesselring's assertion.[77] Röttiger reminded Kesselring that, even at an earlier date of surrender, more troops would have fallen into the hands of the Western powers had Kesselring ordered the troops to retreat with sufficient lead time, rather than ordering them to hold their ground. Here Röttiger formulated what later became the central argument for the cease-fire: a feeling of responsibility for the welfare of the troops. He concluded: "What is easier, to order your men to fight until the last bullet or instead to assume complete responsibility for a voluntary surrender? Thanks to my own bitter experience, I myself have no doubt how to answer this question. Röttiger."[78]

If Kesselring could perhaps dismiss Röttiger's actions as a rather presumptuous intrusion, this was not possible when an officer of nearly equal rank intervened, specifically his successor as supreme commander of Army Group C, Colonel General Heinrich von Vietinghoff-Scheel. Vietinghoff, who had been stripped of his post by Kesselring and threatened with court-martial execution for treason during the aforementioned putsch, also wrote to Kesselring. He, too, pointed out historical falsifications in Kesselring's memoirs: "By the way, I ask the Field Marshal to check once more whether this study could not unintentionally give new impulse to rumors or legends that the Party actually attempted to have spread during the war. The Field Marshal knows better than I what bitter injustice would thus be done. Germany could never and under no circumstances have won this war against nearly the entire world. It is the fatal blame of the 'highest office' alone that the German people were put in such a situation. Signed: v. Vietinghoff."[79]

In 1949, Vietinghoff was playing with the idea of publishing his own memoirs.[80] He decided definitely against the idea in 1951—out of consideration for Kesselring. In 1951 Kesselring personally had a lot at stake. While serving his sentence in a British POW prison, he pinned his hopes on possible denazification and a pardon. In order not to endanger Kesselring's chances, Vietinghoff, ever the gentleman comrade, retracted his manuscript from the *Corriere della Sera,* even though Kesselring had humiliated him, degraded him, and threatened him with death in the final days of April 1945. Vietinghoff emphasized: "Owing to various background information that I have received just recently, I can no longer release for publication my memoirs, sent to you a year ago, without first editing these myself. The need is to assess the actions of several key figures. Therefore I ask you to please return the manuscript to me."[81]

In Vietinghoff's account, the "key figures" were indeed criticized harshly. About Kesselring, he wrote in his manuscript in 1946: "He emphasizes . . . that an end [to the fighting] will not be considered at all as long as the Führer is still alive."[82] Vietinghoff maintained that Kesselring wanted to know nothing about the negotiations in order to avoid the necessity to intervene; but he then ordered Vietinghoff to appear before him on April 30, 1945, to threaten him with dismissal. Vietinghoff reacted by offering his resignation: "So ended this ignoble comedy—ignoble especially because the Field Marshal knew everything and silently approved it, but had dared not profess it out of timidity toward [*Gauleiter*] Hofer."[83] In 1952 the field marshal was pardoned, and the topic of surrender was not mentioned by any of the rivals.[84]

The debate among the veterans heated up again in 1953—after Kesselring left prison and prior to the publication of his memoirs—when a prerelease of his account was distributed among the higher-ranking officers who had served in Italy. In his memoirs, Kesselring justifies his refusal to accept the early surrender initiated by Vietinghoff and Röttiger in Italy on May 2, 1945, as a fait accompli: "It was now no longer the struggle to achieve a respectable peace. It was solely about fulfilling an absolute duty of camaraderie, not to allow German comrades to fall into the hands of the Russians. For this and only this reason, the continuation of the fight was necessary to the bitter end."[85] Despite the historical evidence, Kesselring maintained that he had "known of the secret plans for a cease-fire in Italy since October 1944."[86] He had wanted to be the one to choose the proper moment for such a cease-fire, but his officers went behind his back and took the initiative themselves. Kesselring's version was backed by the generals Schulz and Wentzell, who were not at all interested in having their determination to fight to the end understood as dumb vassal loyalty to Hitler.[87]

Now Kesselring's comrades broke their silence and argued for the importance of Wolff's role. At a meeting in Heidelberg in late June 1953, Röttiger; the field marshal's former first officer within the general staff in Italy, Josef Moll; Wolff; and Rahn agreed to have a memorandum sent to Kesselring. As Vietinghoff had died unexpectedly in 1951, his 1948 comments on Sunrise gained even more weight. This is one of the rare examples in which former officers of the Wehrmacht and the SS came together to form an alliance that countered the ruling narrative of the separation of Wehrmacht and SS in wartime actions. However, Wolff remained the only witness from the ranks of the SS, even though other participants such as Wenner or Dollmann could have testified. The divide between the Wehrmacht and the SS was a distinct one after the war, despite their shared success in the Sunrise story, and apparently only Wolff, reimagined as a Waffen-SS general and not as the police leader that he was, was accepted in the Wehrmacht's circles.

Apparently group cohesion was still strong enough to prevent a public debate about Sunrise, so as not to damage the "clean" reputation of the Wehrmacht in Italy. These men evidently felt obligated to maintain their public silence out of the Wehrmacht esprit de corps and also in light of the fierce debate on German rearmament; one was at a "point when it is crucial to restore confidence in the German officer," as one of them noted.[88] In their memorandum, the authors deliberately alluded to Kesselring when they emphasized that the real blame lay "with all of those" who "assumed or hoped until the very last days in April 1945 that the situation on the fronts would again take a favorable turn of events." Therefore, contradictory narratives were to be repudiated: "out of the abovementioned conviction, we the undersigned [Röttiger, Wolff, Rahn, and Moll] find the kind of remarks expressed about the cease-fire in Italy as an unfair and insulting defamation of their actions, the correctness of which has been fully affirmed by political developments in recent years."[89]

Kesselring did not react to the memorandum but neither was any further edition of the memoirs—Kesselring's revised version of the surrender—ever published.[90] This permanently burdened Kesselring's relationships with his former comrades—particularly with Röttiger, who later became the Bundeswehr's first inspector of the army, whereas the former field marshal was never asked for his expertise.[91]

The group of generals led by Röttiger did, however, succeed in publicly setting the record straight and embedding an accurate account of Sunrise in German society's collective memory. A broadcast by the Nordwestdeutsche Rundfunk in Cologne on April 25, 1955, basically followed the account presented in the memorandum written by Röttiger and Vietinghoff-Scheel. The narrator openly read Vietinghoff's verdict on Kesselring from the former's unpublished memoirs, which until then no one else had dared to publicize: "The Field Marshall approves Wolff's action but does not want to go out on a limb as long as the Führer is alive."[92] Kesselring first had to be convinced by Wolff in a long late-night telephone conversation to approve the surrender ex post facto.[93] By 1955 it had become possible to publicly criticize Kesselring, because his popularity had suffered considerably after a few unfortunate appearances as an expert witness in court. The press even openly speculated whether Kesselring had been a "Nazi general."[94]

Karl Wolff was later the only one to express publicly his opinion on Sunrise, and he had personal motives for doing so: he wanted to draw attention to his own good deeds, for in 1962 he was awaiting trial. Sunrise could serve to exonerate him. Already back in 1955, the *Süddeutsche Zeitung* had published an interview with Wolff in which he expressed the accusations against Kesselring in detail. He directly accused Kesselring of letting himself be "influenced" by *Gauleiter* Hofer to remove Vietinghoff and Röttiger from their commands.[95] It was the first public criticism of the commander-in-chief expressed by a participant. Moreover, it came from an SS general who openly linked Kesselring to a Nazi *Gau* leader. The Röttiger group deeply resented Wolff for making this connection, especially since he was an SS *Obergruppenführer*. Not one of the Wehrmacht officers testified on Wolff's behalf at his later trial in Munich, where Wolff was convicted of murder of three hundred thousand Jews from Treblinka, having organized railway transportation for deportation, and sentenced to fifteen years imprisonment.[96]

Much later—in 1966—*Der Spiegel* wrote about Sunrise, when the book *The Secret Surrender* by Allen Dulles and Gero von Gaevernitz was published. By this time, Kesselring and Röttiger were both dead; the trial of Karl Wolff was over; the Bundeswehr had been in existence for ten years; and integration into the West could be regarded as successful.[97] No longer were there any negative reactions, because the merit of persevering in a fight to the bitter end had finally been discredited.

If one seeks to grasp the military group identity of personnel involved in the Italian campaign after 1945, one can observe at least two opposing narratives. The first of these originated with the manifesto of former generals in Nuremberg and advanced further after the formal acquittal of the general staff in 1946 as a "criminal organization." This was the view that while the Wehrmacht had been abused by Hitler and his "clique," it had, apart from individual wrongdoers, remained essentially "decent." This image could only be upheld at the cost of demonizing the SS troops, as was done at Nuremberg. When one takes a closer look, however, it is apparent that both groups (Wehrmacht and SS officers), despite their efforts to exclude the other officials from their own concepts of dignity and comradeship, still shared the concept of "military honor." Both groups referred frequently to it—in trials as well as in private correspondence.

Thus, the slogan of "restoring honor" was associated with the idea that the Wehrmacht had not lost its honor as a result of the way in which it had conducted itself during the war; rather, it was claimed that the Allies had taken away the officers' honor—by the trial and conviction of representative leaders, by the imposition of humiliating collective measures, and by the deliberate social degradation of German soldiers. In subsequent trials, such as Kesselring's, the defense further advanced such claims.

This view was then bolstered by the clemency campaigns of the 1950s to release convicted soldiers. Motivated by foreign policy interests, such as the aim to integrate West Germany into the emerging bloc system of the Cold War and its potential as a future ally, Germany's erstwhile opponents granted additional concessions—more than any evidence warranted. This recasting was bolstered by a political turn in 1949, when West German Chancellor Konrad Adenauer and other members of the Parliament spoke in favor of the former elite, restoring them to good positions in order to achieve the political goal of building a new German military and a new secret service.

Nevertheless, as a whole, the Allies' war crimes trials program did create a different narrative. Although prosecution did not have access to anything like the details known about Wehrmacht and SS atrocities today, the trials—with the one against Kesselring as a striking example—demonstrated clearly to a majority of the German people that Hitler's Wehrmacht had been involved in the planning and execution of a war of aggression. In this war, certain units were not only witnesses but also perpetrators of and responsible for crimes that had been committed behind the front line.

However, thanks to the manner in which the Kesselring trial was conducted and the pictures of the crimes that were drawn in the courtroom, the proceedings still helped to mold a myth of a "clean Wehrmacht" in Italy; this development can be traced back to Laternser's defense strategy during the trial. It was then fortified additionally by studies written by German officers for the Historical Division of the U.S. Army. This myth accompanied Kesselring through all phases of his clemency campaign, and it was eventually incorporated into the collective war memory of postwar German society. Even today, it is repeatedly said that "it had been impossible to prove" Kesselring's involvement in war crimes.[98]

The combination of the two narratives—innocent General Staff and innocent field marshal in Italy—was, however, challenged by individual memory and led, behind the scenes, to a significant memory battle about military codes such as "duty" and "honor." At stake, as is underlined clearly by the private correspondence analyzed in this chapter, was the reframing of these terms for postwar use. Again, the "decent war" was the key term of this debate, even though it took on a new meaning.

The German officers of Army Group C in northern Italy benefited from their recasting as honorable soldiers who had acted decently and independently from Nazi hardliners and had surrendered early, pragmatically recognizing defeat. This recast group identity, with reference to a "decent war" in Italy, benefited most officers in this group for quite some time—no matter whether Wehrmacht or SS officer. In fact, after the reemergence of the German Army in 1956, many of this group enrolled in veterans' associations, influenced defense policy by taking on government positions, or even advanced to new military ranks. One of them was General Hans Röttiger.[99] He later became the first general inspector of the new Bundeswehr in 1956, advocating all his remaining life for what he termed the "Gewissensentscheidung" (a decision of honor and conscience, and not of ideology) as the highest virtue of a decent army officer.

Given the close involvement of SS-*Obergruppenführer* Wolff in the events leading to surrender, it is particularly striking how the group first tried to integrate Wolff into the positive narrative by pointing to his military service as a general of the Waffen-SS, which in the immediate postwar years was perceived as equivalent to an ordinary army commander—a notion that changed in the early 1950s. The group's unity only broke open in the late 1950s when Wolff's involvement in the Holocaust was discussed publicly and a trial was scheduled—connecting him back to his "dirty" SS past and relocating him to the dark side of memory.

Notes

The author wants to thank Katrin Paehler for her valuable help with the English manuscript of this chapter, making it read more smoothly.

1. The standard work on Operation Sunrise continues to be the extensive study written in 1979; the authors take approaches endemic to political science: Elena Agarossi and Bradley F. Smith, *Operation Sunrise: The Secret Surrender* (New York: Basic Books, 1979); Kerstin von Lingen, *SS und Secret Service: "Verschwörung des Schweigens": Der Fall Karl Wolff* (Paderborn: Schöningh, 2010). The English translation is available as Kerstin von Lingen, *Allen Dulles, the OSS and Nazi War Criminals: The Dynamics of Selective Prosecution* (Cambridge: Cambridge University Press, 2013). See also the books of participants: Allen Dulles and Gero v. Schulze-Gaevernitz, *The Secret Surrender* (New York: Weinfeld and Nicolson, 1967); and Max Waibel, *1945-Kapitulation in Norditalien: Originalbericht des Vermittlers* (Basel: Helbing und Lichtenhahn, 1981).

2. N 431/935, Vietinghoff to Laternser, June 21, 1946, attached to the draft of the study "Der Feldzug in Italien," 7, Federal Republic of Germany, Bundesarchiv-Militärarchiv, Freiburg (hereafter BA-MA).

3. Research on the German occupation of Italy is quite vast. See, as a selection, Lutz Klinkhammer, *Zwischen Bündnis und Besatzung: Das nationalsozialistische Deutschland und die Republik von Salò 1943–1945* (Tübingen: Niemeyer, 1993); Michael Wedekind, *Nationalsozialistische Besatzungs- und Annexionspolitik in Norditalien 1943 bis 1945* (Munich: Oldenbourg: 2003); Gerhard Schreiber, *Deutsche Kriegsverbrechen in Italien: Täter, Opfer, Strafverfolgung* (Munich: Beck, 1996); Carlo Gentile, *Wehrmacht und Waffen-SS im Partisanenkrieg: Italien 1943–1945* (Paderborn: Schöningh, 2012).

4. Gerhard Schreiber, "Partisanenkrieg und Kriegsverbrechen der Wehrmacht in Italien 1943 bis 1945," in *Repression und Kriegsverbrechen: Die Bekämpfung von Widerstands- und Partisanenbewegungen gegen die deutsche Besatzung in West- und Südeuropa*, ed. Guus Mershoek (Berlin: Assoziation A, 1997), 114.

5. The numbers are taken from Giorgio Rochat, "Una ricerca impossibile: Le perdite italiane nella seconda guerra mondiale," *Storia Contemporanea* 201 (1995): 691.

6. Research into the escalation of brutality within the German Army during World War II offers, for example, Omer Bartov, *Hitler's Army: Soldiers, Nazis and War in the Third Reich* (Oxford: Oxford University Press, 1992); and Thomas Kühne, *Kameradschaft: Die Soldaten des nationalsozialistischen Krieges und das 20. Jahrhundert* (Göttingen: Vandenhoeck & Ruprecht, 2006).

7. Lutz Klinkhammer, *Stragi naziste in Italia: La Guerra contro i Civili (1943/44)*

(Rome: Universale Donzelli, 1997), 102. Lutz Klinkhammer has worked out in detail why the Italian theater of war represented a special case in occupation policy and what emergency regulations were in force on a day-to-day basis. He also calculated that only five out of every hundred soldiers in Italy were involved in war crimes, whereas this ratio was nearly reversed on the eastern front.

8. On the dirty war on the eastern front, see Hannes Heer and Klaus Naumann, eds., *Vernichtungskrieg: Verbrechen der Wehrmacht 1941–1944* (Hamburg: Hamburger Edition, 1995).

9. Georg Meyer, "Soldaten ohne Armee: Berufssoldaten im Kampf um Standesehre und Versorgung," in *Von Stalingrad zur Währungsreform: Zur Sozialgeschichte des Umbruchs in Deutschland,* ed. Martin Broszat, Klaus-Dietmar Henke, and Hans Woller (Munich: Oldenbourg, 1988), 683–750. Research on continuity, that is, the question of whether incriminated individuals were accepted into the Federal Republic's new armed forces, and what influence they had on society, has just started. See Klaus Naumann, *Generale in der Demokratie: Generationsgeschichtliche Studien zur Bundeswehrelite* (Hamburg: Hamburger Edition, 2007); Helmut R. Hammerich and Rudolf Schlaffer, eds., *Militärische Aufbaugeneration der Bundeswehr 1955 bis 1970* (Munich: Oldenbourg, 2011).

10. Michael Salter, *Nazi War Crimes, US Intelligence and Selective Prosecution at Nuremberg: Controversies regarding the Role of the Office of Strategic Services* (London: Routledge-Cavendish, 2007); Kerstin von Lingen, "Conspiracy of Silence: How the 'Old Boys' of American Intelligence Shielded SS-General Karl Wolff from Prosecution," *Holocaust and Genocide Studies* 22, no. 1 (2008): 74–109; von Lingen, *Allen Dulles.*

11. Alaric Searle, *Wehrmacht Generals, West German Society, and the Debate on Rearmament, 1949–1959* (Westport, CT: Praeger, 2003). Jay Lockenour, *Soldiers as Citizens: Former Wehrmacht Officers in the Federal Republic of Germany, 1945–1955* (Lincoln: University of Nebraska Press, 2001). Bert-Oliver Manig, *Die Politik der Ehre: Die Rehabilitierung der Berufssoldaten in der frühen Bundesrepublik* (Göttingen: Wallstein, 2004). Manig comments: "Social degradation and delegitimation, however, are not to be confused with discrimination and defamation, two slogans which soon shaped the group identity of the career soldiers, and would bring it back to life" (585).

12. Norbert Frei, *Vergangenheitspolitik: Die Anfänge der Bundesrepublik und die NS-Vergangenheit* (Munich: Beck, 1996), 14; in English: *Adenauer's Germany and the Nazi Past: The Politics of Amnesty and Integration* (New York: Columbia University Press, 2002).

13. Kerstin von Lingen, *Kesselring's Last Battle: War Crimes Trials and Cold War Politics, 1945–1960* (Lawrence: University Press of Kansas, 2009), 249–88; Oliver von Wrochem, *Erich von Manstein: Vernichtungskrieg und Geschichtspolitik* (Paderborn: Schöningh, 2006), 128–212.

14. Benedict Anderson, *Imagined Communities: Reflections of the Origin and Spread of Nationalism* (London: Verso, 1991); with regard to the German case most

prominently: Aleida Assmann, *Der lange Schatten der Vergangenheit: Erinnerungskultur und Geschichtspolitik* (Munich: Beck, 2006), 17.

15. Basic research about the "frame of reference" is offered by Maurice Halbwachs, *Das Gedächtnis und seine sozialen Bedingungen* (Frankfurt am Main: Suhrkamp, 1985); also Halbwachs, *Das kollektive Gedächtnis* (Frankfurt am Main: Fischer, 1991).

16. Reinhart Koselleck, "Formen und Traditionen des negativen Gedächtnisses," in *Verbrechen erinnern: Die Auseinandersetzung mit Holocaust und Völkermord,* ed. Norbert Frei and Volkhart Knigge (Munich: Beck, 2002), 31.

17. Manfred Messerschmidt, "Vorwärtsverteidigung: Die Denkschrift der Generäle für den Nürnberger Gerichtshof," in *Militarismus, Vernichtungskrieg, Geschichtspolitik: Zur deutschen Militär- und Rechtsgeschichte,* ed. Messerschmidt (Paderborn: Schöningh, 2006), 315.

18. Ibid., 315.

19. Ibid., 317, calls the memorandum one of the most decisive documents in terms of "belittlement of the role of OKW and OKH."

20. N 431/828 (private papers of Hans Laternser), questions for cross-examination of Hans Röttiger, BA-MA. See also Wrochem, *Erich von Manstein,* 113.

21. N 431/829, cross-examination of Röttiger, BA-MA.

22. N 431/828, Fragen an Röttiger, 5 (para. 25 and 26), BA-MA, demonstrates that internally many comrades urged Röttiger to take back his statement. Additionally, Westphal started the rumor among other officers in the witness wing at Nuremberg that Röttiger had been rewarded for this affidavit with immediate release.

23. N 431/828, Fragen an Röttiger; and /829, Vorbereitung Kreuzverhör Röttiger, BA-MA; see correspondence and notes here.

24. On the loss of reality, see Wolfram Wette, *Die Wehrmacht: Feindbilder, Vernichtungskrieg, Legenden* (Darmstadt: Primus, 2002), 192.

25. Wolfram Wette, "Das Bild der Wehrmacht-Elite nach 1945," in *Hitlers militärische Elite,* ed. Gerd R. Ueberschär (Darmstadt: Primus, 1998), 2:297.

26. Lawrence D. Egbert and Paul A. Joosten, eds., *Der Prozess gegen die Hauptkriegsverbrecher vor dem Internationalen Militärgerichtshof (IMT), Nürnberg, Nürnberg, 14. November 1945–1. Oktober 1946; [gemäß den Weisungen des Internationalen Militärgerichtshofes vom Sekretariat des Gerichtshofes unter der Autorität des Obersten Kontrollrats für Deutschland veröffentlicht],* 41 vols. (Nuremberg, 1947); *"When it suits their defense they say they had to obey; when confronted with Hitler's brutal crimes, which are shown to have been within their general knowledge, they say they disobeyed. The truth is they actively participated in all these crimes, or sat silent and acquiescent, witnessing the commission of crimes on a scale larger and more shocking than the world has ever had the misfortune to know"* (1:313).

27. See Valerie Geneviève Hébert, *Hitler's Generals on Trial: The Last War Crimes Tribunal at Nuremberg* (Lawrence: University Press of Kansas, 2010), 5; Kim C. Priemel and Alexa Stiller, eds., *Reassessing the Nuremberg Military Tribunals: Transitional Justice, Trial Narratives, and Historiography* (Oxford: Berghahn Books, 2012);

Kevin Jon Heller, *The Nuremberg Military Tribunals and the Origins of International Criminal Law* (Oxford: Oxford University Press, 2011); see also Wolfram Wette, "Fall 12: Der OKW-Prozess," in *Der Nationalsozialismus vor Gericht: Die alliierten Prozesse gegen Kriegsverbrecher und Soldaten 1943–1952,* ed. Gerd R. Ueberschär (Frankfurt am Main: Verlag, 1999), 199–212.

28. Kerstin von Lingen, "Partisanenkrieg und Wehrmachtjustiz: Italien 1943–1945," *Zeitschrift für Genozidforschung* 2 (2007): 8–40; also Schreiber, "Partisanenkrieg."

29. War Office (WO) 310/127, JAG memorandum, 5, United Kingdom, The National Archives (hereafter TNA). As early as 1945, British investigators had found that the SS forces were not the only ones to get their hands dirty in the fight against the partisans. Individual Wehrmacht units had also been involved in massacres.

30. Lingen, *SS und Secret Service,* 14f.

31. Most prominently, Kesselring himself; see N 431/936, Kesselring to Laternser, October 26, 1946, 12 sheets, sheet 3, BA-MA; WO 310/127, Judge Advocate Halse to the War Crimes Group Caserta, Major McKee, January 1, 1947, TNA. Colonel Halse had indicated confidentially, as early as January 1, 1947, that no concrete charges could be made against SS *Obergruppenführer* Karl Wolff.

32. WO 310/123, Voluntary Statement by SS *Sturmbannführer* Heinrich Andergassen, February 21, 1946, TNA.

33. Ibid.; Andergassen was former head of the Gestapo in Bozen, and the file noted: "He wanted a clean exit and for that reason did not mention who gave him the orders. He said that later or sometime, it will be spoken about by those left behind, and they can say 'Schiffer was a real guy.'" Schiffer was convicted by an American military court in 1946 and subsequently shot; see Gerald Steinacher, *Südtirol und die Geheimdienste* (Innsbruck: Studienverlag, 2000), 267.

34. N 750/3, Kesselring trial diary, February 9, 1947, BA-MA: "The battle commences!"; N 750/7 includes reactions to the death sentence, including Beelitz's and Röttiger's. In N 750/6, Boehme to Laternser, April 27, 1951, BA-MA, Albrecht Böhme offered himself as a witness for Kesselring's denazification proceedings, reasoning as follows: "The defense of the Field Marshal is a defense of the honor of non-Nazi German soldiers who only knew their duty to the Fatherland, and it is one of our most honorable concerns to do the best that we can!"

35. Dept. 47, Hiemer Papers, Keller to Hiemer, January 18, 1947, Archiv Monacense Societatis Jesu, Munich.

36. N 431/932, Laternser to Hamsher, June 9, 1947, BA-MA; Laternser emphasized that Kesselring had not been concerned for himself; rather, he had been concerned "for his honor and the honor of German soldiers and the German military leadership. Kesselring is convinced that he conducted the war in Italy as decently and humanely as possible." In his final address to the court, Laternser stressed that Kesselring had "not defended himself" but had defended "the ideals he represented" (see also Foreign Office 642 [preserved in the Imperial War Museum, London], vol. 5, 59th day, May 6, 1947, TNA).

37. N 431/932, Hauser to Laternser, August 29, 1946, BA-MA; thus General Major Wolf Hauser—former chief of General Staff of the Fourteenth Army—asked Laternser, then still involved in the Nuremberg IMT trial, to take custody of the affidavits he had gathered on behalf of Kesselring and von Mackensen.

38. N 431/933, Laternser to the camp commandants of Dachau, Garmisch, Bridgend, and Rimini and Field Marshal von Manstein, September 21, 1946, BA-MA.

39. Thomas Kühne, "Die Viktimisierungsfalle: Wehrmachtsverbrechen, Geschichtswissenschaft und symbolische Ordnung des Militärs," in *Der Krieg in der Nachkriegszeit: Der Zweite Weltkrieg in Politik und Gesellschaft der Bundesrepublik*, ed. Michael Th. Greven and Oliver von Wrochem (Opladen: Leske & Budrich, 2000), 183–96.

40. Ibid., 186.

41. N 431/888, notes made by Kesselring for Laternser on Halse's opening statement, probably February 17, 1947, 6, BA-MA.

42. Ibid.

43. N 431/935, Laternser to von Seidel in Bridgend, December 21, 1946, BA-MA. Laternser's wording was ambiguous: "Simon, . . . Brunner, . . . Tensfeld . . . should be aware of events in . . ." In his letter he wrote that Simon was in the best position to issue a statement on events in Apuana (this probably referred to the Apuanian Coast near Pietrasanta, especially the reprisal at Sant'Anna di Stazzema), whereas Brunner would be best informed regarding Caprane, Bassano, and Sassina; further, he said that Tensfeld would be able to provide information on Vercelli and Crescentino and that General Roth should issue statements on Valdarno and Fibocchi.

44. N 431/936, Kesselring to Laternser, October 26, 1946, BA-MA; here Kesselring himself suggested SS and police commanders as potential witnesses to antipartisan operations, since they were extremely well informed regarding the war waged on the partisans and in some cases had carried out the alleged actions themselves. Laternser initially advised against seeking statements from SS witnesses. Kesselring thus advised that Laternser should approach former *Gauleiter* Rainer Hofer and SS Commander Alois Brunner, seeking statements on the Caprane and Bassano case.

45. N 431/935, Röttiger to Laternser, October 7, 1946, BA-MA. Ekkehardt Albert was also interned in Allendorf, where he was unable to withstand the pressure exerted by the "defense staff" under Westphal's command.

46. Carlo Gentile, "'Politische Soldaten': Die 16. SS-Panzer-Grenadier-Division 'Reichsführer-SS' in Italien 1944," *Quellen und Forschungen aus Italienischen Archiven und Bibliotheken* 81 (2001): 540; and BA-MA, RH 20–14/41, AOK 14, War Journal No. 4, September 30, 1944, 377.

47. JAG 260 Prozess Kesselring JAG 260/2, Zolling cross-examination, 36th day, April 1, 1947, 2, Federal Republic of Germany, Bundesarchiv-Ludwigsburg, Zentrale Stelle zur Verfolgung von Nationalsozialistischen Gewaltverbrechen Ludwigsburg (hereafter ZSL).

48. N 431/305, Lemelsen, copy of a deposition, February 22, 1946, in London for the War Office (Italian Theatre of War, pt. 2), 2, BA-MA.

49. JAG 260/3, trial transcripts, 46th day, April 16, 1947, 21, ZSL.

50. N 431/933, Lemelsen to Laternser, May 12, 1947, BA-MA. General Lemelsen believed that the media coverage of the trial would expose him to the charge of having incriminated the field marshal. He feared that this view, "if spread at home," could show him in a bad light "vis-à-vis his comrades."

51. JAG 260, trial transcripts, 17th day, March 10, 1947, 29, ZSL.

52. *Times* (London), March 11, 1947, "German 'Softness' to Partisans: Kesselring's Claim," p. 3.

53. Albert Kesselring, *Soldat bis zum letzten Tag* (Bonn: Athenäum, 1953), 444.

54. Lingen, *Kesselring's Last Battle*, 123.

55. Ibid., 171–80.

56. Wette, *Wehrmacht*, 223. Wette pointed out that there was great interest outside Germany in promoting the image of a clean Wehrmacht.

57. WO 310/127, JAG, July 8, 1947, TNA.

58. WO 310/127, letter JAG to War Crimes Group South East Europe, February 19, 1948, TNA.

59. See Lingen, *Allen Dulles*.

60. Lingen, "Conspiracy of Silence," 75, 76.

61. Georg Kreis, "Das Kriegsende in Norditalien 1945," *Schweizer Monatshefte* 65, no. 6 (1985): 515. The concerns of the Western Allies are particularly evident in the correspondence between Churchill and Roosevelt after March 8, 1945; see Francis L. Loewenheim et al., *Roosevelt and Churchill: Their Secret Wartime Correspondence* (New York: Saturday Review Press, 1975), Doc. 905.

62. John R. Deane, *The Strange Alliance: The Story of American Efforts of Wartime Co-operation with Russia* (London: Viking Press, 1947), 165: "It marked a distinct turn in the attitude of the United States toward the Soviet Union and gave notice that we were not to be pushed around."

63. G. A. Lincoln to Dulles, December 27, 1966, box 59, folder 10, Princeton University, Mudd Library, Allen Dulles Private Papers (hereafter DCMLP); Dulles had asked Lincoln to give his opinion on the anti-Communist "background considerations" in respect of Sunrise, since Lincoln was then a staff officer with the Joint Chiefs of Staff and had drafted the outlines sent to Moscow. Lincoln confirmed that attempts had been made to conceal the true extent of the capitulation efforts from Stalin; the goal was to improve the U.S. position around Trieste and Venezia-Guilia. However, the delays and complications surrounding Sunrise meant that these attempts were only partially successful.

64. "Vier Jahre Gefängnis für Wolff: Haftbefehl aufgehoben: Die Anklage konnte keine Belastungszeugen vorführen," *Hamburger Allgemeine Zeitung*, June 7, 1949; "Sie gehen mit fleckenlosem Kleide," SS General Wolff erhielt 4 Jahre Gefängnis, *Die Welt*, June 4, 1949; "Vier Jahre Gefängnis für General Wolff: Der Angeklagte verläßt mit fleckenlosem Kleide den Gerichtssaal," *Hamburger Freie Presse*, June 4, 1949.

65. For more detail, see Lingen, *Allen Dulles*.

66. Lingen, "Conspiracy of Silence," 85.

67. Robert Wolfe, "Coddling a Nazi Turncoat," in *U.S. Intelligence and the Nazis,* by Richard Breitman, Norman J. W. Goda, Timothy Naftali, and Robert Wolfe (Cambridge: Cambridge University Press, 2005), 320, 326; E 4320/17, vol. 101, Dossier on Eugen Dollmann, Swiss Federal Archive, Bern, includes a safe pass dated November 7, 1947, U.S. Counter Intelligence Corps, Miesbach, confirmed in Bad Tölz November 12, 1947; Dollmann and Wenner escaped justice together with the help of U.S. secret service; see Institut für Zeitgeschicte (IfZ), Munich, AG TS/53/4, "Exemption of certain German nationals from denazification" (Eugen Dollmann, Eugen Wenner). See also Richard Breitman, "Analysis of the name file of Guido Zimmer," www.archives.gov/iwg/declassified-records/rg-263-cia-records/rg-263-zimmer.html.

68. Lingen, *Kesselring's Last Battle,* 211–27.

69. Klaus Naumann, "Nachkrieg als militärische Daseinsform: Kriegsprägungen in drei Offiziersgenerationen der Bundeswehr," in *Nachkrieg in Deutschland,* ed. Naumann (Hamburg: Hamburger Edition, 2001), 444–72; Friedrich Gerstenberger, "Strategische Erinnerungen: Die Memoiren deutscher Offiziere," in Heer and Naumann, *Vernichtungskrieg,* 620–33.

70. Lingen, *Kesselring's Last Battle,* 92–127.

71. The only critical memoirs were written by Frido von Senger und Etterlin, *Krieg in Europa* (Berlin: Kiepenheuer & Witsch, 1960). In retrospect, however, Senger also succumbed in his details to the temptation of heroic glory, as is shown in connection with the disarming of the Italians, in Hans Meier-Welcker, *Aufzeichnungen eines Generalstabsoffiziers 1938–1943* (Freiburg: Rombach, 1981), 218.

72. N 422 (Röttiger)/15, Anträge und Einwendungen gegen Art. 33 und 34 des Befreiungsgesetzes, Albert Kesselring, December 14, 1951, 19, BA-MA. Röttiger underlined here "that the soldiers, if these assaults should have happened and should have been committed by my troops—which is not yet proven—then they had acted out of an unleashable warrior's instinct against the brutal partisan bands and their unlawful approach."

73. N 422/15, Affidavit Hans Röttiger, December 20, 1951, 26, BA-MA.

74. This and the following passages refer to Lingen, *SS und Secret Service,* 178–87.

75. Frei, *Adenauer's Germany,* 235.

76. N 422 (Röttiger)/4, Fragment of draft study by A. Kesselring, "Fortsetzung des Krieges," January 8, 1948, BA-MA.

77. See N 422/4, statement of Röttiger on a point raised by Field Marshal Kesselring about the "continuation of the war," January 8, 1948, 8, BA-MA.

78. N 422/4, statement of Röttiger on a point raised by Field Marshal Kesselring about the "continuation of the war," January 8, 1948, 12, BA-MA.

79. N 422/4, statement by Vietinghoff to Kesselring, January 8, 1948, 14, BA-MA.

80. N 574 (Vietinghoff), Montanelli to Vietinghoff, November 26, 1949; and Montanelli to Vietinghoff, January 13, 1950, BA-MA.

81. N 574 (Vietinghoff), Vietinghoff to Montanelli, February 2, 1951, BA-MA.

82. N 574 (Vietinghoff), Vietinghoff to Montanelli, February 2, 1951, 4, BA-MA.

83. N 574 (Vietinghoff), Vietinghoff to Montanelli, February 2, 1951, 6, BA-MA.

84. Lingen, *Kesselring's Last Battle,* 248.

85. A comparison between this study and Kesselring's memoirs reveals that he incorporated the quoted passage nearly verbatim but cleaned up some of the ideological vocabulary, such as Nazi phrases like "the biggest battle for survival" and "the failure of leadership." See Kesselring, *Soldat,* 409–11.

86. Ibid., 409f.

87. See especially the correspondence found in the private papers of Friedrich Schulz, N 318, BA-MA.

88. N 422/4, Moll to Röttiger, March 20, 1953, BA-MA.

89. N 422/4, draft memorandum on cease-fire for Kesselring, July 1953, 2, BA-MA.

90. In his memoirs from 1978, Westphal once again evoked Kesserling's version of events. He writes that Vietinghoff had "temporarily turned over his command, for whatever reasons." But Westphal strongly criticizes his successor Röttiger, whom Schulz and Wentzell simply "locked up." Siegfried Westphal, *Erinnerungen* (Mainz, 1975), 340.

91. N. Bäumler, private papers, Kesselring to Bäumler, January 3, 1958, in author's collection.

92. N 1245 (Lindner)/45. Manuscript from the broadcast program "Fünf Minuten vor Zwölf" of the Nordwestdeutschen Rundfunks Cologne, written by Dr. Edgar von Schmidt-Pauli and broadcast April 25, 1955, 7:15–8:00 p.m., Federal Republic of Germany, Bundesarchiv Koblenz.

93. MC 019/72, 20 ("Secret Surrender correspondence"), Rahn to Dulles, July 1, 1965, DCMLP. This account was taken up in particular by Dulles in his later book *Secret Surrender* (see note 1). Rahn pointed out once again to Dulles in this letter the importance of this clarification.

94. Lingen, *Kesselring's Last Battle,* 274–83.

95. *Süddeutsche Zeitung,* April 22, 1955, "Der Sturz ins Dunkel: Die Sondervereinbarungen an der Italien-Front: Interview mit General der Waffen-SS Karl Wolff."

96. Marcus Riverein, "Das 'einwandfreie' Leben des Waffen-SS Generals Karl Wolff: Der Münchner Prozess gegen Himmlers Adjutanten 1964," in *NS-Prozesse und deutsche Öffentlichkeit: Besatzungszeit, frühe Bundesrepublik und DDR,* ed. Jörg Osterloh and Clemens Vollnhals (Göttingen: Vandenhoeck & Ruprecht, 2011), 323–48.

97. Allen Dulles and Gero von Gaevernitz, "'Warum kämpft ihr nicht, statt zu verhandeln?' Die Entscheidung im Unternehmen 'Sunrise,'" *Der Spiegel* 43 (1966): 139–53.

98. Even today, the fact that Albert Kesselring—of all people—was brought to trial occasions some surprise. This surprise has been voiced not only in publications issued by veterans' associations but even in encyclopedia articles. See, for example, the article "Albert Keßelring [sic]," by Thilo Vogelsang, *Neue Deutsche Biographie*

(Berlin: Propyläen, 1977), 11:542–43; Hans-Dietrich Ahrens, "Albert Kesselring," in *Alte Kameraden* 48, nos. 7–8 (2000): 8–9; and Karl-Heinz Meissner, "Gedenkfeier zum 40. Todestag des GFM Kesselring," September 2000, unpublished manuscript, Deutsche Montecassino Vereinigung.

99. Kerstin von Lingen, "Von der Freiheit der Gewissensentscheidung: Inspekteur des Heeres, Generalleutnant Hans Röttiger," in Hammerich and Schlaffer, *Militärische Aufbaugeneration*, 383–409.

Part 3

Unique Recastings in Postwar Germany

8

"I Am the Man Who Started the War"

Alfred Naujocks and His Postwar Stories
about His "Adventures"

Florian Altenhöner

"I am the man who started the war." This quote by Alfred Naujocks opens his biography written by Günther Peis. In this book, published in 1960 in London, the Austrian journalist narrates Naujocks's career with the SS and the SD. The book is full of dramatizations, faultiness, and exaggerations; yet these point to a key element of Naujocks's postwar biography, for his was the story of a perpetrator, told again and again in order to recast his wartime past of murder and crime as nothing more than an adventure.

Naujocks joined the SD in 1934 and rose within the ranks over the course of the next few years. In 1938 he was promoted to SS-*Sturmbannführer*, a rank roughly equivalent to a major in the Wehrmacht.[1] In times of peace, such a rank was hard to reach for a man of Naujocks's age—when World War II began, he was only twenty-eight years old. In January 1939 the SD-Hauptamt (SD Main Office) numbered 865 officials, and only 28 of them held SS-*Sturmbannführer* or higher ranks.[2] Even if Naujocks did not belong to the SD's inner circle around Heydrich, he was definitely part of the SD's leadership. Yet Naujocks was no ordinary high-level perpetrator; his status in the SD and the Reichssicherheitshauptamt (RSHA [Reich Main Security Office]) cannot be explained by his rank and position alone. Within the SD he was used for covert operations. Missions like the mock raid on the Gleiwitz radio

Naujocks wearing the uniform of a
SS-*Untersturmführer*, likely 1935–1936. The
photo was probably taken after the murder of
Rudolf Formis. *Quick,* September 6, 1964.

station at the beginning of World War II and the kidnapping of British intelligence officers in Venlo in November 1939 made him well known in the SD.
Some of these missions were ordered by high-ranking SS officers such as
Reinhard Heydrich, Heinrich Müller, Ernst Kaltenbrunner, Gottlob Berger,
and even Heinrich Himmler. These missions make it hard to define Naujocks
as an average perpetrator, a mere bureaucrat, or a desk murderer; his exceptional career cannot be categorized within the common types of Nazi perpetrators. He was working at his desk but also in the field as forger, kidnapper,
and assassin.

Yet even more intriguing was Naujocks's life after 1945—not his private
life during the 1950s and 1960s, but how he told and retold his SD war stories. Naujocks admitted his deeds but did not cast his personal history as that
of a perpetrator; he described himself instead as an intelligence professional
who did his duty: "I did what my Government told me to do and was decorated for it."[3]

Naujocks's postwar life resembles those of his comrades and colleagues
from the SD: internment, investigations by the Allies, and return to Ger-

many, reentering civil life—all in all a path rather untroubled by justice. Yet, unlike most other members of the SD, the SS, or the Gestapo, Naujocks was one of the very few men who told his tale again and again. In the 1950s and 1960s he did not "disappear" from public life as other SD or Gestapo officials did. Although he had murdered several people during his Nazi career, he told his story to a number of journalists. In various magazines Naujocks was presented not as a Nazi perpetrator, but rather as an adventurer. In this way his wartime activities were reduced to trivial and harmless narratives, adjusted for German postwar popular culture—Nazi pulp fiction. Magazines such as *Stern, Quick,* and *Revue* offered his past as stories, not history. In order to do that, these stories were highly selective: full of gaps, omissions, and misrepresentations, all necessary to recreate Naujocks as an adventurer; murder and other crimes were absent.

Writing an accurate account of Naujocks's postwar life is severely hampered by the lack of reliable sources. Although police officers and state attorneys interrogated him several times, their questions focused on matters of wartime guilt and not on his present life. Only a very few documents offer a window into the process of postwar recasting and the writing of a different biography as well as into Naujocks's cooperation with journalists. He received money for his assistance—but the sources available do not make clear which articles were the product of collaboration and which were more the accomplishments of the individual journalists.[4] This chapter first gives a brief overview of Naujocks's life and his career with the SD and then analyzes the representations of his biography in East and West German magazines, paying particular attention to Naujocks's own role in the recasting of his life in Nazi Germany.

Life, 1911–1966

Alfred Naujocks was born in 1911 in Kiel-Gaarden, a working-class neighborhood. His father ran a small business. At age sixteen, he left school and began an apprenticeship as an orthopedic technician. In 1930 he gave up this apprenticeship and worked as a car mechanic, because it seemed more interesting. In the summer of 1931, before his twentieth birthday, he became a member of the NSDAP and the SS. At that time the SS in Kiel was a rather small organization of some sixty to seventy members. The background for Naujock's decision to join the party and the SS is hard to determine. In 1945 he justified his decision by highlighting the increasing political tensions in his hometown, noting that he simply had to decide for one side or the other, Left or Right. Between 1931 and 1933, he took part in several street battles between Nazis and Communists, and all over town he was known as a notorious rowdy. A newspaper called him a rough fighter ("rauher Kämpfer").[5]

In the beginning of 1934, Naujocks moved to Berlin. Werner Göttsch, one of his SS comrades in Kiel, arranged a job for him with the SD-Oberabschnitt Ost (SD Superior District East), which controlled all SD operations in Berlin and the neighboring provinces.[6] Nothing qualified him for intelligence work, the SD's mainstay. Billeted by his office, he initially worked as a driver and was used as such during the so-called Röhm-Putsch in June 1934. After the war he stated that he had driven some of the people who were arrested to the barracks in Berlin-Lichterfelde, where they were executed.[7]

In January 1935 Naujocks killed the German emigrant Rudolf Formis in Czechoslovakia. For this murder, he was promoted to the rank of SS-*Untersturmführer* (lieutenant) and transferred to the counterespionage department of the SD-Oberabschnitt Ost. Little is known about the work of this department. Before the RSHA was formed in 1939, counterespionage and foreign intelligence were within the responsibility of Amt III of the SD Main Office (SD-Hauptamt), headed by Heinz Jost. In the SD's early years, no centrally organized, permanent foreign intelligence service existed, although from its beginnings there was a clear SD interest in foreign countries, especially neighboring countries.[8] Still, most contacts in foreign lands were efforts by individual SD officials. This did not change until the RSHA came into being in 1939.

In 1945 Naujocks stated that in 1935 his work consisted "almost entirely of internal espionage and the enforcement of security measures designed to protect the clandestine armaments industry. This involved the careful watching of all people known to be opposed to the regime, and considered to be at all dangerous; [they] were rounded up and either thrown into concentration camp or liquidated." After a few years, Naujocks began to work in the field of foreign intelligence. The SD's foreign-intelligence mission initially developed from cooperation with businessmen traveling abroad; the SD also used the foreign branches of German companies for intelligence purposes. Naujocks set up a network of agents operating all over Europe by contacting branches of AEG, the electronics giant. He proved himself capable and in 1937 was promoted to head of the counterespionage department in the SD's main regional office in Berlin (SD-Oberabschnitt Ost). In 1938 he was posted to the SD Main Office and was attached to the emerging foreign-intelligence department. Although he lacked expertise and language skills, he was promoted to SS-*Sturmbannführer* in March 1938 and became head of its south-eastern Europe section.[9] When the RSHA was created in 1939, Naujocks was put in charge of the technical section of the SD's foreign intelligence service. He was responsible for all of the foreign-intelligence service's technical affairs: coding and decoding, secret inks, forgery of documents and bank notes, developing radio equipment, and explosives.

The SD deployed Alfred Naujocks as a hit man, a counterfeiter, an agent, and a terrorist. On August 31, 1939, he set up the mock raid on the Gleiwitz radio station, which Nazi propaganda then used as a pretext for the German invasion of Poland. During the raid the pro-Polish Silesian Franz Honiok was killed and his body was left behind as evidence for an alleged Polish assault. Earlier in 1939, Naujocks was deeply involved with the dissolution of Czechoslovakia and the proclamation of Slovak independence.[10] He arranged for a series of bomb explosions in Bratislava that carried all the hallmarks of a Czech assault on Slovaks; they were meant to provoke an even greater rift between the two main ethnicities in the state and lead to a Slovak declaration of independence. In November 1939 he was heavily involved in the kidnapping of two British intelligence officers from the neutral Netherlands. During a shoot-out, the Dutch intelligence officer Dirk Klop was killed. From 1939 to 1941 Naujocks was involved with the forgery of British banknotes. By 1941 he was discharged from the SD after being accused of corruption; he was then drafted into the Waffen-SS. Naujocks survived the carnage of the Russian front; by 1942 he headed the Fahndungsdienst, an investigative and surveillance office focusing on economic matters such as black-market trades, in the German Military Administration in Belgium. In 1944 he was appointed head of the German counterterrorism campaign (Gegenterror) in Denmark, and in the fall of the same year he defected to the Western Allies. A British intelligence officer stated in 1945 that "over a period of many years he was regarded by the leaders of Nazi Germany as desperado and a thug who could be relied upon to carry out any mission, however dangerous and however disreputable."[11]

His discharge from the SD in 1941 meant that Naujocks lost any benefits from his SS rank and his job with the SD. A soldier like millions of other Germans, he fought in the Russian campaign until early 1942. It is quite likely that his assignment to the SS-Waffen division Leibstandarte Adolf Hitler prevented him from being deployed with one of the *Einsatzgruppen,* for their leadership was recruited mainly from RSHA officials. Consequently, he was not directly involved with the mass shootings of Jews—a precondition for recasting his biography after the war.

Despite being kicked out of Berlin, Naujocks still drew upon his contacts. After spending only a short time on the eastern front, he managed, based on his connections, to get a safe and comfortable position with the German military government in Brussels in 1942. Soon after arriving, he was charged with combating the black market and corruption. But this was only one part of his mission. At the same time he was working against General Alexander von Falkenhausen, head of the military government of Belgium. Acting on orders from Ernst Kaltenbrunner, as of 1943 head of the RSHA, Naujocks collected information to cause von Falkenhausen to be removed from his post.

After having organized Gegenterror in Denmark, Naujocks returned to Brussels. Although there is no doubt that he had been rehabilitated within the SS since his dismissal in 1941, after 1942 Naujocks's SS rank and his position in the SD are not entirely clear. The 1944 official listing of all SS officers does not mention him. But correspondence from that year reveals that he was an SS-*Sturmbannführer* (SS major) again.[12] Neither in Brussels nor in Copenhagen was he formally subordinated to an SD office. Naujocks remained in Brussels until the Allies liberated Belgium. Rather than following the retreating German troops, he went into hiding. In October 1944 he defected to the Allies, claiming membership in an Austrian Resistance movement. His defection was most probably his last mission on behalf of the SD, which wanted to undermine contacts between German and Austrian resistance groups and the Western Allies. His British interrogators were convinced that he was only posing as an Austrian and that he was in fact still working with the SD.[13]

Naujocks was interrogated in detail by American and British authorities. In 1945 he was brought to Nuremberg and testified at the International Military Tribunal regarding some of his activities.[14] In the following months, Allied authorities had to decide where Naujocks should be indicted for his crimes. There were no doubts about his character and his deeds: "Naujocks is a thug of the New Order. His crimes are many, but as murder is included among them, the question of his disposal is simplified. The man should most certainly be put to death, and it may well be that the Czech Government will be glad to discharge that duty."[15] Ultimately, it was decided to extradite him to Denmark rather than to Czechoslovakia or Poland. When Naujocks was turned over to Danish authorities in 1947, he feared a death sentence. Together with the heads of the Gestapo and the SD in Denmark, he was brought to trial in Copenhagen in 1948. But although Danish courts sentenced seventy-eight Danes to death (forty-six were executed), in the end, none of the Germans had to fear death. Their verdicts in the last instance were relatively mild. In January 1949 Naujocks was sentenced to fifteen years in prison, which an appellate court reduced to five years in 1950. Until his death in 1966, this was Naujocks's sole conviction for his crimes.

In June 1950 Naujocks was released and deported to Germany. First he returned to his hometown of Kiel but soon moved to Hamburg; he worked as a salesman, traveling five thousand miles a month, and in other jobs. In 1960 he wrote: "Today I live from hand to mouth. . . . For twenty years I had to burgle, steal, kidnap and lie. . . . All that counts with me in 1960 is that I know no other life well enough to live and that in peace I am a failure."[16] But although his postwar career was no continuation of his SD career, his life in West Germany cannot be considered a failure. Interrogated by the police in 1960, he stated that he worked as a "businessman"; in 1966 he was head of the Hamburg branch of the Erkrath-based Lichttechnische Werke GmbH firm, a company that produced neon signs.[17] There have been many assumptions about his life in West Germany, for example that "he ended his life as a one-eyed bouncer in a brothel-cum-bar in Hamburg's red light district, the Reeperbahn."[18] In the 1965 BBC documentary *The Man Who Started the War,* on the other hand, he was presented as a rather well-off, average German.[19] The documentary showed him driving a Volkswagen and described him as having "a weakness for mohair suits. He married for the second time twenty months ago and has a ten-month-old baby daughter. . . . He earns fifty pounds a week, complains that he is overtaxed. But he has enough left over to rent a sixteen guinea a week flat in one of Hamburg's most exclusive suburbs."

Even though Allied intelligence services, as well as the West German Bundesnachrichtendienst (BND [Federal Intelligence Service]), recruited many former SD and Gestapo officials, it is wrong to presume a general continuity of West German intelligence services from the Nazi past. There was no such automatic recruitment. Naujocks was not employed by any intelligence service after his release from prison in 1950, even though the federal commissioner for the Stasi Archives holds some documents showing that the East German Stasi was convinced that Naujocks worked for the BND.[20] But the sources are weak, and in any case such an affiliation seems implausible: in the 1950s and 1960s a number of articles and books were published about Naujocks. He was thus a far too prominent man to be used for any undercover work. According to Hans-Henning Crome, who in 1963 was assigned to screen the BND for war criminals, Naujocks was not among the BND's employees.[21] In Werner Göttsch's CIA file, Naujocks is briefly mentioned in the 1960s—but only with the remark "no traces."[22]

In 1962 the historian Jürgen Runzheimer interviewed Naujocks in Ham-

The historian Jürgen Runzheimer explains the course of the robbery. *Bild und Funk,* August 30, 1964.

burg while writing an article on the mock raid on Gleiwitz radio station. Naujocks, in this interview, was still proud of his work with the SD: "I was an intelligence professional beyond good and evil." Asked about Gleiwitz specifically, he said he only remembered setting up the mock raid alongside his other work. He could not remember the details because to him the raid had been "small fry" ("ein kleiner Fisch"). As an intelligence professional, he had to execute too many missions like that, he said.[23]

Not the least because of statements like these, Runzheimer regarded him as a typical intelligence officer. The historian described Naujocks as a gifted autodidact, a semi-educated man, well-spoken, and knowledgeable and conversant about a good many things. He stated explicitly that Naujocks did not give the impression of a gangster or of a rowdy, as Gerald Reitlinger had characterized him in his book.[24] Naujocks seemed to be, instead, petit bourgeois (*kleinbürgerlich*), a person who, despite his dirty collar and worn cuffs, attempted to appear like a cosmopolitan man (*weltmännisch*). At the time of the interview, Naujocks's financial situation was dire. He mentioned that once in a while a bailiff came looking for him, that he was insolvent and did not want to be found by local authorities. Runzheimer characterized him as canny and cynical but not unpleasant. He seemed to be unburdened by a conscience and ready to take any orders and to return to a life as an intelligence officer—suited equally well for U.S. or Soviet intelligence services.[25]

But even if there is no evidence that Naujocks worked for various intelligence services, there have always been speculations about his connections to the mysterious ODESSA (Organisation der ehemaligen SS-Angehörigen [Organization of Former SS Members]). Frederick Forsyth, for instance, refers briefly to Naujocks in his 1972 bestseller *The Odessa File*, in which he brought several historical characters into his plot.[26] Even if the real Naujocks was not participating in a completely fictitious ODESSA network, there is no doubt that in the 1950s and 1960s he was in touch with former colleagues from the SD. Heinz Jost, Naujocks's former superior in the SD, in 1962 still was deeply impressed by him: "Naujocks was a great comrade, someone you could always rely on."[27]

In 1966 Alfred Naujocks died from a heart attack at age fifty-four. After his release from the Danish prison, he was never charged for his crimes by a West German court. He was, however, questioned as authorities conducted various investigations into wartime crimes. In the 1960s, for example, Naujocks visited his former driver; the two men discussed the Gleiwitz and Venlo incidents before they were both interrogated about them.[28] Indeed, there were five preliminary investigations into Naujocks's actions; investigators had an eye on Naujocks because he was regarded as an expert for special missions.[29] None of the investigations led to an indictment. At the time of his death, the state attorney in Hamburg was still investigating Naujocks for the murder of Rudolf Formis in Czechoslovakia in 1935, the murder of Franz Honiok in Gleiwitz in 1939, and the shooting of Dirk Klop in Venlo in November 1939.[30]

It is quite remarkable that most of these investigations did not originate from the prosecuting authorities, but rather from the outside. In 1960 the Society of People Persecuted by the Nazi Regime (Vereinigung der Verfolgten des Naziregimes) reported Naujocks to the Central Office of the State Justice Administrations for the Investigation of National Socialist Crimes in Ludwigsburg for the murder of Rudolf Formis. It took German authorities almost three years to identify and locate Naujocks in Hamburg, which is surprising since several newspapers and magazines had written about him, mentioning that he lived in Hamburg, where he was even listed in the telephone book.[31] Regarded as a flight risk, Naujocks was arrested in July 1963 but released from custody after a few days. Both men accused, Naujocks and Göttsch, stated that Heydrich had only ordered the kidnapping of Formis, not his assassination. Both denied having fired the deadly shots and blamed each other. During his investigation the state attorney could not refute their claim that Formis's death was nothing but a failed kidnapping. Premeditation would have been a condition for a conviction of murder. In 1965 the state attorney wanted to dismiss the case, and after Naujocks's death, the case against Göttsch was dismissed in 1966. However, the state attorney had ignored a tiny detail: the SS-Dienstaltersliste, an official listing of all SS officers, reveals that both men were promoted one day after Formis's death. Naujocks became SS-lieutenant (*Untersturmführer*), and Göttsch became SS-captain (*Hauptsturmführer*). The date of these promotions indicates clearly that they had fulfilled their mission and exposes as a lie their claim of a failed kidnapping.

In 1961 Naujocks was suspected of being involved in the murder of Theodor Lessing, a German Jewish philosopher who had been assassinated by Nazis in Mariánské Lázně, Czechoslovakia, in 1933. The investigators assumed that Naujocks was the man mentioned by several witnesses but known only by his first name ("Karl"). There was no evidence that linked Naujocks to the crime, only that "Karl" was tall and blond and spoke with a north German accent. The case against him was dismissed.

In 1965 Robert Kempner, who during the International Military Tribunal at Nuremberg was assistant U.S. chief counsel and later a lawyer in Frankfurt am Main, requested that the Hamburg state attorney examine the Venlo incident of 1939; he also reported Naujocks for the murder of the Dutch intelligence officer Dirk Klop during the ensuing shoot-out. Under questioning, Naujocks and his accomplice Werner Göttsch stated that they only returned the fire Klop had opened on them. Consequently, they were accused of manslaughter rather than first-degree murder. As at the time of the investigation, this offense fell under the statute of limitations, and the case was dismissed.[32]

The investigation into Naujocks's role in the Gleiwitz raid began after the East German movie *Der Fall Gleiwitz* (*The Gleiwitz Case*) was shown in Hamburg in 1963. After a person from the audience reported Naujocks to the police for murder, the state attorney began to investigate. When Naujocks died in 1966, the case had not yet been brought to court, for at that time many details of the mock raid, for example, the identity of the person killed in Gleiwitz, were still unknown. Only by 1968 did investigators identify the victim as Franz Honiok. They then proceeded to charge in absentia Heinrich Müller, former head of the Gestapo, for the crime.

Although Naujocks told Runzheimer that he did not read about Nazi Germany, he was well informed about the statute of limitations and the Central Office of the State Justice Administrations for the Investigation of National Socialist Crimes in Ludwigsburg.[33] There is no doubt that Naujocks considered himself innocent; no statement of regret, self-doubt, or remorse by him is documented. In the 1950s he applied to German authorities for compensation for his imprisonment in Denmark. It is unknown whether this request was approved, but this episode shows that he thought he had acted dutifully and legally.

Criminal in East Germany

In August 1961 the movie *The Gleiwitz Case* (*Der Fall Gleiwitz*) premiered in East German cinemas. Blow-by-blow, the film reveals how SD officer Naujocks staged the outbreak of war in 1939 at the Gleiwitz radio station in cold blood, unaffected by any emotions. A brief flashback shows the paradigmatic life of a young Nazi: a bad student from a nationalistic home, who had conservative teachers; a member of the SS; a snitch, a torturer, and a secret agent, whose activities resulted in promotion. Besides documenting the events leading to the mock raid, the movie offers deep insights into the character of a typical Nazi.[34] The movie's story kept close to the facts known up to then. Director Gerhard Klein underlined: "We have adhered to the facts. But it is no documentary, rather a documentation with artistic means."[35] The movie was, indeed, shot at the radio station at Gliwice, and the scenes showing the raid were shot in the station's broadcasting studio.

From the beginning, reviews of the film were deeply influenced by events in Germany in the 1960s. The initial screenplay used as a framework a story about NATO maneuvers during which West German soldiers dressed in Soviet uniforms; East German propagandists clearly meant to draw attention to the unbroken continuity between Nazi Germany and the Federal Republic of Germany.[36] However, the directors' and the screenwriters' protest prevented such overt political influence on the final product. Yet even without this explicit reference, East German newspapers linked the Gleiwitz incident to current affairs. After the building of the Berlin Wall on August 13, 1961, which was labeled an "anti-fascist protective rampart" (*antifaschistischer Schutzwall*), reviews hinted that current Western actions were nothing more than continuations of fascist provocations. According to one newspaper, the movie showed the essence and the activities of the many little and big "Naujocks" who, on behalf of the West German government, were preparing for war today and who might have set up another "Gleiwitz Case"—had it not been for a world more alert and the forces of peace being stronger than ever.[37]

Most reviews alluded to the fictional character and the real Naujocks. One East German newspaper saw in Naujocks, as played by the actor Hannjo Hasse (1921–1983), exactly the disturbing mélange of blond beast and egotistic petty bourgeois rioting on the western side of the Berlin Wall.[38] To the *Neue Deutschland,* the official party newspaper of the East German Socialist Unity Party, Naujocks was an "evil piece of work" (*ein übles Subjekt*), "who repeatedly has shown himself to be a snitch, a spy, and a bruiser."[39]

This is not the place to give a complete and exhausting outline of the movie and its reception in East Germany. However, it is worth noting that, all things considered, the reviews were ambivalent. On the one hand, critics praised the achievements of the director and the cameraman; yet, on the other hand, they lamented the lack of an overt antifascist perspective. Indeed, *The Gleiwitz Case* is told without the clear assignment of roles of fascists and antifascists that were typical for the DEFA (Deutsche Film-Aktiengesellschaft), the East German state-owned film studio.[40] On the contrary, with its focus on Naujocks and his perspective, the movie refrains from any narration of Communist resistance. His antagonist is a mute, anonymous inmate of a concentration camp, who is murdered by Naujocks at the radio station. Unlike the scenario in most East German films, this man was not portrayed as a Communist hero who stood up against the forces of evil.

The Gleiwitz Case was not screened in West German cinemas, but a few privately organized film clubs presented it there. The reviews by West German newspapers were generally favorable. The rather conservative daily *Welt,* published by the Axel Springer Publishing House, usually free of any sympathies for the German Democratic Republic (GDR), praised the movie as "excellent."[41] To the *Bonner Rundschau,* the movie was an almost perfect example of a semidocumentary motion picture.[42] Notwithstanding this praise, the very few screenings caused irritations between East and West Germany. When the left-wing Friends of Nature Youth organization (Naturfreunde-Jugend) in Frankfurt am Main presented the film in October 1963, the police interrupted the screening and confiscated the reels. Their action was justified by the claim that the East German movie lacked the needed import license and that the West German motion picture rating organization run by the movie industry (Freiwillige Selbstkontrolle) had not approved the movie.[43] The East Berlin daily *BZ am Abend* was outraged: "DEFA-movie confiscated."[44] Only a few days after the incident, the movie was approved by the West German Freiwillige Selbstkontrolle after all and screened by other West German film clubs.[45]

In Hamburg in 1963, the local film club organized a presentation of *The Gleiwitz Case* and invited Naujocks to comment on the incident. The former SD officer agreed to give a factual account and to participate in a discussion.[46] East German papers interpreted the planned event as further clear evidence for West Germany's neofascist tendencies.[47] Soon the screening was canceled: Hamburg's school authority—in charge because the movie was to be screened in a school auditorium—announced that Naujocks's presence was undesirable.[48] Thereupon the *Hamburger Abendblatt* editorialized that "adult citizens, knowledgeable about the facts, should not be deprived of the possibility to encounter those men who during the 'Third Reich' co-determined the evil tragedy of our history." The article closed by stating, "We also come to terms with history by countering the statements of the persons involved. Thus the school authority's decision was ham-fisted."[49]

Adventurer in West Germany

The film incident in 1963 was by no means the first time Naujocks appeared in the West German press. The story of Naujocks's postwar public life began in 1953 when the first major article on him was published in the illustrated magazine *Stern.* The portrait was part of a serial on the alleged mysteries of World War II, entitled "The Invisible Front" ("Die unsichtbare Front"). The article was accompanied by photos of Naujocks in the 1930s but did not include contemporary photos that would have made him recognizable. The only current picture of Naujocks illustrating the article showed him in a murky tunnel, thus obscuring his features. The caption states that "nowadays" Mr. "Naujox of Hamburg" (his name was slightly altered for this piece) "does not care much for pictures anymore." He "simply wants to be left alone. He had to suffer grievously and for a long time for following official orders."[50] The article itself focused mainly on the Gleiwitz incident and presented it as a secret service operation that caused Europe's tragedy (*Europas Tragödie*).

After this, throughout the 1950s and 1960s, Naujocks was often featured in West German weekly magazines such as *Stern, Revue,* and *Quick.* The weekly news magazine *Spiegel,* for example, interviewed him in 1963.[51] One cannot overestimate the influence of journalists in shaping the popular image of Nazi Germany in the 1950s and 1960s. Their research and writing was filling gaps of the public's knowledge about the years between 1933 and 1945. Sometimes even state attorneys had to rely on articles published in popu-

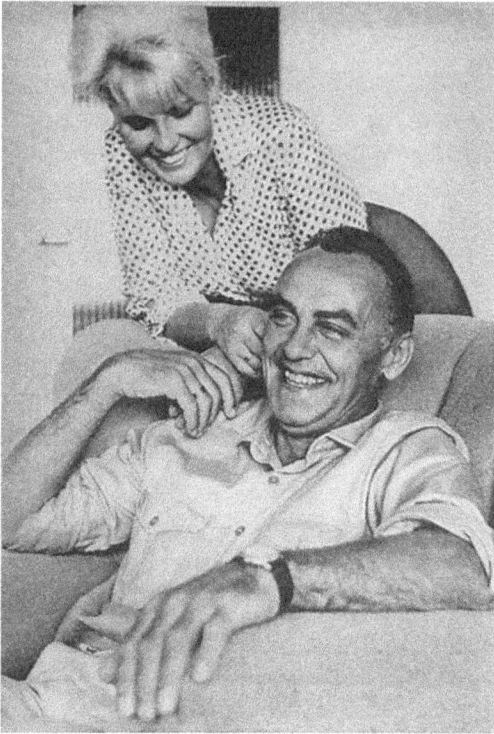

"An adventurer settles down.
. . . He is living with his
family in Hamburg, solidly
middle class (*gutbürgerlich*),
inconspicuously." *Quick,*
September 6, 1964.

lar magazines: when a serialization of Peis's book was published in *Quick* in 1964, the state attorney in Hamburg who investigated Naujocks pointed to the article for his colleague in Berlin, for he thought it contained "good information." The Berlin colleague had the article copied immediately.[52]

Naujocks clearly collaborated with journalists such as Günther Peis, who wrote the primary biography; it is obvious that the pieces were written with Naujocks's approval and his cooperation.[53] One of the few known details about this cooperation is that Naujocks received money from Peis, but the total sum is unknown. Naujocks obviously agreed with Peis's reading of his life and career, as their cooperation did not end with this book. In 1964 Peis wrote an article on Naujocks for *Quick;* Naujocks contributed up-to-date private photos showing himself with his wife and daughter. Consequently, and even though the details of their cooperation are unknown, Naujocks has to be regarded as a coauthor of the process by which his biography was recast.

About what did journalists like Peis write, and which stories about Nazi Germany were featured in magazines like *Quick?* On which crimes and which perpetrators did these articles focus, and which issues were not considered? The 1950s popular magazines like *Stern, Quick, Revue,* and *Kristall* were some of the most important forms of media in West Germany. Around 1955 their circulation peaked at 1 million, with about 20 million Germans reading these magazines every week. They not only presented current events but also featured reports on historical events, such as stories about Nazi Germany—whether as serializations of books or as so-called factual reports (*Tatsachenberichte*). There were also article series that promised the readers historical and political authenticity, although the story's protagonists were frequently fictional characters presented as if they had been historical characters.[54] It would be wrong to assume that the Nazi era was eliminated from West German popular culture. As Michael Schornstheimer has shown, these media sources told Nazi history with "excitement, commitment, and enthusiasm."[55] But they remained silent about war crimes and the murder of millions. In the popular media, as well as in the historical scholarship of the early Federal Republic, the Holocaust did not matter.

Whereas the East German film *The Gleiwitz Case* pictured Naujocks as acting cool and businesslike, almost like a machine, West German magazines presented a completely different character. According to them, he was a hot-headed secret agent and adventurer. Such portrayals left Naujocks occupying a niche of German popular culture that linked him to his actual activities but did not incriminate him. So what is an adventurer? An adventurer experiences thrilling and extraordinary adventures, behaves boldly, and faces an uncertain outcome. Adventure stories are usually not told within politicized surroundings, for the political world is nothing more than the action's framework. Within narrations that treat historical events as adventures, Naujocks's actions are thrilling stories, not crimes.

In these articles and books, Naujocks's biography was not meant to tell the history of Nazi Germany; rather, the biography served simply as a means to tell stories and anecdotes. Articles on Naujocks did not focus on reporting a historical truth in any factual sense but tended to narrate adventures. The telling and retelling of the Gleiwitz incident serves as a good example in this context, as does the shoot-out at Venlo, for the stories focus on the incidents' special-operations character and the danger and thrills associated with them. That Nazi Germany fabricated the events at the Gleiwitz radio station as a pretext for its war of aggression against Poland, leading to millions of people's deaths, falls to the narrative's wayside. The Venlo incident, an actual tactical triumph for German intelligence without any direct impact on politics, is presented as a thrilling shoot-out; not discussed are its consequences on existing (and future) contacts between the British government and the German resistance. Tall tales of spies and dangers like the ones encountered at Venlo and Gleiwitz dominate representations of Naujocks's biography and thereby of Nazi Germany. Anecdotes have replaced analysis.

From the 1950s to the beginning of the 1960s, representations of Nazi perpetrators and their activities were deeply influenced by very schematized patterns. A basic element was the clear distinction between the principal culprits like Adolf Hitler, Heinrich Himmler, and Reinhard Heydrich and the rest of Nazi Germany's population. Only the leaders were sketched as truly guilty and fully responsible for Nazi crimes. In contrast to this, most members of the police, the Gestapo, and the SD were characterized as followers or fellow travelers to varying degrees, who struggled to remain as decent and honorable throughout the Nazi era as they had been before. The Nazi era, for its part, was interpreted as outside of regular German history and demonized as a breeding ground of the abnormal, a period understandable only in terms of pathological categories.[56] The perpetrators who had committed crimes were regarded as "demons and desperadoes" with whom German society at large had nothing in common. They were seen as the absolute other or as the incarnation of evil.[57] A fine example of this mentality was the German translation of the subtitle of Gerald Reitlinger's book on the SS. Originally published as *The SS: Alibi of a Nation,* it was entitled, in German, *Die SS: Tragödie einer deutschen Epoche* (*The SS: Tragedy of a German Epoch*).[58]

In the following years, Naujocks was mentioned in several serials on Nazi Germany published by major West German magazines. These magazines presented him as a low-level subordinate to Heydrich, who, in turn, was presented as an embodiment of evil who had misled others to follow him in his crimes. Accordingly, one key element of Naujocks's representations was his relationship with Heydrich: "Reinhard Heydrich, the intelligent, ice cold Mephisto of the Third Reich had met Naujocks during the movement's time of struggle [*Kampfzeit*] in Kiel. Naujocks was the complete opposite of Heydrich. He was sentimental, emotional, full of fantasy, but with the disposition of a mercenary [*Landsknechtnatur*][;] a daredevil, a womanizer, Heydrich was intelligent, a matter-of-fact person, insensible, a clear and businesslike realist."[59] Whereas Heydrich was sketched as a man of cold reasoning, Naujocks was characterized as emotional and impulsive.

While West German authors distinguished between low-ranking bureaucrats and officers like Naujocks on the one hand and principal perpetrators like Hitler, Himmler, or Heydrich on the other, East German authors emphasized the commonality between the two groups. The lower-level men differed from their leaders mainly in the willingness to comply with orders. West German magazines presented Naujocks as an adventurer and secret agent but not as a villain. East Germany's *The Gleiwitz Case* cast Naujocks as a National Socialist and devoted follower of Heydrich and also as a cold-blooded killer. West German articles almost never described Naujocks's "adventures" as crimes with a judicial aftermath, and there was almost no coverage of the investigations against him. The *Hamburger Morgenpost* was one of the very few papers that published an article—under the headline "Three Bodies Indict!"—on the investigations against Naujocks in 1965.[60] More consistently, East German newspapers demanded a conviction, decried the failings of West German courts, and pointed out the continuities between Nazi Germany and the Federal Republic.

Episodes from Naujocks's life that might incriminate him were faded out of the narrative or were altered and sanitized. Many articles, for instance, tried to explain Naujocks's demotion in 1941 as a consequence of Heydrich's resentment against him. Heydrich was annoyed with Naujocks and thus "was looking for means to get rid of Naujocks," as a *Stern* article put it.[61] According to the same magazine, Heydrich used a present given to Naujocks by Wolfgang Sanner to charge Naujocks with corruption, to let him go from the SD, and to post him with the Waffen-SS, hoping that this would spell Naujocks's end at the front. Another article claimed that Naujocks, formerly a favorite of Heydrich's, fell out of grace on account of an affair. Allegedly, he had eavesdropped on his superior while the latter visited the infamous Salon Kitty—supposedly a brothel operated by the SD to snoop on diplomats and German dignitaries—and was therefore prosecuted by Heydrich and finally dismissed from the SD.[62]

No article or book mentioned the actual reasons for Naujocks's demotion: in 1940 he and Wolfgang Sanner were involved in selling visas to Dutch Jews. A story that involved Jewish refugees would have been too close to the Holocaust, which was only rarely referred to in those magazines—and the context of mass murder would have spoiled the recasting of Naujocks as a rather harmless adventurer.

Also omitted from these stories and articles was Naujocks's participation in a number of counterterrorism murders, as well as his conviction in Denmark for these crimes. Without any explanation, Peis, for instance, mentioned only Naujocks's SD activities in Denmark.[63] While murders of innocent civilians were ignored, stories about Naujocks's role in the deaths of Rudolf Formis, Franz Honiok, and Dirk Klop seem to be justifiable, since they were embedded into adventurous stories of spy games.

Given his role in numerous murders from the 1930s through the 1940s, Naujocks seems to have been one of the abnormal and rather pathological perpetrators. Yet he was one of the characters who was allowed a symbolic return to German society. Most articles presented Naujocks as merely an instrument of Heydrich, who treated him like "a cat [that] plays with a mouse knowing it has it in its grip."[64] In articles like these, Naujocks was presented as a perpetrator as well as a victim. On the one hand, he fell prey to the dangerous, begrudging, and alluring Heydrich, who seduced Naujocks to commit his deeds. In that sense he was a perpetrator. Yet Naujocks was also described as a victim of a German postwar society that was ungrateful and unappreciative of his sense of duty as an intelligence agent and set out to prosecute him. Naujocks considered these investigations by German authorities as an unfounded persecution that endangered his peaceful life as a family man. According to *Quick,* Naujocks "was living inconspicuously in Hamburg, neither rich nor poor, neither burdened by guilt nor boastful, one of millions of Germans."[65] The same article presented him as a husband and a family man, showing him with his young wife and his baby daughter. One of the captions read: "An adventurer settles down. . . . He is living with his family in Hamburg, solidly middle class (*gutbürgerlich*), inconspicuously."[66] Reframing the perpetrator as another victim of the war made him a fellow citizen. Recast as an adventurer by the press, a process in which he had played an important part, Naujocks could be integrated into postwar West Germany.

During the 1960s the all-too-naive coverage of the Nazi past finally but slowly came to an end in the Federal Republic, and as it did, traditional views of perpetrators and their deeds were discarded. The turning point was the trial against Adolf Eichmann.[67] The media coverage of his kidnapping (1960), his conviction (1961), and his eventual execution (1962) introduced the German public to a new type of perpetrator, the desk murderer, and broadened the perspective on the range of previously suppressed crimes. Until then Nazi perpetrators had been sketched as rather abnormal personalities, but with Eichmann all those honorable men and bureaucrats and their crimes came into focus.[68] Instead of thrilling adventures and trivial glorifications, the guilt and responsibility of the Germans more and more became the focus of coverage of the Nazi era.[69]

By the 1960s, the methods of journalists and historians changed also. Instead of using the perpetrator as the primary witness, his view was replaced by the voices of the victims and the legitimacy of documents. When the historian Jürgen Runzheimer published his inquiry into the Gleiwitz incident in the scholarly journal *Vierteljahrshefte für Zeitgeschichte* in 1962, Naujocks finally lost control over the interpretation and representation of the events.[70] Until then Naujocks had been the only eyewitness of the incident and had told and retold his story.[71] On the occasion of the twenty-fifth anniversary of the outbreak of World War II, German television began preparing a documentary on the Gleiwitz incident. The original plan held that Naujocks should be questioned about the orders received from Heydrich and the incident's details.[72] But the TV station refrained from this approach, and finally Runzheimer and a former head of the Gleiwitz radio station gave a reconstruction of the events. Even this minor detail shows the changing coverage of National Socialist crimes and the professionalization of reporting on the Nazi past in the 1960s.

In the foreword to the biography written by Günter Peis, Naujocks was enthralled by his own role in history and compared the shots fired at the Gleiwitz radio station with the assassination of the Archduke of Austria in Sarajevo that sparked World War I. He boasted that he had triggered the "chain-reaction of violence and bloodshed" and regarded himself as one of the world's most wanted men.[73] Yet he was neither wanted nor in hiding. When the book was published in 1960, he was living in Hamburg; and contrary to his big words, he was not the man who had started the war. Gleiwitz was an act of propaganda without any impact on the events. Even the German propaganda of September 1939 did not put much faith in this staged attack. Only in the first days of the conflict did the National Socialist newspapers even cover it at all. Naujocks made headlines but not history. His relevance lies not in his doings but in the story of how he and others represented their wartime crimes and thus the German past.

Notes

The author wishes to thank Katrin Paehler for her help with the translation of this chapter from German to English.

1. On the biography of Alfred Naujocks, see Florian Altenhöner, *Der Mann, der den 2. Weltkrieg begann: Alfred Naujocks: Fälscher, Mörder, Terrorist* (Münster: Prospero, 2010). This chapter is based upon this book; references are given only for specific citations.

2. R 58/8001, Federal Republic of Germany, Bundesarchiv Berlin (hereafter BA-B).

3. Alfred Naujocks, foreword to *The Man Who Started the War*, by Günter Peis (London: Odhams, 1960), 14. The book was never translated into German, but in 1964 it served as a model of a serial in German by the same author in the magazine *Quick*.

4. Outside of such public representations of his life, nothing can be said about how Naujocks told his life in private surroundings or to his family. No relatives could be traced.

5. *Schleswig-Holsteinische Volkszeitung,* December 12, 1932.

6. KV 2 (Secret Service Release), 279/129a, United Kingdom, The National Archives, Kew (hereafter TNA).

7. KV 2/280/168b, TNA.

8. On the foreign-intelligence SD before 1939, see George C. Browder, *Hitler's Enforcers: The Gestapo and the SS Security Service in the Nazi Revolution* (New York: Oxford University Press, 1996), chap. 9; Katrin Paehler, "Espionage, Ideology and Personal Politics: The Making and Unmaking of a Nazi Foreign Intelligence Service" (PhD diss., American University, 2004); Michael Wildt, *Generation des Unbedingten: Das Führungskorps des Reichssicherheitshauptamtes* (Hamburg: Hamburger Edition, 2002), 391–410.

9. KV 2/279/129a, TNA.

10. Florian Altenhöner, "SS-Intelligence, Covert Operations and the Slovak Declaration of Independence in March 1939," *Journal of Intelligence History* 8 (2008): 15–24.

11. KV 2/280/183a, TNA.

12. SSO Alfred Naujocks, BA-B.

13. KV 2/280/169a, TNA.

14. Document PS 2751, *Trial of the Major War Criminals* (Nuremberg, 1948), 31:90–92.

15. KV 2/ 279/ 129a, TNA.

16. Naujocks, foreword to Peis, *Man Who Started the War,* 14.

17. Staatsarchiv Hamburg Staatsanwaltschaft Landgericht/Strafsachen 18135/68, vol. 1.

18. Charles Whiting, *Heydrich: Henchman of Death* (Barnsley, UK: Leo Cooper, 1999), 35.

19. *The Man Who Started the War,* Gordon Thomas, TV Documentary, British Broadcasting Cooperation, London, 1965. It is not entirely clear why the BBC was interested in Naujocks in 1965. Probably the documentary's author had come across some German articles on Naujocks.

20. MfS All. P. 15667/78, Federal Republic of Germany, Archives of the Federal Commissioner for the Stasi Archives (hereafter BStU).

21. Hans-Henning Crome, message to the author, October 31, 2010.

22. RG 263 Records of the Central Intelligence Agency, ZZ 18, box 43, U.S. National Archives and Records Administration, College Park, MD.

23. Hauptstaatsarchiv Düsseldorf (hereafter HStAD) 8 I Js 532/66, Alfred Naujocks, interview by Jürgen Runzheimer, May 25, 1961. Runzheimer was researching the Gleiwitz incident on behalf of the Institut für Zeitgeschichte (IfZ) in Munich. Jürgen Runzheimer, "Der Überfall auf den Sender Gleiwitz im Jahre 1939," *Vierteljahrshefte für Zeitgeschichte* 10 (1962).

24. Gerald Reitlinger, *The SS: Alibi of a Nation, 1922–1945* (London: Heinemann, 1956), 122–23.

25. 8 I Js 532/66, Naujocks interview, HStAD.

26. On the ODESSA myth, see Uki Goni, *The Real Odessa: How Perón Brought the Nazi War Criminals to Argentina* (London: Granta, 2002); Heinz Schneppen, *Odessa und das Vierte Reich: Mythen der Zeitgeschichte* (Berlin: Metropol, 2007).

27. Rep. 382/ 1512, Heinz Jost, interview by Jürgen Runzheimer, February 17, 1962, HStAD.

28. 8 I Js 532/ 66, Handakte, HStAD.

29. NDS. 721 Hannover Acc. 90/99 Nr. 71, 71/1 and 71/2, Hauptstaatsarchiv Hannover.

30. The first investigation dates from 1950. Its reasons remain unknown; only the investigation's file number is still available.

31. MfS HA IX/11, RHE-West, Nr. 289, BStU.

32. B 162/20569, Federal Republic of Germany, Bundesarchiv Ludwigsburg.

33. 8 I Js 532/66, Naujocks interview, HStAD.

34. The screenplay by Günther Rücker, *Die Verlobte: Der Fall Gleiwitz: Texte zu 7 Spielfilmen* (Berlin: Henschel, 1988), 11–62. See the final report on the film's production, DR 117/A 131 b, BA-B.

35. *Filmspiegel* 8 (February 24, 1961).

36. DR 117 A 131 b, BA-B.

37. *Junge Welt,* July 29, 1961.

38. *Wochenpost,* September 6, 1961.

39. *Neues Deutschland,* August 27, 1961.

40. Konrad Schwalbe, "Der Fall Gleiwitz," *Beiträge zur Film und Fernsehwissenschaft* 30 (1989): 19.

41. *Die Welt,* September 14, November 27, 1963. On the censorship of DEFA movies in West Germany, see Andreas Kötzing, "Zensur von DEFA-Filmen in der Bundesrepublik," *Politik und Zeitgeschichte* 59 (2009): 1–2.

42. *Bonner Rundschau,* November 11, 1963.

43. *Frankfurter Rundschau,* October 14, 16, 1963.

44. *BZ am Abend,* October 14, 1963.

45. An assessment of the movie produced nothing subversive, and the film was approved. *Die andere Zeitung* (Hamburg), October 24, 1963.

46. Handout by the Filmklub Hamburg, HStAD 8 I Js 532/66.

47. *Thüringer Tageblatt,* March 18, 1963.

48. *Die Zeit,* September 20, 1963.

49. *Hamburger Abendblatt,* September 17, 1963.

50. Jürgen Thorwald, "Der Mann der den Krieg auslöste," *Stern,* June 7, 14, 1953.

51. *Spiegel,* November 13, 1963.

52. B Rep. 057–01 P n 5, Landesarchiv Berlin.

53. There is a photo showing Naujocks being interviewed by Peis. Lothar Höbelt,

"Günter Peis: Journalist und Historiker: Fact-Finder der Zeitgeschichte," *Das Fenster* 59 (1995).

54. Michael Schornstheimer, *Die leuchtenden Augen der Frontsoldaten: Nationalsozialismus und Krieg in den Illustriertenromanen der fünfziger Jahre* (Berlin: Metropol, 1995), 11.

55. Ibid., 211.

56. Ibid.

57. Gerhard Paul, "Täterbilder—Täterprofile—Taten: Ergebnisse der neueren Täterforschung," in *"Hier wird der Kampf des Menschen exemplarisch ausgefochten": Jüdischer Widerstand gegen den Nationalsozialismus*, ed. Hans Erler (Frankfurt am Main: Campus, 2003), 143–44.

58. Gerald Reitlinger, *Die SS: Tragödie einer deutschen Epoche* (Vienna: Desch, 1957).

59. Wolfgang Löhde, "Geld wie Heu," *Stern*, August 1, 1959. Again and again it was claimed that Heydrich and Naujocks knew each other from their times together in Kiel. But actually they first met in Berlin. It stands to reason that this piece of information was meant to enhance Naujocks's status. On the chronology of Heydrich in Kiel, see Altenhöner, *Der Mann*, 148–49.

60. *Morgenpost*, February 3, 1965.

61. Löhde, "Geld wie Heu."

62. There never was a Salon Kitty—neither Walter Schellenberg or Naujocks mentioned it during their interrogation. See Altenhöner, *Der Mann*, 283–84.

63. Günter Peis, "Der Mann, der den Krieg begann," *Quick*, October 4, 1964.

64. Thorwald, "Der Mann," June 14, 1953. On Thorwald, one of the most influential journalists of postwar West Germany, see the special issue of *Non Fiktion* 6 (2011).

65. Peis, "Der Mann," *Quick*, September 6, 1964.

66. Ibid.

67. Habbo Knoch, *Die Tat als Bild: Fotografien des Holocaust in der deutschen Erinnerungskultur* (Hamburg: Hamburger Edition, 2001), 674.

68. Ibid.

69. On the changing coverage, see Jan Erik Schulte, "'Namen sind Nachrichten': Journalismus und NS-Täterforschung in der frühen Bundesrepublik Deutschland," in *Public History: Öffentliche Darstellungen des Nationalsozialismus jenseits der Geschichtswissenschaft*, ed. Frank Bösch and Constantin Goschler (Frankfurt am Main: Campus, 2009), 24–51.

70. Runzheimer, "Der Überfall."

71. Although at least two other of Naujocks's men who had raided Gleiwitz radio station did survive the war, they never told their tale publicly.

72. 8 I Js 532/66, HStAD.

73. Peis, *Man Who Started the War*, 13–14.

9

"A Man with a Wide Horizon"

The Postwar Professional Journey of
SS Officer Karl Nicolussi-Leck

Gerald Steinacher

In his biography of SS *Obergruppenführer* Werner Best, the German historian Ulrich Herbert coined the phrase *Ausgrenzung in den Wohlstand*, or
"exclusion into prosperity." According to Herbert, "for those excluded from
politics and public service, there remained the liberal professions and business, mostly provided by old contacts, some dating from their student days."[1]
Yet there are few studies on the postwar professional lives of former high-
ranking Nazis and SS officers. Among them are Norbert Frei's edited volume
Karrieren im Zwielicht (*Careers in the twilight*) and a dozen or so biographical studies, such as Herbert's work on Best.[2] Former SS officer Karl Nicolussi-
Leck and his post-1945 network of "comrades"—business associates and
friends—exemplify Herbert's assertion that former Nazis and SS men reinvented themselves after 1945, transforming from political actors into successful "apolitical" businessmen.

Nicolussi-Leck and his circle provide excellent examples of the postwar
careers of former midlevel SS officers and Nazi officials, many of whom managed to start new careers in the private sector, especially with big German
companies in the Rhine-Ruhr region. This traditional heartland of German
industry started to boom again in the 1950s, and with it many careers took
off too. Indeed, it is striking how swiftly and easily former SS officers reintegrated into German and Austrian social and economic life. By no means an
exception, Nicolussi-Leck's career was a product of the Cold War–era eco-

nomic and political climate, and as such it is a telling case. It was not until the late 1980s that hard questions about former Nazi officials began to be asked: To what degree were they involved with the crimes of the Hitler regime? Did they bear any legal or moral responsibility for these crimes? What did they do after the war? While researching Nicolussi-Leck's postwar career, I came across a number of similar cases that can only be touched upon here. Given the scarce research on the postwar careers of former Nazis with major German companies, this chapter seeks to raise awareness of this understudied topic and begin to fill in the gap in scholarship.[3]

Karl Nicolussi-Leck was born to a South Tyrolean farming family on March 14, 1917, in Vadena (Pfatten in German), near Bolzano (Bozen in German). He was one of eleven children. The Nicolussi-Leck family had for centuries lived in the German-speaking enclave of Luserna in the northern Italian province of Trentino in the Dolomites. During World War I, the region erupted in fighting between the Austro-Hungarian and Italian armies. In May 1915, the town of Luserna was shelled from nearby Italian forts,[4] forcing the Nicolussi-Leck family to flee the front for a little farmhouse called Kreithof in Vadena. Karl attended elementary school in Kaltern and later the well-respected Franciscan *Gymnasium* in Bolzano, graduating in 1936. Soon after, he began studying law at the University of Padua.[5]

After World War I, Italy annexed the mostly German-speaking South Tyrol, which had up to that point been part of the Austrian province of Tyrol. Under Benito Mussolini's Fascist regime (1922–1943), South Tyrol's German-speaking population experienced harsh discrimination and oppression. The use of German in schools and on official documents was forbidden, and German names for towns, mountains, and valleys, and even some German surnames, were Italianized. At the same time, tens of thousands of Italians began to pour into the region. Almost overnight, the people of South Tyrol—who had for centuries belonged to the powerful German-speaking majority of the Habsburg Empire—became a powerless ethnic minority in the Italian state.[6]

After Adolf Hitler became German chancellor in 1933, many South Tyroleans placed their hopes for liberation from Italian rule in Nazi Germany.[7] They supported National Socialism mostly because it was German and rejected Fascism mostly because it was Italian. As the South Tyrolean journalist Claus Gatterer explains, in the eyes of the South Tyroleans, "Mussolini's Fascism was more human, more corrupt, and, precisely in its human imponderables, more easily predictable—but it spoke Italian; it was 'alien.' Although Nazism was more brutal and inhuman, many South Tyroleans embraced it 'because it spoke our language.'"[8] South Tyrol was a region where Italian nationalism and German nationalism met and often clashed. This ethnic conflict also burdened the relationship between Hitler and Mussolini.

Nicolussi-Leck became involved as a teenager with the Völkischer Kampfring Südtirol (VKS)—a pro-Nazi movement opposing the Italian Fascists' denationalization policy. According to his friend Christoph Pan, "When VKS leaders were exiled by the Italian rulers in 1936, three people assumed the lead in the movement. One of them was Karl Nicolussi-Leck, at the time just nineteen years old."[9] Beginning in 1933, the VKS came increasingly under Nazi influence. According to the South Tyrolean historian Leopold Steurer, from 1933 to 1939 the VKS's main goal was to lay the groundwork for the *Anschluss* (annexation) to the Third Reich by Nazifying South Tyrol through teaching and propaganda.[10]

In his curriculum vitae, Nicolussi-Leck wrote: "When I was 14 years old, I started my political career in the national fight [*Volkstumskampf*] for the South Tyrolean people and with it, my career as a National Socialist."[11] Nicolussi-Leck soon became one of the leading and most active members of the VKS. On his SS documents, he listed his profession as "political leader and organizational head of the Nazi movement in South Tyrol."[12] He received an appropriate ideological education in Germany at the NS-Schulungsburg in Krössinsee. His superiors ascribed to him a "leader's personality and comradeship." His commitment to Nazi ideology was described as "firm and clear."[13]

Four months after accepting German citizenship in January 1940,[14] Nicolussi-Leck enlisted in the Waffen-SS.[15] "The Second World War had started," wrote Christoph Pan about his friend's decision, "and Karl Nicolussi volunteered immediately after the *Option* . . . because he thought that the war had to be won by Germany if his homeland, South Tyrol, was not to be lost for good."[16] In November 1941, SS-*Scharführer* Nicolussi-Leck was sent to officer-candidate training at the SS-Junkerschule in Bad Tölz. On April 20, 1942, he was promoted to SS-*Untersturmführer*.[17]

SS Man Becomes War Hero

On May 1, 1943, Nicolussi-Leck assumed command of the newly formed Eighth Company of the Viking Division's Fifth Panzer Regiment, a tank unit that initially consisted of volunteers and was chiefly deployed on the eastern front.[18] Formed in 1940, the Viking Division comprised ethnic German, Flemish, Dutch, Belgian, Danish, Swedish, Norwegian, and Finnish soldiers, most of whom had fought earlier against the Soviet Union as volunteers in a kind of "Germanic Army."[19] Armed with the new Panther tanks and a deep sense of comradeship, Nicolussi-Leck turned his company into "a tight-knit unit."[20] Just six months later, on November 9, he was promoted to SS-*Obersturmführer*.[21]

On January 26, 1944, while on leave, he married the politically active Maria Troy (nicknamed Mutz) of Bolzano. She was a senior leader in the League of German Maidens (Bund Deutscher Mädel), the girls' wing of the Nazi youth movement. Nicolussi-Leck's friend Robert Kukla, himself a high-ranking Nazi, vouched for the bride's Aryan and pro-Nazi background. Karl and Maria could not marry before receiving authorization from the SS in Berlin; thus by the time of their wedding, their daughter Reinhilde had already been born.

By March 1944, Nicolussi-Leck had rejoined his company and set off for the eastern front on a special assignment in the Ukrainian city of Kovel, which was encircled by strong Soviet forces. The German defenders inside the city were poorly armed and consisted of mostly railway men and supply troops. Nicolussi-Leck received orders to break through the Soviet forces, get into the city, and hold out until the siege could be broken. His unit's advance was slow and incurred heavy losses. After ten hours, the group had covered barely half the distance to the city. The situation looked hopeless, and the officers received orders to withdraw. Determined to get inside the city, however, Nicolussi-Leck ignored the orders. Heavy snowfall covered the group's advance, enabling it to penetrate the encirclement. Once inside the city, Nicolussi-Leck's men fought successfully for a week against the far superior Soviet forces, securing the orderly retreat of the German defenders and wounded soldiers.[22] In honor of his courage at Kovel, in April 1944 Nicolussi-Leck was awarded the Knight's Cross of the Iron Cross—one of the Third Reich's highest decorations—and Nazi propaganda in South Tyrol celebrated his heroism.[23]

After the German defeat at Stalingrad and Reich propaganda minister Joseph Goebbels's announcement of "total war," all available home-front forces were mobilized. In a telegram to SS chief Heinrich Himmler on February 3, 1943, the South Tyrolean Nazi leader Peter Hofer declared his willingness to "completely mobilize the forces of the *Volksgruppe.*" Nicolussi-Leck, who had been criticizing the South Tyroleans' unwillingness to mobilize for the Third Reich and accusing them of *Verschweizerung* (Swissification), was a key proponent of this crusade. In all his speeches, he voiced support for the SS as the "elite troop of the Reich."[24]

Nicolussi-Leck's wartime service showed his daring and fearlessness, qualities that also served him well in his postwar life. During the last year of the war, he served with distinction while leading his tank company. He was promoted to SS-*Hauptsturmführer* in January 1945 and awarded the German Cross in gold in March 1945 after being wounded several times on the eastern front.[25] In early April 1945, Nicolussi-Leck was transferred with a unit of 150 men from Hungary to northwest Germany. After fighting fierce battles while retreating, Nicolussi-Leck finally gave the order in mid-April to dissolve the unit. Each soldier had to make his own way home. Nicolussi-Leck and most of his men either surrendered or were captured and then interned in U.S. prisoner-of-war camps in Austria and Germany.[26]

In 1947 Nicolussi-Leck was released from the Glasenbach camp near Salzburg and began to work as an "escape agent" for SS men and Nazis fleeing to South America via Italy. Like Nicolussi-Leck, they had been interned for two years in Glasenbach. "The American internment camp for the bad Nazis [was] well known all over Austria," remarked one former SS man.[27] The friendships forged in the confines of Glasenbach evolved into escape networks. In the period leading up to their escapes, the "bad Nazis" were less concerned with politics than with camaraderie and mutual assistance, keys to starting over after 1945. One Glasenbach prisoner wrote, "We are closely connected and help each other as much as we can."[28] Indeed, groups of SS comrades helped one another, mostly to start over at home but also to emigrate overseas. Word began to spread that SS men were escaping from Europe, and the group from Glasenbach knew there must be a reliable friend facilitating the getaways—Karl Nicolussi-Leck.

From Prisoner to Escape Agent: The Man behind ODESSA

After his release from Glasenbach, Nicolussi-Leck returned to Bolzano and soon met former SS-*Hauptsturmführer* Horst Carlos Fuldner, a German Argentine who was one of the masterminds behind Nazi escape assistance in Italy. Fuldner acted as a liaison with the Argentine immigration office to secure visas and employment for the fugitive Nazis.[29] He had contacts all over Italy, notably along the route to Genoa via the Brenner Pass. The U.S. Central Intelligence Agency knew about Fuldner and his activities. One CIA document stated: "An Argentine-born SS leader named Fultner (aka Fuldner or Fuster), was reported to be Col. Gonzalez' liaison with the Argentine Office of Immigration. In 1948, Fultner was made a member of the Argentine Immigration Delegation for Europe, and was stationed in Genoa. From this key position he was able to help many Wehrmacht, Gestapo, and Waffen-SS veterans to enter Argentina."[30]

In a 2004 interview, Nicolussi-Leck recounted that after he got to know Fuldner in 1947 in Italy, Fuldner revealed that he was helping to smuggle people out of Europe and into Argentina. Nicolussi-Leck agreed to assist him. The two became friends, and even late in life Nicolussi-Leck spoke with respect of "Don Carlos."[31] They were ideal complements for each other. Nicolussi-Leck knew many SS men and smugglers, and he was familiar with the safe routes across the Austrian-Italian border. He and his network escorted the fugitives over the border to Genoa, and Fuldner handled the next stage of the journey. Nicolussi-Leck worked with former Nazis and their family members as well as the smugglers, coordinating his efforts with Fuldner and the Argentine authorities.

Nicolussi-Leck was one of the most important organizers of escape assistance via Italy for Nazi fugitives. Among those whom he smuggled into Italy and then hid in Bolzano were the well-known Luftwaffe fighter pilots Hans-Ulrich Rudel, Adolf Galland, and Herbert Bauer.[32] The Argentine government under Juan Perón—desperate for specialists, particularly technicians, in every profession—welcomed German experts with open arms.[33] Nicolussi-Leck knew this. Fuldner had told him that "Perón was going to buy out all of Germany" and bring the German experts to Argentina.[34] Indeed, it was likely Nicolussi-Leck who guided colleagues of airplane designer Kurt Tank, who went on to build the first fighter jet for the Argentine air force, over the Brenner Pass to Bolzano.[35] Holocaust perpetrators like Adolf Eichmann also escaped overseas via South Tyrol. Eichmann and other high-ranking Nazis received new papers and new identities from the town of Tramin (Termeno). This is how Eichmann became the South Tyrolean "Riccardo Klement" from Bolzano.[36] We still don't know who provided these Nazi criminals with new papers and identities, but certain possibilities should be researched further. One of the closest friends of Nicolussi-Leck was the former Nazi official Kurt Heinricher. Heinricher was the brother-in-law of Viktor Walch, who belonged to the richest and most influential families in Tramin and was the powerful *Nazi-Kreisleiter* (district leader) there. Is this just a remarkable coincidence?[37]

The escape route via Austria and Italy was an open secret. A 1953 CIA document stated that "many Wehrmacht and SS veterans went from a center in Munich through Innsbruck, Bern and Rome, to Beirut and Damascus. Some of those going to Spain and South America also passed through Rome. A transit and recruiting center existed there under the protection of German [actually, Austrian] Bishop Alois Hudal."[38] The Austrian police believed that the flight of Nazis across the Brenner Pass was controlled and financed by a "secret organization." As early as 1949, after receiving tips about well-organized Nazi human-smuggling operations, the Austrian Public Prosecutor's Office launched an investigation that uncovered Nicolussi-Leck's escape network and even caught some smugglers, including Nicolussi-Leck's brother-in-law. It was not until 1969, however, that the Austrian government connected Nicolussi-Leck's group to the mythical Organisation der ehemaligen SS-Angehörigen (Organization of former SS members), known as ODESSA. That year, the Austrian Ministry of Justice placed a new cover page titled "ODESSA Organization" in the file for the Tyrolean human smugglers.[39]

Nicolussi-Leck himself longed to start a new life "away from ruined Europe." His professional and political prospects in South Tyrol were bleak. Because of his Nazi past, the Italian government very likely refused to restore his citizenship. A business career in Argentina seemed to be a realistic alternative. In a 2004 interview, Nicolussi-Leck said that the Argentines had invited him to go to Argentina.[40] So, in 1948, using the same routes along which he had guided so many others, Nicolussi-Leck headed for South America via Italy.

On August 31, he applied for a Red Cross travel document in Rome together with the family of Luftwaffe officer Otto Behrens.[41] Nicolussi-Leck had no need to lie on his application forms. He could declare his citizenship truthfully: he was "stateless." But he had no proof of identity. Fortunately, he had close contacts with the Fascist Croatian priest Krunoslav Draganović in Rome. According to Nicolussi-Leck, "the good Father Draganović was the most important contact and colleague of Fuldner's in Italy."[42] On the morning of August 31, 1948, Nicolussi-Leck met with Draganović in Rome. The Vatican aid mission for refugees issued Nicolussi-Leck a letter of recommendation, and Draganović himself signed his application for the Red Cross travel document. Nicolussi-Leck and his wife were placed on Draganović's list of 169 Croatians and received their visas for Argentina as "Croatians." Nicolussi-Leck deliberately left his nationality of origin open, saying only that he was stateless and that his place of birth was "Wadena" (Vadena). The lack of data seemingly enabled Draganović to present him as an ethnic German from Croatia.[43]

Once their papers were in order, Nicolussi-Leck and his wife and daughter immigrated to Argentina. With Fuldner's help, Nicolussi-Leck became a business manager for a group of industrial designers that included former Wehrmacht, Luftwaffe, and Nazi technicians and other experts who had formed the Compañía Argentina para Proyectos y Realizaciones Industriales (CAPRI).[44] As early as 1950, Nicolussi-Leck worked in agricultural planning, probably within the framework of CAPRI, for the Argentine provinces of Tucumán and Santiago de Estero. In 1952 in Buenos Aires, he founded Nicolussi-Leck Aspersión, a watering-system company, which was a great success.[45] He also lectured on thermodynamics at Buenos Aires University. At this point, Nicolussi-Leck and Fuldner shared an office on the sixth floor of 375 Avenue Córdoba in Buenos Aires. Their firms in the Argentine capital employed former Nazis and even war criminals such as SS-*Brigadeführer* Hans Fischböck.[46] Nicolussi-Leck and his comrades in Argentina won numerous contracts from President Perón and quickly established new companies.

A New Beginning Abroad: The Mannesmann Era

The origin of Nicolussi-Leck's connection with the powerful Düsseldorf-based corporation Mannesmann AG is unclear, but it most likely began in Argentina, perhaps while he worked as an agricultural-machinery salesman (a job he acquired through his acquaintance with Ferdinand Porsche) for Porsche-Diesel-Motorenbau, a division of Mannesmann.[47] Mannesmann was one of Germany's biggest enterprises. According to sociologist Rolf Wiggershaus, "Mannesmann was not just any company. It was a founding member of the Anti-Bolshevik League and financed the Nazi Party. During the Second World War, it took over factories in occupied countries."[48]

Several high-ranking Nazis had successful careers with Mannesmann after the war. Wilhelm Zangen, a key figure in the German war economy, was the supervising chairman of the board of Mannesmann's pipe company from 1948 to 1952, chairman of Mannesmann AG from 1934 to 1957, and supervising chairman of Mannesmann AG from 1957 to 1966. So integral was he to the firm that Mannesmann proudly commemorated Zangen's accomplishments in 1990 with his portrait under the general motto "Continuity within Change."[49] Yet Zangen, who had joined the Nazi Party in 1937, had served in myriad positions for the Reich, including director of the Reichsgruppe Industrie, substitute director of the Reichswirtschaftskammer (the Reich's economic ministry), and war industry leader.[50] His name was even on the U.S. list of suspected Nazi criminals to be called to justice, but he never was. Instead, in 1956 he received the Bundesverdienstkreuz mit Stern (Federal cross for merit with star) from the West German government. The historian Tim Schanetzky makes the point that "in this context, the processes carried out in Nuremberg after 1947 against a total of 36 owners, leaders and managers of the concerns Flick, IG Farben and Krupp could be interpreted as a symbolic and substitute accusation of the German Industry."[51]

In addition to Zangen, SS-*Obersturmbannführer* Bernhard Baatz, ex-leader of the Einsatzkommando 1 and commander of the Sicherheitspolizei and the SD in Estonia, became director of Mannesmann-Wohnungsbau-gesellschaft in Duisburg.[52] And, at Zangen's urging, in 1962 Egon Overbeck, ex-officer of the Wehrmacht chief of staff, was made general director of Mannesmann ("through a *Zangengeburt"*—a forceps delivery—according to the German weekly *Der Spiegel*).[53]

Despite a short interruption owing to war damages and Allied intervention, Mannesmann managed to reconstruct its international organization by 1949 and to open sales offices in the United States and Canada.[54] It also quickly resumed its operations in Argentina and Brazil. U.S. authorities recognized that Argentina was the perfect locale for German interests: "The German commercial and political penetration in Argentina went so deep that it was disturbed only slightly by Germany's military defeat. Neither domestic nor foreign anti-Axis forces were able to induce the Argentine government to take effective action against the principal German [businesses] which had provided funds and cover for Nazi operations."[55]

Notwithstanding Allied interferences, Mannesmann regained the Sociedad Tubos Mannesmann in Buenos Aires, with its numerous branch offices in Argentina as well as in Chile and Brazil. Soon Mannesmann's Milan-based partner company Dalmine established a pipe factory in Argentina. According to Zangen, "The demand increases steadily. Who satisfies it is another question. It is impossible to stop a country from industrializing, and the international concerns must ask themselves if they will deal with the question. Mannesmann will always be present in foreign countries." Mannesmann also hoped to profit from Perón's ambitious plans for modernizing Argentina. Zangen talked about *Entwicklungshilfe* ("assistance in development").[56] Nicolussi-Leck later explained that "Mannesmann . . . was very interested in regaining its influence all over the world."[57]

It was not only in Argentina that former SS men helped one another professionally. In Europe, groups of former Nazis set up thriving businesses, sometimes working with their friends in South America. Perón's escape assistants in Italy again played a key role. Connections from Germany, Italy, Spain, and Argentina often came together in companies and SS circles in South Tyrol. Thus the borderland evolved from an escape hub into a business hub. A good example is the company Mengele & Steiner in Merano (Meran) and Ora (Auer). Founded in 1969, it was probably established to provide financial security for Nazi doctor Joseph Mengele's wife and son, who had returned from South America and settled down in South Tyrol. In South Tyrol, Mengele's family could rely on old networks. Joseph Mengele himself had escaped justice in 1949 under the alias "Helmut Gregor," thanks to a South Tyrolean ID from the town of Tramin.[58] Like other companies of former comrades in South Tyrol, the Mengele & Steiner Company sold German agricultural equipment in Italy and elsewhere. Harvesters with the company name "Mengele" were soon seen on farms all over Alpine Europe.

Many former Nazis in South Tyrol who needed jobs turned to the agricultural sector.[59] There were ideological networks within the South Tyrolean farming community, which was in large part organized into the Chief Agricultural Association (Landwirtschaflicher Hauptverband).[60] These networks were hardly secret. Based on information provided by local anti-Nazis, the British consulate in Bolzano reported to the embassy in Rome in May 1949 that "the headquarters of the Nazi movement in S. Tyrol is the exhotel Sti[e]gl at Bolzano, now occupied by the 'Hauptverband Landwirtschaftlicher Genossenschaften' (Consorzio delle Co-operative Agricole), a very powerful body[;] the prominent Nazis inside this body [include] . . . Nicolussi."[61] These associations, which were based on friendship, a shared worldview, and business interests, lasted until the 1980s. Nicolussi-Leck's close comrades included Michael (Much) Tutzer, Ferdinand (Ferdl) Lauggas, and Paul Hafner. Tutzer and Nicolussi-Leck may have known each other since their school days.[62] SS-*Sturmmann* Tutzer was one of the top organizers of the Nazi movement in South Tyrol. In 1943, he wrote to his SS superiors: "In 1939, I had to interrupt my university studies, since, due to the . . . relocation of our South Tyrolean people, I had to put myself [completely] at the service of the secret Nazi movement, of which I had been a member since 1933, and in the *Landesführung* (regional direction) since 1934. I could contribute significantly to the achievement of a unique adherence to Germany of the South Tyrolean people."[63]

Tutzer had worked closely with South Tyrolean Nazi leader Peter Hofer, had attended courses on Nazi ideology for "political leaders" at the Ordensburgen in Sonthofen, Krössinsee, and Erwitte, and was decorated with the Alte-Kämpferwinkel.[64] In May 1942, he was severely wounded in the Soviet Union and hospitalized in Italy. SS-*Hauptsturmführer* Robert Kukla and Nicolussi-Leck intervened on his behalf so that he could obtain leave to complete his *Diplomvolkswirt* (economics degree).[65]

Ferdinand Lauggas was also a leading figure in the VKS who was educated

Paul Hafner in Spain. Courtesy of
MOSOLOV-P, "Hafner's Paradise." Special
thanks to Günter Schwaiger.

in the Reich—political courses in Rossiten in 1935 and in Berlin-Hubertus-höhe in 1937, and ideological training at the Ordensburg Hohenwerfen in 1943. He listed his profession that year as "leader for political training in the *Volksgruppenführung.*"[66] Lauggas later became *Nazi-Kreisleiter* of the Bolzano district during the German occupation of Italy in 1943–1945.

Like Nicolussi-Leck, Paul Hafner attended the Franciscan *Gymnasium* in Bolzano and grew close to the leading South Tyrolean Nazis before World War II. After obtaining German citizenship in 1940, Hafner transferred to the Hegelhaus *Gymnasium* in Berlin. It was there that he became a fervent Nazi.[67]

Like other enthusiastic young South Tyroleans, Hafner volunteered for Hitler's war; he joined the Waffen-SS in 1941,[68] initially serving in the SS-Polizei-Ersatz-Bataillon Dresden.[69] In 1942–1943, he fought in the ranks of the Waffen-SS-Gebirgsdivision Nord at the Finnish-Soviet border.[70] Hafner was wounded several times there and was highly decorated for his efforts. Beginning in September 1943, he attended the SS-Junker School[71] and then Oberjunkerlehrgang officers' training, both in in Bad Tölz in southern Germany.[72] The following summer, he became an instructor at the SS-Junker School in Bad Tölz, where he helped to set up the SS Grenadier Division Nibelungen, one of the last SS squads.[73] Like so many others, he spent several months in U.S. custody as a POW. After he was released, he studied business at the University of Innsbruck and graduated in 1949. The combination of his academic studies and his contacts from his SS days positioned him well for a prosperous postwar career.

With a Little Help from Their Friends

Nicolussi-Leck's companies provided a livelihood and a professional community for many former Nazis and SS men. In 1950 in Bolzano, Nicolussi-Leck and Tutzer founded the Aedes-Landmaschinen agricultural machinery company, which sold German agricultural equipment in Italy.[74] Later that year, Tutzer and Nikolaus Christanell, owner of Tenax Import-Export in Bolzano, founded the successful Allgemeine Beregnungsgesellschaft mbH (ABG)—also known as Società Generale Pioggia—which installed sprinkler systems and made and distributed irrigation devices in Italy and abroad.[75]

Nicolussi-Leck was at the time still in Argentina working in the field of irrigation, but his comrades in Italy kept him informed about the status of joint agricultural projects in the homeland as well as politics and the "Südtiroler Volkskörper." In a letter to Nicolussi-Leck in Buenos Aires, they wrote: "Best greetings from your comrades at the firm; they work like crazy."[76] Given his close ties with his colleagues in Europe, Nicolussi-Leck was also probably involved with the founding of ABG. His friend Ferdinand Lauggas was certainly in on it from the start.[77]

When Nicolussi-Leck returned from Argentina in 1953, he was named general manager of ABG. He remained in control of the Argentine firm Nicolussi-Leck Aspersión as well and made sure that the two companies were not competing with one another, noting that ABG's work was primarily in "the Italian Republic, the Balkan States, the Near East, and North Africa."[78] As head of ABG, Nicolussi-Leck did not forget about the old "combatants in the national struggle" for South Tyrol. He found Hafner a position as technical director with ABG, and in 1954 Nicolussi-Leck made Kurt Heinricher an authorized representative of the company.[79] Heinricher had been an important Nazi activist in South Tyrol and was de facto head of the northern Italian province of Trento during the Nazi occupation in 1943–1945.[80] Heinricher defined himself as *gottgläubig* (an adherent to Nazi ideology). His teachers in a 1940 course on Nazi ideology in Krössinsee had praised him as "very knowledgeable in all areas of Nazi *Weltanschauung*" and considered him to be a good candidate for *Kreis-leiter* (Nazi district leader) or *Gauamtsleiter* (a high official in Nazi provincial governments).[81]

In 1955, Georg Thaler, an Austrian and former SS-*Unterscharführer* who was close to Nicolussi-Leck, became a special representative for ABG.[82] Five years later, he was promoted to technical director, and in 1964 he became Nicolussi-Leck's second-in-command. The chair of the supervisory board, Anton Lun of Bolzano, had attended courses at the Nazi Ordensburg Sonthofen in 1940 and in Hohenwerfen in 1943. He stated that he had been involved in the "illegal movement" of South Tyrolean Nazis in 1943 and had served as the economic expert for the Südtiroler Volksgruppe.[83]

Former SS-*Hauptsturmführer* Nicolussi-Leck's postwar career was flourishing. His position at ABG was secure, and his businesses were profitable, particularly in the area of irrigation devices. The market was strong for Mannesmann sprinklers, used for agricultural frost protection and irrigation, from South America to North Africa. According to the introduction to Mannesmann's 1959 irrigation handbook, "The increasing linkage of agriculture and economic development presents serious challenges, the solution to which must interest industry as well as agriculture. Mannesmann addresses these challenges, further developing techniques with its two firms, Porsche-Diesel Motorenbau and Mannesmannregner."[84]

In December 1956 ABG became a subsidiary of Mannesmannregner GmbH in Düsseldorf, thereby substantially raising ABG's capital.[85] During these years, Mannesmann's business in Italy was growing, and Nicolussi-Leck frequently worked with Dalmine and other companies in Milan.

In 1954, Hafner took a job with Mannesmann in Spain. He gained the position via his connections with Nicolussi-Leck and Tutzer.[86] Hafner started a small company for Mannesmann in Madrid that specialized in sprinkling systems for large agricultural areas and sold Mannesmann pipes. It eventually branched out into steel silos and livestock breeding. The company grew to fifty-five employees. Hafner later started a pig-breeding business, boasting in 1999 that "there are at least two million Spanish pigs with German blood in their veins today!"[87] He also joined the community of exiled Nazis in Madrid—playing tennis with SS officer Otto Skorzeny, who had rescued the imprisoned Benito Mussolini in 1943, and becoming acquainted with the prominent Belgian Waffen-SS officer Leon Degrelle.[88] Hafner also attended yearly gatherings of former Waffen-SS members to celebrate Hitler's birthday. Even as an old man, he still believed that "Hitler [was] the most important personality in world history."[89] He also denied the Holocaust to the end, claiming that "Hitler was not the gasser of the Jews, but the promoter of efforts to establish the Jewish national state (Zionism!). . . . Not a single Jew was killed because he was a Jew! For me, Hitler is the savior of Europe and Christianity!"[90]

The Irrigation Expert

While Hafner had found his "paradise" in Spain in the late 1950s, Nicolussi-Leck was busy making money in Europe, North Africa, and South America in the field of multipurpose irrigation. He planned large irrigation complexes in Italy and, in 1956, obtained a huge contract for ABG for the construction of the then-largest irrigation installation in Europe, on the Natz plateau in South Tyrol.[91] Frost-protective irrigation for the booming apple plantations in South Tyrol was lucrative business. Together with Mannesmann, ABG built the gigantic installation in a year,[92] making Nicolussi-Leck a good deal of money. He worked closely with Mannesmann's specialists on this project as well as with old Nazi acquaintances, including the former Nazi party member Baron Rudolf von Unterrichter, who was secretary of the supervisory council for the Natz project.[93] The assistant chief of the project, Hans Stanek, had been mayor of Bressanone (Brixen) during the Nazi occupation of South Tyrol.[94] The Natz plant opened in 1958. Among the honorary guests at the grand opening were members of the state parliament such as Mario Günther von Unterrichter, a key figure in the Consorzio Agrario, and Italian MP Karl Tinzl, who had been governor of South Tyrol during the Nazi occupation,[95] as well as many representatives of Mannesmann AG from Düsseldorf.[96]

Nicolussi-Leck held a variety of positions with Mannesmann through the years. He was active as technical consultant for the agricultural-industrial sector for Mannesmann AG Düsseldorf from 1957 until 1969. Between 1960 and 1967, he also worked for Mannesmann-Export GmbH in Düsseldorf.[97] When Mannesmann bought Nicolussi-Leck Aspersión in 1957, Nicolussi-Leck purchased some property near Bolzano with the profits and built a villa, using Mannesmann pipes.[98] In 1957, Nicolussi-Leck's old friend Michael Tutzer started the Bolzano-based Agria Mediterranea firm, which distributed agricultural machinery as a subsidiary of the Agria Werke engineering works in Möckmühl in Germany.[99] In 1959, with the assistance of Mannesmann, ABG's capital was again increased, and the board gave Nicolussi-Leck "far-reaching authority" to realize the firm's ambitious goals.[100]

Over the years, ABG changed names several times. In 1963, it was renamed Mannesmann Agrotecnica GmbH.[101] "This decision was made," wrote Nicolussi-Leck, "by the Administrative Council, in order to adapt the name of our company to those of the Mannesmann branches that are active in the agricultural sector in European countries."[102] According to Hafner, in 1972 the Mannesmann main office in Germany decided to abandon its business in agriculture and instead to focus on major projects such as oil pipelines from Siberia to Germany. With the retreat of Mannesmann from the agricultural sector, Mannesmann Agrotecnica slid into crisis. In 1978, it was dissolved.

The Master in the Magic Garden

Nicolussi-Leck's career both before and after 1945 must also be understood in the context of the history of South Tyrol. There was no *Stunde Null* ("zero hour") in the region in May 1945, making this borderland a unique case—a region shaped more by a continuity between the prewar and postwar periods than by a break. According to the historian Leopold Steurer, "In South Tyrol, the year 1945 did not signify a hiatus in the political, cultural, and spiritual life of the region, but rather a continuity."[103] The Allied Military Government in northern Italy ended in December 1945. Thus South Tyrol became one of the first German-speaking regions in Europe not under Allied control. Given the lack of an Italian Nuremberg, attempts at denazification and defascistization in the region were extremely short-lived, aborted in their infancy. Former Tyrolean Nazis and former Italian Fascists soon returned to their posts in public life. The dividing line in South Tyrol continued (and continues) to be drawn along ethnic lines: Italian *or* German. Nazism was identified with the pro-German camp and Mussolini's Fascism with the pro-Italian camp. As a consequence, South Tyrol is one of the few regions in the world (and maybe the only one) where one could be an anti-Fascist and a Nazi at the same time. And many German-speaking South Tyroleans were. On the other hand, many Italians in the region were anti-Nazi but pro-Fascist. Nicolussi-Leck's purported "anti-Fascism" was therefore nothing other than anti-Italianism born of his desire to defend the German identity of his native South Tyrol. The Südtiroler Volkspartei, the political party of the German-speaking South Tyroleans, received the "Wehrmacht generation" with open arms after the war. But Nicolussi-Leck had no postwar political career in mind.

In the postwar era, Nicolussi-Leck, who always valued his wartime relationships, shifted his focus away from politics and toward culture. He founded the South Tyrolean Educational Center (Südtiroler Bildungs-zentrum) and the Museum for Modern Art in Bolzano, of which he was a long-serving president. His villa, not far from Bolzano, became a center of cultural life in South Tyrol. Over the years, he adorned the walls of his home and the surrounding vineyard with modern art and resided there like a "Master in the Magic Garden."[104]

Nicolussi-Leck was also at the center of the community of former Wehrmacht soldiers and members of the Waffen-SS in South Tyrol. In 1975, the *Südtiroler Kamerad,* the journal of war veterans, wrote of him: "Karl Nicolussi needs no introduction. He is one of those comrades who has distinguished himself a thousand times on the battlefield, as his decorations clearly show."[105] He gave big speeches at gatherings commemorating the "war heroes." In 1959, for example, he spoke together with former high-ranking SS officer Sepp Dietrich, who had been commander of the Leibstandarte Adolf Hitler. Dietrich was sentenced to life in prison at the 1946 trials in Dachau for his involvement in the murder of U.S. prisoners of war during the Battle of the Bulge in December 1944–January 1945.[106] But Dietrich spent only a few years in prison and was released in 1955. In 1957 he was again imprisoned but set free six months later—just in time for the memorial speech with Nicolussi-Leck.[107] This was not unusual. German Nazi officials and SS officers could expect a warm welcome in the *German* South Tyrol (*im deutschen Südtirol*). It is therefore not surprising that during the Cold War era, many former Wehrmacht and SS officers, including SS general Karl Wolff, Himmler's right-hand man, enjoyed their vacations in South Tyrol and were even sometimes honored by the local tourist boards.[108] Until his death, Nicolussi-Leck liked to spread the word about his "heroic deeds," sending all over the world letters with an enclosed autographed picture of himself wearing his SS uniform.

The French author Jean Mabire, in his book on the Viking tank division, wrote that Nicolussi-Leck "came from Bozen in South Tyrol—which the Italians renamed Bolzano in 1918—and thus belongs to the southernmost German minority abroad. He was a young, slim, and dashing daredevil, who waged war in the Hussar style, and attracted attention even in the battles in the Caucasus."[109] Journalist Erich Kern, a former SS-*Sturmbannführer,* described him as a "courageous officer from South Tyrol" who, with the help of his unit, "destroyed the plans of the Communists, at least [in Kovel]."[110] Indeed, Nicolussi-Leck's reputation for being a "reckless daredevil" endures even today, especially online.

In 2006 Nicolussi-Leck wrote the foreword to Peter Mooney's book *Waffen-SS Knights and Their Battles.* He seems to assert there that Hitler's war of aggression and annihilation was fought based on "knightly ideals" and that the majority of SS officers served honorably: "In the first decades after the war, the public opinion was stamped by the victor powers. Nevertheless, not even in those days could it be denied that also on the German side brave soldiers and extraordinary achievements were to be found. . . . Actions led by knightly ideals occurred far more often than the opposite and after sixty years of peace this should be admitted in any publication."[111] Nicolussi-Leck died in the summer of 2008 as a respected art collector in Bolzano. In an obituary in the widely read South Tyrolean cultural magazine *Der Schlern,* not a word was devoted to his involvement in National Socialism, the SS, or helping Nazis to flee Europe.[112] His obituary in the South Tyrolean daily *Dolomiten,* titled "A Man with a Very Wide Horizon," stated that the "greatest patron of the arts in South Tyrol has died . . . at the age of 91." The notice makes no mention of his Nazi and SS past, but the accompanying photo of his funeral shows members of a veterans' organization carrying a large flag bearing the black cross of the Wehrmacht.[113]

The impressive postwar business careers of Karl Nicolussi-Leck and his circle of former Nazi and SS comrades were not exceptions. By 1950, as the Cold War was heating up, the Nuremberg trials and the denazification process were basically over, and former SS men and Nazis were being integrated into the new democratic society—whether they had renounced Nazism or not. And few did. According to Ulrich Herbert, "West Germany's political and economic ascent offered former Nazi elites the possibility of . . . social elevation"; thus "their interest in new political activity, particularly in the field of the radical right, constantly diminished."[114] Yet this does not mean that they ever broke with their Nazi pasts, or that they stopped glorifying their "heroic deeds" during Hitler's Thousand Year Reich. At heart, Nicolussi-Leck, Michael Tutzer, Ferdinand Lauggas, and Paul Hafner remained proud Nazis until the end. At least it very much appears that way.

Just as Cold War geopolitics encouraged the reintegration of former high-ranking Nazis, West Germany's postwar "economic miracle," or *Wirtschaftswunder,* rewarded the old comrades for staying out of politics and tolerating democracy. Private-sector enterprises, including the large German industrial firms on the Rhine and the Ruhr, offered many opportunities to men such as Nicolussi-Leck. Rudolf Rahn, the former Nazi ambassador to Italy, became secretary-general of the Coca-Cola Company in Essen; Konstantin Canaris, commander of the security police in Belgium, found a position with Henkel-Werke in Düsseldorf. Both Werner Best, the former Reich commissioner for occupied Denmark, and the former Hitler Youth leader Heinz Wilke worked for the Hugo Stinnes Company in Mülheim.[115] Franz Hofer too, the former *Gauleiter* of Tyrol, became an entrepreneur in Mülheim, and SS-*Oberführer* Reinhard Hoehn became West Germany's leading expert in management training.[116]

Even more than Germany in some ways, South Tyrol presented an ideal locale for starting over after the war. There was no Italian Nuremberg, no consequent defascistization or denazification. Moreover, the war had done nothing to diminish the long-standing tensions in the region between German-speaking South Tyroleans and Italian immigrants, which continued to dominate the sociopolitical landscape there. Thus many Tyroleans, Austrians, and Germans of the Wehrmacht generation revered men like Nicolussi-Leck for having fought on what they deemed to be the "right" side of important battles—opposing the Italianization of South Tyrol during Mussolini's Fascist regime and battling against the Soviets during World War II. Given the impressive "anti-Fascist" and "anti-Communist" credentials of Nicolussi-Leck and his ilk, West German companies could easily and openly welcome such men into their folds.

Notes

Much of the detailed information about Nicolussi-Leck and other Nazi businessmen in this chapter is new and based on years of research. All the former Nazis discussed in this chapter were highly respected businessmen, men of the arts, or men of politics after 1945. Thus I faced considerable resistance and am therefore extremely grateful for the support that I did receive while researching this paper. In particular, I would like to thank Leopold Steurer and Franz Haller for sharing important archival and library sources. Tracy Brown did a fantastic job copyediting and proofreading this chapter. For the larger context, see Gerald Steinacher, *Nazis on the Run: How Hitler's Henchmen Fled Justice* (Oxford: Oxford University Press, 2011). All translations are mine or are taken from *Nazis on the Run*.

1. Ulrich Herbert, *Best: Biographische Studien über Radikalismus, Weltanschauung und Vernunft, 1903–1989* (Bonn: J. H. W. Dietz, 1996), 475.

2. Norbert Frei, ed., *Karrieren im Zwielicht: Hitlers Eliten nach 1945* (Frankfurt am Main: Campus, 2001). See also the important book by the Austro-American historian and political scientist Kurt P. Tauber, *Beyond Eagle and Swastika: German Nationalism since 1945*, 2 vols. (Middletown, CT: Wesleyan University Press, 1967). For South Tyrol, see Gerald Steinacher, "Ausgrenzung in die Wirtschaft? Karrieren von Südtiroler Nationalsozialisten nach 1945," in *Regionale Zivilgesellschaft in Bewegung/Cittadini innanzi tutto: Festschrift für/Scritti in onore di Hans Heiss*, ed. Hannes Obermair, Stephanie Risse, and Carlo Romeo (Bozen: Folio 2012), 272–86.

3. A recently published novel by Ferdinand von Schirach dramatizes such a case. In *The Collini Case: A Novel* (New York: Viking, 2013), Schirach tells the story of a former SS officer and war criminal who after 1945 went on to an impressive career in a big German company, before his dark past caught up with him.

4. Franz Kurowski, *Panzer Aces II: Battle Stories of German Tank Commanders of WWII* (Mechanicsburg, PA: Stackpole, 2010), 273.

5. Christoph Pan, *Lebenspfade des Karl Nicolussi-Leck* (Bozen: Eigenverlag, 2007), 3–4.

6. See Stefan Lechner, *"Die Eroberung der Fremdstämmigen"*: *Provinzfaschismus in Südtirol 1921–1926,* Veröffentlichungen des Südtiroler Landesarchivs 20 (Innsbruck: Wagner, 2005). See also Leopold Steurer, *Südtirol zwischen Rom und Berlin 1919–1939* (Vienna: Europa, 1980), 256–71. See also Martha Verdorfer, *Zweierlei Faschismus: Alltagserfahrungen in Südtirol 1918–1945* (Vienna: Gesellschaftskritik, 1990). See also Günther Pallaver and Leopold Steurer, eds., *"Deutsche! Hitler verkauft euch!"*: *Das Erbe von Option und Weltkrieg in Südtirol* (Bozen: Raetia, 2010).

7. See Anthony E. Alcock, *The History of the South Tyrol Question* (London: Joseph, 1970); Rolf Steininger, *South Tyrol: A Minority Conflict of the Twentieth Century* (New Brunswick, NJ: Transaction, 2003).

8. Claus Gatterer, "Südtirol 1930–45: Eine politische Landschaftsskizze," in *Aufsätze und Reden* (Bozen: Raetia, 1991), 171–84 at 177; see Steinacher, *Nazis on the Run,* 33.

9. Pan, *Lebenspfade des Nicolussi-Leck,* 5–6.

10. Leopold Steurer, "Südtirol zwischen schwarz und braun," in *Teilung Tirols: Gefahr für die Demokratie,* ed. Godele von der Decken, Beiheft Sturzflüge No. 23 (Bozen: Redaktion "Sturzflüge," 1988), 25–40, at 32.

11. RG 242, Berlin Document Center (BDC), RuSHA, roll E0295, File Karl Nicolussi-Leck. "Als 14-jähriger begann ich meine politische Betätigung im Volkstumskampf der Südtiroler und damit meinen Werdegang als Nationalsozialist." Handgeschriebener Lebenslauf Karl Nicolussi-Leck, 1943, U.S. National Archives and Records Administration (hereafter NARA).

12. RG 242, RuSHA, roll E0295, File Karl Nicolussi-Leck, R. u. S.-Fragebogen, Karl Nicolussi-Leck, NARA.

13. RG 242, RuSHA, roll E0295, File Karl Nicolussi-Leck, Personalbogen und Beurteilungsbogen Karl Nicolussi-Leck, Schulungsburg Krössinsee, November 23, 1940, NARA.

14. RG 242, EWZ, Südtiroler, File Karl Nicolussi-Leck, Einbürgerungsurkunde, January 24, 1940, NARA.

15. His SS number was 56.834.

16. Pan, *Lebenspfade des Nicolussi-Leck,* 8–9.

17. Kurowski, *Panzer Aces,* 276.

18. Ibid., 401.

19. Bernd Wegner, *Hitlers politische Soldaten: Die Waffen-SS 1933–1945: Leitbild, Struktur und Funktion einer nationalsozialistischen Elite* (Paderborn: Ferdinand Schöningh, 1997), 310ff., 315.

20. Kurowski, *Panzer Aces,* 401.

21. RG 242, RuSHA, roll E0295, File Karl Nicolussi-Leck, Gebührniskarte, NARA.

22. Kurowski, *Panzer Aces,* 401.

23. Ibid., 398, 400.

24. Leopold Steurer, "Meldungen aus dem Land: Aus den Berichten des Eil-Nachrichtendienstes der ADO (Jänner–Juli 1943)," *Sturzflüge: Eine Kulturzeitschrift,* 29–30 (1989): 31–125, at 41. See also Ulrich Saft, *Der Krieg in der Heimat: Das bittere Ende zwischen Weser und Elbe* (Langenhagen: U. Saft, 1990), 54.

25. RG 242, RuSHA, roll E0295, File Karl Nicolussi-Leck, Gebührniskarte, NARA; see Wilhelm Eppacher and Karl Ruef, *Hohe Tapferkeitsauszeichnungen an Tiroler im Zweiten Weltkrieg,* Veröffentlichungen des Innsbrucker Stadtarchivs 6 (Innsbruck: Stadtmagistrat, 1975), 41.

26. Saft, *Der Krieg in der Heimat,* 53–66.

27. U.S. Army Intelligence and Security Command, Fort George G. Meade, MD. Counter Intelligence Corps, 430th CIC Detachment, City of Vienna, "Subject: Possible Nazi Group," June 1948 (Confidential), Records concerning Austrian Intelligence Services ZF400006WJ, Department of the Army, 107ff. (copies of the files in the possession of the author).

28. U.S. Army Intelligence and Security Command, Fort George G. Meade, MD. Counter Intelligence Corps, 430th CIC Detachment, City of Vienna, Letter from Ambros Murbitzer, Vienna, Civil Censorship Group Austria, APO 777 U.S. Army, Vienna Station, March 20, 1948 (Confidential).

29. Uki Goñi, *The Real Odessa: How Perón Brought the Nazi War Criminals to Argentina* (London: Granta, 2002), 65ff.

30. RG 263, Records of the Central Intelligence Agency, 62-00865R, box 0003, folder 0003, 22, NARA. "German Nationalist and Neo-Nazi activities in Argentina," July 8, 1953.

31. Karl Nicolussi-Leck, video interview by Franz Haller and Gerald Steinacher, May 10, 2004, Film-Archives Franz Haller, Meran, Italy. Statement by Franz Haller, July 10, 2010.

32. Steinacher, *Nazis on the Run,* 236ff.

33. For more information about Argentina and its immigration policy after 1945, see Holger Meding, *Flucht vor Nürnberg? Deutsche und österreichische Einwanderung in Argentinien 1945–1955* (Cologne: Böhlau, 1992).

34. Nicolussi-Leck interview.

35. Jürgen Leyerer, *Argentinien der Flieger und wir* (Vienna: Liber Libri, 2010), 300–301.

36. Steinacher, *Nazis on the Run,* 52ff.

37. RG 242, EWZ Südtiroler, File Viktor Walch, born in Tramin on April 22, 1906, NARA; Walch attended the *"Schulungsburgen"* Sonthofen and Hohenwerfen and is referred to in these files as *"Kreisleiter der Bewegung."* Trude Heinricher married Viktor Walch on July 15, 1933. See letter from the town of Tramin to the author, August 14, 2012. See also obituary for Ida Heinricher in *Dolomiten,* July 29, 1942. Thanks to Leopold Steurer, Meran, for important information and materials in this case.

38. RG 263, 62-00865R, box 0003, folder 0003, 11–12, "German Nationalist and Neo-Nazi Activities in Argentina," July 8, 1953, NARA.

39. Bestand Landesgericht, Akt 10 Vr 873/49, Bundesministerium für Inneres an das Landesgericht Innsbruck, "Betr.: Organisation 'Odessa,'" July 1, 1969, Tiroler Landesarchiv.

40. Nicolussi-Leck interview.

41. "Titres de Voyage CICR 1945–1993," application 83,520, International Committee of the Red Cross (ICRC) Archive, Geneva; Barbara Kummer-Behrens, Mosaiksteine aus Rom. Ein alter Filmstreifen führt zurück in die Vergangenheit, Manuskript, 2003; see also "Titres de Voyage CICR 1945–1993," application 83,520, "Application for a Travel Document for Gertrud Behrens," August 31, 1948, ICRC Archive.

42. Nicolussi-Leck interview.

43. "Titres de Voyage CICR 1945–1993," application 83,519, Application for a Red Cross travel document for Karl Nicolussi-Leck, Italian Red Cross in Rome, August 31, 1948, ICRC Archive.

44. RG 263, 62-00865R, box 0003, folder 0003, 22, "German Nationalist and Neo-Nazi Activities in Argentina," July 8, 1953, NARA.

45. Nicolussi-Leck interview; Uki Goñi, email, July 28, 2010.

46. Uki Goñi, email, July 28, 2010.

47. Nicolussi-Leck interview.

48. Rolf Wiggershaus, *The Frankfurt School: Its History, Theories, and Political Significance* (Cambridge, MA: MIT Press, 1994), 479.

49. Horst A. Wessel, *Kontinuität im Wandel: 100 Jahre Mannesmann 1890–1990* (Düsseldorf: Mannesmann-AG, 1990), 211.

50. Ernst Klee, ed., *Das Personenlexikon zum Dritten Reich: Wer war was vor und nach 1945?* (Fischer: Frankfurt, 2005), 690, states that Zangen joined the SS and the Nazi Party in 1927; Zangen's Nazi Party membership card at the National Archives in College Park gives the year 1937. I found no evidence for his membership in the SS in the BDC files at NARA; see RG 242, NSDAP Ortsgruppenkartei, roll 2065, NARA. NSDAP-Karteikarte Wilhelm Zangen, born September 30, 1891.

51. Tim Schanetzky, "Unternehmer: Profiteure des Unrechts," in Frei, *Karrieren im Zwielicht,* 73–129, at 84.

52. Herbert, *Best,* 475. See also Schanetzky, "Unternehmer," 73–129, at 96.

53. "Mannesmann AG: Zangen-Geburt," *Der Spiegel,* October 17, 1962, 37.

54. Wessel, *Kontinuität im Wandel,* 284.

55. RG 263, 62-00865R, box 0003, folder 0003, 17, "German Nationalist and Neo-Nazi Activities in Argentina," July 8, 1953, NARA.

56. Wessel, *Kontinuität im Wandel,* 284–85.

57. Nicolussi-Leck interview, "Mannesmann war damals interessiert wieder in der Welt Fuss zu fassen."

58. Steinacher, *Nazis on the Run,* 41ff.

59. Steurer, "Südtirol zwischen schwarz und braun," 25–40, at 36.

60. See also Walter Pichler and Konrad Walter, *Zwischen Selbsthilfe und Marktlogik: Geschichte des Genossenschaftswesens in Südtirol* (Bozen: Raetia, 2007).

61. British Consulate in Bolzano to British Embassy in Rome, Savingram, May 27, 1949 (Confidential), copy in the possession of the author.

62. Karl Kompatscher, interview by Franz Haller, February 5, 2011.

63. RG 242, EWZ, Südtiroler, roll S028, Tutzer, Michael, April 18, 1916, Much Tutzer CV, June 18, 1943, NARA.

64. RG 242, EWZ, Südtiroler, roll S028, Tutzer, Michael, April 18, 1916, "Personalbogen Ordensburg Sonthofen," 1940, NARA; RG 242, EWZ, Südtiroler, roll S028, Tutzer, Michael, April 18, 1916, "Beurteilungsbogen Reichsschulungsburg Erwitte," 1941, NARA.

65. RG 242, EWZ, Südtiroler, roll S028, Tutzer, Michael, April 18, 1916, Robert Kukla and den Reichskommissar für die Festigung des deutschen Volkstums, June 18, 1943, NARA.

66. RG 242, EWZ. Südtiroler, roll 0006, Lauggas, Ferdinand, November 9, 1906, Personalbogen Ferdinand Lauggas Schulungsburg Hohenwerfen, February 17, 1943, NARA.

67. Georg Mair, "Ein Leben als Nazi," *FF-Südtiroler Illustrierte*, May 2008, 32–37.

68. His SS number was 490,167.

69. RG 242, SS Lists, roll SS-A0006, p. 1732, List number 1396 Hafner, Paul, February 24, 1923, "Liste der zur Waffen-SS einberufenen volksdeutschen Freiwilligen," March 1941, NARA.

70. RG 242, SS Lists, roll SS-A0009, pp. 2798ff., Hafner, Paul, February 24, 1923, "Amt Führerausbildung, SS-Gebirgsdivision Nord," 1942, NARA.

71. RG 242, SS Lists, roll SS-A0012, p. 4199, Hafner, Paul, February 24, 1923, "Kriegs-Junkerlehrgang an der SS-Junkerschule Tölz," October 7, 1943, NARA.

72. RG 242, SS Lists, roll SS-A0014, Hafner, Paul, February 24, 1923, "Kriegsjunkerlehrgang an der SS-Junkerschule Bad Tölz," March 14, 1944, NARA.

73. RG 242, SS officers, roll 051A, SS File Paul Hafner, February 24, 1923, NARA; CV Pablo Hafner für die Universität Innsbruck, July 3, 1999. Copy in possession of author.

74. Steurer, "Südtirol zwischen schwarz und braun," 25–40, at 36.

75. Verbale, assemblea straordinaria, December 22, 1953, Anhang, Statut der Generalpioggia, Bolzano-Bozen, Files of the company Agrotecnica Bolzano, Handelskammer Bozen, Archiv.

76. Letter to Karl Nicolussi-Leck, September 17, 1951 (copy in possession of the author).

77. Files of Agrotecnica Bolzano, Gründungsakt, Allgemeine Beregnungsgesellschaft mbH, August 25, 1950, Handelskammer Bozen, Archiv.

78. Pan, *Lebenspfade des Nicolussi-Leck*, 15; files of the company Agrotecnica Bolzano. Verbale, assemblea straordinaria, December 22, 1953, Anhang, Statut der Generalpioggia, Bolzano-Bozen, Handelskammer Bozen, Archiv.

79. George Tinzl, interview by the author, September 6, 2004.

80. RG 242, NSDAP-File, Zentralkartei, Rolle H058, Kurt Heinricher, June 15,

1911, NARA. See Michael Wedekind, *Nationalsozialistische Besatzungs- und Annexionspolitik in Norditalien 1943 bis 1945—die Operationszonen "Alpenvorland" und "Adriatisches Küstenland,"* Militärgeschichtliche Studien, 38 (Munich: Oldenbourg, 2003), 124.

81. RG 242, EWZ, Südtiroler, Rolle M008, Dr. Kurt Heinricher, June 15, 1911, Personalbogen Schulungskurs Krössinsee, November 24, 1940, NARA.

82. RG 242, RuSHA, Rolle G0197, SS-File Georg Thaler, July 7, 1923, NARA; Tinzl interview; files of the company Agrotecnica Bolzano, Procura Speciale, November 15, 1955, Handelskammer Bozen, Archiv.

83. RG 242, EWZ, Südtiroler, Rolle 0014, File Dr. Anton Lun, August 31, 1906, NARA.

84. Mannesmannregner GmbH, *Beregnungs-Taschenbuch,* 2nd ed. (Düsseldorf: Mannesmann, 1959), foreword, 3.

85. Files of the Agrotecnica Bolzano, Verbale di Assemblea Straordinaria, Repubblica Italiana, December 28, 1956, Handelskammer Bozen, Archiv.

86. Mair, "Ein Leben als Nazi," 32–37.

87. CV Pablo Hafner for the University of Innsbruck, March 7, 1999 (copy in possession of author). "Für Spanien ein großer Erfolg, denn es gibt so mindestens 2 Millionen spanische Schweine mit deutschem Blut in den Adern!"

88. Mair, "Ein Leben als Nazi," 31–37, at 31. See Paul Hafner on Leon Degrelle in the documentary *Hafner's Paradise,* 2007, directed by Günter Schwaiger. Special thanks to Günter Schwaiger for helping me with this research and for the photo of Hafner in Spain. Courtesy of Mosolov-P (Günter Schwaiger). For more information about the documentary, see www.mosolov-p.com.

89. Paul Hafner in *Hafner's Paradise:* "Ich betrachte Hitler als die bedeutendste Persönlichkeit der bisherigen Weltgeschichte."

90. Pablo Hafner to the University of Innsbruck, February 24, 1999 (copy in possession of the author). "Hitler war nicht der Judenvergaser, sondern der Förderer des jüdischen Nationalstaatsbestrebens (des Zionismus!). . . . Nicht ein einziger Jude wurde umgebracht, weil er ein Jude war! Für mich ist Hitler der Retter Europas und des Christentums!"

91. Ernst Überbacher, *Wasser auf durstige Äcker: 50 Jahre Bodenverbesserungskonsortium Natz* (Brixen: Weger, 2008), 42.

92. *Dolomiten,* June 19, 1958, 9; Überbacher, *Wasser auf durstige Äcker,* 67.

93. RG 242, NSDAP-Zentralkartei, File Rudolf Unterrichter, May 2, 1914, Aufnahme: January 1, 1940 (handwritten correction, December 1, 1940), NARA.

94. Überbacher, *Wasser auf durstige Äcker,* 41. See Wedekind, *Nationalsozialistische Besatzungs- und Annexionspolitik,* 147.

95. See Wedekind, *Nationalsozialistische Besatzungs- und Annexionspolitik.*

96. *Dolomiten,* June 19, 1958, 9; Überbacher, *Wasser auf durstige Äcker,* 67.

97. Pan, *Lebenspfade des Nicolussi-Leck,* 13, 15.

98. Nicolussi-Leck interview.

99. Handelskammerauszug aus dem Firmenregister bezüglich der "AGRIA Mediterranea Spa," March 9, 2005, Handelskammer Bozen. Cf. Company charter for "AGRIA Mediterranea," December 13, 1957, articles of incorporation, "AGRIA Mediterranea," Handelskammer Bozen, Archiv.

100. Akten der Firma Agrotecnica Bolzano, Verbale di Assemblea Straordinaria, August 31, 1959, Handelskammer Bozen, Archiv.

101. Akten der Firma Agrotecnica Bolzano, Schreiben Karl Nicolussi-Leck an Walter von Walther, Handelskammer Bozen, December 1962, Handelskammer Bozen, Archiv.

102. Akten der Firma Agrotecnica Bolzano, Karl Nicolussi-Leck to Walter von Walther, Handelskammer Bozen, December 1962, Handelskammer Bozen, Archiv.

103. Steurer, "Südtirol zwischen schwarz und braun," 25–40, at 37.

104. Marina Kramper "Meister im Zaubergarten," *Bunte*, May 26, 2007, www.stern.de/reise/europa/hochfrangart-der-meister-im-zaubergarten-589622.html.

105. Quoted by Leopold Steurer, foreword to *Die versteinerten Helden: Kriegerdenkmäler in Südtirol,* by Elmar Heinz (Bozen: Raetia, 1995), 7–12, at 11.

106. For more information on the Malmédy case, see James J. Weingartner, *A Peculiar Crusade: Willis M. Everett and the Malmédy Massacre* (New York: New York University Press, 2000); James J. Weingartner, *Crossroads of Death: The Story of the Malmédy Massacre* (Berkeley: University of California Press, 1979); John M. Bauserman, *The Malmédy Massacre* (Shippensburg, PA: White Mane, 1995).

107. Mair, "Ein Leben als Nazi," 32–37, at 33.

108. For Karl Wolff, see Kerstin von Lingen, *SS und Secret Service: "Verschwörung des Schweigens": Die Akte Karl Wolff* (Paderborn: Schöningh, 2010).

109. Jean Mabire, *Die SS-Panzer-Division "Wiking"* (Eggolsheim: Dörfler, 2002), 282–97, here 282.

110. Erich Kern, *Kampf in der Ukraine 1941–1944* (Göttingen: Plesse, 1964), 134.

111. Karl Nicolussi-Leck, foreword to *Waffen-SS Knights and Their Battles: The Waffen-SS Knight's Cross Holders,* vol. 1, *1939–1942,* by Peter Mooney (Atglen, PA: Schiffer, 2008), 7–8.

112. Christoph Pan, "In Memoriam Karl Nicolussi-Leck," *Der Schlern,* August 2008, 48–49.

113. "Ein Mann mit sehr großem Weitblick," *Dolomiten,* September 3, 2008, 17. "Der wohl größte Kunstmäzen Südtirols war am vergangenen Samstag 91-jährig verstorben."

114. Herbert, *Best,* 475.

115. Ibid.

116. Tim Schanetzky, "Unternehmer," 73–126, at 116. For postwar networks, see also Nina Grunenberg, *Die Wundertäter: Netzwerke der deutschen Wirtschaft 1942–1966* (Munich: Siedler 2006).

10

Revision of Life Story/Revision of History

Gertrud Slottke, from National Socialist
Coperpetrator to Expellee Official

Elisabeth Kohlhaas

National Socialism's women's and gender history has witnessed a particularly productive phase in the past few years. The majority of these studies show a broad spectrum of participation in National Socialist crimes by nonpersecuted women. Having documented the mobilization of women for the war—both on the "home front" and in German-occupied Europe[1]—scholars have focused on women who could be considered perpetrators or coperpetrators, despite concerns about the terminology's appropriateness; this is particularly true for women in the SS and the police.[2]

The current scholarship also considers the post-1945 period but largely focuses on the judicial treatment of women's (co-)perpetration. Questions as to how denazification took place and whether and how women were punished by Allied or German courts stand at the fore.[3] The impact of female gender roles and stereotypes of female perpetration on these judicial proceedings plays an important role in these investigations as well.[4] Additional studies consider gender-specific aspects of memory, commemoration, and writing about National Socialism.[5]

Many female perpetrators and coperpetrators had a simple answer to this volume's guiding question of how individuals hushed up their Nazi past and recast it into a presentable biography: they simply did not encounter this problem. Very few women were held responsible for their participation in Nazi crimes or genocide and punished for it rather than simply acquitted. Female participation in crimes often escaped the judicial category of guilt. Most strongly affected by the search for postwar justice were those women who, as doctors, nurses, and orderlies, took part in the euthanasia program, thereby committing murder, as well as women who worked as concentration camp guards, such as Irma Grese, sentenced to death in the first British Bergen Belsen trial and executed in December 1945. However, no woman stood trial in front of the International Military Tribunal at Nuremberg. And among the 209 defendants during the Subsequent Trials, only two women could be found: the physician Herta Oberheuser and the "special representative" of the SS-Lebensborn, Inge Viermetz.[6] And even though the IMT had declared the Gestapo a criminal organization, it had also extended a blanket exemption from this designation to personnel in charge of "non-official routine tasks"—in effect, all of the Gestapo's female administrative and office staff.

This chapter focuses on the Gestapo employee Gertrud Slottke. It investigates how this particular (co-)perpetrator dealt with her past after the end of the war and how she recast her (co-)perpetration in order to go on to an unblemished existence for most of the next twenty years. During the war, Slottke worked as a clerk (*Sachbearbeiterin*) for the Jewish Section (Judenreferat) of the Gestapo in the Netherlands. Even though she was only an administrative employee, she gained exceptional influence that substantially exceeded her formal standing.[7] As an eager desk murderer, she energetically carried out her part in the persecution and deportation of the Dutch Jews.

After the war, Slottke, who hailed from Danzig, remade herself into an active functionary of the expellee organization Bund der Danziger in Württemberg, a province in West Germany. This voluntary activity became the most important element of her life for the next twenty years. In the 1960s, though, her past caught up with her. Jointly with her former supervisors, she was brought to trial at the Landgericht München in 1967; in the then much-noted lawsuit, she was sentenced to several years in a women's penitentiary. Slottke was thus one of the very few female former Gestapo employees who stood trial in the Federal Republic of Germany.

Following a brief biographical sketch, this chapter discusses Slottke's life in Nazi Germany and in the 1950s and 1960s. It focuses on her work in the Netherlands, describes the scope of her work in the Jewish Section, and analyzes the exact type of her (co-)perpetration. Subsequent sections draw attention to the judicial side of Slottke's post-1945 biography: initially, the

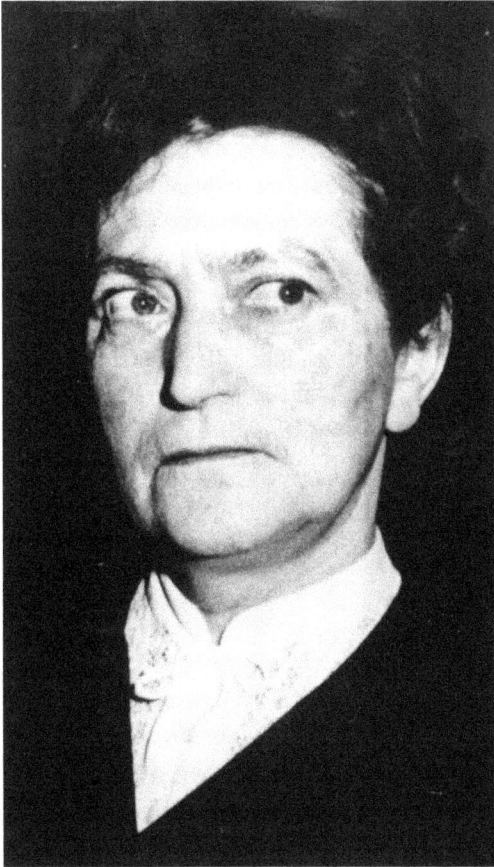

Gertrud Slottke, 1967.
Image Bank, Image no. 37269,
WW2/NIOD, Netherlands
Institute for War, Holocaust
and Genocide Studies,
Amsterdam.

main topic is denazification, and Slottke's self-image as a victim is what first becomes visible. Next, I turn my attention to her trial in 1967, especially her defense strategies and the perspective of the Munich court on Slottke's role as a perpetrator. The final section focuses on her activism for expellees—the first time ever that the Women Services Section (Frauenarbeit) of the Bund der Danziger becomes a topic of historical investigation; I am particularly interested in gaining a perspective on Slottke's understanding of her voluntarism. This discussion makes use of the term *Handlungsräume* (scopes for action), which was coined in German women's history in the late 1990s, to investigate women's participation in Nazi Germany. It postulates that nonpersecuted women could be found "at vastly different places, differently far removed from the centers of power" in Nazi Germany.[8] The question, then, becomes how women acted in these different places. This investigation of

Gertrud Slottke not only uses the concept of *Handlungsräume* for her activities in Nazi Germany but also applies it in the postwar period.

This inquiry into Slottke is based on archival sources—most notably the documents from her denazification proceedings and those dealing with the later trial in Munich. Unfortunately, Slottke left no private papers.[9] However, many of her own statements can be found in those judicial files, giving us some sense of her voice in the process of investigation and recasting. Despite their judicial origin, these statements have to be treated with the greatest care, for they can be characterized best as apologias. Yet, they allow insights into Slottke's attitudes after the war all the same. Also of importance are the trial reports by Robert Kempner, who participated in the Munich trial, and Heiner Lichtenstein, who observed it.[10] On Slottke's work for the Bund der Danziger, its newsletter serves as the main source.

Interest in Working Abroad—Slottke's Biography until 1941

Gertrud Slottke was an experienced secretary, almost forty years old, when in 1941 she took her position in the Netherlands. She was unmarried and had thus far lived with her parents in Danzig.[11] Born in 1902 in Sensburg, East Prussia, she was the oldest daughter of a peasant-artisan family. She spent her early years with her three younger siblings and her parents on different mills in the West Prussian countryside; in 1913 the family settled in Danzig, where her father, a miller, became the manager of a flour factory. After attending school, she and one of her sisters were tutored privately. Subsequently, for one year she attended a trade school for girls. Like many other young women, she thus, in a comparatively short time, acquired an education that allowed her to take on simple secretarial positions—as opposed to the multi-year office-apprenticeship path.[12] After finishing trade school in 1917, she worked for many years as a shorthand typist in various businesses, including shipping companies, some of them involving international shipment, in Danzig. In 1934 she took a position with the Danzig State Bank.

It might have been important for her first position with an official entity of the Free City of Danzig that she joined the NSDAP on May 1, 1933.[13] As early as 1930, the NSDAP was the second-strongest party, behind the Social Democrats (SPD), in Danzig, and during the elections in late May 1933, the NSDAP reached the absolute majority in the Danzig Volkstag (parliament). The city's administration was soon Nazified.[14] Yet there is no way to infer Slottke's ideological convictions from the timing of her entry into the party. In postwar interrogations she noted that her parents' household leaned toward the Social Democrats and that her father had kept his distance from the Nazi Party. This can be confirmed to the extent that her father did not join the NSDAP; however, her mother became a member in 1937.[15] Slottke stated after the war that she had believed that the NSDAP would lift Germany out of its economic slump.[16]

After Danzig became yet again part of the Reich in the aftermath of the German attack on Poland on 1939, Slottke transferred to the newly created administration of the Nazi *Reichsstatthalter* Albert Forster; she was with the Department for Employment and Economy. Aside from her more than twenty years of professional experience, Slottke's party membership likely played a role in securing this position. However, scholarship on women during the Nazi era has also shown that party membership was not a requirement for employment in the Nazi administrative or persecutory apparatus.[17]

Slottke embarked for her position in the Netherlands in early summer 1941. During her first interrogation in the preliminary proceedings against her in Munich, she said she had been interested in employment abroad and that acquaintances had facilitated the assignment.[18] It is also possible that she applied for an assignment abroad with Heinrich Himmler's Reich Security Main Office (Reichssicherheitshauptamt [RSHA]), as other female employees had. Because her statement would have indicated personal agency, Slottke tried to correct this later with a frequently used postwar justification: she claimed to have been conscripted during an *Auskämmaktion* (a search for qualified people) and thus was subject to coercion.[19] Today it is known, however, that even in cases of conscription for service (*Notdienstverpflichtung*), women could exert influence with the local employment office about their specific posting.[20] It is quite possible, then, that Slottke's personal motivations and wartime necessities went hand in hand: while she was able to make true her wish for an assignment abroad, she was also a valuable resource for the Security Police. There was much need for qualified female clerks in German-occupied Europe.

"Usually Merciless"—*Sachbearbeiterin* with the BdS Niederlande

The Gestapo, Department IV, formed the core in the office structure of the Representative of Sipo and SD (Befehlshaber der Sipo and des SD [BdS]) in the Netherlands.[21] Gertrud Slottke worked for its Jewish Section—designated IV B 4. Headed by Wilhem Zoepf, it had been created in the aftermath of the Wannsee Conference in February 1942, and it was subordinated directly to

BdS Dr. Wilhelm Harster. It had thirty-six employees and was thereby one of the biggest sections in the office structure of the BdS—even though it was not particularly strongly staffed for such a section. Slottke quickly became indispensable. She was one of the two clerks, both women, whose higher wages—among other things—distinguished them from other administrative staff members. Slottke was soon in charge of the intricate system of deferrals (*Rückstellungen*), after having initially been responsible for waiver applications regarding the mandated display of the Star of David.

Deferrals exempted certain groups of Jews from deportation and, in the process, structured the course of the deportations. More than a dozen different categories for deferment existed, mostly for (war) economic, diplomatic, or judicial reasons. Under the deferment policy fell, for example, members of the Jewish Council, Jews whose (racial) background needed to be rechecked, and diamond polishers. The highest number of Jews exempted from deportation, forty-two thousand persons, was reached in fall 1942. For those who qualified for exemptions, this perfidious system meant a short-term postponement of deportations. The hope for deferral also caused many Jews to hold back from going underground. Beginning in winter 1942, the different deferral groups were abolished. All in all, the Germans deported approximately 107,000 of the 140,000 Dutch Jews—most of them to the extermination camps Auschwitz and Sobibor.[22]

This was not Slottke's only area of substantial responsibility. She also functioned as Wilhelm Zoepf's right-hand woman, for he was frequently absent.[23] She prepared Zoepf's meetings with BdS Harster, wrote his reports to the Reich Commissar, and prepared his correspondence for signature. In all of it, she worked independently and held a large "scope for action": she maintained communication with the RSHA and answered diplomatic inquiries about the whereabouts of deportees; she participated in central discussions in Amsterdam and traveled several times to the concentration camp Bergen-Belsen, where, in the so-called Star Camp, those Dutch Jews slated for exchange for Germans interned abroad were held hostage. Most importantly, though, she traveled regularly to the Westerbork transit camp, which, from mid-1942 on, fell under the authority of the Jewish Section. Most Dutch deportation trains originated there. At Westerbork she had at her disposal a number of existing deferral and transport lists, and, working closely with the camp leader, she determined who would have to leave the camp with the next transport. For the victims, this was a life-or-death decision. In his book on the persecution and murder of the Dutch Jews, historian and Dutch Holocaust survivor Jacob Presser describes Slottke's conduct: "She insisted on seeing everyone whose case she had to review. On the whole, she was to the point and friendly, although more often than not she would give a negative decision. While she pretended to be friendly, she was in fact an inhuman automaton, working from early morning to late at night."[24]

Gertrud Slottke had the authority to make assessments and decisions, even though she had to act within the given guidelines. During the investigations in the 1960s, she tried to pretend that she held no decision-making responsibilities, but stacks of documents show that she did, indeed, make decisions. An impression of her former powers can be gleaned from a postwar interrogation during which she stated that she "checked and qualified" Jews who had distinguished themselves during World War I and had filed applications for deportation deferrals.[25] This was a distinctive slip in her defense strategy that focused on portraying herself as a small-time clerk without any individual "scope for action." Zoepf, quite to the contrary, described her independent "scope for action" with the following words: "Slottke only gave to me for decision issues from her own work sphere if there was doubt or for signature of [her] suggestion; other than that, she decided herself— within the given regulations. . . . [She] knew, as I was aware, her regulations [by heart] and never needed to be pushed."[26]

Slottke's work was in the administration; she was a desk murderer. Her work's focus was the bureaucratic decision whether Jews were to be deported or whether their deportation, for reasons of National Socialist expediency, was to be deferred for a brief time. Her activity can thus be described as "selection by radical administrative action." She worked with a level of independence that has not been documented for any other female employee of the Security Police, even though it has been noted that the competencies and responsibilities of female Gestapo employees became broader over the course of the war.[27] In Slottke's case several factors led to this development. Wilhelm Zoepf, the leader of the Jewish Section, left a supervisory vacuum that could be filled. Slottke, on her part, had the personality traits—ambition and diligence—that led her to grasp the opportunity. She was a few years older than both of her supervisors, Zoepf and Harster, and her age and her work experience made her an employee who could be confidently expected to do reliable work. And her work ethic made her pour all her energy into her activities for the Jewish Section. Harster characterized the situation this way after the war: "The broadening of her area of responsibility presumably related to the fact that a lack of any interests outside of her work made her particularly work-eager and that based on her actual age and her seniority she could be employed for demanding [*qualifiziert*] tasks. This led to a situation in which she was entrusted tasks that are normally not given to a police employee."[28] She acted rigorously against Jews. According to Zoepf, she made decisions radically and consistently. Regarding her attitude, he remarked pointedly that "within the given regulations," she "never . . . tried to decide as open-heartedly as possible for the benefit of the Jews. Rather the opposite[;] for several deferral groups she pressed for a sharper RSHA gait."[29]

Within the National Socialist machinery of persecution, Gertrud Slottke exemplifies many activists who operated on seemingly subordinate hierarchical levels. They contributed to a radicalization from below, for as members of the "fighting administration," they again and again took the path of deciding life and death without mercy.[30] Participants such as Gertrud Slottke in these Nazi crimes were not small cogs in a big machine, as they portrayed themselves after the war. They had room for initiative, pressed for acceleration and intensification, steered clear of delays, and formulated ideas for an ever-more-concentrated organization of the persecution.

Like many other women in "Security Police deployment" in German-occupied Europe, Slottke was awarded the Kriegsverdienstkreuz (War Merit Badge) in 1943. She remained part of the Jewish Section in Den Haag until the end. After the end of the war, she was detained briefly in the Netherlands but released at the end of May 1945. By June, she made her way to her sister in Württemberg. She was, in the judgment of the historians De Mildt and Meizhuizen, "expelled overly quickly," because the Dutch judicial system had a difficult time with the prosecution of Germans in the immediate aftermath of the war—and thereafter.[31]

Nazi Member Based on Idealism—Denazification

Until the late 1950s, when the investigation against her first began, and her initial interrogation in April 1960, Gertrud Slottke lived without a bother from the judicial system—initially in Waiblingen in northern Württemberg and later in close-by Stuttgart. She was not subject to automatic arrest, and, living in the U.S. zone of occupation, she made it through unspectacular denazification proceedings in front of the *Spruchkammer*, the local denazification panel, in Waiblingen. In her denazification questionnaire, she had checked the box stating that she had not been a Gestapo member, but she had also freely provided information on her position as an office employee for the Security Police in Den Haag. It was possibly this piece of information that led to Slottke's categorization as *belastet* (offender), since other women who had been part of the Gestapo's administrative and office staff fell under the IMT blanket exemption right then and there. However, the increasing permeability of the denazification regulations made it possible to recategorize some "offenders" as "followers," effectively rehabilitating them. And so-called followers fell under the Christmas Amnesty of 1947. Early in the new year, Slottke's denazification proceedings simply ended.[32]

Slottke's experience mirrored that of most female Gestapo employees: denazification did not present a serious obstacle. If they did not fall under amnesty—mostly the youth amnesty of 1946, as many of these women were young—then the denazification entities followed the instructions of the Allied Control Council Directive No. 24 of January 1946. It held that people employed in subaltern positions in which they only conducted "regular work," such as office work, were to be exempt from denazification.[33] The Law for the Liberation from National Socialism and Militarism, which was based on Control Council Directive No. 10 and enacted in the U.S. zone of occupation, provided for the same exceptions.[34] Before this backdrop, many female former Gestapo employees made it through denazification proceedings without any problems.[35] Female guards formerly employed in the Work Education Camps of the Gestapo fared differently.[36] As Kathrin Meyer's research shows, they received comparatively harder sentences than their male counterparts.[37]

Gender mattered greatly in denazification proceedings. Powerful stereotypes of femininity led to gender-specific indictments and exonerations. The notion of an allegedly natural peacefulness of women had particular effect. Meyer describes it as such: "The higher moral expectations brought to bear on women were frequently the reason to blame them more strongly for violent acts than men. These expectations also led to a situation in which those women whose activities did not diverge from common gender roles could expect exoneration even when politically more strongly implicated."[38]

In the denazification of Gertrud Slottke, who had worked in the classic position of an office employee and had not herself inflicted violence on others, the latter explication seemingly carried the day—that is if the Denazification Court was even aware of what was hidden behind the term "Security Police." Most effective was probably Slottke's representation of herself as a victim of National Socialism. She described herself as someone betrayed by National Socialism and punished by the march of history, for a number of close family members had been killed in the violence committed against Germans by the Red Army and the Poles in Danzig in 1945. In addition, Slottke's mother had died in Thuringia in November 1945, after her expulsion from Danzig. In her written statement for the denazification proceedings, Gertrud Slottke wrote that she had joined the NSDAP, which had promised "work and bread," for "idealism."[39] For that she was punished heavily with the "Russians' deluge" (*Russeneinbruch*) at the war's end.[40] This image of herself as victim later on also shaped her statements in the Munich courtroom.

"Not a smidgen of penitence, not even shame or empathy": The Munich Trial

With a few exceptions, female Gestapo employees got out scot-free from trials for National Socialist crimes in the Federal Republic of Germany. Gertrud Slottke was initially in this category but eventually became one of the exceptions. Jointly with her former supervisors in the Netherlands, the BdS Dr. Wilhelm Harster and the head of the Jewish Section Wilhelm Zoepf, she had to answer for the deportation of 110,000 Jews from the Netherlands at the Landgericht Munich II in early 1967. After eleven days in court, the judges sentenced Harster to fifteen years in the penitentiary, Zoepf to nine, and Slottke to five; they were convicted of joint accessory to murder (*gemeinschaftliche Beihilfe zum Mord*).[41] Thus, Slottke was one of the very few women who stood trial for their activity with the Gestapo—and of that group, fewer still were, like Slottke, sentenced rather than acquitted.

In this trial the defendants Harster and Zoepf represented two of the so-called desk murderers of the middle or higher Nazi functional elite, people who had not committed murder themselves but had run the administrative machinery that performed the essential spadework for systematic murder. The trial relied exclusively on documentary evidence; no witnesses took the stand. Among the trials in the Federal Republic, it also represented an oddity, as for the first time confessions had been entered by some of the defendants.[42] Harster and Zoepf admitted to knowing that the Jews, after their deportation, were murdered. Gertrud Slottke did not confess. From the beginning she stuck with her defense that she "neither knew nor suspected" that the deported Jews were killed in the (extermination) camps.[43] While she assumed that they would meet a terrible fate, she claimed to have learned about their murder only after the end of the war. The court, however, saw it as proven that Slottke, too, knew about the systematic murder of those who were deported. The court held that she could have recognized and known this by March 1943 at the latest.

In its verdict, the Munich court drew the picture of a tremendously reliable, competent, dutiful, and ambitious employee of the Nazi persecution machinery in the Netherlands: Slottke's "factual competence" had been "almost total." In the view of the judges, it was, above all, her "diligence" and her "factual knowledge in all Jewish issues" that made her an indispensable resource.[44] The court also emphasized her independent and far-reaching work: "[Her] area of responsibility extended to the entire area of the Netherlands and [extended beyond] the regular tasks of a police employee." It also noted that "the focus of her work evolved from . . . pure administrative work to security policing."[45]

The court fastened on her "zeal" (*Diensteifer*) for the "smooth implementation" of the deportations as the most important reason for Slottke's rigorous activities. The court concluded that the three defendants' zeal for their work was motivated less by ideological commitment to Hitler's race policies and more by their desire to be effective managers and to gain professional recognition.[46] This evaluation, once out there, foregrounded a nonideological drive for action that was detached from National Socialism, giving minor relevance to motivations that could have been connected to Nazi ideology and anti-Semitism. The court here followed a perspective on Nazi perpetrators that had gained currency with Hannah Arendt's characterization of Adolf Eichmann and her descriptive phrase "banality of evil."[47] Under these terms, Slottke was a diligent, ambitious woman desk murderer, a female Eichmann in the Netherlands. In the evaluation of anti-Semitism as a potential motivation, the court assumed that mitigating circumstances—such as the conditions of the time and the effects of anti-Semitic Nazi propaganda—also played a role but were not as central.[48]

Rather unsurprisingly, Slottke drove the same point and presented herself as a woman who was not anti-Semitic at all but was defined strongly by Prussian secondary virtues, most importantly the desire to be seen as committed to her job. Yet she also clearly showed the extent to which she had integrated brutality into her daily work. Her pithy words revealed a social coldness. She knew that "Jews were not handled all that humanely at Auschwitz," as she put it in one of her interrogations. She did not have "any thoughts" about the deportation of old and sick people, for it was said that the Auschwitz was a big camp.[49] And she "thought nothing" about the deportation of fourteen-year-old children.[50] On her visits to Bergen-Belsen, she saw that the Jews there were "miserable."[51] Her statements lacked even belated empathy and were defined by Slottke's cold detachment. Trial observer Heiner Lichtenstein noted that "not a smidgen of penitence, not even shame or empathy" crossed her lips—an eerie echo of the cold and efficient professionalism she displayed while on the job with the *Judenreferat*.[52]

"Indefatigable service": Voluntary Functionary for the Bund der Danziger

Immediately upon her arrival in Waiblingen in 1945, Gertrud Slottke became active for expellees from Danzig. Her voluntary activities for the Bund der Danziger were her life's focus for the next twenty years. She was primarily responsible for women's services (*Frauenarbeit*) in (Baden-)Württemberg, but she also held numerous other positions. And she was repeatedly given awards. She resigned from her positions in March 1967, after the Munich court handed down the sentence against her.[53] In her day job she led the pale existence of a secretary—first for the Raiffeisenverband and thereafter for the Südwestdeutschen Pflanzenzüchterverband of the Landwirtschaftliche Hochschule (Agricultural College) in Stuttgart-Hohenheim. In 1965, at age sixty-three, she took early retirement.

Over the course of the years, Gertrud Slottke took on more and more positions with the Bund der Danziger. She initially served as an assistant district representative (*Bezirksbeauftragte*) for North Baden–North Württemberg until, after the 1957 restructuring of the State Association (Landesverband) of Baden-Württemberg, she was appointed state women's leader (*Landesfrauenleiterin*).[54] This made her a member of the state board. She also held influence on the national level, because she was a delegate to the general meetings of the Bund der Danziger and, as such, cast a vote for the organization's national board. While she did not count among the organization's highest officers and did not hold national office, she was very active at the next-lower, secondary level of the state and local chapters. In addition, she was active in expellee umbrella organizations in the state. In short: in Baden-Württemberg, Slottke took on much association work beyond the Bund der Danziger.

Slottke's sphere of influence was women's services and thus cultural and social activities in an area that, according to prevalent gender images, was left to the women to organize. The Bund der Danziger developed women's services as a separate field beginning in the mid-1950s and soon gave it its own structures. A leading position for women's services was created at the national level; the different state associations appointed state women's leaders who, as of 1958 and after an internal discussion, sat on the respective state board—as Gertrud Slottke did in Baden-Württemberg. Women's circles also emerged in local chapters.

Women became increasingly important to the association, because they were seen as "the guardians of the Danzig traditions in the family."[55] In view of the low level of organizational membership among former residents of Danzig—about 30 percent—and the difficulties of reaching younger people, women were to concern themselves, above all, with ensuring children's and adolescents' commitment to the goals of the Bund.[56] Already in 1950, in a piece entitled "The Tasks of the Danzig Women: Believing, Loving, Hoping," Bremen district leader Anni Kalähne noted that the women's "greatest duty for the homeland and task" was to ensure that the young people do not forget their home and pursue the goal of returning to Danzig: "We Danzig women should and have to be the guardians of the young generation's feelings; [we] should advise them! Help [them]! And guide them on the proper path."[57] Parallel to the strengthening of women's services was the founding of children's groups on the local level; the state and local women's leaders were also put in charge of the youth movement. That Gertrud Slottke, who was both unmarried and childless, took on a leadership position in women's work did not run counter to the fulfillment of this mandate. The Bund der Danziger's image of women maintained that, by their very nature, all women were potential mothers: in addition to biological mothers there were also spiritual mothers.[58]

For all practical purposes, the Bund der Danziger women's services focused on social and cultural activities. The women's circles looked after the old and the needy; they concerned themselves with former Danzig residents who, in the 1960s, still lived in camps; they organized neighborhood support, found spots in sanatoriums for mothers, organized vacation housing, and founded children's groups. An important focus, beginning in 1951, was the shipment of packages to Germans in Danzig or those who were from Danzig but now lived in the GDR. Cultural work focused on the maintenance of Danzig traditions.

As state women's leader, Slottke was responsible for the guidance and coordination of the local chapters in Baden-Württemberg. For example, she transmitted to chapter leaders guidelines, formulated at the national level, for the work and programming to be done in the women's circles. From time to time she called meetings of all chapter leaders in Baden-Württemberg. She also regularly attended supraregional meetings of state leaders. She organized the shipment of clothing and food packages to the GDR and to Danzig. As a member of the state board, she also took part in numerous representative appointments. And she quite frequently visited the local chapter in Ludwigsburg, near Stuttgart. Owing to the large number of expellees in the region, this chapter had a large membership and was quite active.[59]

Slottke poured all her energy into her voluntarism and its associated positions. One reads repeatedly in the newsletter *Unser Danzig* about her achievements and honors she received. In 1958, for example, she was given the silver honor badge as a "symbol of high appreciation" for her "indefatigable service."[60] During the delegates' meeting in April 1963, the national leader for women's services highlighted as "exemplary" Slottke's work in the shipment of packages from her state to the GDR and to Danzig.[61] And when Slottke was first detained in 1960, the Stuttgart priest Kurt Walter, the regional representative of the Bund der Danziger, wrote in support of her to the State Attorney's Office in Munich. His letter indicates that she filled her voluntary position as expertly and efficiently as she had participated in the deportations of Jews from the Netherlands. His words are strikingly similar to those used by her former supervisors of BdS Netherlands: Slottke, stated Walter, temporarily took on the leadership position in Stuttgart and worked independently in it, for he himself had been sick for a long time. "Her efficiency and lack of self-interest then brought her into leading positions," he noted further.[62] As a state women's leader, she created a new field of responsibility from scratch—and she did so independently. He praised her willingness to sacrifice, for she had devoted to her voluntary position her entire free time, much money, and her private life.

According to Walter, Slottke's engagement for the Bund der Danziger had been close to boundless. In contrast, there is little information on how she herself conceptualized her voluntarism. As indicated above, there are no materials authored by Slottke; and, with one exception, she also did not write for the Bund der Danziger's newsletter. She remained largely invisible to the public; it was always others who talked about and praised her. Just once she is cited in the newsletter, and her remark indicates that she held a politicized-militant understanding of women's services and women's tasks in the Bund der Danziger. She had emphasized during a general delegates' meeting that women had to be educated politically, to have the "armor [*Rüstzeug*] for the political fight for the East."[63]

Slottke's activities in the Bund der Danziger could not possibly contribute to a questioning of her self-image as someone seduced by National Socialism and as a victim of World War II. There is no detailed study on the personnel structure of the Bund der Danziger, and the existing scholarship cannot gauge how much of a National Socialist spirit and related mind-sets remained in effect in expellee organizations in general.[64] It can be determined, though, that Danzig—much like all the other eastern regions of the Reich—was a stronghold of the Right before 1933. "Indubitably, there were members with burdened pasts [*belastete Vergangeheit*] in the expellee organizations, for in the immediate postwar years local elites, who before 1945 determined the tone in the old homeland, reconnected," writes Andreas Kossert about postwar continuities.[65] He also notes that well into the 1960s, leading offices in the expellee organization were staffed by people who had been active in Nazi organizations before 1945.[66] From the trauma of the expulsion and the loss of home emerged a distinctive memory culture in the Bund der Danziger. Peter Oliver Loew describes it with the term "encapsulation."[67] "Silence" and "embitterment" reigned among Danzig expellees, who, at the same time, created a new, overarching narrative that subsumed under it both silence about Nazism and concealment of one's role in it, glorified the prewar period, and conserved from a distance the image of an idyllic Danzig.[68] This memory left out the war and the loss of Danzig. The same happened to Slottke and her role during the Nazi era, for neither her environment nor its memory culture gave her a reason to reflect on her own activities during Nazism, let alone to call them into question the slightest bit. She could simply fade her own war years out of memory as well.

This development is all the more remarkable since, from the very beginning and for about a decade, Gertrud Slottke worked very closely with the above-mentioned pastor Kurt Walter; they remained close until his death in 1963. As an expression of their good relationship, she wrote his obituary for the newsletter of the Bund der Danziger—her only known postwar document.[69] In the obituary, Slottke called herself his "closest co-worker." Walter, who had been a cofounder of the Confessing Church in Danzig, had been persecuted under Nazism and had been imprisoned in the "pastors' block" in Dachau.[70] It cannot be determined whether Slottke and Walter knew each other from Danzig, but as of summer 1945 the formerly persecuted pastor and the former participant in the organization of deportations worked together closely. Even that did not lead Slottke to reflect on her activities during the Nazi era. Quite to the contrary, she claimed for Walter and herself a narrative of immediate postwar opposition to Allied rules and regulations.

Owing to the Allied meeting ban, early get-togethers of former Danzigers in Stuttgart took place clandestinely and were code-named "Die Kogge" (The Cog). In the obituary, Slottke described how an Advent celebration in December 1945 almost led to their arrest. Walter had mustered "a lot of courage and boldness" to call meetings despite the Allied ban.[71] Here Slottke indirectly also talked about herself. In her words resonates her self-perception as someone persecuted and victimized by restrictions imposed by the American victor's justice.

In July 1968 Slottke started her prison term in the women's penitentiary Gotteszell in Schwäbisch Gmünd. After rejecting numerous applications for early release, the Bavarian Ministry of Justice granted her medical parole in May 1971. Harster and Zoepf, who had confessed during the trial, had been released from prison significantly earlier. At the time of her parole, Slottke had been in a Stuttgart hospital for nine months already; this is also where she died from a neurological disease on December 17, 1971. She was sixty-nine.

Gertrud Slottke's biography described here is that of a woman who—during the Nazi era and thereafter—actively and aggressively filled her "scope for action." She grabbed her chances to influence and to shape, politically as well as otherwise, even though she always acted from subordinate positions. After the war she remade her participation in Nazi crimes as a committed administrative employee into the biography of a victim. She regarded herself, without any notable fractures and with multiple overlays, as a victim of the Nazi government and of Germany's military defeat. And after the Munich trial, Slottke also came to see herself as a victim of the Federal Republic's judicial system. "I had to pay for my idealism with a pretty penny [*bitteres Lehrgeld*]" became the mantra of her postwar life; she thus expressed how National Socialism had disappointed and betrayed her.[72] Her 1967 sentence she called a "miscarriage of justice."[73]

The environment in the Bund der Danziger, as well as, to use Norbert Frei's term, the "politics of the past" prevalent in the society of the Federal Republic, which was silent about the Nazi past while downplaying it all the same, provided the context for the recasting of Slottke's life story.[74] After the war, West Germans, in need of shared modes of identification, fashioned a myth of victimization. They put at its center the "German victims" of the war: the expellees, the prisoners of war, and, in the most general terms, themselves. In this process, they overlooked the "victims of the Germans": Jews, Sinti and Roma, homosexuals, and many others.[75] Slottke epitomized this self-victimization that was so dominant in the 1950s and 1960s. While certainly presenting a heightened version of this narrative, she fit into her times. Her recasting was both exceptional and all too common.

Notes

The author would like to thank Katrin Paehler for the translation of this chapter from German to English.

1. Elizabeth Harvey, *"Der Osten braucht Dich!" Frauen und nationalsozialistische Germanisierungspolitik* (Hamburg: Hamburger Edition, 2010); Franka Maubach, *Die*

Stellung halten: Kriegserfahrungen und Lebensgeschichten von Wehrmachthelferinnen (Göttingen: Vandenhoeck & Ruprecht, 2009); Nicole Kramer, *Volksgenossinnen an der Heimatfront: Mobilisierung, Verhalten, Erinnerung* (Göttingen: Vandenhoeck & Ruprecht, 2011).

2. For a discussion about the usage of the term *perpetrator,* see Christina Herkommer, "Frauen im Nationalsozialismus: Ein diskursgeschichtlicher Überblick," *Terezin Studies and Documents* 14 (2007): 288–327. On women with the SS and the police, see Simone Erpel, ed., *Im Gefolge der SS: Aufseherinnen des Frauen-KZ Ravensbrück* (Berlin: Metropol, 2007); Jutta Mühlenberg, *Das SS-Helferinnen-korps: Ausbildung, Einsatz und Entnazifizierung der weiblichen Angehörigen der Waffen-SS 1942–1949* (Hamburg: Hamburger Edition, 2010); Bettina Blum, "Weibliche Polizei—soziale Polizei? Weibliche (Jugend)Polizei zwischen Demokratie und Diktatur 1927–1952," in *Die Polizei im NS-Staat: Beiträge eines internationalen Symposiums an der Deutschen Hochschule der Polizei in Münster,* ed. Wolfgang Schulte (Frankfurt am Main: Polizeiwissenschaft, 2009), 511–38; Elisabeth Kohlhaas, "Weibliche Angestellte der Gestapo: Tätigkeiten, biografische Profile und weltanschauliche Formierung," *Beiträge zur Geschichte der nationalsozialistischen Verfolgung in Norddeutschland* 15 (2013): 136–46.

3. Ulrike Weckel and Edgar Wolfrum, eds., *"Bestien" und "Befehlsempfänger": Frauen und Männer in NS-Prozessen nach 1945* (Göttingen: Vandenhoeck & Ruprecht, 2003). Compare also the relevant contributions in Erpel, *Im Gefolge der SS.*

4. Anette Kretzer, *NS-Täterschaft und Geschlecht: Der erste britische Ravensbrück-Prozess 1946/47 in Hamburg* (Berlin: Metropol, 2009); Alexandra Przyrembel, "Ilse Koch—'normale' SS-Ehefrau oder 'Kommandeuse von Buchenwald'?," in *Karrieren der Gewalt: Nationalsozialistische Täterbiographien,* ed. Klaus-Michael Mallmann and Gerhard Paul (Darmstadt: Wissenschaftliche Buchgesellschaft, 2004), 126–33.

5. Elke Frietsch and Christina Herkommer, eds., *Nationalsozialismus und Geschlecht: Zur Politisierung und Ästhetisierung von Körper, "Rasse" und Sexualität im "Dritten Reich" und nach 1945* (Bielefeld: Transcript, 2009); Insa Eschebach, Sigrid Jacobeit, and Silke Wenk, eds., *Gedächtnis und Geschlecht: Deutungsmuster in Darstellungen des nationalsozialistischen Genozids* (Frankfurt am Main: Campus, 2002); see also *Gedenken und Erinnern: Perspektiven der Aufarbeitung des Nationalsozialismus,* special issue, *Ariadne* 59 (2011).

6. Harald Schmid, "Gender gap Erinnerungskultur: Frauen in der westdeutschen Auseinandersetzung mit dem Nationalsozialismus—eine Spurensuche," *Ariadne* 59 (2011): 6. On Oberheuser, see Wendy A.-M. Sarti, *Women and Nazis: Perpetrators of Genocide and Other Crimes during Hitler's Regime, 1933–1945* (Palo Alto, CA: Academica Press, 2011), 169–88; on Viermetz, Andrea Böltken, "Inge Viermetz: Eine weibliche Karriere im Dritten Reich," in *Historische Rassismusforschung: Ideologen, Täter, Opfer,* ed. Barbara Danckwortt, Thomas Querg, and Claudia Schöningh (Hamburg: Argument, 1995), 179–207.

7. Elisabeth Kohlhaas, "Gertrud Slottke: Angestellte im niederländischen Juden-

referat der Sicherheitspolizei," in Mallmann and Paul, *Karrieren der Gewalt*, 207–18. Parts of this article are used here.

8. Kirsten Heinsohn, Barbara Vogel, and Ulrike Weckel, eds., *Zwischen Karriere und Verfolgung: Handlungsräume von Frauen im nationalsozialistischen Deutschland* (Frankfurt am Main: Campus, 1997), 13.

9. Spruchkammerakte Gertrud Slottke, Staatsarchiv Ludwigsburg, EL 902/24, Az. 49/1/8373 (hereafter Spruchkammerakte); Spruchkammer Waiblingen; Verfahren vor dem Landgericht München II gegen Dr. Wilhelm Harster, Wilhelm Zoepf und Gertrud Slottke, Bayerisches Staatsarchiv München, Staatsanwaltschaften 34879 (hereafter Prozessakten).

10. In Munich, Robert Kempner represented the families of Anne Frank and Edith Stein, who were coplaintiffs (*Nebenkläger*); Heiner Lichtenstein followed the trial as an observer. Robert M. W. Kempner, *Edith Stein und Anne Frank: 2 von 100000* (Freiburg im Breisgau: Herder, 1968); Heiner Lichtenstein, "Dr. Wilhelm Harster: Der niederländische Holocaust," in *Im Namen des Volkes? Eine persönliche Bilanz der NS-Prozesse*, ed. Heiner Lichtenstein (Cologne: Bund, 1984), 163–73.

11. Many women, most of them unmarried, allowed themselves to be mobilized for the war effort and to be deployed in German-occupied Europe. However, generally speaking, these women were significantly younger than Slottke. Nazi Germany thus achieved a very public upgrade of a time period in a woman's life that thus far had been regarded solely as a waiting period before marriage. See Elizabeth D. Heineman, *What Difference Does a Husband Make? Women and Marital Status in Nazi and Postwar Germany* (Berkeley: University of California Press, 1999). For biographical information, see Slottke's statements for the trial in Munich as well as press reports about the trial in Harster's file. Wilhelm Harster, 16.2.-Ende 1967, Niederländisches Institut für Kriegsdokumentation Amsterdam, KB I, Nr. 3027.

12. Ute Frevert, "Traditionale Weiblichkeit und moderne Interessenorganisation: Frauen im Angestelltenberuf 1918–1933," *Geschichte und Gesellschaft* 7, nos. 3–4 (1981).

13. NSDAP-Mitgliedsnachweis Gertrud Slottke, BArch, NSDAP-Zentral- und Gaukartei. The possibility remains that she joined the party before Hitler's ascension to chancellor and that her membership came into effect on May 1, 1933.

14. Martin Broszat, "Die Anfänge der nationalsozialistischen Herrschaft in Danzig (1933–1936)," in *Gutachten*, ed. Institut für Zeitgeschichte, vol. 1 (Munich: Institut für Zeitgeschichte, 1958), 392–94; Dieter Schenk, *Hitlers Mann in Danzig: Albert Forster und die NS-Verbrechen in Danzig-Westpreußen* (Bonn: Dietz, 2000), 125–43.

15. NSDAP Membership Record Maria Slottke, BArch, NSDAP-Zentral- und Gaukartei; no such record for Leopold Slottke.

16. Vernehmung Slottke vom 19.1.1966, Prozessakten, Bd. 6, Bl. 1188–95.

17. Lavern Wolfram, "KZ-Aufseherinnen—Parteigängerinnen der NSDAP?," in Erpel, *Im Gefolge der SS*, 187–97.

18. Vernehmung Slottke vom 14.4.1960, Prozessakten, Bd. 2, Bl. 287–92.

19. Vernehmung Slottke in der Hauptverhandlung am 23.1.1967, ebd., Bd. 8, Bl. 1685–1704.

20. Stefanie Oppel, "Marianne Eßmann: Von der Kontoristin zur SS-Aufseherin: Dienstverpflichtung als Zwangsmaßnahme?," in Erpel, *Im Gefolge der SS,* 81–88; Mühlenberg, *SS-Helferinnen,* 62–84.

21. In 1936, Himmler combined the Gestapo and the Kripo—the criminal police—in the Main Office Security Police. The Befehlshaber der Sipo und des SD (BdS) and the subordinated Kommandeure (commanders), established in the occupied territories, mirrored the structure of Heinrich Himmler's main instrument of persecution, policing, and genocide, the RSHA. Regarding the German occupation of the Netherlands, see Johannes ten Houwink Cate, "Der Befehlshaber der Sipo und des SD in den besetzten niederländischen Gebieten und die Deportation der Juden 1942–1943," in *Die Bürokratie der Okkupation: Strukturen der Herrschaft und Verwaltung im besetzten Europa,* ed. Wolfgang Benz, Johannes ten Houwink Cate, and Gerhard Otto (Berlin: Metropol, 1998), 197–222. With a focus on the murder of the Dutch Jews, see, in addition, Jacob Presser, *Ashes in the Wind: The Destruction of the Dutch Jewry* (Detroit: Wayne State University Press, 1988); Guus Meershoek, "Machtentfaltung und Scheitern: Sicherheitspolizei und SD in den Niederlanden," in *Die Gestapo: Mythos und Realität,* ed. Klaus-Michael Mallmann and Gerhard Paul (Darmstadt: Wissenschaftliche., 1995), 383–402.

22. Of all Western European countries, the Netherlands had the highest deportation rate. Eberhard Jäckel, Peter Longerich, and Julius H. Schoeps, eds., *Enzyklopädie des Holocaust: Die Verfolgung und Ermordung der europäischen Juden,* 4 vols. (Munich: Piper, 1995), 2: 1008; Marnix Croes, "The Holocaust in the Netherlands and the Rate of Jewish Survival," *Holocaust and Genocide Studies* 20, no. 3 (2006): 474–99.

23. Vernehmung Dr. Harster vom 30.10.1959, Prozessakten, Bd. 1, Bl. 43–48. Zoepf was not the most eager to fulfill his duties and frequently went on trips or spent large amounts of time in the sanatorium Hohenlychen, where he had formerly worked as a PE instructor. In those instances, he had his employees represent him—including the other female clerk of the Jewish Section, Margarete Frielingsdorf. It was therefore said that "in his office, the women wore the pants."

24. Presser, *Ashes in the Wind,* 343.

25. Vernehmung Slottke vom 16./17.2.1966, ebd., Bd. 6, Bl. 1266ff.

26. Vernehmungen Zoepf vom 31.1. und 23.2.1966, ebd., Bd. 6, Bl. 1223–33, 1297–1304.

27. Elisabeth Kohlhaas, "'Meine Tätigkeit bestand darin, die Frauen der Juden körperlich zu durchsuchen': Frauen als Beschäftigte der Gestapo und ihre Handlungsfelder 1933–1945," in *Frauen als Täterinnen und Mittäterinnen im Nationalsozialismus: Gestaltungsspielräume und Handlungsmöglichkeiten,* ed. Viola Schubert-Lehnhardt (Halle: Martin-Luther-Univ. Halle-Wittenberg, 2006), 133–46.

28. Vernehmung Dr. Harster vom 8.2.1966, ebd., Bd. 6, Bl. 1234ff.

29. Vernehmung Zoepf vom 23.2.1966, ebd., Bl. 1297–1304.

30. The concept of a "fighting administration" originated with Reinhard Heydrich: here I follow Michael Wildt, *Generation des Unbedingten: Das Führungskorps des Reichssicherheitshauptamtes* (Hamburg: Hamburger Edition, 2002), 227.

31. Dick de Mildt and Joggli Meihuizen, "'Unser Land muss tief gesunken sein . . .': Die Aburteilung deutscher Kriegsverbrecher in den Niederlanden," in *Transnationale Vergangenheitspolitik: Der Umgang mit deutschen Kriegsverbrechern in Europa nach dem Zweiten Weltkrieg*, ed. Norbert Frei (Göttingen: Wallstein, 2005), 283–325, esp. 304.

32. Einstellungsbeschluss des öffentlichen Klägers der Spruchkammer Waiblingen vom 5.1.1948, Spruchkammerakte, Bl. 18.

33. Kontrollratsdirektive Nr. 24: Entfernung von Nationalsozialisten und Personen, die den Bestrebungen der Alliierten feindlich gegenüberstehen, aus Ämtern und verantwortlichen Stellungen vom 12. Januar 1946.

34. Gesetz Nr. 104 zur Befreiung von Nationalismus und Militarismus vom 5. März 1946.

35. These are also the findings of my research on the female employees of the Staatspolizeistelle Frankfurt am Main.

36. Gabriele Lotfi, *KZ der Gestapo: Arbeitserziehungslager im Dritten Reich* (Stuttgart: Dt. Verl.-Anst., 2000).

37. Kathrin Meyer, *Entnazifizierung von Frauen: Die Internierungslager der US-Zone Deutschlands 1945–1952* (Berlin: Metropol, 2004).

38. Kathrin Meyer, "'Die Frau ist der Frieden der Welt': Von Nutzen und Lasten eines Weiblichkeitsstereotyps in Spruchkammerentscheidungen gegen Frauen," in Weckel and Wolfrum, *"Bestien" und "Befehlsempfänger,"* 132; see also Daniel Kück, "Bei den Gefangenen trug die L. den Spitznamen 'das blonde Gift': Die Stenotypistin Margarethe Lücke als informelle Gestapo-Beamtin?," in *"Was verstehen wir Frauen auch von Politik?": Entnazifizierung ganz normaler Frauen in Bremen (1945–1952)*, ed. Eva Schöck-Quinteros and Jan-Hauke Ahrens (Bremen: Universität, Institut für Geschichtswiss., 2011), 231–72.

39. Beide Zitate aus schriftl. Äußerung Slottkes vom 19.2.1947, Spruchkammerakte, Bl. 2.

40. Anhang Slottkes zum Meldebogen vom 28.6.1946, ebd., Bl. 1.

41. Urteil vom 24.2.1967, Prozessakten, Bd. 12, S. 1–625; esp. 498; also BArch Ludwigsburg, B 162/Vorl. SA 192. The sentence is published in *Justiz und NS-Verbrechen: Die deutschen Strafverfahren wegen nationalsozialistischer Tötungsverbrechen*, ed. Rüter and Dirk de Mildt (Amsterdam: Amsterdam University Press, 2001); Bd. 25: Die vom 24.11.1966 bis zum 16.03.1967 ergangenen Strafurteile, lfd. Nr. 645.

42. Christian Ritz, *Schreibtischtäter vor Gericht: Das Verfahren vor dem Münchner Landgericht wegen der Deportation der niederländischen Juden (1959–1967)* (Paderborn: Schöningh, 2012).

43. Ibid., 175.

44. Urteil vom 24.2.1967, Prozessakten, Bd. 12, 493–94.

45. Beschluss des OLG München vom 29.4.1966, ebd., Bd. 6, Bl. 1387–90. Urteil vom 24.2.1967, ebd., Bd. 12, 498.

46. Beschluss des OLG München vom 29.4.1966, ebd., Bd. 6, Bl. 1387–90. Urteil vom 24.2.1967, ebd., Bd. 12, 572.

47. Hannah Arendt, *Eichmann in Jerusalem: Ein Bericht von der Banalität des Bösen,* 9th ed. (Munich: Piper, 1995).

48. Urteil vom 24.2.1967, Prozessakten, Bd. 12, 571–72.

49. Vernehmung Slottke vom 14.4.1960, ebd., Bd. 1, Bl. 287–92.

50. Vernehmung Slottke vom 16./17.2.1966, ebd., Bd. 6, Bl. 1266–78.

51. Vernehmung Slottke vom 20., 21. und 26.10.1960, ebd., Bd. 4, Bl. 631–52.

52. Lichtenstein, *Im Namen des Volkes?,* 171.

53. Karteikarte Gertrud Slottke, Kartei des Bundes der Danziger. Sie trat rückwirkend zum 31.10.1965 aus.

54. "Bericht aus der Ortsstelle Schwenningen," *Unser Danzig* 9, no. 11 (1957): 23.

55. "Wachsende Aufgaben und Pflichten: Mitarbeit der Frauen tut dringend not," *Unser Danzig* 7, no. 11 (1955): 4.

56. Andreas Kossert, *Kalte Heimat: Die Geschichte der deutschen Vertriebenen nach 1945* (München: Siedler Verlag, 2009), 146.

57. "Die Aufgabe der Danziger Frauen: Glauben, Lieben, Hoffen," *Unser Danzig* 2, no. 9 (1950): 7.

58. Thus argued the national women's leader in her article "Die Leistungen der Frau: Aus verborgenen Quellen strömen entscheidende Wirkungen," *Unser Danzig* 9, no. 13 (1957): 16.

59. Landkreis Ludwigsburg, ed., *Die Eingliederung der Vertriebenen im Landkreis Ludwigsburg: Ein Rückblick auf die vier Jahrzehnte seit 1945* (Ludwigsburg: Landkreis Ludwigsburg, 1986).

60. "Bericht über die Landesarbeitstagung der Danziger Frauenkreisleiterinnen in Baden-Württemberg," *Unser Danzig* 10, no. 22 (1958): 8.

61. "Bericht von der 15. Delegiertenversammlung am 20./21.4.1963 in Travemünde," *Unser Danzig* 15, no. 9 (1963): 3–5.

62. Brief des Pfarrers Walter an die Staatsanwaltschaft in München vom 20.4.1960, Prozessakten, Bd. 2, Bl. 301–2.

63. "Bericht über die Delegiertentagung in Travemünde," *Unser Danzig* 11, no. 11 (1959): 11.

64. Matthias Stickler, *Ostdeutsch heißt Gesamtdeutsch: Organisation, Selbstverständnis und heimatpolitische Zielsetzungen der deutschen Vertriebenenverbände 1949–1972* (Düsseldorf: Droste, 2004), 321.

65. Kossert, *Kalte Heimat,* 184.

66. Ibid., 182.

67. Peter O. Loew, "Vertriebene aus Danzig, Vertriebene in Danzig seit 1939/45: Trauma, Einkapselung und die langsame Entdeckung des anderen," in *Verflochtene Erinnerungen: Polen und seine Nachbarn im 19. und 20. Jahrhundert,* ed. Martin Aust, Krzysztof Ruchniewicz, and Stefan Troebst (Cologne: Böhlau, 2009), 221–44.

68. Ibid., 226.

69. Gertrud Slottke, "Pfarrer Kurt Walter," *Unser Danzig* 15, no. 14 (1963): 13.

70. Kurt Walter, "Danzig," in *Die Stunde der Versuchung: Gemeinden im Kirchenkampf 1933–1945. Selbstzeugnisse,* ed. Günther Harder and Wilhelm Niemöller (Munich: C. H. Kaiser, 1963), 37–56. Immediately after the war, Walter took on the position as the state representative for Danziger in the U.S. and French occupational zones. Later—after admission of the Bund der Danziger in 1948 and the fast growth of the association—he held the position of regional representative for Nord-Württemberg und Nord-Baden; he also belonged to the first "Rat der Danziger," the freely elected council of thirty-six delegates that regarded itself as the parliament of the Free City of Danzig in exile. During all these years, he also headed the local chapter in Stuttgart.

71. Ibid.

72. Schriftl. Äußerung Slottkes vom 19.2.1947, Spruchkammerakte, Bl. 2.

73. So die niederländische Illustrierte Kwik vom 23.2.1967: "Mijn veroordeling is een rechterlijke dwaling."

74. Norbert Frei, *Vergangenheitspolitik: Die Anfänge der Bundesrepublik und die NS-Vergangenheit* (Munich: C. H. Beck, 1996).

75. Robert G. Moeller, "Deutsche Opfer, Opfer der Deutschen: Kriegsgefangene, Vertriebene, NS-Verfolgte: Opferausgleich als Identitätspolitik," in *Nachkrieg in Deutschland,* ed. Klaus Naumann (Hamburg: Hamburger Editions, 2001), 29–58.

11

The Gehlen Organization and the Heinz Felfe Case

The SD, the KGB, and West German Counterintelligence

Norman J. W. Goda

The case of the Gehlen Organization and Heinz Felfe is one of the Cold War's great espionage tales. Felfe was a former Sicherheitsdienst (SD) officer recruited in 1950 by the Soviet Ministry for State Security (MGB), known after 1954 as the Committee for State Security (KGB). In 1951 he entered the Gehlen Organization, West Germany's foreign intelligence service, known after 1956 as the Bundesnachrichtendienst (BND). Felfe moved up the ladder in BND counterintelligence, becoming the chief officer charged with counterespionage against the Soviets by 1956. Because he in fact worked as a penetration agent for the KGB rather than for the BND, he wrecked BND counterintelligence operations against the Soviets as well as U.S. counterintelligence operations run by the Central Intelligence Agency (CIA). In the process he revealed hundreds of West German and U.S. agents in East Germany.

After Felfe's arrest in 1961, both the BND and the CIA tried to assess the damage. "The BND damage report," wrote David Murphy, chief of the CIA's European Division, "must have run into tens of thousands of pages."[1] To this day, the BND has not made public its damage assessments—or any other materials from the Felfe affair. Murphy's own assessment noted that "all major BND CE [counterespionage] operations were compromised" and that "the majority of the [BND]'s tactical sources in East Germany were compromised or under hostile control." And because Felfe worked with the CIA's Berlin Operations Base, numerous CIA operations there were similarly compromised.[2]

Historians have not joined journalists in looking more deeply. Partly they view the Soviet penetration of the BND as an intelligence tale rather than an episode of *Vergangenheitspolitik*—Germany's fraught politics of memory—and thus less appealing to the contemporary academic eye.[3] But the latter term applies. The Felfe case involved a clandestine yet very effective reinvention of numerous SD officers in the Federal Republic, all within the context of broader reinvention and venality at the highest levels of West German intelligence and the West German state. Yet historians also struggle with source problems regarding work on West German intelligence. In 2010 the BND opened bits of information revealing 47 partial names of 216 BND members (as of 1960) who had careers in the SS or related police organizations.[4] And though the BND appointed a commission of academic historians in 2011 to examine the BND's formative years, it is also true that the BND, as revealed the same year, had destroyed more than 250 relevant files, including a very large file on Aloïs Brunner, one of Adolf Eichmann's top deputies, who worked for Syrian intelligence after the war.[5] It is unclear at this writing whether the commission will be able to produce a study on par with that recently completed on the wartime and postwar German Foreign Ministry, a study that itself suffered at times from official obstruction and the earlier destruction of relevant documents.[6]

On the other hand, the U.S. government after 2001 released hundreds of CIA files on former SS and SD officers, owing to the 1998 Nazi War Crimes Disclosure Act. Many of these officers worked for the Gehlen Organization (and some for the Soviets as well). Hundreds of relevant files from the U.S. Army Counterintelligence Corps (CIC) concerning the Gehlen Organization and its employees have also been released under this law.[7] It is possible from these records to write on the Gehlen Organization in general and the Felfe case specifically as never before, because both the CIC and the CIA penetrated the Gehlen Organization where they could, even coming to understand certain matters that surely did not make their way into the BND's own records. The result is unusually rich information on the complicated intersection of *Vergangenheitspolitik* and espionage, to be understood within the broad framework of the Gehlen Organization's struggle for independence from both the U.S. and West German governments. In the Felfe case, these factors opened the BND to Soviet manipulation to create the greatest intelligence disaster of the Cold War.

Understanding the Felfe case depends on a contextual understanding of the Gehlen Organization and its founder, General Reinhard Gehlen.[8] From 1942 until Hitler dismissed him in April 1945, he was chief of the German Army General Staff's Fremde Heere Ost office, where he made (mostly incorrect) intelligence predictions concerning the Red Army.[9] Gehlen surrendered to U.S. Army forces on May 22 in Bavaria and quickly recast himself as a knowledgeable, anti-Communist army officer willing to work for the Americans. He offered a trove of documents, his expertise, his staff, and his intelligence assets to the United States. Gehlen and several staff members were taken to Fort Hunt, Virginia. They returned to Germany in July 1946, where they became an intelligence-gathering and -evaluation group known as the Gehlen Organization or by its U.S. Army cryptonym, RUSTY.[10] In December 1947 Gehlen established his own headquarters at Pullach.

Gehlen, in fact, viewed himself as working for a reconstituted conservative German state. Able to create intelligence jobs while solidifying his power base, he and his staff quickly hired former German Army staff and intelligence (Abwehr) officers, but also former Reichssicherheitshauptamt (Reich Security Main Office [RSHA]) officers, including former SS and SD personnel, who fell within Allied automatic arrest categories but who also could be blackmailed by the Soviets as potential war criminals.[11] The CIC quickly noticed a spiraling mess. In the summer of 1946, shortly after Gehlen's return to Germany, the CIC arrested a number of his agents. "Some of the agents," read a later report, "were SS personnel with known Nazi records and, in most cases, undesirable people."[12] In 1948 the CIC learned that Gehlen had hired former SD officers, some of whom tried to recruit still other SD and Gestapo officers, who themselves—in an ironic twist—already worked for the CIC.[13] "This state of affairs," said one CIC officer, "should definitely be considered a security menace."[14] In 1949, Gehlen's chief U.S. Army liaison, Colonel William Philp, complained that RUSTY was at best a reconstitution of German Army staff without firm U.S. control and at worst a potentially hostile organization that had been penetrated by the Soviets. The Gehlen Organization, he said, was becoming "increasingly uncooperative," U.S. field agents were "intentionally kept uninformed," and discipline and security were "unsatisfactory."[15]

The U.S. Army wanted the CIA, which was created in 1947, to assume firmer control of RUSTY. CIA assessments, conducted by James Critchfield, then the CIA's chief of station in Karlsruhe, were mixed. "In the recruitment methods," reported Critchfield, "no attention was paid to the character of the recruits, security, political leanings, or quality with the result that many of the agents were blown almost immediately."[16] But, Critchfield said, the organization's four thousand associates made it Germany's foremost intelligence group, whose nucleus would be part of any future German state's defense establishment. It also produced certain types of intelligence, such as Soviet air force radio traffic, that the U.S. could not obtain otherwise. Critchfield argued that better control by the CIA, typified by closer liaison and a tighter budget, would alleviate past problems.[17] The CIA assumed control of the Gehlen Organization, now code-named ZIPPER, on July 1, 1949. Critchfield became the chief CIA liaison at Pullach. He established ground rules for cooperation within an anti-Communist partnership to be dominated by the CIA. Gehlen was to follow U.S. directives and to provide "complete details of operational activities," including agent backgrounds.[18]

But Gehlen refused to act as a subordinate. Western Germany, he argued, was on the front line of the East-West divide. Its intelligence organization had to make snap decisions and assume risk. The "mechanical application of American principles," which stressed central control, was inefficient. "We operate with German methods," he explained, "applying to [the] German mentality." He further refused to produce agent files owing to the operational delays that it would cause. "If such red tape spreads out," Gehlen insisted, "every creative impulse also from the lower ranks will disappear."[19] The CIA still controlled Gehlen's funding. But it could never adequately supervise Gehlen's operations or his security methods.

The West German government, formed in October 1949, had similar frustrations, though the available records on the relationship between the government and the Gehlen Organization are spotty.[20] As it moved toward sovereignty and integration into NATO in 1955, the West German government created an armed forces establishment, the Bundeswehr, which, unlike past German military establishments, was under civilian control. It sat under a cabinet-level minister of defense who in turn answered to a defense committee within the elected Bundestag. Officer candidates were carefully screened to weed out those without commitment to democratic principles. The Bundestag launched inquiries to discuss even public speeches by officers that seemed like apologias to the Nazi years.[21]

Gehlen avoided parliamentary oversight. In 1956 the Gehlen Organization left CIA tutelage and became a legal part of the West German state as the Bundesnachrichtendienst. But the Gehlen Organization had come into existence four years before the West German government did, and Gehlen had prepared for the eventuality of state control. From 1949 to 1955 he out-maneuvered his potential intelligence rivals and gained the ear of Chancellor Konrad Adenauer and his trusted state secretary Hans Globke. Gehlen convinced Adenauer that his intelligence mission was too sensitive for parliamentary meddling. The BND thus became a free-floating organization within the Bundeskanzleramt. Gehlen developed an especially close relationship with Globke.[22] Outspoken SPD leader Kurt Schumacher expressed misgivings over this extraconstitutional arrangement. He also wondered aloud how many former RSHA officials worked for Gehlen.[23] But Schumacher died in 1952, and his successors were unable to press for effective oversight or even personnel screening.

Even within the Bundeskanzleramt, Globke liked to talk intelligence with Gehlen rather than perform actual supervision. Globke's appointment calendar refers to Gehlen as "Dr. Schneider," Gehlen's cover name, suggesting that Globke was too taken with spy craft to press Gehlen on hard questions. German records of their discussions are either nonexistent or closed to scholars, but CIC files record an instance in September 1952 when Globke asked Gehlen for information on Karl Schütz, a former SS officer who was then working in counterintelligence. Adenauer himself, Globke said, had expressed "personal interest in the man." Gehlen replied that he could furnish nothing on Schütz because, as he put it, the British held Schütz's background information. Schütz had indeed submitted a sanitized career history to the Gehlen Organization in April 1951, but his SS file—which included Schütz's service in wartime Lodz and Rome—was available under U.S. control had Gehlen wished to have Schütz's past traced.[24] Indeed, Gehlen had enough background information on Emil Augsburg, a former SD officer wanted for war crimes in Poland and now a counterintelligence officer, that he had Augsburg work outside of the Pullach complex after 1954.[25]

After 1956 Bundestag leaders managed to create a small, nonpublic intelligence committee (Vertrauensmännergremium) that met with Gehlen and Globke once a year, but like Globke, the committee discussed the intelligence product rather than the methods of its collection. The chief topic of the 1956 meeting was Nikita Khrushchev's secret speech to the Twentieth Communist Party Congress. SPD leaders expressed concern about former RSHA personnel in the BND, but Gehlen put them off. Only in the meeting of June 1958 was the issue of former RSHA personnel discussed—that is, whether they could be employed by the BND. Gehlen assured his listeners that each case would be examined thoroughly and that it "was self evident, that they could not be considered for influential leadership positions."[26] Numerous examples show that party leaders in the new West German state had no control over Gehlen's hires, even in leadership positions.[27]

That the Soviets penetrated the Gehlen Organization under these circumstances is not surprising. The CIA posited in 1969—based partly on information from Soviet defectors—that the Soviets had

> a well-targeted, well-developed recruitment campaign directed against former police and intelligence officers of the Nazi Reich. The thesis was simple: old intelligence hands will flock together, will seek to return to what they know best. Some of these people might be susceptible to a Soviet approach because of their general sympathies. Others, such as former Elite Guard (SS) and Security Service (SD) members, many of whom were now war criminals able to make their way only by hiding a past which had once put them among the elite, would be vulnerable to blackmail. . . . The future West German intelligence and security services could be penetrated almost before they were created.[28]

It remains difficult to discern the degree to which the Soviets actually recruited through blackmail. The U.S. war crimes program was winding down by 1948, and not until the mid-1950s did West German society react to former RSHA officers living in its midst.[29] Surely, compromised Germans from wartime police formations did not want their records publicly discussed. But though blackmail might have been effective in some cases, many Soviet recruits surely had their own motivations, ranging from bitterness toward the Americans to a more basic attraction, perhaps some of it financial, to the game of double-agent work. Their allegiance to the new Federal Republic, meanwhile, was less than whole.

Whatever the motivations of their recruits, the Soviets went to work immediately after the formation of the Gehlen Organization, targeting its counterintelligence wing, designated Generalvertretung L (GV L). The chief of GV L was Alfred Benzinger, who served in the army's Geheime Feldpolizei (GFP) behind the lines of the eastern front. The GFP engaged in war crimes that included the murder of Soviet commissars and Jews as well as ordinary civilians assumed to be partisans, including women and children.[30] Critchfield later wrote that Benzinger "openly recruited SD officers. . . . The word quickly got around, and the recruitment of one former

SD officer soon led to the recruitment of his friend, which led to another, and so on."[31]

Benzinger's key hire in 1948 was Wilhelm Krichbaum, the GFP's former chief. Krichbaum's trajectory with the Soviets is not clear. The Soviets knew who he was—he provided testimony as a witness at the Trial of the Major War Criminals at Nuremberg—and he was certainly subject to blackmail. Krichbaum worked for the MGB as early as 1950. Suspicion within the Gehlen Organization that Krichbaum was a double agent brought his dismissal in April 1952.[32] He died in 1957, before any full investigation was launched. In the meantime Krichbaum hired another cadre of former SD members who were Soviet spies, most notably his fellow Dresdeners Hans Clemens and Felfe himself in 1951.[33]

The city of Dresden, firebombed by the Allies in February 1945, might have been critical. In 1949 the MGB recruited Hans Clemens, a former SD officer from Dresden. "Clemens," noted one local, "was greatly feared in Dresden as an SS leader" in the 1930s.[34] In 1944 Clemens was reassigned to northern Italy, where he became known as the "Tiger of Como." He took part in the Ardeatine Caves massacre, where the SS killed 335 civilians in reprisal for an attack on an SS column in Rome.[35] On his return to Dresden in 1949, the MGB detained and recruited Clemens through an MGB officer known as "Max." Clemens agreed for two reasons. One, according to a later CIA assessment, was "his culpability as an SD criminal," and the other, according to Clemens, was "because he hated the Americans like [poison]" for bombing Dresden. "Max" sent Clemens west with instructions to join the Gehlen Organization and "to recruit known former SD co-workers for the Soviets." This was easy once Clemens met Krichbaum, who informed Clemens that "he was with the old gang again." The Gehlen Organization officially hired Clemens in 1951.[36] Clemens recruited fellow Dresdener Heinz Felfe the same year.

Unlike Clemens, Felfe was something more than a common thug. Felfe was born in Dresden in 1918. He joined the Hitler Youth in 1931 and the SS in 1936. He served in a Wehrmacht construction unit during the Polish campaign but was discharged in 1940 owing to health problems. He entered the Security Police in 1941 as an officer in the Criminal Police branch, and by 1943 he was a member of the SD. Felfe was assigned to the Amt VI (RSHA Foreign Intelligence) Swiss Desk, where he worked at least partly on matters related to the Red Orchestra, an extensive Soviet espionage network in western Europe. In December 1945 he was sent to the Netherlands as the deputy head of Amt VI in Enschede, which the Allies liberated on April 1.[37]

Felfe's superiors stated that he had fine capabilities and a strong work ethic. And there was, said one SS report, "no doubt concerning his political reliability." He finished the war at the rank of *Obersturmführer* (first lieutenant). Felfe had an ego, often telling his superiors that he was destined for greater responsibilities.[38]

Canadian forces in the Netherlands arrested Felfe on May 31, 1945. The British interrogated him at length concerning SD men who broke through Allied lines late in the war. Felfe's British interrogators noted: "He admits freely to having been an ardent Nazi and to having great hopes of what the party could do for GERMANY." At the same time, Felfe displayed contempt for the poor organization of Amt VI, while giving the British full breakdowns of its operations in Switzerland and the Netherlands.[39] He was, in fact, already reinventing himself for the postwar world as a seemingly reliable spy for the West. Later CIA assessments of his SS file and of earlier British interrogations noted that Felfe was "a highly intelligent man with very little personal warmth; a person with high regard for efficiency, and for authority, but susceptible to flattery; venal; and capable of almost childish displays of vindictiveness. . . . Infinitely cool and brazen in the face of danger, thoroughly aware at all times what he was doing, Felfe was the 'ice-cold calculator.' . . . The only emotions detectable in him are his enjoyment of the game and his disdain for his fellow man."[40]

After the British released Felfe in October 1946, he settled in the British occupation zone and struggled to make ends meet for himself and his family, which had moved west from Dresden. In the summer of 1947, Felfe offered to work for the British, who employed him and a few other former Amt VI officers in the Cologne region. Felfe provided intelligence on the German Communist Party (KPD) and left-leaning student groups at the University of Bonn. In his capacity as a British agent, he joined the KPD, traveled to Soviet-controlled Berlin several times to attend student rallies, and attended Communist meetings including the third People's Congress (Volkskongress) in the Soviet sector of Berlin.[41] Here he was so eager to read the list of attendees that a U.S. source at the meeting had to snatch it away from him.[42]

The British dropped Felfe in April 1950. Nearly twenty years later, the CIA noted that "as early as April 1950, British files contained sufficient information on Felfe to make anyone wary at the very least."[43] Felfe tried to sell information collected for the British to other intelligence agencies and to the East German Socialist Unity Party (SED). He had also, despite British objections, maintained contact with former colleagues in the RSHA from Dresden.[44] Not until after Felfe's arrest by German authorities in November

1961, however, did the British share with Gehlen that Felfe was dropped for security reasons—namely that he accepted money from the KPD to work as a double agent and that he provided false intelligence on the KPD to the British.[45]

For now, Felfe looked for work in the West German government, initially in the Bundeskriminalamt. He sanitized his past carefully. His application to the Ministry of the Interior for a position in the Bundeskriminalamt in January 1950 noted that his last residence in Germany was Gleiwitz, where he had been stationed for four months in 1943 but which was now part of Poland. This, said Felfe, made him a refugee. And though Felfe mentioned his training and employment in the Criminal Police, he said nothing about his service in the SD. He further maintained that in 1947 and 1948 he had worked for the British government, but with the Geographical Survey Unit. The Interior Ministry did a thorough background check and eventually determined in 1954 that Felfe was lying.[46] Felfe had already begun working in the West German Ministry for All-German Affairs in February 1950.[47] He interrogated refugees from the newly formed German Democratic Republic (DDR) and gathered information on the East German Volkspolizei, the Soviet order of battle, and Soviet agents.[48] To get this position, Felfe used wartime contacts. And by the time the Interior Ministry noted that he had lied about his past, the Gehlen Organization had hired him.

In September 1951 Hans Clemens set up a meeting with "Max," who recruited Felfe into the MGB. Like Clemens, Felfe was sent west, where Krichbaum hired him into GV L.[49] Other figures hired in this wave included former SD associates of Clemens, all with wartime criminal backgrounds stretching from France to Poland.[50] But Felfe emerged as the most dangerous. Once hired, Felfe rose in the Gehlen Organization more quickly than his SD comrades. From November 1951 to August 1953 he served as a GV L assistant in Karlsruhe and as a branch leader in the Rhineland. By August 1953 he was moved to the counterintelligence section at the Pullach headquarters.

From 1952 to their arrest in 1961, an MGB/KGB officer called "Alfred" handled Felfe, Clemens, and other SD penetration agents. He created an excuse—a dummy source code-named "Balthasar" who provided fake information on a Soviet uranium plant—for Clemens to travel periodically to Berlin. In 1952 and 1953 Felfe and Clemens reported to "Alfred" on GV L's bases in Karlsruhe, Stuttgart, Cologne, and the Pullach headquarters. By 1953 Gehlen's counterintelligence operations in East Berlin and the DDR suffered. His sources there were either recalled or arrested. The East German press even revealed where Gehlen's field bases were located.[51]

Yet it was in 1954 that Felfe began to run immensely complicated operations whereby the increasingly venal Gehlen depended on him in order to
impress his own superiors in the Bundeskanzleramt. Felfe built his reputation that year with the so-called LENA case. LENA was the CIA cryptonym for
Günther Hofe, an East German publisher and senior member of the National
Democratic Party of Germany. He traveled often to West Germany, providing information to the Gehlen Organization on East German politics. In
March 1954 Hofe revealed that the Soviets had recruited him to gather information on personnel within different West German agencies, including the
Foreign Ministry and the Bundeskanzleramt itself. Felfe received the mission
of turning Hofe into a double agent and playing him back against the Soviets.

LENA became typical of Felfe's increasingly bold operations, run from
positions of leadership within West German intelligence. Felfe convinced
Gehlen that LENA's Soviet handlers in Bonn were loose talkers who, in the
midst of conversations with LENA, revealed details of Soviet agents in West
Germany. Such information, he said, was invaluable for counterintelligence
work. LENA, Felfe argued, should thus provide the Soviets with information
in order to keep them talking, whereby they would unwittingly provide far
more sensitive information themselves. Gehlen subsequently persuaded
Adenauer and Globke to allow LENA to pass information already known to
the Soviets as "build-up" information—that is, true information that was not
particularly sensitive that would "build up" LENA's own bona fides—thus
making him reliable and valuable to the Soviets.

In return LENA supposedly elicited information on Soviet agents in West
Germany, which Felfe ostensibly developed in order to uncover them. But
in this particular operation, the KGB gave up nothing more than pawns and
decoys, many from rival Soviet services such as Soviet military intelligence.
In the meantime the dummy KGB orders to LENA contained statements to
the effect that information unknown to the KGB was actually already known.
Felfe was thus able to pass new and sensitive information through LENA,
which led to further Soviet successes. In 1955 the KGB used this information even to recruit a construction worker to place microphones in the newly
built Bundeskanzleramt.

In the meantime, Felfe's apparent value grew in Pullach. He became more
trusted by Gehlen, who in turn became more trusted by Globke and Adenauer. In 1956, when the Gehlen Organization was reorganized as the BND,
Felfe became the deputy chief of the Soviet Operations Section of the Counter Espionage Group.[52] His place secure, Felfe worked after 1956 to protect
KGB espionage operations against West Germany. He provided "Alfred" with

information on West German–run anti-Soviet operations in West Germany, Berlin, or the USSR. Felfe had reinvented himself so convincingly as a reliable West German official and security expert that officials in the Federal Office for the Protection of the Constitution (Bundesamt für Verfassungsschutz [BfV]) outlined their counterespionage cases for Felfe in order to elicit his opinion. In this way Felfe wrecked BfV operations against Soviet spies such as Dmitry Ivanovich Kirpichev, a KGB operative with the Soviet Freight and Transport Office. Shortly before Kirpichev's planned arrest by the BfV in February 1961, Kirpichev made a "business" trip to East Berlin, became mysteriously ill, and did not return.[53] Only later was it apparent that Felfe's curiosity about the operations of other agencies blew their operations against eastern bloc spies.

Felfe neutralized more elaborate BND counterintelligence operations. In 1959 he was in charge of a scheme to tap Soviet Embassy telephones and the apartments of Soviet officials in Bonn. The Soviets thereafter used the tapped phones to put forward deceptive information while using the untapped phones for more secure communications. Felfe foiled efforts to improve phone tapping through bureaucratic delays or the staged technical failure of audio equipment. Soviet officials, moreover, conveniently moved out of newly tapped offices and apartments while less important officials moved in.[54] In the meantime Felfe protected his co-workers in GV L. In October 1956 the CIC learned that Felfe had interceded with Gehlen personally to protect the aforementioned Karl Schütz from an investigation that Adenauer had requested. Gehlen, as mentioned earlier, told Globke that the British held the information on Schütz's past.[55]

Few imagined the kind of damage that Felfe was causing, in part because his activities themselves were so bold. He simply did not fit the profile of a low-level operative passing messages with invisible ink. But a few imagined something. In February 1954 the KGB counterintelligence chief in Vienna, Peter Deriabin, defected to the Americans. He provided the code names of three KGB agents within the Gehlen Organization, two of whom—"Peter" and "Paul"—were the Soviet code names of Felfe and Clemens. The same year James Critchfield, still the CIA's liaison with Gehlen, suspecting more than the usual trouble, discussed with CIC officials the "future need for [high-level] penetration of the Gehlen Group" once it became part of the West German government.[56] CIC penetration would provide information while keeping the CIA's hands clean in its relationship with the West Germans.

The CIC soon managed to penetrate GV L through a senior counterintelligence official named Ludwig Albert. Albert was a former GFP official who, it turned out, was a triple agent, working for Gehlen, the CIC, and the East German Stasi. His true loyalties may never be determined. But in 1954 Albert provided a stream of reports to CIC special agent Rodney C. Ruffine that clearly pointed to Felfe as a Soviet spy. Seventy percent of the information leaked to the Soviets, Albert said, could only have come from the clique within GV L, which was made up of "former Sicherheitsdienst people [with] rather unsavory backgrounds."[57] Felfe, he noted, had a propensity to interest himself "in other matters which were none of his business."[58] Albert further reported that officials within the Gehlen Organization were investigating Felfe, Karl Schütz, and Walter Vollmer, another former SD member. In April Vollmer was dismissed, Albert said, "because of the volume of unsavory information regarding his past."[59] Yet Felfe and Schütz remained.

In October 1954 Ruffine reported, "ALBERT has become more and more frustrated and discouraged on the subject of Gehlen security."[60] He reported soon after that, "The suspicion that Heinz Felfe and the SD . . . clique which followed him into the organization are 'enemies' has been growing steadily."[61] How, then, was Felfe allowed to remain? Albert had several theories. One was that Gehlen and his top officials simply did not perform sufficient background checks. Another was that they feared a scandal shortly before the granting of West German sovereignty.[62] Another still was that there were too many former SD men in the counterintelligence section to effect a full investigation.[63] The CIA later added that Deriabin's defection prompted the Soviets to divert any investigation in such a way that the most important KGB agents were protected.

The victim in 1955 was Ludwig Albert himself. Albert, as mentioned, was a triple agent. Gehlen ran him against the CIC, and the East Germans ran him against both the CIC and Gehlen. Albert truly despised Felfe and the SD clique, but he also wished to divert attention from himself. The question was who would be exposed first, Albert or Felfe. The Soviets seem to have protected Felfe by exposing Albert through a man named Herbert Weinmann, who was surely a KGB plant. Albert was arrested in May 1955, and his home was searched. West German authorities found wads of cash, intelligence reports, correspondence with CIC, and a microfilm reader manufactured in East Germany. "If he can't explain," said Albert's wife, "he can hang himself." Indeed, after a series of interrogations by Emil Augsburg, Albert did just that.[64]

The Gehlen Organization refused to share much information on the Albert case with the Americans. But the CIA surmised that the immediate effect of the Albert case was that Gehlen trusted Felfe more than ever. Gehlen believed, evidently, that Albert, the "true" mole, had tried to divert attention from himself to Felfe as a deception maneuver. It was now that Felfe began his true ascent within the BND. As Critchfield put it, "FRIESEN [the CIA cryptonym for Felfe] enjoys a peculiar close relationship to UTILITY [the CIA cryptonym for Gehlen]. While he is not one of UTILITY's 'boys' in the sense of having served with him during the war, he appears to have made a rapid-rise prestige-wise within UPSWING [the BND] and now certainly enjoys a great measure of UTILITY's confidence."[65] The CIA later noted, "One thing is clear: The net effect of the Albert case was to solidify, rather than weaken, Felfe's position."[66] A senior Gehlen official noted, not until 1962, "It now seems obvious that Albert and Felfe were parallel KGB penetration agents . . . unwitting of each other, and that once Felfe was placed in headquarters the KGB apparently went to a good bit of trouble to neutralize Albert."[67]

But at the time, Felfe also managed to build unusual trust with the CIA. He complained to Critchfield about what he called "ALBERT's vendetta against former GV L members who had been transferred to UPSWING headquarters."[68] Despite seeing Felfe's SS file, Critchfield even swallowed Felfe's nonsensical tale that he became an SD officer by accident. "His story," reported Critchfield, "is that he happened to be in Berlin and available one day when [RSHA Amt VI Chief Walter] SCHELLENBERG went to the Kripo [Criminal Police] headquarters and levied a request for 20 bodies. . . . My guess," Critchfield added, "is that [Felfe] is more reconstructed in his political orientation than are a number of his colleagues. . . . He is a man who apparently ties his personal future to the West and has made a decision to fight Communist ideologies and practice within the best framework available to him."[69]

It was with this trust that Felfe targeted CIA operations, and particularly the CIA's Berlin Operations Base, which worked against Soviet military headquarters in Karlshorst. In September 1956 Felfe was part of a delegation that visited CIA headquarters in Washington. As a hook, he gave a talk on the LENA case, "revealing" that it had produced valuable intelligence on KGB operations from Karlshorst, including safe-house addresses and license plate numbers. He offered to provide information garnered by LENA. As CIA analysts put it later, "We responded with alacrity. Not only did we wish to keep our foot in the door now that the newly legalized BND was often eager to dispense with us. . . . Even more important was the need to have as many sources as possible within Soviet controlled territory such as Karlshorst." The Soviets now even allowed LENA to provide early warning on a few minor developments, and the CIA believed that it had additional coverage of the Karlshorst compound.[70]

Felfe, meanwhile, collected information on the CIA's operations against Karlshorst. He was briefed by the CIA three times in 1958 and 1959 and managed to place a BND liaison officer (whom he himself supervised) with the U.S. Army Berlin Base and the CIA's Berlin Operations Base. He met with "Alfred" in December 1959 to report on CIA operations against Karlshorst.[71] Felfe thus revealed not only the identities of hundreds of BND sources and agents in the east. He also blew the identities of numerous CIA sources and agents there.

The Soviets often reacted with care. Rather than arrest one key female CIA recruit in their compound in Karlshorst, they limited her access to information, thus protecting Felfe, since her sudden disappearance would have caused CIA suspicion of him. Until the construction of the Berlin Wall in August 1961, other CIA agents identified by Felfe received similar treatment. Afterward the KGB moved in, made arrests, or doubled CIA agents for work against the CIA and BND. "As a result of such aggressive manipulation by Felfe and the KGB," a major CIA report concluded, "the hitherto unilateral Berlin Base program against Karlshorst was largely compromised."[72]

CIA suspicion of Felfe resurfaced in 1959 owing to Michal Goleniewski, Poland's deputy chief of army counterintelligence, who worked for the KGB and who in that year began funneling information to the CIA (he defected in 1961). Goleniewski revealed that two KGB agents were part of the BND delegation that visited CIA headquarters in September 1956. He further revealed that the KGB had an agent who reported on joint BND-CIA operations. It could only have been Felfe. The CIA soon began to study Felfe seriously, but without telling the BND.[73] They followed him on his visits to Berlin and Rome in 1959 and 1960. They tapped the phone in his Munich apartment. They also discovered, much to their surprise, that there had seemingly been no check of Felfe's SS file in the CIA-controlled Berlin Document Center as of January 1960.[74]

As they looked over past reports, Felfe indeed seemed suspicious to his CIA interlocutors. He had asked repeatedly about his SS file in the Berlin Document Center. He owned a second home in Oberaudorf, conveniently on the border with neutral Austria. He disappeared briefly during a trip to Berlin with Critchfield in March 1957. But Felfe's treachery was hard to believe, partly because he seemed so reliable and competent. "There is not much doubt that he should be ranked high," wrote Clare Edward Petty, now the CIA liaison to Gehlen in Munich. "Of course, the tendency to give him very good marks is affected . . . by the fact that we compare . . . him with his UPSWING [BND] colleagues, and a fair number of these would be quite easy to beat on any rating test." Petty concluded, "[Felfe] is undoubtedly a man who will be around a long time. . . . All the little items *could* mean he has eastern contacts. They *could* mean nothing. . . . For my part I tend to conclude, at least on the basis of what we now have to go on (or do not) that . . . FRIESEN [Felfe] is not a penetration agent. . . . Certainly if he is such an agent, it must be presumed that he is a very good one."[75] Indeed he was. During a meeting with Petty in January 1960, Felfe pressed for a closer operational relationship with the CIA. There was much, said Felfe, that he did not know about operational possibilities against Soviet intelligence.[76]

But the circumstantial and accumulated evidence against Felfe was strong enough that the CIA informed Gehlen himself in February 1961. Gehlen, according to later CIA studies, "immediately agreed that his heretofore favorite case officer—Felfe—was the major suspect."[77] Gehlen set up a small task force under his security chief Walrab Rudolf von Buttlar (code-named BERN-HARDT), and the subsequent investigation was code-named Fall Mexiko. Buttlar picked up the leads Ludwig Albert had developed back in 1953. He reviewed all information on Krichbaum. He discovered that Kurt Ponger, a Soviet spy arrested by the Americans in Vienna in 1953, had been in contact with Krichbaum and other Gehlen Organization members.[78] Emil Augsburg, meanwhile, closely reviewed the LENA case. Buttlar told Petty in March 1961 that he had in fact had his eye on Felfe since 1957. He further relayed that "FRIESEN [Felfe] was a dangerous man because he was an inordinately skillful manipulator and elicitor, was much sharper than most of the people around him, and was the sort of guy who could really, without being too obvious, get his hands on almost anything." Buttlar noted, however, that, "even UTIL-ITY [Gehlen] had succumbed to FRIESEN's [Felfe's] charm and that FRIESEN, unlike almost any other officer of his level at UPHILL [the BND], for many years had had the privilege of personally briefing UTILITY on especially interesting and sensitive Soviet matters." Gehlen's comments in these briefings surely reached the Soviets thereafter.[79]

Gehlen's task force concluded by April 1961 that Felfe was a penetration agent.[80] Buttlar placed Felfe's Oberaudorf home under visual and telephone surveillance. He discovered that Felfe and his former SD colleague Hans Clemens spoke often about secure matters, that Clemens retained contacts in Dresden, and that Felfe became aggressively inquisitive after his visits to Clemens in Cologne (Clemens having relayed Soviet orders to Felfe there).[81] The CIA diverted personnel in Germany and Austria to help in the surveillance of Felfe, Clemens, and another former SD counterintelligence officer named Friedrich Busch, all of whom traveled to Berlin in August 1961 and to

Vienna in September, allegedly on operational business. The British, meanwhile, helped with surveillance of Clemens in Cologne.[82]

But Gehlen remained indecisive. In August 1961—after the Berlin Wall's construction somehow surprised the Western world—Gehlen told his CIA liaison that "some concrete action must be taken by [the] end [of] September [to] neutralize leading security subjects, especially UJDROWSY [Felfe] himself." But Gehlen spoke only of moving Felfe away from the Pullach headquarters.[83] As late as October 25, Gehlen talked about creating a new Munich *Dienststelle* for Felfe, compartmentalized from the rest of the BND. It is likely that Gehlen did not want Adenauer or Globke to know how badly Felfe had fooled him. Or, as the CIA posited, maybe he wished to have a channel to the Soviet government via the KGB, owing to the tense political situation.[84] Why he finally approved the arrest of Felfe and Clemens on November 6 is not entirely clear and must await the opening of BND records.[85]

Felfe and Clemens were tried for treason in 1963, receiving fourteen- and ten-year sentences, respectively. Felfe was released in 1969 in exchange for the freedom of two West German students—Walter Neumann and Peter Sonntag—who had been arrested by the Soviets for espionage in September 1961. He spent the rest of his life in East Germany, later spreading more disinformation through his memoir *Im Dienst des Gegners* (1986) and eventually outliving the German Democratic Republic and the Cold War themselves (he died in 2008). In the meantime, the scandal relating to the Felfe trial resulted in Gehlen's estrangement from Adenauer, a slow, albeit incomplete, housecleaning of the BND that included Gehlen himself in 1968, and proper government oversight thereafter. In retirement, Gehlen bitterly complained, "For week after week the [Felfe] affair continued to hold the newspaper headlines: his character, his Nazi past, and his subsequent treachery were all grist for their mill, resulting in exaggerated reports about us." He insisted, "I have reason to believe that [Felfe] did not work as successfully as Moscow had hoped."[86]

More importantly, the treason trials of Felfe and Clemens in 1963 resulted in national scandal. In 1954 the cover of *Der Spiegel* referred to Gehlen as "the Chancellor's favorite general."[87] Now newspapers wondered aloud how many former SS members polluted the West German foreign intelligence establishment, the degree to which they compromised national security owing to their vulnerability to blackmail, and the degree to which the Bundeskanzleramt had learned their pasts after the BND became part of the West German government in 1955. Publicly anyway, Globke insisted in 1963 that fewer than 1 percent of Gehlen's men had held rank in the SS, his inference being that it was not a significant problem.[88]

Indeed, we know more now concerning these questions than was known at the time. But complete answers must await the opening of BND records that have not been destroyed, and an analysis of these records against U.S. intelligence files. Thorough consideration will reveal the number of SS officers in the BND and the operational ways in which the shadow of the SD carried forward into Cold War intelligence. At the same time, it will reveal a tale of *Vergangenheitspolitik* by which we can discern the reasons for those individuals' continued inclusion in the most sensitive of agencies, as we broaden the early conflicted political history of the Federal Republic of Germany.

Notes

1. Christopher Andrew, *The Sword and the Shield: The Mitrokhin Archive and the Secret History of the KGB* (New York: Basic Books, 1991), 439.

2. David E. Murphy, Memorandum for Deputy Director (Plans), February 7, 1963, "Heinz Felfe Damage Assessment," RG 263, Records of the Central Intelligence Agency, entry ZZ-19, box 35, Felfe, Heinz: Damage Assessment Report, U.S. National Archives and Records Administration, College Park, MD (hereafter NARA).

3. Studies on East German intelligence under the Ministry for State Security (Stasi) form an exception. On operations, see primarily Kristie I. Macrakis, *Seduced by Secrets: Inside the Stasi's Spy-Tech World* (New York: Cambridge University Press, 2008); Kristie I. Macrakis, Thomas Wegener Friis, and Helmut Müller-Engbergs, eds., *East German Intelligence: Myth, Reality and Controversy* (London: Routledge, 2009). Much work on the Stasi concerns the relationship between East German citizens and the police state. See, for example, Barbara Miller, *Narratives of Guilt and Compliance in Unified Germany: Stasi Informers and Their Impact on Society* (London: Routledge, 1999).

4. An assessment of the BND's limited revelations in 2010 is in Stephen Tyas, "Smoke and Mirrors: The German Foreign Intelligence Service's Release of Names of Former Nazi Employees," *Holocaust and Genocide Studies* 25, no. 2 (Fall 2011): 290–99.

5. The commission's official title is the Unabhängige Historikerkommission zur Erforschung der Geschichte des Bundesnachrichtendienstes 1945–1968. Its website is www.uhk-bnd.de/. On its formation, see Sven Felix Kellerhoff, "Nazi Verstrickungen des BND werden endlich geklärt," *Die Welt,* January 13, 2011. On the destruction of relevant files, see Georg Bönisch and Klaus Wiegrefe, "Braune Vergangenheit: BND vernichtete Akten zu SS-Verbrecher Brunner," *Der Spiegel,* July 20, 2011; Klaus Wiegrefe, "BND vernichtete Personalakten frühere SS-Leute," *Der Spiegel,* November 29, 2011. Poor BND record-keeping is also a factor in limiting what we might learn from that agency's records. Unit 85, a task force created in 1961 to discern the Nazi backgrounds of BND members, depended on help from the Zentrale Stelle der

Landesjustizverwaltung zur Aufklärung nationalsozialistischer Verbrechen in Lud-wigsburg, an investigative authority set up in 1958 to investigate Nazi crimes. Unit 85 concluded that BND chief Reinhard Gehlen simply did not want to know the back-grounds of the men that his organization hired in the 1950s. See Peter Carstens, "NS Verbrecher im BND: Eine 'zweite Entnazifierung,'" *Frankfurter Allgemeine Zeitung*, March 18, 2010.

6. See Eckhart Conze, Norbert Frei, Peter Hayes, and Moshe Zimmermann, *Das Amt und die Vergangenheit: Deutsche Diplomaten im Dritten Reich in der Bundesre-publik* (Munich: Blessing, 2010). On the destruction of Foreign Ministry records, see Eckhart Conze, Norbert Frei, Peter Hayes, and Moshe Zimmermann, "Panzerschrank der Schande," *Frankfurter Allgemeine Zeitung*, May 5, 2012. The independent com-mission researching the BND reported in 2014 that its research on the Gehlen Orga-nization/BND from 1945 to 1968 would be complete in 2016. A study appeared in the interim, based on papers presented in December 2013. See Jost Dülffer, Klaus-Dietmar Henke, Wolfgang Krieger, and Rolf-Dieter Müller, eds., *Die Geschichte der Organisation Gehlen und des BND 1945–1968: Umrisse und Einblicke*, posted at www .uhk-bnd.de/wp-content/uploads/2013/05/UHK-BND_Bd2_online-12.pdf. It men-tions the Felfe affair but provides little analysis.

7. Researchers should be aware that the CIA files at NARA that have been made public under the Nazi War Crimes Disclosure Act underwent two separate releases between 2000 and 2007. Files in the first release of CIA Name Files and CIA Sub-ject Files (RG 263, Entries ZZ-16 and ZZ-17, respectively) have more redactions and more pages withheld. CIA Name and Subject Files in the second release (RG 263, Entries ZZ-18 and ZZ-19) are of higher quality. For an online guide to these entries, see www.archives.gov/iwg/declassified-records/rg-263-cia-records/. U.S. Army Counterintelligence Corps Records based on names and subjects are in RG 319 (Records of the Army Staff, Counterintelligence Corps Collection, Records of the Investigative Records Repository), NARA. Various entries are relevant, but addi-tional entry 134A contains three thousand pages, released in 2004, specifically on the Gehlen Organization. Online guides to the relevant records include www.archives .gov/iwg/declassified-records/rg-319-army-staff/rg-319-records.html.

8. For Gehlen's own self-serving account, edited by Holocaust denier David Irving, see Reinhard Gehlen, *The Service: The Memoirs of General Reinhard Gehlen* (New York: World, 1972). For older journalistic attempts, see Heinz Höhne and Her-mann Zolling, *The General Was a Spy: The Truth about General Gehlen and His Spy Ring* (New York: Coward, McCann and Geoghegan, 1972); and the more academic Mary Ellen Reese, *General Reinhard Gehlen and the CIA Connection* (Fairfax, VA: George Mason University Press, 1990), 143–73. More recently, see Timothy Naftali, "Reinhard Gehlen and the United States," in *US Intelligence and the Nazis*, by Rich-ard Breitman, Norman J. W. Goda, Timothy Naftali, and Robert Wolfe (New York: Cambridge University Press, 2005), 375–418; Peter-Ferdinand Koch, *Enttarnt: Dop-pelagenten—Namen, Fakten, Beweise* (Salzburg: Ecowin, 2011), 158–205; Rolf Dieter-

Müller, "Frühe Konflikte: Annäherung an eine Biographie Reinhard Gehlens," in Dülffer, et al., *Die Geschichte der Organisation Gehlen und des BND*, 17–25.

9. A good assessment of Gehlen's failings is in Geoffrey P. Megargee, *Inside Hitler's High Command* (Lawrence: University Press of Kansas, 2000).

10. Documents on the U.S. relationship with Gehlen until 1949 are in Kevin Ruffner, ed., "Forging and Intelligence Partnership: The CIA and the Origins of the BND, 1945–1949," RG 263, entry ZZ-19, box 30–31, NARA, now also available at the online National Security Archive, www.gwu.edu/~nsarchiv/NSAEBB/NSAEBB146/index .htm. See also Kevin Ruffner, "American Intelligence and the Gehlen Organization 1945–1949," *Studies in Intelligence*, RG 263, entry ZZ-19, box 61, NARA. The memoirs of Gehlen's CIA liaison James H. Critchfield, *Partners at the Creation: The Men behind Postwar Germany's Defense and Intelligence Establishments* (Annapolis, MD: U.S. Naval Institute Press, 2003), 21–108, are illuminating but best used cautiously. See also Reese, *General Reinhard Gehlen*, 37–103.

11. A recent analysis, which points to the decentralized structure of the Gehlen Organization as the cause of this questionable recruiting, is Gerhard Sälter, "Nazi Netzwerke und die Rekrutiering hauptamtlicher Mitarbeiter," in Dülffer et al., *Die Geschichte der Organisation Gehlen und des BND*, 41–52.

12. Chief of Station Karlsruhe to Chief, Foreign Branch M, August 19, 1948, Ruffner, ed., "Forging an Intelligence Partnership," document 63.

13. These Gehlen recruits included former Gestapo officer Anton Mahler, former SD officer Emil Augsburg, and former SD officer Kurt Auner. All had criminal records. See Agent Herbert Bechtold, 7970th CIC Group, TIB Attempts to Penetrate the KPD, April 25, 1949, RG 319, entry ZZ-7, file XE 260030, NARA; TIB Penetration of KPD, Special Agent Jack E. Heibler, June 12, 1948, RG 319, entry ZZ-7, file MSN 57281, TIB Operatives Salzburg, NARA. On Mahler, see Richard Breitman and Norman J. W. Goda, *Hitler's Shadow: Nazi War Criminals, US Intelligence, and the Cold War* (Washington, DC: National Archives and Records Administration, 2010), 43–49. On Augsburg and Auner, RG 263, entry ZZ-18, box 5, Name File Emil Augsburg, Name File Kurt Auner, NARA.

14. Chisel Report, Report No. 981, June 25, 1947, RG 319, entry ZZ-7, box 14, file XE 185968, Rusty Personalities, Pt. 2, NARA.

15. Chief of Station Karlsruhe (James Critchfield) to Chief, Foreign Branch M, April 18, 1949, Ruffner, ed., "Forging an Intelligence Partnership," document 89.

16. Chief of Station Karlsruhe (James Critchfield) to Chief, Foreign Branch M, August 19, 1948, Ruffner, ed., "Forging an Intelligence Partnership," document 63.

17. Chief, Munich Operations Base (Critchfield) to Chief, OSO, December 17, 1948, Ruffner, ed., "Forging an Intelligence Partnership," document 72.

18. Basic Agreement included in Chief of Station Karlsruhe (Critchfield) to Chief, Foreign Branch M, June 13, 1949, Ruffner, ed., "Forging an Intelligence Partnership," document 93.

19. Gehlen to Critchfield, October 10, 1949, enclosed in Chief of Station Karls-

ruhe (Critchfield) to Chief, Foreign Branch M, October 12, 1949, Ruffner, ed., "Forging an Intelligence Partnership," document 97.

20. On the source problem, see Stefanie Waske, *Mehr Liaison als Kontrolle: Die Kontrolle des BND durch Parlament und Regierung 1955–1978* (Wiesbaden: Sozialwissenschaften, 2009), 15–17.

21. See the case of Captain Hans-Adolf Zenker, discussed in Norman J. W. Goda, *Tales from Spandau: Nazi Criminals and the Cold War* (New York: Cambridge University Press, 2007), 160–66.

22. On their relationship, see Future Federal Military Security and Intelligence Agencies, November 12, 1951, RG 319, entry 134A, box 140A, file ZF015120WJF, v. II, f. 1, NARA.

23. Waske, *Mehr Liaison als Kontrolle*, 26.

24. 348/52, September 12, 1952, RG 319, entry 134A, box 140A, file ZF015120WJF, v. II, f. 1, NARA; Memo regarding Carl [*sic*] Schuetz, November 2, 1954, RG 319, entry 134A, box 141A, file ZF015120WJF, v. III, f. 1, NARA. Schütz was not dropped from the BND until 1964 for his closeness to Felfe. EGMA-64930, July 27, 1964, RG 263, entry ZZ-18, box 116, Name File Carl [*sic*] Schuetz, NARA.

25. RG 263, entry ZZ-18, box 5, Name File Emil Augsburg, NARA. He was later suspected of working with Felfe and in 1966 dismissed from the BND owing to his SS record.

26. Quoted in Waske, *Mehr Liaison als Kontrolle*, 49.

27. Ibid., 52–54. Even in his memoirs, Gehlen argued that his organization hired civilian officers "provided they had had a clean slate during the Third Reich." Gehlen, *Service*, 131.

28. RG 263, entry ZZ-19, box 35, Felfe, Heinz: KGB Exploitation, 13, NARA.

29. Patrick Tobin, "Crossroads at Ulm: Postwar West Germany and the 1958 Ulm *Einsatzkommando* Trial" (PhD diss., University of North Carolina at Chapel Hill, 2013).

30. On the GFP, see Paul B. Brown, "The Senior Leadership Cadre of the Geheime Feldpolizei, 1939–1945," *Holocaust and Genocide Studies* 17, no. 3 (Fall 2003): 278–304.

31. Critchfield, *Partners at the Creation*, 163.

32. At the time of Krichbaum's dismissal in 1952, it was known that he had associated with Kurt Ponger and Wilhelm Höttl, both of whom U.S. authorities arrested as Soviet agents in early 1953. But the CIA believed that Krichbaum was "at most an unwitting informant of Kurt PONGER . . . who displays symptoms of a creeping senility." See Chief of Base, Pullach, to Chief, EE, EGLA-3418, April 24, 1953, RG 263, entry ZZ-18, box 72, Name File Wilhelm Krichbaum, NARA.

33. For the versions of the hiring wave that emphasize the initiative of Krichbaum and Oskar Reile, see RG 263, entry ZZ-19, box 35, Felfe, Heinz: KGB Exploitation, NARA; RG 263, entry ZZ-18, box 72, Name File Wilhem Krichbaum, NARA. See also the BND's chronological account of Felfe's career dated July 3, 1961, RG 263,

entry ZZ-18, box 34, Name File Heinz Felfe, v. II, NARA. For a version that empha-sizes Felfe's own role more, see Lt. Col. Sam Boone to Commanding Officer, 66th CIC Group, III-35714, June 23, 1954, RG 319, entry 134A, box 141A, file ZF015120WJF v. III, f. 3, NARA.

34. See statements from Georg Weickert and Willi Papenfuss, January 25, 1962, RG 263, entry ZZ-18, box 24, Name File Hans Clemens, v. II, f. 2, NARA.

35. Bern to OSS Headquarters, IN 18776, received August 31, 1944, and CSDIC-CMF/SD 7, First Detailed Interrogation Report on SS Hauptsturmfuehrer Clemens, Hans, May 23, 1945, both in RG 263, entry ZZ-18, box 21, Name File Hans Clemens, v. I, NARA.

36. Chief of Base, Bonn, to Chief, EE, EGNA-27257, March 23, 1964, RG 263, entry ZZ-18, box 21, Name File Hans Clemens, v. III, f. 2, NARA. See also RG 263, entry ZZ-19, box 35, Felfe, Heinz: KGB Exploitation, 20, NARA.

37. Chronology based on Felfe's SS file, RG 242, Microfilm Publication A3343 SSO (Records of the Berlin Document Center, SS Officer Files), roll 201, NARA. On the Red Orchestra, see Attachment A to EGMA 54025, March 23, 1961, RG 263, entry ZZ-18, box 34, Name File Heinz Felfe, v. I, NARA.

38. Beurteilung über den SS-Unterstürmführer Heinz Felfe, November 3, 1943, RG 242, Microfilm Publication A3343 SSO, roll 201, frames 257–58, NARA.

39. Tactical Interrogation Report, July 14, 1945, RG 263, entry ZZ-18, box 34, Name File Heinz Felfe, v. I, NARA; Tactical Interrogation Report, August 4, 1945, RG 319, entry ZZ-6, box 4, file XE 220949—Felfe, Heinz, NARA.

40. RG 263, entry ZZ-19, box 35, Felfe, Heinz: KGB Exploitation, 15–16, NARA.

41. See the card on Felfe dated April 12, 1950, RG 319, entry ZZ-6, box 4, file XE 220949—Felfe, Heinz, NARA.

42. See the card on Felfe dated June 23, 1950, RG 319, entry ZZ-6, box 4, file XE 220949—Felfe, Heinz, NARA.

43. RG 263, entry ZZ-19, box 35, Felfe, Heinz: KGB Exploitation, 81, NARA.

44. RG 263, entry ZZ-19, box 35, Felfe, Heinz: KGB Exploitation, 17, 81–82, NARA.

45. Memorandum on Felfe dated January 1962, RG 319, entry 134A, box 142A, file ZF015120WJF, v. VIII, f. 1, NARA.

46. Felfe to Bundesminister des Innern, January 13, March 10, 1950; Vermerk, May 18, 1954, RG 263, entry ZZ-18, box 34, Name File Heinz Felfe, v. I, NARA.

47. See Lt. Col. Ira Ewalt to Commanding Officer, 66th CIC Group, III-35714, July 13, 1954, RG 319, entry ZZ-6, box 4, file XE 220949—Felfe, Heinz, NARA.

48. The information is from Ludwig Albert in the Gehlen Organization. See the report dated June 10, 1954, III-35714, RG 319, entry ZZ-6, box 4, file XE 220949—Felfe, Heinz, NARA. See also the report of June 23, 1954, III-35714, RG 319, entry ZZ-6, box 4, file XE 220949—Felfe, Heinz, NARA.

49. For the versions of Felfe's hiring emphasizing the roles of Krichbaum and Oskar Reile, see RG 263, entry ZZ-19, box 35, Felfe, Heinz: KGB Exploitation, NARA.

See also the BND's chronological account of Felfe's career dated July 3, 1961, RG 263, entry ZZ-18, box 34, Name File Heinz Felfe, v. II, NARA. For a version that emphasizes Felfe's own role more, see Lt. Col. Sam Boone to Commanding Officer, 66th CIC Group, III-35714, June 23, 1954, RG 319, entry 134A, box 141A, file ZF015120WJF, v. III, f. 3, NARA. On Krichbaum's own hiring of Felfe, see RG 263, entry ZZ-18, box 72, Name File Wilhelm Krichbaum, NARA.

50. Clemens recruited the aforementioned Karl Schütz, a former SS major who served in Lodz in 1939 and 1940 and who later joined the SD and worked in Rome. In 1954 he was transferred to headquarters to work in counterintelligence. RG 263, entry ZZ-18, box 116, Name File Carl [sic] Schuetz, NARA. Clemens also recruited Friedrich Busch, another former SD officer, convicted in France for war crimes and released in 1952. See Clemens, Hans Max, Att [EGLA-2254], page 3 [1955], RG 263, entry ZZ-18, box 21, Name File Hans Clemens, v. I, NARA; Chief, EE to Chief, Munich Liaison Base, October 6, 1961, RG 263, entry ZZ-18, box 34, Name File Heinz Felfe, v. II, NARA; RG 263, entry ZZ-18, box 19, Name File Friedrich Busch, NARA. Felfe in 1953 recruited Friedrich Frank, who escaped war crimes prosecution in the Netherlands. See Contact Report, @BERNHARDT, @FLEMING, May 29, 1961, RG 263, entry ZZ-18, box 34, Name File Heinz Felfe, v. I, NARA. Other hires in this period whose loyalties cannot be determined were Hans Sommer and Walter Vollmer. Sommer was a former member of Amt VI in France, fired in 1952 for falsely claiming travel expenses. Gehlen sources said that he worked for French intelligence thereafter. Vollmer joined the SS in 1931 and served the SD after 1936. After working for the Gehlen Organization, he was dismissed in 1953. On Sommer, see RG 263, entry ZZ-18, box 122, Name File Hans Sommer, NARA. On Vollmer, RG 263, entry ZZ-18, box 133, Name File Walter Vollmer, NARA.

51. See the BND's chronological account of Felfe's career dated July 3, 1961, in RG 263, entry ZZ-18, box 34, Name File Heinz Felfe, v. II, NARA.

52. On the LENA case and its significance, see RG 263, entry ZZ-19, box 35, Felfe, Heinz: KGB Exploitation, 44–52, NARA.

53. RG 263, entry ZZ-19, box 35, Felfe, Heinz: KGB Exploitation, 59–61, NARA.

54. RG 263, entry ZZ-19, box 35, Felfe, Heinz: KGB Exploitation, 58–59, NARA.

55. Central Clearance Unit, American Consulate General, Munich, Request for Records Check, Date illegible, RG 319, entry ZZ-6, box 4, file XE 220949—Felfe, Heinz, NARA.

56. DAD/G2 USAREUR Conference on Control of Gehlen Group, Annex B, RG 319, entry 134A, box 140A, file ZF015120WJF, v. I, f. 2, NARA.

57. See the report dated June 10, 1954, III-35714 and the CIC report of June 24, 1954, in RG 319, entry ZZ-6, box 4, file XE 220949—Felfe, Heinz, NARA.

58. See the report dated June 10, 1954, III-35714, RG 319, entry ZZ-6, box 4, file XE 220949—Felfe, Heinz, NARA.

59. Lt. Col. Ira Ewalt, report to Commanding Officer, 66th CIC Group, USAREUR, III-35714, June 24, 1954, RG 319, entry ZZ-6, box 4, file XE 220949—Felfe, Heinz, NARA.

60. Lt. Col. Ira Ewalt, report of October 29, 1954, RG 319, entry 134A, box 140A, file ZF015120WJF, v. I, f. 3, NARA.

61. See card concerning FELFE, Heinz, November 16, 1954, RG 319, entry ZZ-6, box 4, file XE 220949—Felfe, Heinz, NARA.

62. Summary of Information, Region III, 66th CIC Group, July 13, 1955, Gehlen Organization, entry 134A, box 140A, file ZF015120WJF, v. I, f. 2, NARA.

63. Summary of Information, Region II, 66th CIC Group, April 26, 1955, Gehlen Organization, RG 319, entry 134A, box 144A, v. I, f. 2, NARA. Albert also provided the names of Gehlen officials whom he deemed security risks who were not former RSHA members. See Summary of Information, Gehlen Organization, Region III, 66th CIC Group, November 22, 1954, RG 319, entry 134A, box 144A, v. III, f. 1, NARA.

64. Pull 1352 (IN28850), p. 2, July 25, 1955, RG 263, entry ZZ-18, box 34, Name File Heinz Felfe, v. I, NARA.

65. Memorandum for the Record, EGLA 22991/2, undated, RG 263, entry ZZ-18, box 34, Name File Heinz Felfe, v. I, NARA.

66. RG 263, entry ZZ-19, box 35, Felfe, Heinz: KGB Exploitation, 35–41, NARA.

67. Chief, EE to Chief, Munich Liaison Base, EGMW, 11494, February 9, 1962, RG 263, entry ZZ-18, box 21, Name File Hans Clemens, v. II, f. 2, NARA.

68. Memorandum for the Record, March 29, 1956, RG 263, entry ZZ-18, box 34, Name File Heinz Felfe, v. I, NARA.

69. Memorandum for the Record, EGLA22991/2, undated, RG 263, entry ZZ-18, box 34, Name File Heinz Felfe, v. I, NARA.

70. RG 263, entry ZZ-19, box 35, Felfe, Heinz: KGB Exploitation, 55–56, NARA.

71. RG 263, entry ZZ-19, box 35, Felfe, Heinz: KGB Exploitation, 56, NARA.

72. RG 263, entry ZZ-19, box 35, Felfe, Heinz: KGB Exploitation, 57–58, NARA.

73. EGMA-46721, January 5, 1960, RG 263, entry ZZ-18, box 34, Name File Heinz Felfe, v. I, NARA.

74. EGMA-46721, January 5, 1960, RG 263, entry ZZ-18, box 34, Name File Heinz Felfe, v. I, NARA.

75. Attachment A to Chief of Munich Base to Chief, EE, Chief of Station, Germany, EGMA-47248, January 25, 1960, RG 263, entry ZZ-18, box 34, Name File Heinz Felfe, v. I, NARA. Emphases in original.

76. Attachment B to Chief of Munich Base to Chief, EE, Chief of Station, Germany, EGMA-47248, Meeting with @FRIESEN on January 29, 1960, RG 263, entry ZZ-18, box 34, Name File Heinz Felfe, v. I, NARA.

77. RG 263, entry ZZ-19, box 35, Felfe, Heinz: KGB Exploitation, 85, NARA.

78. Munich Liaison Base Contact Report: April 12, 1961, RG 263, entry ZZ-18, box 34, Name File Heinz Felfe, v. I, NARA. In reviewing its own records from the Ponger case, the CIA found that information on Ponger, Krichbaum, and Wilhelm Höttl (a former SD officer who was probably also a Soviet agent) was kept in a single file, suggesting that indeed Ponger tried to penetrate the Gehlen Organization

through Krichbaum and Höttl. Chief, EE to Chief, Munich Liaison Base, EGMW-10731, no date, RG 263, entry ZZ-18, box 34, Name File Heinz Felfe, v. I, NARA.

79. Attachment A to EGMA-54025, March 23, 1961, RG 263, entry ZZ-18, box 34, Name File Heinz Felfe, v. I, NARA.

80. Munich Liaison Base Contact Report: April 12, 1961, RG 263, entry ZZ-18, box 34, Name File Heinz Felfe, v. I, NARA.

81. Attachment to EGMA-54269, April 5, 1961, RG 263, entry ZZ-18, box 34, Name File Heinz Felfe, v. I, NARA; Contact Report, @BERNHARDT, @FLEMING, May 31, 1961, RG 263, entry ZZ-18, box 34, Name File Heinz Felfe, v. I, NARA.

82. Documents on this surveillance are in RG 263, entry ZZ-18, box 34, Name File Heinz Felfe, v. II, NARA.

83. Munich to Director, August 21, 1961, RG 263, entry ZZ-18, box 34, Name File Heinz Felfe, v. II, NARA.

84. Munich to Director, IN 11604, October 25, 1961, RG 263, entry ZZ-18, box 34, Name File Heinz Felfe, v. II, NARA.

85. Gehlen later ascribed the delay to "our quaint West German laws" of evidence. See Gehlen, *Service,* 247. Also arrested was Erwin Tiebel, a former SD officer recruited into the KGB, who entered the Gehlen Organization and served as a courier to "Max" in Berlin.

86. Gehlen, *Service,* 245.

87. I am grateful to Thomas Boghardt for this reference to *Der Spiegel*'s cover story of September 22, 1954.

88. Marion Gräfin Dönhoff, "Gehlens Geheimdienst: Der Mann im Zwielicht und die Männer im Dunkeln," *Die Zeit,* July 26, 1963.

Acknowledgments

We, the editors, wish to thank the contributors for their hard work to see this volume through to publication. In addition to exchanges via e-mail and at conferences, we benefited from many conversations with our contributors that have expanded our own understandings of recast identities and postwar developments in West Germany and beyond. It has been a pleasure to work with such a diverse group of excellent and committed historians.

We would like to thank the anonymous reviewers of the manuscript for their comments and suggestions, which improved the manuscript greatly. Special thanks go to Jonathan Wiesen for his prescient comments that helped us tremendously with the introduction. His assistance went well above and beyond the call of duty, and his generosity reminded us that some of the smartest people are also some of the kindest.

Allison Webster and Stephen Wrinn at the University Press of Kentucky have been patient supporters of this project from the outset. Working with the Press has been a real pleasure.

Finally, the editors would like to thank each other. This project developed from a sideline conversation at a conference quite a few years ago, and while putting plenty of work into the project, we also acquired new levels of patience and discovered, to our great delight, that our talents are quite often complementary. The editor is, as the saying goes, the chief herder of cats: it was good to share this responsibility, for this volume could not have been completed by one of us alone. It has been a joy to see a project move from conversation, to idea and proposal, to completion.

Contributors

Florian Altenhöner, the recipient of numerous prestigious scholarships in Germany and Great Britain, is an independent historian based in Berlin. He is the author of two books: *Kommunikation und Kontrolle: Gerüchte und städtische Öffentlichkeiten in Berlin and London, 1914/1918* (2008) and *Der Mann, der den Zweiten Weltkrieg began: Alfred Naujocks (1911–1966)* (2008). He edited *Kollektive Identitäten und Kulturelle Innovationen: Ethnologische, Soziologische und Historische Studien* (2001) with K. Buchenau, G. Knauthe, and W. Rammert and has authored a host of scholarly articles on intelligence history.

Hilary Earl is associate professor of European history at Nipissing University, North Bay, Ontario, Canada. She has published extensively on genocide, war crimes trials, and perpetrator testimony. Her book *The Nuremberg SS-Einsatzgruppen Trial, 1945–1958: Atrocity, Law, and History* (2009) won the 2010 Hans Rosenberg book prize. She is currently working on an examination of the reintegration of war criminals into German (and Canadian) society.

Norman J. W. Goda is the Norman and Irma Braman Chair in Holocaust Studies at the University of Florida. He is the author of *Tomorrow the World: Hitler, Northwest Africa, and the Path toward America* (1998), *Tales from Spandau: Nazi Criminals and the Cold War* (2007) (both also in German and Spanish editions), and the coauthor with Richard Breitman of *US Intelligence and the Nazis* (2005) and *Hitler's Shadow: Nazi Criminals, US Intelligence and the Cold War* (2010). He has served since 2001 as a congressional consultant for U.S. government declassification efforts under the Nazi War Crimes Disclosure Act.

Elisabeth Kohlhaas is an independent scholar whose research focuses on National Socialism, the Holocaust, child survivors, and female perpetrators, as well as Jewish history of the nineteenth and twentieth centuries, oral history, gender history, and history education. Her most recent publications include edited volumes on women and the Holocaust and on Jewish knowledge cultures.

Kerstin von Lingen is lecturer in the Department of Contemporary History at Heidelberg University and is the independent research group leader on "Transcultural Justice—War Crimes Trials after 1945" at the Cluster of Excellence: Asia and Europe in a Global Context, Heidelberg. She has testified in court as an expert witness in recent war crimes trials concerning Nazi war crimes committed in Italy during World War II, and between 2009 and 2012 she was appointed to be a scholar for the German-Italian Historical Commission, an intergovernmental working group related to World War II history. She is the author of *Allen Dulles, Nazi War Criminals and Selective Prosecution* (2013) and *Kesselring's Last Battle: War Crimes Trials and Cold War Politics, 1945–1960* (2009) and numerous articles for journals such as *Holocaust and Genocide Studies.*

Thomas W. Maulucci is assistant professor of history at American International College in Springfield, Massachusetts. He is the author of articles and book chapters on West German foreign policy as well as on depictions of Cold War Berlin in film and the book *Adenauer's Foreign Office: West German Diplomacy in the Shadow of the Third Reich* (2012). He also contributed sections on the denazification and new postwar careers of German diplomats for *Das Amt und die Vergangenheit: Deutsche Diplomaten im Dritten Reich und in der Bundesrepublik* (*The office and the past: German diplomats in the Third Reich and in the Federal Republic*), edited by Eckart Conze, Norbert Frei, Peter Hayes, and Moshe Zimmermann (2010).

David A. Messenger is associate professor of history and director of the Global and Area Studies Program at the University of Wyoming. He is the author of *Hunting Nazis in Franco's Spain* (2014) and *L'Espagne Républicaine: French Policy and Spanish Republicanism in Liberated France* (2008). He has also written chapters in edited volumes and several articles in journals such as *Contemporary European History, Journal of European Studies,* and *Intelligence and National Security.* His research interests focus on World War II and its immediate aftermath, particularly in Spain, early Cold War Europe, and on the memory of war and dictatorship in contemporary Spain.

Katrin Paehler is associate professor at Illinois State University. In her research and teaching she specializes on Nazi Germany, the Holocaust, foreign intelligence, genocide, and mass violence, as well as on history and memory and their representations. She is the author of chapters and articles on the Nazi Security and Intelligence Service, on foreign intelligence and the Holocaust, and on memories of World War II. Her monograph on Office VI of the RSHA is forthcoming from Cambridge University Press.

Daniel E. Rogers is professor of history at the University of South Alabama, where he teaches courses on modern Germany, the world wars, the Holocaust, and contemporary Europe. He is the author of *Politics after Hitler: The Western Allies and the German Party System* (1995) and coeditor, with Alan E. Steinweis, of *The Impact of Nazism: New Perspectives on the Third Reich and Its Aftermath* (2003)

Susanna Schrafstetter is associate professor of history at the University of Vermont. She is the author of *Die dritte Atommacht: Britische Nichtverbreitungspolitik im Dienst von Statussicherung und Deutschlandpolitik, 1952-1968* (1999), and coauthor, with Stephen Twigge, of *Avoiding Armageddon: The United States, Europe and the Struggle for Nuclear Non-Proliferation, 1945–1970* (2004). She has also published numerous articles on nuclear diplomacy and on the role of the Nazi past in the West German debate over acquisition of nuclear weapons. Her most recent research focuses on indemnification for victims of National Socialist persecution and on West German government officials and their Nazi pasts for journals such as *German History.* She is currently working on a book about the role of reparations for victims of National Socialism in Anglo-German relations, 1945 to the present.

Gerald Steinacher is assistant professor of history and Hymen Rosenberg Professor of Judaic Studies at the University of Nebraska–Lincoln. He has served as Joseph A. Schumpeter Research Fellow at the Center for European Studies at Harvard University and in 2006 was a Visiting Fellow at the U.S. Holocaust Memorial Museum in Washington, D.C. He was also an independent researcher for the museum's Oral History Project. He is the author of three books and has edited seven volumes. His latest book, *Nazis on the Run: How Hitler's Henchmen Fled Justice* (2011), which was translated into four languages, was awarded the 2011 National Jewish Book Award.

Index

Page numbers set in *italics* refer to photographs.

www.ingramcontent.com/pod-product-compliance
Lightning Source LLC
Chambersburg PA
CBHW030256100426
42812CB00002B/457